CONFRONTING SLAVERY

CONFRONTING SLAVERY

Edward Coles and the Rise of Antislavery Politics
in Nineteenth-Century America

SUZANNE COOPER GUASCO

NIU Press
DEKALB

Published by the Northern Illinois University Press
DeKalb, Illinois 60115

Library of Congress Cataloging-in-Publication-Data

Guasco, Suzanne Cooper.
    Confronting slavery : Edward Coles and the rise of antislavery politics in
nineteenth-century America / Suzanne Cooper Guasco.
        pages cm. — (Early American places)
    Includes bibliographical references and index.
    ISBN 978-0-87580-689-1 (pbk.)
    ISBN 978-1-60909-082-1 (e book)
    1. Coles, Edward, 1786–1868. 2. Antislavery movements—Illinois—
History—19th century. 3. Antislavery movements—United States—History—
19th century. 4. Abolitionists—Illinois—Biography. 5. Governors—Illinois—
Biography. 6. Illinois—Politics and government—To 1865. I. Title.
F545.C695G83 2013
977.3'03092—dc23
[B]
                                                                    2012045346

For my Mom,
Suzanne Lankford Duncan
(1942–2011)

Contents

Illustrations

Note on Illustrations

Several of the images included in this book were the product of a collaboration between the author and graphic artist Mike Wirth, Assistant Professor of Art and New Media Design at Queens University of Charlotte. What follows is an explanation of the sources used to create those images. All of the images can be viewed at http://www.MikeWirthArt.com.

1.1. Enniscorthy, ca. 1805. Created by Mike Wirth and Suzanne Cooper Guasco. The image of the Coles family estate in Albemarle County, Virginia, was created from the following sources: *Mutual Assurance Society Declaration & Revaluation of Assurance, 1796–1867*, Volume 36, #472 (microfilm, Miscellaneous Reel 4124), Library of Virginia; Enniscorthy, National Register of Historic Places Registration, August 1992; and Elizabeth Langhorne, K. Edward Lay, and William D. Rieley, *A Virginia Family and Its Plantation Houses* (Charlottesville: University Press of Virginia, 1987).

3.1. The Journey of Edward Coles, 1819. Created by Mike Wirth and Suzanne Cooper Guasco. The following sources were used to recreate the path of Coles's 1819 journey to Edwardsville, Illinois: Aaron Arrowsmith, *Map of United States of North America* (1819), P. F. Tardieu, *Map of United States of North America* (1820), and John Pope Melish, *Map of Illinois* (1820), David Rumsey Map Collection, www.davidrumsey. com (accessed April 15, 2012); Edward Coles to John Coles, April 11, 1819, Carter-Smith Family Collection, University of Virginia; Edward Coles to Mother [Rebecca Coles], April 24, 1819, and Rebecca Coles, Almanac Memorandum, Edward Coles Collection, Historical Society of

Pennsylvania; Edward Coles to James Madison, July 20, 1819, Edward Coles Papers, Chicago Historical Society.

3.3. Illinois Settlement Pattern, 1820. Created by Mike Wirth. This image was adapted from Ronald E. Nelson, ed., *Illinois: Land and Life in the Prairie State* (Dubuque, Iowa: Kendall/Hunt, 1928), 118; and George H. Ryan, *Origin and Evolution of Illinois Counties* (Springfield: Printed by the Authority of the State of Illinois, 1996), 36–37.

3.4. Coles, Crawford, and Lee farms. Created by Mike Wirth and Suzanne Cooper Guasco. Coles's Prarieland farm and the farms owned by Robert and Kate Crawford as well as Polly Crawford and her husband Michael Lee were located between five and seven miles east of Edwardsville, Illinois. Coles did give several of the adult slaves he liberated 160 acres of land. The gifts, however, were located in the Military Bounty Tract District in what would become Knox County. According to the land and tax records in the Coles financial papers, none of the ex-slaves lived on those lands. The following sources were used to plot the location of Coles's Madison County property and the farms occupied by several of the slave families he emancipated in 1819: the maps of Henry S. Tanner, *Illinois and Missouri* (Philadelphia: Henry Tanner, 1823) and Lewis C. Beck, *Map of the State of Illinois and Missouri* (Albany: Charles R. & George Webster, 1823); Edward Coles, Land Transactions Ledger, 1818–1869 and Account Book, 1818–1839,volume 4, Edward Coles Collection, Historical Society of Pennsylvania; and Illinois Public Domain Land Sales Database, Illinois State Archives.

Edward Coles purchased at public auction and through private transactions the following tracts: T4N R7W SE 6 160 acres on May 13, 1819; T5N R7W SW33 160 acres on May 13, 1819; T4N R7W SE5 160 acres from William L. May on May 20, 1819; T4N R7W SW4 160 acres from John Rice Jones on June 11, 1819; T4N R7W NE 6 148 acres from George Coventry on June 11, 1819; T4N R7W NWNW9 40 acres, T4N R7W NENW9 40 acres and T4N R7W NW9 80 acres on June 18, 1832.

Robert Crawford purchased at public auction T4N R7W NENE9 40 acres on October 6, 1832 and T4N R7W SENE9 40 acres on August 16, 1836.

Michael Lee purchased at public auction T4N R7W W2SW10 40 acres on May 25, 1831 and T4N R7W NENE15 40 acres on September 15, 1836.

3.5. Gubernatorial Election, August 5, 1822. Created by Mike Wirth. This image was created from George H. Ryan, *Origin and Evolution of Illinois Counties* (Springfield:Printed by the Authority of the State of Illinois, 1996), 36–37; and Theodore Calvin Pease, ed., *Illinois Election*

Returns, 1818–1848 (Springfield: Illinois State Historical Library, 1923), 14–18.

4.1. Convention Contest, August 2, 1824. Created by Mike Wirth. This image was created from George H. Ryan, *Origin and Evolution of Illinois Counties* (Springfield:Printed by the Authority of the State of Illinois, 1996), 36–37, and Theodore Calvin Pease, ed., *Illinois Election Returns, 1818–1848* (Springfield: Illinois State Historical Library, 1923), 27–29.

ACKNOWLEDGMENTS

Convention dictates that every author acknowledge the debts they have accumulated as they produced a book. Traditionally, as well, scholars insist that any failings or mistakes left uncorrected rest solely in the hands of the author. I am no different from anyone else. The book you are about to read is much better because of the generous help of many people. Any faults belong to me alone. Yet this brief recognition does not do justice to the debts I owe, nor does it reflect the journey I have traveled to arrive at this moment.

Fortunately for me, the formula for an acknowledgment allows a writer to do what historians are not supposed to do in their books—cross the barrier between the professional and private worlds we all occupy. Still, the expectation is that no author will venture too far into the personal, reveal too much about themselves. I hope, then, that you will forgive me for moving further into my personal world than you might expect. The biographer in me cannot avoid explaining the gratitude I feel without situating it within the very personal context that informed the creation of this book.

Truth be told, I was convinced in January 2009 that this book would never come to be. This might seem strange, given the momentum the project had developed by that time. The dissertation I completed in 2004, while still not ready for publication, offered a strong base for the current book thanks to the guidance of my mentors at The College of William and Mary. The advice and encouragement of Fredrika Teute, Chandos Brown, and Carol Sheriff were essential to that project and the published book the emerged afterward. Moreover, I had been presenting my work steadily at various national conferences since 1993. Commentators, moderators, and audience members at several annual meetings of the Society for Historians of the Early American Republic, Southern Historical Association, and Organization of American Historians, as well as a Filson Historical Society Symposium, had offered insightful observations and provided helpful advice on nearly every chapter that follows. At every one of these events I left with new friends and a renewed sense of confidence that the manuscript I was writing was worth the effort. I had also published an award-winning article in *Civil War History*, portions of which are reprinted here in Chapter 4 with the permission of Kent State University Press. In the summer of 2005, I participated in a NEH Summer Seminar designed and led by John Larson and Mike Morrison. The manuscript benefitted greatly from the discussions generated over the six-week seminar. I also made quite a few friends. The most transformative and important relationship that I developed that summer was with Mike Morrison. He has become a valued and cherished friend and mentor. He has read this manuscript from beginning to end in all of its iterations and has never failed to offer insightful comments and suggestions for revision. Without his guidance, the best parts of this book would not exist. I cannot express fully the affection and gratitude I hold for him. He is a kind man, a generous friend, a brilliant scholar, and one of the most compassionate human beings I know. I will be grateful forever that our paths crossed in Philadelphia in the summer of 2005.

I came to know several other scholars in the years before 2009, and all of them have given generously of their time and intellect. Nichole Etcheson, Gary Kornblith, Carol Lasser, Matt Mason, Drew Cayton, Tom Chambers, Holly Shulman, and Sally McMillen all read and commented on this manuscript or substantial parts of it. The book is much stronger because of their help. For much of 2007 I was also a member of a wonderful writing group composed of nineteenth-century scholars from a variety of disciplines. This "Davidson Group" met monthly to discuss various projects, drink wine, and share our lives. I am immensely grateful to Vivien Dietz for organizing the group and inviting me to join. Comments, particularly on Chapter 1, by her, Trish Tilburg, Anne Wills, Annie Ingram, and Suzanne Churchill improved this work greatly. Even more important, our monthly meetings kept me sane and reminded me that it was possible to be a scholar, a teacher, a friend, and a parent without losing my mind.

Additionally, librarians and archivists at a variety of organizations ensured that I had access to all of Edward Coles's bountiful supply of papers as well as the collections of so many of his contemporaries. The staffs at the Illinois State Historical Society, Chicago Historical Society, and Illinois State Archives aided my efforts to explore and understand frontier politics and society in the Prairie State. Funding from the King V. Hostick Award ensured that my trips in Springfield and Chicago were productive. The archivists and librarians at the College of William and Mary, University of Virginia, Virginia Historical Society, the Library of Virginia were also helpful and funding provided by the Mellon Foundation (as well as the kindness of my dear friends Rob and Kim Galgano) made my sojourns in Charlottesville and Richmond fruitful and enjoyable. During the last stages of my research and writing, I traveled repeatedly to the Historical Society of Pennsylvania, the Library Company of Philadelphia, and Duke University where I encountered men and women eager to share their expertise. For their time and effort, I am immensely grateful. The staff at Davidson College's library was particularly helpful. Jean Coates, Joe Gutekanst, Susanna Boylston and Sharon Byrd provided access to the college's impressive collection of books and journals, electronic databases, microfilm and interlibrary loan services, and gave permission to include in this book the 1836 Thomas Sully portrait of Mrs. Edward Coles, which is published here for the first time.

By early 2008, the idea that my dissertation might actually become a book did not seem too outrageous. I had revised significant portions of the manuscript and had re-imagined it as a very different book. What as a dissertation had been an investigation of elite authority became a book about the rise of antislavery politics. The improvements I had made as a result of presenting at conferences, participating in writing groups, and absorbing and responding to the comments of other scholars had energized me, and my enthusiasm for the project had never been stronger. In the fall of 2008, Queens University of Charlotte gave me a semester leave. I used that time to write and submit a book proposal. I also spent a month at the Library Company of Philadelphia finishing my research. James Green generously provided a place to live and a community of scholars to join, and invited me to present my research before an engaging audience. An invitation to participate in a symposium on Abraham Lincoln and Jefferson Davis at the Filson Historical Society in November of that year was also valuable. In Louisville, I met a group of scholars whose work I greatly admire, and their influence on me is clearly evident in the notes at the end of this book. Also, my time with them led directly to a publication in *American Nineteenth Century History*, portions of which are reproduced in Chapters 3 and 5. Even more important, the sabbatical resulted in a book contract with Northern Illinois University Press. The year 2008 had been very productive.

All of this momentum halted in January 2009 when I was diagnosed with breast cancer. Every ounce of energy I had was redirected toward managing this crisis. The book and my job (beyond distracting me from the potential consequences of my diagnosis) no longer mattered. I resented how this disease disrupted my life and brought fear and sadness into my family. But after the initial shock wore off and I adjusted to the treatments (as well as the metallic taste in my mouth and the loss of my hair), a strange thing happened. I became obsessed with the idea of leaving behind some kind of legacy if the treatments failed. Of course, I had my children, my husband, and my wonderful extended family as proof that I had made an impact on the world. Yet selfishly I still wanted the sense of academic accomplishment that only comes with publishing a book. So, when my treatments were over and I began to recover, I refocused my attention on the book project. I read, revised, edited, and rewrote various chapters. More colleagues and friends read and commented on my revisions. I could not have navigated this post-cancer path, however, without Jane Mangan. This dear friend, a woman I admire greatly for her intelligence, compassion, and determination, has shared her life and work with me over beers at The Brickhouse and coffee or tea at Summit Coffee. I know I am a better person (and scholar) because of our evenings together. My conversations with her helped alleviate my seemingly ever-present anxieties and, along the way, allowed me to clarify my ambitions for myself, my family and my work. Without her friendship and her willingness to read and comment on the final draft of the manuscript, I would not have had the confidence to forge ahead. Two years had been added to a process I thought would only take a few months, but by the summer of 2011, I had submitted a manuscript for review. The fears I had felt in the winter of 2009 were gone, replaced by the joy and relief that comes with finishing a book manuscript.

I must confess, however, that the determination and the will to finish this book and see it published did not come solely from me, or my friendship with Jane. It came from four other people in particular. First, it came from my mother, Suzanne Duncan. Because of her I was no stranger to cancer. She was diagnosed with a blood disorder in the fall of 2002 and was given a grim prognosis. Yet, she never yielded to that disease and stoically, bravely, and on her own terms fought to defeat the cancer. She defied her doctor's predictions, and for a few years it looked as though she had triumphed. But as is often the case with this disease, the cancer came back (if it was ever really gone), and it has stolen from my children their "Gaga." Witnessing her struggle taught me the value of perseverance and of the importance of pursuing your passions even when the obstacles seem great. That I finished this project is largely due to the example she set for me to follow.

My two children, Joseph and Amelia, also inspired me to finish this book. They have been very patient with me and more forgiving than any son or daughter should ever have to be. I have never been very good at putting work aside, but they have led me to temper my ambition and have reminded me that they are my true legacy. They are the true center of my world and I could never be happy if they were not around to interrupt me with requests for snacks or a partner for a game. They (and I) are very glad to know that Edward Coles will no longer demand the attention of their mother.

By far the most important person in my life has been and always will be my husband, Mike Guasco. He suffered more than anyone, including myself, when I got sick. He has grey hair because of me. He delayed finishing his own book because of me. Yet, his strength and his compassion gave me the will I needed to overcome the crisis that cancer brought to our family. And, his humor, patience, and generosity helped me survive writing a book—which as anyone who has done it knows, is an ordeal in and of itself. He is my best friend, and though I too often cast my gaze on Edward Coles, it is Mike who will always have my heart and my soul.

Confronting Slavery

Introduction

On a cold February day in 1862, Edward Coles opened the latest edition of the *Philadelphia Inquirer* only to discover that his son Roberts had been killed in the Battle of Roanoke Island. Initial reports were spare. Extracts republished from southern newspapers recorded only that a "Captain Coles" was "among the killed." There was a chance that this Captain Coles was not his son, but on February 15, a more detailed account of the two-day battle appeared in the paper. As he scanned the two pages of reports, his weary eyes stopped at the end of a long article entitled "The Great Victory!" There, in bold capital letters, was the name Roberts Coles. In this section presenting scenes from the battlefield, the war correspondent described "dead bodies lay[ing] about in every conceivable position" and a landscape littered with a "great variety of articles which had been cast aside by the retreating foe." One particular casualty had caught the reporter's attention. There amid the thicket and underbrush lay the body of "a well-dressed officer . . . with his face upward and eyes partially closed, as if resting in delicious and dreamy sleep." This initial impression was a mere illusion; for upon closer examination it became clear that "the hue of life had departed." What a shame, the writer observed, that this Rebel soldier, whose parents lived in Philadelphia, had allowed his "impulsive spirit" to overwhelm his "better judgment." Coles's youngest son, a captain in the 46th Virginia Infantry Regiment, was indeed dead.[1]

A lifetime of moving back and forth from Philadelphia to Albemarle County, Virginia, had led Roberts to see himself not as a Philadelphian

FIGURE I.1. "Gallant Charge of Hawkins's Zouaves upon the rebel batteries of Roanoke Island," *Harper's Weekly,* March 1, 1862. (Courtesy of the North Carolina Collection, University of North Carolina, Chapel Hill.)

but as a Virginian. In so large and affectionate a family with such diverse views, Roberts probably assumed that, as had always been the case, a difference of opinion would not weaken any bond of affection. "I do not believe," he wrote to his Uncle John Rutherfoord in October 1861, that "father ever supposed my entering the army was in want of respect for him; he knows too well the love I bear him, & which he so well deserves at the hands of all his children." The truth of the matter was, declared Roberts, that although Philadelphia was the place of his birth, Virginia was where his heart belonged. He had never kept these feelings a secret. Indeed, "my father and mother know my feelings as well as I do." It was this devotion to Virginia as well as his determination to "claim my share of paternity in Enniscorthy," the Coles family plantation, that had led Roberts to declare "the corresponding right to defend it" by joining the Confederate Army. Roberts consoled himself with the hope that "in spite of his objections to its institutions," his father "would shudder at the thought of" the Old Dominion "being overrun by any invader" and, for this reason, would respect if not support his decision "to strike for Virginia." Coles learned of his son's enlistment in the fall of 1861 and responded despondently: "From what has occurred, and will probably occur, there is little or no prospect of my ever being again happy."[2]

Edward Coles was hardly the first or the last nineteenth-century father to experience the tragedy of a beloved son's death in the American Civil War. During the two-day battle for Roanoke Island, sixty Confederate and Union men lost their lives. This relatively small number paled in comparison to the thousands of young men who had died on battlefields in Missouri, Kentucky, Tennessee, Virginia, and along the Gulf Coast and Mississippi River in 1861 or the hundreds of thousands of men who would perish before the war's conclusion in 1865.[3] But the death of Roberts Coles, and the pain felt by his father, was somewhat different, for his death proved to be the last in a series of difficult sacrifices Edward Coles made in a lifelong struggle against slavery. More than forty years earlier, he had made the difficult decision to abandon the South rather than remain in a slaveholding state. In doing so, he forfeited the wealth and status he had inherited from his father. A few years later, he fell in love with Richmond belle Marie Antoinette Hay, but she was unwilling to marry a man whose opposition to slavery promised an uncertain future. He remained a bachelor until the age of forty-six. Even when his public campaign against slavery in Illinois succeeded, and his reputation spread up and down the Atlantic coastline, Coles became a political pariah and was unable to transform his victory into long-term political influence in the Prairie State. Then, thirty years later, when the nation finally elected a president who shared his antislavery views and the gradual demise of slavery appeared likely, his twenty-two-year-old son died defending the South and the institution of slavery. His only consolation was that in a short three years it would become clear that these sacrifices had not been made in vain. When the Federal Army claimed victory in the spring of 1865, Edward Coles bore witness to the final triumph of his antislavery ambitions. America had become the Union that Coles believed the founders had always intended it to be—a nation without slavery.

Born into a wealthy slaveholding Virginia family in 1786, Edward Coles was destined to join the Old Dominion's gentry planter class. But, while a student at the College of William and Mary, he concluded that slavery was morally and ideologically wrong. When he confessed his convictions to his family and revealed his intention to liberate all of the enslaved property he inherited from their father, Coles's siblings immediately objected, declaring that doing so would destroy any hope he had of a prosperous future. Coles refused to relent and made plans to move westward to free territory, where he could emancipate his enslaved men and women and start a new life. The unexpected arrival of an invitation from James Madison in the winter of 1809, however, led Coles to defer his antislavery ambitions while he served as the president's private secretary.

Although his duties in the President's House kept him busy, Coles's opposition to slavery never diminished. In fact, it intensified. During his tenure in Washington, he challenged Madison to explain how slavery could persist in a nation celebrated the world over for its republicanism. When hostilities between the United States and Great Britain erupted, the fear of slave insurrection gripped the nation's capital, ensuring that few of the city's residents could ignore the issue. It was also during the War of 1812 that Coles famously wrote Thomas Jefferson to request that he come out of retirement and lead a movement against slavery in Virginia. Jefferson refused, citing age and infirmity as well as poor timing as an excuse for his inaction. He recommended that Coles remain in Virginia and wait until popular opinion matched his antislavery zeal before pressing the state's leaders to embrace emancipation. As disappointed as he was with this response, Coles was reassured by Jefferson's optimistic prediction that slavery was destined to end eventually.

Coles remained committed to emancipation, but by 1819 he was no longer willing to be as patient as Jefferson instructed. In the spring of that year, he migrated to Illinois, where he liberated his human property and built a new home in a free state. To sustain his experiment in frontier freedom, Coles secured an appointment as Register of the Land Office, purchased a farm, and became a prominent member of the Edwardsville community. He discovered almost immediately that Illinois was not nearly as hospitable to free blacks as he had anticipated. Instead, a potent and pervasive antiblack prejudice tarnished the experiences of the former slaves and ensured that the state's free black population generally encountered more obstacles to economic prosperity than opportunities for advancement.

Coles's position as Register also provided him with an intimate view of the hardships many of his white neighbors endured as they struggled to achieve more than a mere competency. When in the early 1820s a small group of local leaders offered slavery as an antidote to the region's economic woes and racial anxieties, Coles attempted to thwart their efforts by running for the governorship. He was the only outspoken antislavery candidate and won the election, a victory secured with a mere plurality of the vote. He then boldly called on the legislature to eliminate the last remnants of territorial slavery and instructed them to repeal the state's black codes. This action precipitated a call for a constitutional convention, a move many residents believed would legalize slavery through constitutional reform. In the eighteen-month contest that followed, pro- and antislavery residents debated the economic and social merits of the institution. Coles led the antislavery forces and successfully prevented Illinois from becoming a slave state in 1824.

Much of this narrative is familiar to historians of the Early American Republic and the trans-Appalachian West. Coles has been recognized for the remarkable nature of his decision to follow through with his antislavery convictions when so many of his contemporaries failed to behave similarly.[4] His role in the Illinois convention contest in the early 1820s is also well known. Most scholars, however, have found his performance in the Prairie State more disappointing than satisfying. Since the 1950s, a variety of scholars have argued that Coles was a man of limited political skill who was, in the end, out of step with the political and social changes transforming nineteenth-century America. One historian, for example, argues that Coles's years in Illinois exhibited "a curious mixture of sunlight and shadow—of success and failure, with the failures seeming to clearly outweigh the successes." More recently, scholars have acknowledged his "commitment and energy" and have given him credit for the anticonvention victory in 1824, but they still assert that Edward Coles was little more than "a common man who made uncommon history." Moreover, although they argue that resurrecting his story reveals that emancipation was possible, these historians ultimately see Coles as a local figure who had little impact on the national debate about slavery in America.[5]

Edward Coles is rightly famous for his role in the history of early Illinois, but his place in the broader history of American political culture and the nation's critical engagement with slavery remains underappreciated. He was an often pragmatic and innovative, if not always effective, politician. During his tenure in Illinois, he adapted the political tactics he had absorbed in Washington during Madison's presidency to the frontier environment of Illinois. He did so by exploiting the advantages of his personal associations with important men while simultaneously employing the more popular political tactics emerging in many western communities. He believed that personal associations mattered, especially when his connections were to men as prominent as Thomas Jefferson and James Madison. He remained convinced that his intimacy with them gave him credibility on the public stage. Moreover, Coles continued to employ the political tactics he refined on the frontier throughout the remainder of his life. During his post-Illinois public career, he developed an even more extensive network of associations and used the power of the printed word to promote his antislavery goals. After 1830, he self-consciously formed friendships with Whigs and Democrats as well as northerners, southerners, and westerners. He believed that by doing so he might help the nation's leaders come together to resolve the problem of slavery. He also embraced the more pragmatic tactics of democratic politics, such as organizing, campaigning, and participating in partisan politics. Over the course of a long public career, then, Edward Coles developed a hybrid political style that combined elements of an eighteenth-century elite political culture with the popular political habits emerging during the first half of the nineteenth century.

Because they have focused their attention exclusively on his frontier career, historians have also failed to understand how the lessons Coles learned in Illinois anticipated and shaped the rise of antislavery politics during the decades immediately preceding the Civil War. Here is where the story of Edward Coles's lifelong confrontation with slavery has much to add to the history of the rise of antislavery politics in nineteenth-century America. Generally, scholars have explored the American debate over slavery by organizing their scholarship into three distinct time periods: Revolutionary (1760–1800), Early National (1800–1830), and Antebellum (1830–1860) America. Historians of Revolutionary America have long sought to understand how and why slavery persisted in a political climate that celebrated equality and freedom. Some scholars have identified the Revolutionary era as a missed opportunity to achieve emancipation on a nationwide scale, indentifying a concern for national unity, economic interest, racism and political ambition as obstacles to abolition.[6] Others have challenged this narrative by arguing that there was little chance for national abolition in the years following the War of Independence. These scholars have insisted that the new American nation was a slaveholding union from the beginning, ruled by leaders who made political and economic decisions that they knew would create a proslavery nation.[7] Whether the result of individual failings or institutional commitments, slavery persisted and became more entrenched in American society, even as some Americans called for the institution's demise.

Although slavery endured and political elites retreated from the battle, scholars of the Early National period have argued that many Americans continued to challenge the institution of slavery during the first third of the nineteenth century. These historians have explored the complex ways

Americans from all walks of life contested the institution even as slave-holders consolidated their control of the national economy and political system. These recent works have documented a vibrant antislavery culture at the local level in many communities throughout the country and among members of nearly every political persuasion. According to this new scholarship, debates over slavery were ubiquitous during the first third of the nineteenth century. Yet, as much as they have brought attention to a previously neglected period of slavery agitation, these scholars still reinforce the prevailing temporal framework by producing studies that emphasize the politics of slavery during the Early National period and leave to others the task of explaining the political and cultural challenges to the institution that emerged after 1830.[8]

The story of the struggle against slavery in the Antebellum era has been fleshed out by other scholars, whose work often concentrates on Garrisonian abolitionism and the Free-Soil movement.[9] These historians have demonstrated that although very effective at provoking a discussion of slavery, immediate abolitionists were purposefully apolitical and produced few emancipations. Within fifteen years, the movement was overtaken by the reemergence of antislavery politics, when the leaders of the Free-Soil and Republican parties confronted the problem of slavery and westward expansion.[10] With a few notable exceptions, scholars have provided insightful examinations of the agitation over slavery in the Antebellum era, but they rarely explicitly connect the ideas or activities of abolitionists or Free-Soilers to the debates of the Early National era, nor do they situate the colonization movement within the broader spectrum of antislavery activism.[11] The current antislavery chronology, then, has remained compartmentalized, and the connections between the Revolutionary antislavery impulse and the Antebellum political antislavery movement still demands attention.

Edward Coles participated in early nineteenth-century challenges to slavery, lived through the 1830s, when political antislavery voices were least welcome, and eagerly joined the fight in the 1840s and 1850s, when the Free-Soil movement and the new Republican Party climbed onto the national political stage. His life and activities reveal the ways antislavery efforts persisted from the era of the American Revolution to the Civil War. Even though the work to end slavery ebbed and flowed over time, it continued as Coles and others made creative adaptations to the changing times and their own changing circumstances. Coles, in particular, crafted an antislavery nationalism that emphasized that slavery violated the nation's republican principles and hindered economic development, and he called on the public to honor the founders' antislavery legacy. He enjoyed considerable success in Illinois, where his ideological arguments combined with a pragmatic free labor critique to prevent the legalization of slavery in the state. Illinois confirmed for him that a southern-born population could support his antislavery agenda. He also attributed his victory to his willingness to accommodate the residents' strong antiblack prejudice. Principle, prejudice, and the recognition of a shared antislavery past together became an approach to the problem of slavery that he would promote for the rest of his life.

To his dismay, he could not transfer the success he enjoyed on the frontier to Virginia. In his native state, many slaveholders acknowledged that slavery was ideologically inconsistent with the nation's founding principles, but they remained unwilling to sacrifice on the altar of principle the political and economic power their property bestowed. As he learned in 1829, nonslaveholding western reformers, though open to emancipation, lacked the political will to link their reform effort with emancipation. When they were confronted with a violent slave insurrection two years later, Coles was disappointed to discover that the Old Dominion's leaders still refused to embrace liberation. Instead, they ignored the popular demand for emancipation and strengthened the slave system. Although his arguments proved effective at preventing the expansion of slavery into new regions, Coles's antislavery nationalism, even when coupled with a colonization scheme (which called for removing free blacks to Africa), failed to make any progress in a slave society. Not until the Mexican-American War revived the slavery extension issue did he have an opportunity to resurrect his antislavery appeal and work once again to transform a slaveholding republic into the free nation the founders had originally envisioned.

In the late 1840s, the question of slavery in the western territories reemerged, and the nation's leaders were forced to confront the slavery issue directly. Coles published essays, organized and participated in public ceremonies, and encouraged Free-Soil and Republican politicians to make the antislavery nationalism he first constructed in Illinois a central feature of their public pronouncements. With Abraham Lincoln's ascendance to the presidency, he optimistically hoped that the nation had finally elected a leader as devoted to freedom and equality as the founders, but more determined than they had been to enact those principles for all Americans, black and white. Coles, however, failed to recognize that the antislavery strategy which seemed moderate in the 1820s and 1830s had become radicalized in the sectional environment of the 1850s and, as a result, contributed to the destruction of the Union it was designed to preserve. Still, as the story of his lifelong confrontation with slavery reveals, the challenges to slavery that first emerged in the Revolutionary era and continued into the first decades of the nineteenth century were dormant during the 1830s but never disappeared. Indeed, the eventual triumph of Lincoln's Republican Party can only be understood within this longer history of the rise of antislavery politics in America. And, although slavery was a formidable institution, woven into the nation's political, economic, and social order and often vigorously protected, men like Edward Coles persistently and consistently promoted a political antislavery appeal designed to destroy the institution that gave the lie to the nation's political and social ideals.

1 /   Becoming Antislavery

In the winter of 1805, a young Virginian rode his horse down Williamsburg's deserted Duke of Gloucester Street and viewed the remnants of a once-vibrant capital. The town's residents remained closed inside the many buildings that lined the main thoroughfare, protected from the cold December weather. At one end of the main street lay the old capital building. Years earlier colonial representatives in that building had challenged the authority of the king of England, but now the rooms were empty and the voices silent. At the other end sat the second oldest college in America. Once a place of learning that produced many of the state's most prominent revolutionary leaders, the College of William and Mary now struggled both to remain financially solvent and to keep students enrolled through graduation. At first glance, the appearance of departed grandeur, bare trees, empty streets, and an overcast sky presented a portrait of dreary isolation. Nineteen-year-old Edward Coles, who harbored grand expectations for his tenure at the college, arrived in town only to be "disappointed in the idea that I had formed of Williamsburg."[1]

Southern elite planters had been sending their sons to the College of William and Mary for decades. They did so because they expected the school to transform the students into enlightened gentlemen who would become civic leaders in the young nation. As early as 1785, Thomas Jefferson had bragged to Englishman Richard Price that "the college of William and Mary in Williamsburg is the place where are collected together all the young men of Virginia under preparation for public life." Thomas Todd, a Virginia-born Supreme Court Justice, sent his son to Williamsburg because he believed a young man's college years were a "golden period for improvement, . . . the most important . . . in the course of your whole life." It was during these years, insisted this father, that the young man would "form [the] character—habits of industry & study . . . which . . . last you forever." Edward Coles's father similarly recognized the value of a refined education and sent three sons to the College of William and Mary. Isaac attended the college from 1796 to 1798, and Tucker was a student from 1801 to 1803. Edward entertained such high expectations for the school because his older brothers and their friends frequently celebrated their experiences there as transformative. Carter Henry Harrison, who was Isaac's classmate and a cousin of future president William Henry Harrison, boasted endlessly of the "Gaiety and myrth which Williamsburg affords." Isaac, who also enjoyed carousing with his friends, emphasized a different aspect of his experience. He venerated the school as "the best place on the continent for the education of young men."[2]

Edward's initial impression of the school and town hardly matched these descriptions. "I see nothing very prepossessing," lamented Coles, "either in the town or College." In fact, he feared that his stay in Williamsburg would provide few of "the advantages of improvement" he had expected to encounter.[3] Coles soon discovered, however, that appearances could be deceiving. As he had been led to believe, Williamsburg and the college both offered plenty of opportunities to refine his manners, cultivate friendships, and acquire a useful education. In one important way, however, his two-year stay at the College of William and Mary produced an outcome few would have predicted. While most of his fellow collegians became slaveholding planters and prominent public servants after graduation, Edward Coles become an antislavery idealist who would eventually emancipate the enslaved property he inherited from his father.

"the ease and self-indulgence of being waited on"

Edward Coles was born in Albemarle County, Virginia, on December 15, 1786, and he enjoyed an almost idyllic childhood. As a member of the third generation of the Coles family in Virginia, he benefited from a lifestyle remarkably similar to Virginia's colonial planter elite, and he had little reason to doubt that he would continue to enjoy such a high standard of living. He grew up at Enniscorthy, an elegant plantation house situated on the ridge of Green Mountain in the Piedmont region of Virginia. It was here that enterprising planters like his father managed diversified homesteads sustained by enslaved labor. Like most eighteenth-century Virginians and southerners generally, the Coles family never questioned their dependence on enslaved labor. They took it for granted that they lived in a hierarchical society with planters at the top and enslaved men and women at the bottom. Coles and his siblings spent much of their youth socializing with Virginia's wealthiest families on their plantations, at western springs, and in Richmond. Moreover, life at Enniscorthy was rarely dull. During the late eighteenth and early nineteenth centuries, it was not uncommon to find Thomas Jefferson, Patrick Henry, or James Monroe visiting for a few days, playing whist and discussing farming and politics. Distant relatives from the Carter, Cabell, and Tucker families also visited regularly. Edward grew up, then, in the prosperous world of Virginia's great slaveholding planter families. Indeed, as he recalled many years later in his autobiography, his upbringing amid "the rich planters of the Southern States" had so habituated him to "the ease and self-indulgence of being waited on" that he could not help but feel acutely the sacrifice he made when he emancipated his bound laborers and abandoned the Old Dominion to resettle in a non-slaveholding state.[4]

The Coles family prosperity and rise to prominence began decades before Edward's birth, when John Coles I arrived in the colony of Virginia in the late 1720s or early 1730s. He was among the early settlers of Richmond, a town emerging at the falls of the James River. Founded by William Byrd II in 1733 and laid out by Major William Mayo in 1737, Richmond was the ideal place to locate. As Byrd declared, the new town was situated "on the uppermost landing of [the] James" and will serve as a "mart where all the traffic of the outer inhabitants must center." Indeed, John I was among the first to purchase lots, establish a store, and build a warehouse. As befitted a town founder, he chose to erect a large house atop Church Hill, a location that gave him a beautiful view of the waterway that would be so essential to his financial success. By the late 1740s he was married to Mary Ann Winston, was the father of three children, and had become a prominent merchant and member of the church vestry.[5]

Although a merchant and town dweller at heart, John I recognized that land and slaves were the key to prosperity and prominence in Virginia's genteel planter society. Accordingly, he supplemented the income from his urban landholdings and merchant business by acquiring plantations in the Richmond hinterland. Along with the Carter, Epps,

Cabell, Fry, and Jefferson families, he obtained land in the Piedmont region, skipping over the Tidewater, where land was scarce and tobacco had begun to drain the soil of its nutrients. John I purchased nearly four thousand acres situated along the Blue Ridge Mountains in 1745. The Coles property was called Green Mountain, named for the bright poplar tree foliage that was the first to emerge each spring. John I never lived on the property, but he fully expected the next generation of the Coles family to make their fortune by settling in the western part of the colony and, in turning west, he set a precedent that several of his grandchildren would emulate.⁶

John I died at the relatively young age of forty-two in 1747, leaving behind a twenty-seven-year-old widow and five young children. In his will, he distributed his extensive land holdings in Richmond and the surrounding countryside to his children. His daughters (Sarah and Mary) each received money, livestock, and slaves, while his sons (Walter, John, and Isaac) each gained a portion of his town holdings, a plantation, slaves, and livestock. John II, who was Edward Coles's father, inherited nine slaves and Green Mountain, a 3,854-acre plantation in Albemarle County.⁷ When he divided his property among them, John I provided his children with a strong base from which to build a prosperous future; yet, if they aspired to maintain their gentry status, they too would have to be shrewd in their investments and accumulate more land and slaves.

Unlike his father, who preferred town life in Richmond, John Coles II chose to establish himself as a planter on the Enniscorthy lands he inherited. Born in 1745, John II was only two years old when his father died, but as his father's will directed, the Albemarle County lands were maintained until he could assume control of them. An overseer directed the slaves on the property to clear a small portion of the land, construct a few outbuildings, and build a road (the Green Mountain Road) to transport tobacco to the river and market. John II did not take formal possession of the lands until 1766, when he reached his majority. Three years later, he married Rebecca Elizabeth Tucker, a half-sister of his brother-in-law Henry Tucker, and in this way the Coles family remained part of a close-knit group of elites who preserved their status and authority through endogamous marriages. They had a child every two years without fail, and by 1784 the Coles clan had grown to eight, including all six of Edward's older siblings (Walter, John III, Mary Elizabeth—called Polly—Isaac, Tucker, and Rebecca).⁸

The economic potential of the property he inherited was evident from the beginning, and John II flourished as a planter. Like most of

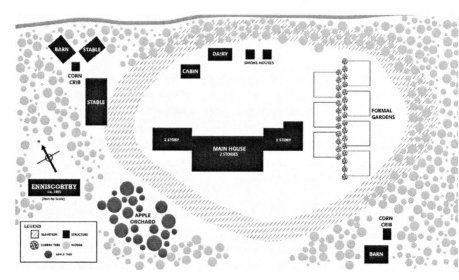

FIGURE 1.1. Enniscorthy, ca. 1805. (Created by Mike Wirth and Suzanne Cooper Guasco, www.MikeWirthArt.com.)

his neighbors, he used enslaved labor to cultivate tobacco, hemp, and, eventually, wheat, but he also diversified his enterprise to protect himself from the risks of the market and the vagaries of overseas trade. Enniscorthy, like many eighteenth-century plantations, was self-sufficient. He raised livestock and slaughtered, cured, and sold meat to his neighbors and the local store. He cultivated cotton and hired a local weaver to make clothes for his family and his enslaved laborers. He also ran a tannery and distributed leather products to less-well-to-do neighbors who bartered their labor to pay for their orders. He likewise operated a grist mill on the Hardware River, where he ground wheat and corn into flour, shipping thirty-three barrels to Richmond in 1783, for example. He also owned several distilleries, producing a fine brandy, cider, and whiskey for trade and entertaining.[9]

He became most famous for two other products assiduously raised on the property—horses and fruit. As his account book testifies, John II maintained between thirty-five and fifty horses on his estate and charged relatively high stud fees. Occasionally he sold his steeds for a significant profit. In 1805, for example, he sold Mountaineer for $560 and six slaves. He likewise raised an impressive orchard, cultivating grafts that he distributed to neighbors and friends throughout Virginia. Mrs. Drummond, a resident of Williamsburg, claimed that "Mr. Coles" possessed "the choicest Englis fruite" in Virginia and suggested to Thomas Jefferson that he secure some for himself. Jefferson, however, was already well aware of his neighbor's valuable tree grafts, for many of the fruit trees at his Monticello came from Enniscorthy orchards. Throughout the second half of the eighteenth century, John Coles II built a prosperous plantation and established his reputation as "a genial, horse-loving, hospitable Virginia gentlemen of the old school."[10]

Like his father before him, John Coles II recognized that acquiring additional land and slaves would preserve his gentry status and ensure his ability to provide a strong start for his children. By the late eighteenth century, however, the conflict with Great Britain severely undermined Virginians' efforts to achieve these goals. John II looked beyond "these horrid times" and saw opportunity where others observed danger. Between his marriage in 1769 and the conclusion of the American Revolution in 1783, he steadily increased his property holdings. In 1771 he purchased one thousand acres of land contiguous to his original inheritance, increasing his holdings to five thousand acres. He added another one thousand acres by 1783. John II also augmented the number of slaves he owned throughout the Revolutionary era. In the spring of 1780 he eagerly relinquished his continental currency, which was rapidly diminishing in value, by investing in slaves. A family friend in Williamsburg praised this strategy. "That you intend my good sr. to lay out the vile trash, which we call money in Young Negroes," he declared, "is wisely determine'd." By 1782, John II owned sixty-four enslaved laborers, a number that increased to seventy-nine by 1791. Two years later, he purchased five more slaves from Thomas Mann Randolph, increasing his holdings to eighty-four. He made several more purchases during the initial years of the nineteenth century, spending as much as one thousand dollars in the effort. Slavery and enslaved laborers were a regular part of Edward Coles's upbringing, and his family no doubt viewed the sale and purchase of bound laborers as hardly unusual or fraught with anxiety.[11]

The prosperity of the Coles clan contrasted sharply with the experience of many Virginia planters during and following the Revolutionary War. The tobacco market had always been volatile in Virginia, with prices rising and falling from decade to decade. Declines already present before the war only grew worse during the conflict. Great Tidewater families such as the Tuckers, Pages, Nelsons, Byrds, Randolphs, and Carters all absorbed the brunt of the unstable financial conditions. Disrupted trade, inflation, and a diminishing money supply conspired to nearly bankrupt these families who were land rich, cash poor, and severely in debt to Scottish and British merchants.[12] Even after the war, economic conditions in the state remained dire. In 1786, Virginian John Banister lamented that "Our Planters and Merchants are much dispirited. The first cannot pay what they owe and the Last cannot sell the goods they have on Hand." Complaints about "the dullness of Trade and the Scarcity of Money," he continued, are "common . . . among our Citizens." Historians have argued that the economic dislocation of the war and the simultaneous decline of the Tidewater gentry fueled the emergence of a generation of conservative Virginians who bitterly resented the political and cultural decline of the Old Dominion and its ruling planter class. This post-Revolutionary generation, many scholars insist, longed for the past and nostalgically, but unsuccessfully, tried to recreate the world of their planter forefathers. No two men epitomized this view more than John Randolph of Roanoke and Nathaniel Beverley Tucker, both of whom were on intimate terms with members of the Coles clan. Both men spent much of their adult life blaming their father, St. George Tucker, for not bequeathing to them a patrimony that could sustain the gentry lifestyle they craved.[13]

John II's sons were not among those who made such complaints, because they grew up amid prosperity and an enthusiastic optimism for the future. In fact, when Edward Coles was born in December 1786, the Coles family was at the beginning of a golden age that stretched well into the nineteenth century. John Coles II had improved upon his inheritance by amassing thousands of acres of prime Piedmont acreage and commanding more than eighty slaves. His plantation generated a comfortable income from slave-produced tobacco, wheat, hemp, and corn. In 1795, for example, he sold nearly 700 bushels of wheat for just over $200. Five years later, his harvest increased to nearly 1,200 bushels and sold for $505. That same year, he sent an additional 889 bushels of wheat to his mill on the Hardware River, where his enslaved laborers converted it into flour to sell at the market in Petersburg.

John II's children were healthy and happily growing into adulthood. They lived in a well-appointed plantation house and were constantly surrounded by extended family and friends. And, although he avoided politics as a rule, John II served his community as a senior member of the church vestry and a colonel in the county militia. He also enjoyed intimate social connections to many of the state's most prominent public leaders, St. George Tucker, Robert C. Nicholas, Edward Carter, Thomas Jefferson, James Madison (who married Dolley Payne Todd—a Coles family cousin—in 1794), James Monroe, and Patrick Henry among them.[14]

As other Virginia families began to worry about the future, the Coles family continued to grow in size and prosper financially. Edward's mother Rebecca gave birth to several more children before the end of the century. Sarah, who was affectionately called Sally and would become a favorite of their cousin Dolley Madison, arrived in 1789, followed by Elizabeth in 1791 and Emily Ann in 1795. John II passed intact to the next generation much of the prosperity he had accumulated. Nothing symbolized this transition more than his ability to build large plantation houses for three of his children. In 1796, he built Woodville for his son Walter and his new wife Eliza Fontleroy Cocke. Two years later, he constructed Calycanthus Hill for John III, who assumed control of his inheritance in 1798. Redlands, the most extravagant of the houses he built, was for his favorite daughter, Polly. Construction began in 1799, a year after her marriage to Robert Carter, whose declining financial situation mirrored the condition of most Virginians. All of these houses were located on land contiguous to the Enniscorthy estate. As the older siblings moved out of the family homestead and began their own families, the Coles clan remained a close-knit group that easily expressed affection for one another. Their prolific correspondence stretching throughout the eighteenth and nineteenth centuries is filled with family news, expressions of concern, and messages of love and support, demonstrating the depth and persistence of their affection for one another. Edward and his siblings grew up in the prosperous world of Virginia's great slaveholding planter families and never doubted that they would not only replicate but improve upon the ease and comfort of their life at Enniscorthy.[15]

"not one shilling went in the way of dissipation"

Edward Coles was the fifth of five sons and stood to inherit the smallest portion of his father's estate. Not surprisingly, then, John II recognized that Edward would need every advantage available if he was to improve his circumstances. The College of William and Mary offered just such an opportunity; for it was through a more formal education that planters' younger sons gained access to alternative careers in the law and public service. Perhaps equally attractive was the chance for his son to join a refined cosmopolitan society of gentlemen in Williamsburg. John II had already successfully employed this strategy with Edward's two older brothers, Isaac and Tucker. After earning his Bachelor of Arts degree in 1798, Isaac moved to Richmond, where he studied the law, passed the bar, and then combined his professional skills with a family association to secure an appointment as President Thomas Jefferson's private secretary. Tucker graduated in 1803 and followed his brother's example by studying the law, as well. He passed the bar and became deeply involved in county and state politics. Both of Edward's older brothers, then, used their formal education and the connections they forged in college to launch successful public careers.[16]

In December 1805 Edward Coles joined the junior class at the College of William and Mary, and in his first letter home he took great pains to reassure his father that he was devoted to his studies. He explained that his schedule of courses included natural history, mathematics, modern languages, and natural philosophy. He had discovered that the library was nonexistent and that students were expected to acquire the texts for these courses on their own. Coles immediately informed his father that "I shall . . . require all the books . . . that you have" and asked him to "send them down with my other books on philosophy and other subjects." Coles also confessed to his father "that I have spent all my money" and was desperate for additional funds. Worried that his father would suspect that he had spent his allowance irresponsibly, Coles assured him "that not one shilling went in the way of dissipation" and catalogued his expenditures. "I was obliged to buy Adam's philosophy which cost me 14 dollars." The "masters fees came to 25, and for sundries for my room" he paid another 7 dollars. He had also been informed that he had to pay in advance for "shoe cleaning and washing," which cost "8 dollars a quarter." Together, these expenses had exhausted his store of cash, and if he was to continue his studies he would need additional funds.[17]

Ten days later, John II responded to his son's request for books and funds. He reported that Tucker had packed more than eighteen books and that they would arrive shortly by way of the public stage from Richmond. As it turned out, Edward had worried about requesting more money for no reason, for his father was rather generous in his stipends. John II forwarded "forty or fifty dollars" without complaint and encouraged his son not to be shy about asking for financial support because he expected him "to be prudent and frugal but not niggardly with respect to your money." John II was so generous with his funds partly because he recognized that the full college experience included activities outside of the classroom. Moreover, he knew that social intercourse was by definition reciprocal. Students could not be perpetual guests without risking offense. They were expected, at least among their fellow students, to host one another occasionally. If the surviving record provides an accurate representation of student life, they did so often.[18]

In fact, John II was not really concerned about the practical details of books and finances. Instead, he was more interested in his son's experiences with other students and the residents of the town. In his response to his son's first letter home, John II chastised Edward for not providing a more detailed description of his circumstances. He wanted to know if "you have met with any of your old acquaintances" from home. He knew, as many of Coles's contemporaries reported, that developing a circle of friends was important. Garrett Minor acknowledged that "one great source of improvement . . . is the Social intercourse of fellow students." While several students complained that their social commitments "sometimes encroached on my studies," they felt confident that the time spent "in this way" was not "altogether lost." Socializing, they insisted, "will tend to give a polish to the manners that is absolutely essential to enable us to glide smoothly thro' society."[19] Indeed, most students acknowledged that their associations with one another "could serve as a stimulus" to their own improvement. As Edward's older brother Isaac had declared during his tenure at the college, "man in general is indebted for his passions & character to those by whom he is surrounded."[20]

Edward Coles associated with a variety of elite young men and formed friendships that he sustained well beyond his years as a student. Like both of his brothers before him, Coles rented a room at the James Moir House, located a few blocks from the college in the heart of Williamsburg. This establishment could house up to a dozen students, two to a room. Coles informed his father that he shared his quarters with Henry W. Tucker, a young man he described as "a very good scholar and more moral and less dissipated than young men generally are here." Coles's circle of acquaintances also included Joseph C. Cabell, his older brother Isaac's best friend, who had returned to Williamsburg to continue studying the law and to court Mary Walker Carter. He also spent his leisure time with Hodijah Meade, Nathaniel Nelson, John Page, John Madison, William Fitzhugh Carter, and Benjamin Harrison, all of whom came from prominent Virginia families. Several of his other friends became well-known national figures after college. Winfield Scott, who would eventually become a general in the United States Army and run for the presidency in 1852, became a lifelong friend, as did eventual Kentucky governor and senator John J. Crittenden, future president John Tyler, and William S. Archer and Armistead T. Mason, both of whom became U.S. senators. Coles would have agreed with Cabell, who had concluded long before he arrived in Williamsburg that it was at the College of William and Mary that Virginia's young men "formed the firmest of friendships" and benefited immensely from "the society of congenial souls."[21]

The old colonial capital offered Coles and his friends plenty of opportunities to socialize. The town itself contained no fewer than five taverns, boasted several boarding houses, and was the site of a variety of public and private social gatherings. Although he repeatedly informed his parents that "I have not a moment to bestow on pleasure," Coles was routinely drawn into student social functions. Even his slow recovery from a broken leg, an injury he sustained while wrestling with St. George Tucker's son Nathaniel Beverley, failed to deter him. In November 1806, Coles informed his parents that he was continually "tempted to dance" at one of the numerous balls and parties that occurred during the session. Like Coles, most William and Mary students entered Williamsburg's "circle of fashionable company" by attending parties and public balls. Benjamin Howard reported to a friend that "we are going on pleasantly," entertained by the balls and parties hosted by the local inhabitants. "There will be a good deal of dancing," he continued, and "I wish to God you were here" to enjoy the entertainment. Similarly, one of Coles's friends, who had pledged "to shun the gay scenes of pleasure and dissipation" while pursuing his law studies, admitted that "scarcely a single Ball or Party of pleasure has escaped me."[22]

Recognizing that an invitation to dine with the elite families of Williamsburg was also an important part of the student social experience, Edward's father likewise inquired "if you have been invited out by any of the Town Gentlemen." Coles regularly reported that he visited several prominent residents, often closing his letters home abruptly by declaring that he "barely [had] time to dress" for dinner "where I am invited." In November 1806, for example, he visited Colonel Samuel Travis, who served as the justice of York County and provided access to the elite social circles of the town. Col. John Ambler, who lived in Richmond but frequently visited Williamsburg, was among the men Coles may have met in Travis's home. Ambler was one of the wealthiest and most influential men in Virginia, and a friendly association with him certainly held the promise of future advancement. Travis also socialized with several leading men in town, including Judge Samuel Tyler, William Coleman, and St. George Tucker. Tucker, who had resigned his position as law professor in 1804, continued to influence the young men who came through the college by visiting with them at informal dinners and public social gatherings. Edward's mother was a Tucker, and several members of the Coles family were also close friends with the jurist's children. Edward's older brother, for example, corresponded regularly with Henry St. George. It is not difficult to imagine Coles attending dinners at the Travis house where he conversed with Tucker about family, contemporary events, and his education. By inserting himself into the elite social circles of Williamsburg, Coles was supplementing his more formal education in the lecture hall. As the father of one of Coles's fellow collegians explained, "it is by associating with the virtuous & respectable part of the community that we learn & imitate laudable Actions 'till they become habitual & familiar."[23]

"I will derive some practical knowledge"

At the beginning of his second year in Williamsburg, Coles informed his father that he was once again boarding in the Moir House and that the cost was as expensive as the previous session. He assured his father that "this would be the last year that I would be here." Coles arranged to take courses six days a week, leaving only Sunday free of academic commitments. "I attend Mr. Madison's political class two days in the week," he reported, his natural philosophy course on a third day, "and the other three days I attend Mr. Blackburn's mathematical class." In addition, he also attended Mr. Girardin's natural history class two nights a week. Bishop Madison expected the students to attend an additional set of lectures two nights a week with Mr. Blackburn, but Coles doubted the students would consent to the additional work load and he did not believe he could shoulder the extra burden. "From this statement you see," he declared, "that I have my hands full." Indeed, Coles feared "that I have aimed at too much," but as his mentors reminded him, "'he who has most to do, will do most.'" Coles assured his father that "I will derive some practical knowledge" from his studies and declared his refusal to allow his tenure in Williamsburg to become "so much money and time thrown away."[24]

The most important and influential course Coles took in Williamsburg was Bishop James Madison's course in moral philosophy. Bishop Madison, the president of the college and an Episcopal minister (and the future president's second cousin), was an ardent revolutionary patriot who championed American independence and extolled the virtues of republicanism. Throughout the Revolution, he consistently demonstrated a commitment to John Locke in his understanding of natural rights, and was forever distrustful of developments that might threaten the hard-earned liberties of the people. During the post-Revolutionary

period, he increasingly came under the influence of such French philosophes as Rousseau, Abbé Raynal, and Gabriel de Mably, believing
even more firmly in social equality, political freedom, and the value of
a government that served the public will. Such a perspective led him to
view with skepticism the movement for a new constitution and the Federalists' apparent distaste for equality. As president of the college, Madison defined the central mission of the institution to be the diffusion of
these ideas. Writing to Jefferson in 1786, he declared that at William and
Mary "the spirit of Republicanism is infinitely more pure as well as more
ardent . . . than among any other class of Citizens." Yet Madison placed
equal emphasis on the importance of free inquiry and the individual's
duty to recognize right from wrong. He intended the College of William
and Mary to produce independent-minded republican men of virtue
who were capable of protecting the liberties of the people and worthy of
leading the new nation.[25]

Every post-revolutionary college required its students to take a moral
philosophy course that included lectures on ethics, the relationship
between Man and God, and the nature of government. The course at
William and Mary, however, differed significantly from those offered at
Harvard, Princeton, Columbia, and Yale in its greater emphasis on politics, and a brand of politics that many critics complained was dangerously partisan and radical in nature. Madison claimed that his objective
as an instructor was to inspire a healthy skepticism and a devotion to
republican principles among his students. As he explained in 1795, he
believed that America's sons should "be trained not only to a knowledge,
but [also] to a just sense of the duty of asserting and maintaining their
rights." Even more important, he continued, they should cultivate "a love
of equality" because it was "the basis of all rights and all social happiness." Accordingly, he assigned authors that appeared in curriculums at
every post-revolutionary college. Students read, for example, Emmerich
von Vattel, John Locke, Adam Smith, William Paley, Jean-Jacques Burla-
maqui, and Charles Louis, Baron Montesquieu. These authors celebrated
the superiority of the republican form of government and the role of
public virtue as a powerful defense against corruption.[26]

Madison, however, taught many of these authors differently from
his colleagues elsewhere. Nearly every college president, for example,
assigned Adam Smith's *Wealth of Nations* and Madison, as one student observed, "extols and recommends him continually." They all used
Smith's text because he argued that the pre-revolutionary economic
relationship between Great Britain and the colonies was detrimental to

FIGURE 1.2. Portrait of Bishop James Madison. (Courtesy of the Virginia Historical Society.)

the prosperity of America. Smith also celebrated the republican form of government, believing that its design best protected private property and ensured the prosperity of society. These ideas, the instructors claimed, explained why colonists pursued independence, supported the decision to call a constitutional convention, and approved the Constitution. Yet Smith also contained an aggressive critique of the British economic system. From his perspective, the best economic policy left the individual unimpaired by government regulation. Additionally, Smith was critical of corporations and the influence of powerful financiers on public policy. In Bishop Madison's hands, then, Smith became a vehicle for criticizing Alexander Hamilton's fiscal programs and the Federalist administrations of Washington and Adams.[27] Similarly, while Timothy Dwight and Joseph Willard, presidents of Yale and Harvard, respectively, assigned William Paley's *Principles of Moral and Political Philosophy* because of its warning against the excesses of democracy, the author's defense of the unequal distribution of property, and his support for a strong tie between the church and state, Madison emphasized the portions of Paley that favored utilitarianism, instructing his students to engage in actions that promoted the common good.[28]

Madison also countered the conservative tendencies of many authors like Paley by expanding his list of readings to include a number of Scottish Common Sense writers and radical French philosophes. He augmented the standard commonwealth cannon by assigning authors who celebrated democracy and popular sovereignty, writers such as Count Constantine de Volney, Joseph Priestley, Jean-Jacques Rousseau, Marquise de Condorcet, Thomas Paine, and Thomas Reid. Like their commonwealth predecessors, these authors warned their audiences that the decline of civilization resulted from corruption. But while Whig theorists remained critical of the promise or potential of human nature, these more optimistic contributors to the Revolutionary Enlightenment displayed an unerring confidence in the triumph of Man, whose reason equipped him to overcome superstition, overthrow oppression, and pursue the path of virtue. More important, they viewed revolution, violent or otherwise, as a natural and potentially beneficial part of progress. As Cordorcet and Priestley both claimed, human progress, as exhibited by the spreading influence of the Enlightenment, allowed man to break from his past and encouraged him to rely on the general will as a guide for charting a new future. Rather than warn of the excesses of democracy and popular sovereignty, these authors advised readers to question institutional authority generally and called on leaders to harness the will of the people to ensure a successful break from an oppressive and tyrannical past.[29]

Madison insisted that he taught these authors "not because they suit a particular administration" but because "they are the touchstone by which we try the verity of every political hypothesis, and the purity of all political conduct." Yet few of his contemporaries would have denied that the school produced a decidedly anti-Federalist and democratic student body. Indeed, the students eagerly absorbed the lessons Madison offered in the political course, a subject that one student proclaimed was "studied with so much ardour, and . . . which . . . is considered so preeminently a favorite." As Joseph C. Cabell declared in 1798, when "Rousseau, Montesquieu, Smith, and [Vattel] are the textbooks on Politics at this college, how can the Political tenets of the young men be wrong?" He was pleased to report that all of the students at the College "are purely Democratic." Three years later, he proudly observed that "the College is still famous for Republicanism."[30]

The political preferences of the student body were never more apparent than during the late 1790s and early years of the nineteenth century. Convinced that the Adams administration pursued a foreign policy detrimental to "the future destiny of the Country," a sizeable group of students published in the *Philadelphia Aurora* an address in the spring of 1798 warning of the consequences of continued hostilities between America and France. Echoing the lessons they learned in their classical history and moral philosophy readings, the students reminded their representatives that "all governments, and particularly representative governments," were susceptible to the corruption and eventual ruin that accompanied the expansion of executive power during a time of war. They expressed the fear that, as had occurred under Caesar, the raising of a standing army would become "an engine for the destruction of our liberties." Joseph C. Cabell similarly viewed the spring and summer of 1798 as a time of "crisis, when . . . a mode of thinking both dangerous & illusory, is spreading among us." He found comfort, however, in the knowledge that, at least in Williamsburg, the majority opposed the administration's policies. To ensure that no one doubted their disgust with Adams and his policies toward France, several students "paraded through the streets of Williamsburg" during the 1798 Fourth of July celebration and concluded their march by burning John Adams in effigy.[31]

Federalist opposition among William and Mary students remained intense through the election of 1800, when Thomas Jefferson, a Virginia native, William and Mary alumnus, and leader of the republican opposition, ran for the presidency. As he anxiously awaited the election results, one student, Joseph Shelton Watson, contended that "the conduct of the late administration threatened us with a relapse, which would be ruinous to America, joyous to tyrants, and unfortunate for the human race." One of his classmates agreed and credited "the number of innocent victims of the oppressive sedition law, the repeated and frequent violations of the Constitution, . . . [and] the operation of Congressional taxes" with forcing "the people to reflect and endeavor to avoid the dangerous abyss" they faced by voting the Federalists out of office. Once news of Jefferson's victory was confirmed, William and Mary's student body erupted in celebration. "The students assembled in the number of nearly 60 and marched in body down the street, with shouts, huzzas, [and] whirling . . . hats." Two years into Jefferson's first term, support for his administration remained strong at the college. In January 1802, Thomas L. Preston reported that "politics in this place have entirely subsided. We are, however, all republicans, and consequently read the President's message with ecstasy and applause."[32] Although all of the nation's post-revolutionary colleges shared a commitment to republican principles, only the College of William and Mary demonstrated a strong preference for Jeffersonian democracy.

Still, Bishop Madison never intended to produce young men who followed blindly the advice or direction of others. Instead, he spent most of his career at the College of William and Mary insisting that "the principle which governs the philosophical school is that truth fears no discussion." He always insisted that every "student is urged to diligent and honest enquiry, and to decide for himself from the best evidence he can collect." As Edward's older brother Isaac claimed as early as 1799, "The spirit of skepticism which so much prevailed & which every student acquired as soon as he touched the threshold of the college is certainly the first step towards knowledge." He recognized that this approach might lead to such radical notions as "Deism [and] atheism . . . but," he warned, many critics might object to the use of reason "on the same grounds." To guard against such dangerous developments, the older Coles trumpeted the virtues of free inquiry. "Skepticism," he insisted, reins in these potentially destructive tendencies. Indeed, students loved Madison because he encouraged their intellectual curiosity. As one student testified, attending Madison's lectures and discussions was the most important part of his experience at the college. Without them, he declared, "no man can boast of a good education."[33]

Edward Coles took Madison's celebration of free inquiry to heart, and like many of his fellow students, worked through the meanings and implications of his moral philosophy readings in his notebooks. In the

few excerpts of his class notes that survive, it is clear that Coles struggled
to make sense of the texts he was reading and reconcile the principles
they contained with the world he inhabited. In his 1806 notes on Rousseau, for example, he recognized the supremacy of the law. "As all sound
engagements are reciprocal," he recorded, "it is impossible for any one
to set himself above the law without renouncing the advantages of it."
Furthermore, he acknowledged that "it is to the law alone that men are
indebted for justice & liberty [and] it is this salutary organ of the general
will which establishes in civil right the natural equality of mankind."
Yet he also recognized that it was by "the precept of public reason" that
every man should "act according to the maxims of his own understanding and not to behave inconsistent with himself." In these lines, Coles
seemed to be exploring how one should behave when the dictates of one's
conscience contradicted the law of the land. A tantalizing clue indicating that slavery was the contradiction he strove to resolve appeared on
the backside of this particular sheet of notes. There Coles wrote: "The
terms Slavery & Justice are contradictory and reciprocally exclusive of
each other."[34]

That Coles was interested in the nature of man as well as the idea of
equality and natural rights is clear from another set of notes that have
survived. In this document, Coles established that "every history of creation . . . agrees in establishing one point, the unity of man." From this
foundation, he concluded that "all men are born equal and with equal
natural rights." He then went on to explore the implications of such a
principle. "By considering man in this light and by instructing him to
consider himself in this light," he declared that "the duties of man are
plain & simple and consist but of two parts—his duty to God and to his
neighbor." He concluded that this meant he had to "do as he would be
done by." In and of itself, this train of thought offers little that was new
or revolutionary. But Coles also attempted to investigate the potential
limits of these maxims. Starting with the premise that "natural rights are
those which appertain to man in right of his existence," Coles concluded
that all men likewise possessed "intellectual rights . . . and also those
rights of acting as an individual for his own comfort & happiness."[35]
Who, Coles seemed to imply, could deny black men the same privileges?

"the state of master & slave"

It should hardly be surprising, then, that Coles would recall in his
often nostalgic 1844 autobiography that it was during Bishop Madison's

moral philosophy course that "I had my attention first awakened to the state of master & slave." For the first nineteen years of his life, Edward Coles apparently never questioned the propriety of owning men as property. The enslaved laborers his father owned ensured that the plantation household ran smoothly and that the crops of corn, wheat, and tobacco made their way from the field to the market. While Coles was in Williamsburg, John II's slaves harvested a particularly profitable crop of tobacco, bringing in more than 62,000 pounds in 1805. Edward also received family letters filled with news that included regular references to the family's bound laborers. It was here that John II revealed both his dependence on and casual objectification of his human property, a perspective the younger Coles probably shared until he attended Bishop Madison's lectures on moral philosophy. In 1805, for example, John II complained to his son about the escape of a favored slave named Nim. Apparently, Edward's older brother, Isaac, had seen Nim at the Washington races. The escaped slave had managed to make his way to the capital city through the aid of another slave, "the famous Gamester Bailey," who claimed Nim had "told so fair a storey of his going on to his young master in Washington that he believed him." John II doubted the veracity of Bailey's claim, expressing astonishment that Bailey would think he "would send a servant without a pass or letter & on foot." To his disappointment, Nim managed to avoid Isaac, but Edward's father still held out hope they might yet recapture their escaped property. He informed Coles that Isaac had "sent handbills & advertised him both in Baltimore and Philadelphia." To his father's considerable annoyance, Nim was never recovered.[36]

That the Coles family objectified the human capital they owned was revealed in another letter John II wrote to his son at college. The winter of 1806 was particularly brutal at Enniscorthy, and John II reported that "the whole face of the earth has been a sheet of ice." As the house slaves conducted their daily work, John II revealed that one of "Salls children [had] attempted to walk to the ice house, [but] *it* fell & never stopped until *it* got to the Spring. I was obliged to send Scipio," he continued, "& have *it* brought home." In this exchange, John II betrays his tendency to objectify his slave property by referring to the slave child not by name or the use of a personal pronoun, but by labeling the child "it." As these experiences reveal, nothing about Coles's early experience with slavery or about his immediate family life would have led him to oppose slavery. Instead, slavery was ubiquitous, and he and his family never questioned the propriety of their family's dependence on the institution. In fact, it was their ownership of enslaved property that secured the Coles family's continued rise to economic prominence in Albemarle County during the nineteenth century.[37]

The inspiration for Coles's antislavery commitment, then, did not come from his immediate family. He did have at least one extended family member who experimented with emancipation. His uncle John Payne, Dolley Madison's father, married John II's cousin, Mary Coles, in 1761, a match that brought together two landed and slaveholding Virginia families. For Payne, the marriage also brought religious conversion. Mary Coles was a Quaker and, like many religious groups at the time, Quakers did not permit their members to marry "strangers," individuals from outside the group. Three years after his marriage to Mary Coles, then, John Payne applied for membership in Cedar Creek Meeting, was welcomed into the faith, and moved with several Cedar Creek families to North Carolina, where they hoped to establish a Quaker community. The decision proved a poor one for Payne, who struggled to succeed in his new home. The Paynes returned to Virginia less than a year later, and once back in Virginia, Payne made another financially risky decision. Whether inspired by the emerging Quaker opposition to slavery or the revolutionary ideals in the air during the War of Independence, John Payne liberated his slaves in 1783, a year after the Virginia legislature liberalized the state's manumission laws. The decision, however, destroyed the Payne family's already precarious economic position. Unable to work the land without enslaved laborers, John Payne moved his family to Philadelphia.[38] Although a series of business decisions and possible failed entrepreneurial ventures probably explain the economic decline of the Payne family more than the decision to liberate slaves, Coles surely recognized in the story of his uncle's experiences the potential economic consequences of emancipation.

Nor did his emerging antislavery impulse reflect a response to the emancipation endeavors of his fellow Virginians. It is unclear how much Edward knew of the experiences of Virginia's late-eighteenth-century manumitters, but his knowledge of their efforts toward emancipation was probably anecdotal at best. Well before Coles's birth, for example, John and Robert Pleasants, prominent Richmond Quakers, had attempted to liberate more than 100 slaves but were prevented because Virginia law did not recognize their decision as legally binding. In 1791, when Coles was five, Virginia's largest slaveholder liberated his slaves. That year, Robert Carter of Nomini Hall emancipated 500 enslaved laborers. Both the Pleasants and Carter tried to employ their newly freed blacks as wage laborers, much to the chagrin of their neighbors, and their benevolent acts were universally criticized by their fellow Virginians. Five years later, Richard Randolph manumitted 150 enslaved people and provided them with land to secure their economic independence, an experiment that produced a vibrant free black community in the heart of slaveholding Virginia. Even more famously, George Washington used his will to liberate nearly 120 slaves upon the death of his wife. Some observers noted that his decision inadvertently placed his wife's life in danger, because it might encourage slaves impatient for freedom to orchestrate her premature demise.[39]

During the 1780s and 1790s, more relatively unknown Virginians also embraced emancipation, as the liberalization of the state's manumission law in 1782 legalized what the Pleasants had been barred from doing ten years earlier. In her study of eight Virginia counties (but not including Coles's Albemarle County), Eva Sheppard Wolf found that 1,045 slaves gained their freedom by deed or will between 1782 and 1806. Extrapolating from these numbers, she estimates that between 8,000 and 11,500 slaves were emancipated during that period. After the failed slave insurrection spearheaded by Gabriel Prosser in Richmond in 1801, however, the number of manumissions diminished, and Virginia's white slaveholders increased their efforts to control and limit the activities of the states' black residents, free and enslaved alike. Indeed, while Coles was in Williamsburg, the state legislature passed a law requiring all emancipated slaves to leave the state within one year or risk re-enslavement, a provision that greatly discouraged manumission.[40] So these early experiences of emancipation, if he knew of them, probably came to Coles as evidence more frequently against than in favor of emancipation.

As he claimed in his 1844 autobiography, then, Coles's antislavery sensibility was most likely born of the enlightenment education he encountered in Bishop Madison's moral philosophy courses at the College of William and Mary.[41] Coles recalled that it was during one of the college president's lectures "explaining the rights of man" that he asked if all men were born free and equal by nature, then "how can you hold a slave—how can man be made the property of man?" While Madison confirmed Coles's conclusion that holding another man in slavery "could not be rightfully done, . . . [and] could not be justified on principle," Coles claimed that the bishop had maintained that the institution persisted "by our finding it [already] in existence, & the difficulty of getting rid of it." Unsatisfied with this response, Coles then asked, "was it right to do what we believe to be wrong, because our forefathers did it?" After several conversations with Madison during class and more casually in the privacy of the college president's residence, Coles recalled that he had concluded that "if he could not reconcile Slavery with his principles, & did not believe man could have a property in his fellow man, he ought not to hold slaves," even if the law permitted him to do so. Echoes of Thomas Reid must have rung through his ears as he arrived at this conclusion. As Reid instructed, Coles ultimately reached his decision by determining what he believed to be his moral duty, not only to himself but to the enslaved men and women he would inherit.[42]

Coles was not the first William and Mary resident to question whether or not slavery was consistent with republican society. Throughout much of its eighteenth-century history, the college contained a small but influential group of students, professors, and board members who questioned slavery—men such as Francis Fauquier, George Wythe, William Small, Richard Graham, St. George Tucker, and Samuel Henley. By the turn of the century, an antislavery sensibility continued to pulse through the student body. William Brockenbrough, an Essex County resident who attended the College of William and Mary between 1798 and 1801 and eventually served in the Virginia House of Delegates, asked if liberty was a perfect right, then "ought our Negroes to enjoy Freedom?" He also wondered if Virginia's enslaved population "would be perfectly right in obtaining it [freedom] by turning upon their masters." For this Virginian, however, the prospect that such actions would result in the destruction of the "Vestige[s] of Virtue & Science," only to have them replaced by "an age of Barbarism & Darkness," required him to deny enslaved blacks their right to freedom. Undoubtedly, fresh memories of the slave revolt in San Domingo shaped the trajectory of his logic. Perhaps, as well, though, Adam Smith's advice that a moral man should allow caution to prevail over even the most noble of passions justified Brockenbrough's moderation. Rather than admit that every individual possessed the right to freedom, he preferred to allow slavery to persist by concluding that "perfect Rights may sometimes be imperfect ones, & imperfect Rights, perfect," especially when such moderation allowed for the preservation of a harmonious society.[43]

Unlike Brockenbrough, who concluded that the prospect of slave rebellion was cause for caution, Chapman Johnson, who graduated in 1802, studied law with St. George Tucker and eventually served in the Virginia Senate, viewed the threat of an insurrection as justification for doubting his commitment to the preservation of the institution of slavery. "We are told," reported Johnson in January 1802, "that a serious alarm has been lately experienced in Notaway. In Williamsburg," he continued, "we have had a slight (though I believe an unfounded) apprehension of disturbance." Shocked by the possibility, Johnson asked "Is it not miserable, is it not shameful, is it not unworthy the character of Virginians, or of men, thus to live the unsafe trembling tyrants of an unhappy people?" While fears of violence and disruption led most Virginians to preserve the institution of slavery regardless of its contradictions with their principles, Johnson felt that the good of society may require drastic action in the opposite direction. Still, referring to the call for restraint issued by Adam Smith and Francis Hutcheson, Johnson reproached himself by proclaiming that "the subject almost deprives me of moderation."[44]

Moderation and a pragmatic approach to the issue of slavery, as Coles would be disappointed to witness, prevailed during the post-revolutionary era. Like Brokenbrough and Johnson, most political leaders preferred to avoid discussing the issue, fearing that any emancipation scheme would threaten the stability of the social order. On the national level, by the early nineteenth century, public leaders had already established the habit of privileging the preservation of the Union over their ethical concerns with the institution. In 1787, the members of the constitutional convention accepted the three-fifths clause (which allowed southerners to count three-fifths of the enumerated slave population toward representation in Congress and in this way granted them a disproportionate share of power in the federal government) to satisfy slaveholders in Georgia and South Carolina, and had similarly pledged not to interfere with the slave trade until 1808. Then during the 1790s, national representatives agreed to table any antislavery petitions submitted to Congress, fearful that any public discussion of the issue would further weaken an already fragile nation.[45] In Virginia, leaders had experimented with liberalizing the state's emancipation laws in 1782 and witnessed an increase in manumissions in the last decades of the eighteenth century, but proslavery petitions, local and international threats of insurrection, and economic concerns conspired to undermine the antislavery impulse generated by the Revolution. Perhaps equally important, the idea that blacks were innately inferior to white Americans was gaining currency at the turn of the century and contributed to the pragmatic inclination to maintain and, indeed, strengthen the slave system in Virginia.[46]

In Virginia, no author did more to popularize a pragmatic approach to the slavery issue, as well as the idea of biological determinism, than Coles's friend and neighbor, Thomas Jefferson, whose *Notes on the State of Virginia* began to circulate privately in 1785 before being published in England by John Stockdale in 1787. A standard text at the College of William and Mary during Coles's tenure in Williamsburg, Jefferson's *Notes* praised the American landscape as particularly suitable for republican society. To preserve this condition, Jefferson recommended the eventual eradication of slavery, a system he described as a "great political and moral evil." He warned, however, that the "deep prejudices entertained by the whites; [and] ten thousand recollections, by the blacks, of the injuries they have sustained" precluded the preservation of a harmonious social order after emancipation if the newly freed blacks remained in America. He also suggested that the inferiority of the black race, whose "imagination is wild and extravagant, [and which] escapes incessantly from every restraint of reason and taste," further prevented them from participating in American society as equals. Emancipation, then, was only practical and proper when it would not disrupt the harmony of American society. Therefore, he could only support a program that included the eventual removal of those set at liberty. In 1806, the Virginia legislature passed a law that reflected, at least in part, Jefferson's view of the situation. To discourage philanthropic slaveholders from emancipating their chattel property and thereby endangering the Old Dominion's social order with a disruptive free black population, the new law required all emancipated blacks to leave the state within one year or be sold back into slavery.[47]

Nevertheless, unlike the majority of his contemporaries, Coles cast aside the predictions and warnings issued by Jefferson, never shared his protoracist views, and ignored the arguments offered by Bishop Madison. Instead, he insisted that he remained unable to tolerate "a state of things which was in direct violation of . . . [our] great fundamental doctrines." Relying on Rousseau, who claimed that individual conscience was the final arbiter of good moral behavior, he maintained that he was "unable to screen myself . . . from the pelting & upbraidings of my own conscience . . . [and] could not consent to hold as property what I had no right to, & which was not, and could not be property, according to my understandings of the rights & duties of man." Apparently, Bishop Madison's decision to assign political and moral authors that encouraged readers to challenge authority and think for themselves led at least one student to the radical conclusion that "I would not & could not hold my fellow-man as a Slave."[48]

"I expect you will be a farmer"

In the early summer of 1807, just a few weeks before his final exams, Edward Coles's college career abruptly ended when his father called him home to Enniscorthy. John II reported that he and Coles's older brother Tucker were "very unwell," and requested that Edward return to "assist us in our harvest." He acknowledged the inconvenience of his request, but forwarded a letter addressed to the college masters conveying "my full consent" to Edward's premature departure. He then informed his son that he did not "believe that you can return to Williamsburg" and instructed him to pack his "clothes, books, etc." and arrange for them to be shipped home. He implored his son not to delay, for there was no one else to help. Walter, the oldest Coles son, had long been married, situated on his own plantation, and was already occupied managing his own harvest. John III was away from home, gone for several weeks attempting to sell the family's stores of tobacco in Richmond and to the south. He was not due to return before the harvest would have to begin. Isaac was also away, traveling along the Atlantic seaboard, and he was not expected home until mid-July, much too late to be of service to his father. So the responsibility had fallen to Edward, the youngest of five sons. To soften the blow, John II reminded Edward that "I expect you will be a farmer," and assured him that "your presence will not only be of service to us but to yourself." Coles dutifully returned home, arriving at Enniscorthy on June 25 (as his mother Rebecca noted in her almanac, where she kept a record of all of the comings and goings of her large family), without a degree, and spent the summer and fall helping his father manage the family plantation.[49]

The following February, John II died suddenly, an event that forced Coles to confront the reality that he was now a slave-owning planter. The experience of his father's death was, as would be expected, devastating for Edward. The Coles family was very close to one another, bound together by regular declarations of affection. Edward opened all his letters home from Williamsburg with "Dear Papa," and concluded his notes by sending "my love to mama and all" the rest of the family. Such affection extended beyond the immediate Coles clan to include uncles, aunts, and cousins, as well. Indeed, even these physically distant but emotionally close members of the family felt the loss acutely. John Tucker, Edward's maternal uncle, wrote soon after John II's death to console his despondent sister and her children. He declared that he was "sincerely sorry for my Sister's loss. . . . I always considered Mr. Coles the best of Husbands and the most affectionate of Fathers," but he hoped that they would all "yield to the decree of the most high God our blessed Creator and Redeemer with fortitude and resignation."[50]

In his will, written and signed in 1795, John II expressed his affection for his immediate family by distributing generous portions of his sizeable estate to his wife and ten children. The five eldest children had already come of age and had received the majority of their inheritance years earlier. To ensure their continued prosperity, John II supplemented Walter and John III's portions by giving them additional livestock and enslaved property at his death. Isaac inherited Enniscorthy, a place he had confessed of dreaming about nightly while in college, along with all of the plantation's improvements, livestock, and the largest portion of bound laborers. He would not assume control of his inheritance, however, until his mother's death in 1826. Tucker owned and managed Tallwood plantation and, like his brothers, he already benefited from his father's generous distribution of livestock and slaves. After his father's death, then, he only received an additional four hundred acres of land. To his four unmarried daughters (Rebecca, Sally, Elizabeth, and Emily), John II bequeathed one thousand pounds and seven slaves each.[51]

For Edward, the distribution of his father's assets was bittersweet. At his father's death, he became the owner of a 782-acre plantation called Rockfish farm and as many as twenty slaves. His father had purchased the tract from Francis Meriwether in 1784, and during most of Edward's childhood an overseer managed the small plantation. The land, located roughly twenty miles southwest of Enniscorthy in Amherst County, was pleasantly situated and consisted of alluvial soil enriched by the river that passed through the estate. In many ways, the site resembled the Enniscorthy property John Coles II had taken control over when he reached his majority. Although smaller, Rockfish farm possessed great potential, and John II probably expected his youngest son to follow his example and become a prosperous planter in his own right. Edward, however, did not care for the rural isolation that accompanied plantation life. Like John I (the grandfather he never met), he preferred the cosmopolitan society of urban life. As he confessed to one of his college friends, "My situation . . . presents a sad & melancholy reverse ever since I left Wmsburg." He complained that his remote situation meant that he "heard from very few, and [had] seen still fewer" of his old friends from school. In fact, Coles left Enniscorthy to visit friends whenever the opportunity presented itself. He craved the company of others, lamenting that plantation life had left him separated from the society of those closest to him. During the two years following his father's death, Edward was away from Green Mountain for more than fifteen months.[52]

Perhaps contributing to his sense of melancholy was his fear that he would not be able to follow through with his antislavery convictions. Ever since his tenure at the College of William and Mary, Edward had been deeply opposed to slavery but had kept his feelings secret from his family. As he recorded in an autobiography written nearly forty years after the fact, Coles revealed soon after his father's estate was settled that he intended to manumit the bound laborers he had inherited. "All," recalled Coles, "disapproved & endeavored to reason me out of this determination." They offered many of "the usual arguments in favor of slavery." When these general arguments failed to dissuade him, Coles recalled that his siblings changed tactics and focused on the personal consequences of his decision. As Coles remembered the conversation, they had reminded him that he had "no profession" other than "the occupation of a planter; how," they asked, "can you carry on your plantation, & support yourself, without Slaves?" They had insisted that just as it would be impossible for a tradesman to perform his craft without his tools, so too would it be impossible "for a Virginian to be an agriculturalist without owning or employing Slaves." He reported that they also reminded him that, as the fifth of ten children, he had inherited "barely enough to enable you to live as a gentleman, even with your Slaves." Emancipate the most valuable portion of his inheritance, they had declared, and Coles would destroy any hope he had for a secure and productive future.[53]

In his decidedly romanticized reminiscence of these events, Coles recalled acknowledging every argument they offered, confessing that he was "fully sensible . . . of the inconveniences & privations I shall subject myself to." He recalled heroically responding to them with the same arguments he had proclaimed to Bishop Madison. "All of this is dust in the balance, when weighing the consolation & happiness of doing what you believe right." His conscience, he smugly boasted, would not allow him to continue to hold men in bondage, a condition that deprived them "of the greatest of all earthy blessings, the enjoyment of . . . liberty, that liberty," he lectured, "which we are taught to believe is the gift of God, & the inherent & inalienable right of man."[54] The blasé tone of his recollection may reflect the naivety he attributed to his youth or an adult desire to remember a difficult decision as easier than it in fact was. Either way, it is impossible to ignore the fact that he could not dismiss so easily the very real practical obstacles to emancipation; for it ultimately took him twelve years to follow through with his pledge—twelve long years of wrestling with his own convictions, his own ambitions, and his own selfish desires.

Still, as he remembered the occasion, he contemplated pursuing several emancipation strategies. First, he considered remaining in Virginia, and hiring "my Negroes as laborers." He reassured his family that he would not record any free papers, but would instead liberate his enslaved property in his will. According to his recollection, his family and neighbors immediately objected to this plan. They assured him that if he implemented his proposal he "should not only incur the displeasure of my relations & neighbors, but I, and my unfortunate Negroes, would be considered and treated as pests of society." Moreover, as mentioned, Virginia law required all liberated slaves to leave the state within a year or risk reenslavement. As a result of both of these circumstances, Coles recorded that this experiment never came to pass.[55]

Unable to free his slaves and remain in Virginia, Coles then concluded that he "could do better for myself, & for the Negroes, to remove & take them with me to the Country North West of the Ohio River," where he could emancipate them without opposition. In many ways, he was following a precedent first set by his paternal grandfather, who in the early eighteenth century had recognized the value of western lands and had purchased Green Mountain for John II's future. Like his grandfather, Edward recognized in the relatively inexpensive land available on the frontier the potential for a promising future. Unlike his grandfather and father, however, the youngest male Coles intended to rely not on enslaved laborers but on the energies of free men to ensure his economic prosperity. Accordingly, in the summer of 1809, Coles rented his Rockfish plantation and embarked on a four-month tour of the Ohio River Valley, "exploring a great part of Ohio and Indiana," as well as Kentucky. His uncle Travis Tucker owned land in the Bluegrass State and had agreed to sign over his deed should Coles decide to settle in the region. Although he enjoyed his journey through Lexington, Louisville, and Frankfort, Coles was determined not to exchange one slaveholding state for another and rejected his uncle's offer. The Old Northwest, however, proved more inviting, and when he returned home in December 1809, Coles "advertised my land for sale" and began making plans for his next departure. Unfavorable economic conditions occasioned by the Jeffersonian embargoes, however, diminished his enthusiasm and put in doubt the likelihood that he would be able to "effect a sale." As a result, this newly minted antislavery idealist spent the winter of 1809 at Enniscorthy fearing that his future as a frontier landholder free of slavery would be delayed indefinitely.[56]

2 / Antislavery Ambition Deferred

On a cold winter morning in January 1810, Edward Coles sat at a desk in the parlor at Enniscorthy and contemplated how best to respond to President James Madison's request that he serve as his private secretary. He could recall the many evenings when Madison, Thomas Jefferson, and James Monroe had joined his father and brothers to discuss politics and farming in that very room. These men were among the most politically powerful in the nation, the American Republic's first generation of natural aristocrats, and they were intimate family friends. Consequently, Coles relished the opportunity to join Madison's presidential family; for doing so would allow him to exchange the isolated rural life at Enniscorthy for the cosmopolitan excitement of Washington City (as the capital was then called). "Nothing has ever more flattered my vanity, or given me more gratification," wrote Coles, "than this token of your esteem and confidence in me." Still, although he coveted the society of Washington City, Coles remained determined to liberate his enslaved property and resettle in free territory on the frontier. Madison's timely offer, then, caused Coles to "feel sensibly a struggle between my inclinations and my reason." In the end, Edward Coles decided to follow the dictates of his reason and informed President Madison that he would have to decline "to accept a place . . . in the bosom of a family for whom I have the greatest respect."[1]

On his way to the post office to deliver the letter, Coles encountered his neighbor and good friend James Monroe. Monroe lived at Ashland, just a few miles east of Enniscorthy, and the two men had formed a close friendship during the year and half after the young Virginian returned home from Williamsburg. As he helped his father manage the plantation, Coles had taken advantage of Monroe's offer of his library to continue his studies. It was during his visits there that the two men engaged in extended conversations about politics and society and Coles's plans for the future. When he learned the purpose of Coles's journey, Monroe immediately discouraged his friend from mailing the letter. As Coles recalled in his autobiography, Monroe "urged me by all means to accept" the president's offer. He insisted "that it was the most desirable situation in the world for a young man . . . one in which I would derive more useful information than in any other." Monroe argued that no other position could prepare him more thoroughly for his western move. "It was particularly desireable," reasoned Monroe, that Coles "associate with non-slaveholding people and form acquaintances with Members of Congress from the Old Northwest." Still, his "anxiety to sell my Farm . . . & as soon as possible to restore to my Negroes their liberty" led Coles to resist Monroe's advice. Only after the future president urged him to reconsider his decision, repeatedly emphasizing how a temporary sojourn in Washington would ease his transition to the frontier, did Coles capitulate and accept Madison's offer.[2]

Washington City offered many of the advantages Monroe described. Every winter, members of Congress, foreign ministers, and other prominent men, along with their wives and children, descended upon the federal city. Eager to catch a glimpse of the nation's great orators from the galleries of Congress or at the Supreme Court, as well as to participate in various social events, these transitory residents of Washington City constructed a community of national ruling elites well known for their conviviality and political character. As one traveler observed, for those "who love dissipation . . . the game of politics . . . and who [wish to] make a study of strong minds under strong excitements," Washington was the place to visit. Indeed, Coles met and became well acquainted with national leaders from all over the country. Of course, he encountered many familiar faces in the Virginia delegation, men such as Wilson Cary Nicholas, James Breckenridge, William A. Burwell, and John Randolph. But he also met prominent men from other states, including Josiah Quincy, Nathaniel Macon, William H. Crawford, Henry Clay, and John C. Calhoun, to name just a few. He came across these men as he performed his official duties as well as during social events at the President's House. In fact, as Monroe predicted, his experiences in the presidential household provided Coles with useful connections and taught him important lessons in political tactics that would become very useful to him after he moved to the frontier.[3]

Yet the distractions of society and politics did not relieve Coles's uneasiness about the slavery issue. When he arrived in the city, Washington contained 5,395 slaves, which was just over 22 percent of the total population. These enslaved laborers worked as domestic servants, coachmen, laundresses, cooks, hack drivers, waiters, messengers, and manservants. More skilled slaves also worked as blacksmiths, bricklayers, and carpenters. The number of slaves in the city also expanded on the eve of every congressional session, when southern political leaders arrived and brought their own slaves with them or hired domestic servants from enterprising slaveholders in neighboring Virginia and Maryland.[4] The nation's capital also boasted a vibrant slave trading industry. Several auction houses were located within blocks of the capital building and presidential mansion. Moreover, although the nation's leaders occasionally debated the propriety of slavery in the capital of a nation founded upon republican principles, the institution remained unreformed. Even more frequently, congressional leaders employed the rhetoric of slavery in their political battles over domestic and international policy.[5] Coles's Washington City was a slave society much like the rest of the South generally, and his opposition to the institution and his determination to liberate his inherited property, though deferred, was only strengthened during his tenure in the nation's capital. Moreover, it was during his tenure in Washington City that he developed the political instincts and skills required to extend his opposition to slavery to a broader community.

"the city is gay"

Edward Coles arrived in Washington City on January 14, 1810, and joined a bustling President's House full of family and friends. Dolley Madison's ne'er-do-well eighteen-year-old son Payne Todd lived in the house when he was not attending a private boarding school in Baltimore. Dolley's younger sister Anna and her husband Richard Cutts, who was a member of Congress from Massachusetts, along with three of their eventual seven children also resided in the executive mansion, as did her other sister, Lucy Washington, a widow with two children. This family circle expanded and contracted as various cousins, nieces, nephews, and close family friends came and went with astounding regularity. During each congressional session, for example, Coles might find his sisters Sally and Betsy, Maria Mayo, Margaret Hamilton, Phoebe Morris and her

FIGURE 2.1. North View of the President's House in the city of Washington, ca. 1810. (Courtesy of the Library of Congress, Prints & Photographs Division (LC-USZ62-63254).)

husband Anthony, as well as William C. Preston, and John G. Jackson staying in the house. Coles, then, joined a busy household that was often overflowing with family connections.[6]

In his first letter home to his family, Coles reported that "the city is gay" and described a crowded social calendar that included public balls, private parties, dancing, and nightly dinners. It was at these social occasions that Coles was introduced to and came to know more intimately the members of Congress, their families, and the younger members of the region's elite families. Every winter the crowds of people who flowed into the city from far and wide took part in a winter social season that coincided with the congressional session. The members worked together closely during the day and then retreated to their boarding houses and rented homes, where they socialized with one another, their families, and other government officials and visitors. Coles's residence as well as his official role as the president's private secretary put him right in the middle of this vibrant social scene, which was far more exciting than the dull evenings spent at his family's secluded estate.[7]

His cousin Dolley Madison was largely responsible for establishing the President's House as the center of this exciting social world. Though not conventionally beautiful, Dolley was vivacious, elegant, and engaging. She captivated the attention of all those who crossed her path or basked in the warmth of her glow at social occasions. Augustus John Foster, a British diplomat disposed to find fault with anything American, described her as "perfectly good-tempered and good humoured" and praised her ability to make her social events "agreeable to all parties." Margaret Bayard Smith, perennially present at Washington social gatherings, claimed that Mrs. Madison possessed such an inviting "social disposition" that everyone around her felt comfortable and at ease. Her reputation for sociability grew from the time she arrived in the city in 1801, when her husband began his service as secretary of state, and continued throughout Jefferson's presidency as she occasionally served as the president's hostess at official state functions.[8]

By the time she became First Lady in her own right, Dolley Madison had cultivated a social style admired by Americans and foreign visitors alike. She hosted her first drawing room gathering in May 1809, and these events quickly became so popular that they earned the nickname "squeezes" because so many people attended. In true republican spirit, she opened these Wednesday parties to a wide variety of people, ignoring party affiliations and the informal social rank that divided ordinary folks from aristocratic gentlemen elsewhere in the world. A member of the British legation who attended his first drawing-room party in June of that year "found a Crowd of Ladies and Gentlemen Walking through the Apartments which were all thrown open. . . . Such a Meeting seems to be much relished," he observed, "& there is the honor of Seeing the President & his Lady." These gatherings, however, provided much more than direct access to the president. It was in the drawing rooms of the executive mansion that congressmen and senators discussed the politics of the day, forged alliances, and cultivated the familiarity required to broker compromises on the floor of Congress. In this way, the Madisons expanded the political arena beyond the formal boundaries of authority and transformed the President's House into the center of an emerging national political culture in which social space became an important arena for conducting public business.[9]

Coles witnessed firsthand the important role sociability played in national politics. James Madison inherited a disintegrating international

FIGURE 2.2. Portrait of Dolley Payne Todd Madison, 1804, by Gilbert Stuart. (Courtesy of the White House Historical Association (White House Collection).)

scene and an increasingly fractious domestic political community when he took office in 1809. Tensions with Great Britain and France had fluctuated between good and bad throughout the early nineteenth century and constantly threatened to break into formal hostilities. The two European belligerents had each issued orders prohibiting Americans from trading

FIGURE 2.3. Portrait of James Madison, ca. 1805–1807, by Gilbert Stuart. (Courtesy of Bowdoin College Museum of Art, Brunswick, Maine, Bequest of the Honorable James Bowdoin, III.)

with their enemies. To enforce their edicts, France and Great Britain routinely seized American ships. The British also impressed American sailors, claiming that the seamen owed service to the British crown, thereby denying their claims of American citizenship. At the same time, the British navy effectively blockaded the Eastern Seaboard, challenging any ship that attempted to carry cargo across the Atlantic. Such behavior angered the American public as well as national leaders, and few could deny that Congress and the Executive would have to respond.[10]

The United States initially attempted to remain aloof from the conflicts brewing between England and France by occupying a middle ground that preserved the nation's right to free trade while simultaneously maintaining political neutrality. By the winter of 1810, however, years of pursuing a policy of economic coercion and commercial restraint had failed to improve the situation or alleviate the anger of the American public over perceived British abuses. Still, the nation's political leadership had yet to determine the course of action to pursue next. "It has been my opinion ever since the meeting of Congress," declared Coles in February of that year, "that that body is not now for war." Instead, Congress was divided into several factions that advocated a variety of different approaches to the intensifying international crisis. Coles found that some leaders were "for patching the old intercourse law, which is found to be leaky." Others sought to substitute "some similar machine in its place." Still others, Henry Clay most prominently, advocated a more aggressive response, earning the nickname of "War Hawks" for their outspoken call for military action.[11]

The inability of the members of Congress to agree on a specific policy, but more significantly the failure of the Republican foreign policy agenda in general, caused conflicts to erupt within the Republican Party and fueled the resurgence of the Federalist opposition. From within his own party, Madison faced opposition from the Virginia Quids who, behind the leadership of John Randolph, repeatedly ridiculed both the president and his policies. One congressman observed that Randolph, a fellow Virginian and one-time political ally of Madison, frequently "came out . . . in a most bitter philippic against the President and the Secretary of State." Madison also encountered the anti-administration sentiment expressed by senators Michael Leib and Samuel Smith, and New York governor DeWitt Clinton. These "Malcontents," as they were often called, transformed the usually secure Republican strongholds of Pennsylvania, Maryland, and New York into doubtful sources of support for the administration. As one ardent Federalist observed, "many of the members styled democrats, like . . . Merino sheep, are some two thirds and others not more than half blooded and often vote with us."[12]

"the whole circle of duties"

As the president's private secretary, Coles understood the important role he must play to prevent the political turmoil from overwhelming the administration. In early February 1810, for example, Coles reported that he had already begun performing "the whole circle of duties" required of his position. He received, cataloged, and organized the president's correspondence and was responsible for delivering all the communications between the president and Congress. Occasionally, he carried collections of documents or informal notes to particular members of the legislature. More often than not, however, he delivered official messages from the president that he then read before Congress. Initially, he described this task as "that ordeal of embarrassment." Undoubtedly, many members of Congress associated him with his older brother Isaac, who had resigned the secretaryship in late December 1809 after attacking a member of the House of Representatives in the name of honor. His brother's behavior and the formal investigation of the events leading to his resignation severely damaged the bond between the executive and the legislature, and at first threatened to hamper Coles's ability to fulfill his responsibilities as the president's secretary.[13] Once the members recognized his more cautious and tempered personality, however, Coles carried out this task with ease.

Additionally, he frequently "presided . . . as master of ceremonies" at official and informal dinners. Jonathan Roberts, a Republican representative from Pennsylvania, remarked that "the members of Congress, are [often] invited to dine with the Pres[ident] in detail. The table would hold about thirty guests," he continued, which generally included "a mixture of parties and locations." Roberts also noted that "Mrs. Madison always [sat at] . . . the head of the table," Edward Coles "at the foot & the President took some convenient seat" in between. In this way, Coles and Dolley Madison controlled the flow of the conversation and occasionally deferred to the president, who strategically selected a seat nearest those with whom he needed to discuss important matters.[14]

Even when the president's dinner companions were limited to the members of the presidential family, the conversations invariably turned to politics. After he observed the activities of the legislature from the galleries of Congress, for example, Coles "would repeat to" Madison the content of the most effective speeches. On several occasions, he reported on the "violent speech of some northern man or a short sarcasm of [John] Randolph." William C. Preston, another young Virginian who frequently stayed at the President's House, observed that Madison expected those who attended meals at the executive's house to provide him with important information otherwise unavailable to him. "He enquired of his brother-in-law, Mr. [Richard] Cutts," he noted in 1810, about "the news of the day, the proceedings of Congress, the audits, and seemed especially interested to know what Chief-Justice Marshall said and did." When he was not acting as master of ceremonies at official dinners, Coles helped the president obtain the most up-to-date information on the extent and content of opposition to his administration.[15]

The political power of dinner parties extended beyond the executive's residence, as well. Each week Coles attended a "number of dinner parties. . . . I have not dined at home in a family way," he confessed to his brother, "more than three times in the last fortnight." While some of the invitations Coles received and accepted were purely social, others came from individuals seeking insight into administration policy. In the fall of 1810, Julien Poydras, the congressional delegate from the Territory of Orleans, "insisted" that Coles dine "with him every Sunday." Poydras, who vigorously supported his territory's desire for statehood, undoubtedly viewed Coles as both a source of information and a potential advocate who might expedite his efforts to transform Louisiana into the newest member of the American union. British minister Sir Augustus John Foster likewise recognized the importance of hosting dinner parties. He admitted that he "had to give dinners three or four times a week" if he intended to remain well informed of or shape government attitudes toward his nation, especially when "questions of peace and war were debating." Like Madison and other Washingtonians, he invited various representatives, executive officers, and staff members, Coles among them, to dinner "to keep a constant and friendly connection with as many Members of Congress and public men as possible."[16]

Coles was also expected to attend and facilitate the exchange of information at executive levees and drawing room parties. At these events, he often greeted guests once they were escorted into the drawing room of the President's House. He then regulated access to Madison by ushering forward those the president wished to see and diverting others by involving them in conversations with other guests. "Mr. Madison," observed one attendee, "had no leisure for the ladies; every moment of his time," she grumbled, "is engrossed by the crowd of male visitors who court his notice." After paying heed to the ladies, it was Coles who directed the president toward the other guests so that "his attention is unavoidably withdrawn to more important subjects." In addition to the dinners, there were weekly presidential levees that attracted crowds of people, both men and women, who, like presidential dinner guests, came to socialize and conduct business with men of importance and authority.[17]

As he became increasingly adept at manipulating social gatherings to collect and distribute important information, Coles discovered perhaps the most valuable characteristic of the political culture he was helping to create. Unlike the colonial period, when an individual's public authority was linked to his local community, political power in the Early Republic was becoming increasingly portable. This was never clearer than during the summer of 1811, when Coles and his older brother John embarked on a northern tour that included sojourns in Baltimore, Philadelphia, New York, Albany, Newport, Boston, and Portland. The timing of the trip was particularly fortuitous, and perhaps purposeful, because American relations with Great Britain and France had deteriorated significantly, and factional opposition to the administration threatened the president's reelection. Over the preceding year, both European nations refused to lift their trade restrictions against the United States, and efforts to increase America's military preparedness had failed to bring either belligerent to the negotiating table.[18]

Simultaneously, while congressional War Hawks increasingly demanded a military response to British insults on the Atlantic and in the West, Federalists and anti-administration Republicans voiced their dissatisfaction with Madison and continually blocked his legislative efforts to prepare for war. Perhaps most disconcerting for the president, Madison had been forced to dismiss his secretary of state, Robert Smith, for betraying him by leaking valuable information to the administration's political enemies. The president feared that the ensuing newspaper battle between Smith and administration loyalists would undermine his credibility. Coles's northern tour, then, provided the president with a unique opportunity to gauge the region's attitude toward the administration, his reelection, and the possibility of war with Great Britain.[19]

Coles's value as an informant proved most useful when he stopped in Baltimore and spent several days visiting Robert Smith's brother Samuel. "I was treated civilly by" the Smiths, Coles reported, but "their displeasure with the President . . . is very apparent." Even more troubling, however, was Coles's discovery that, while they "are said not directly to vent their spleen," the Smiths "spur[red] on their relations & friends, many of whom are extremely abusive of the President." As proof, Coles revealed that "those abusive & scurrilous pieces signed Temolian," in the Baltimore *Whig*, "are now publicly known . . . to be from the pen of George Stevenson . . . the nephew of Smith." Coles concluded his report by stating: "I have said too much about this little clan, whose vanity or weakness is such, as to make them believe that they can make & unmake any administration."[20]

Similarly, Coles found that opposition to the Madison administration in the mid-Atlantic and New England, among Republicans and Federalists alike, remained strong. As he socialized with Dr. Benjamin Rush and Dr. Caspar Wistar in Philadelphia, Coles learned even more about the anti-administration sentiments of men such as William Duane, editor of the *Aurora Gazette Advertiser*, and Senator Michael Leib. While in Boston, a hotbed of Federalist opposition, his stays with Governor Elbridge Gerry and future senator Robert C. Winthrop confirmed the growing strength of Federalist animosity toward the administration. Yet the trip also reassured the president of the loyalty of Gerry, who received Coles hospitably and eagerly provided him with information. During this tour, Coles uncovered pockets of opposition to the president and his administration wherever he traveled and, as he attempted to repair damaged relationships among those he visited by relaying information back and forth, he aided Madison in his effort to prepare for war.[21]

By the spring of 1812, war with Great Britain appeared imminent—developments that would test how well Coles's intelligence gathering and social networking had fortified the administration in the approaching international crisis. Elbridge Gerry, the governor of Massachusetts and one of Coles's hosts during his northern tour, informed Coles in early March that "all eyes are on Congress, & war is expected by the most cool & considerate men." Most of his friends, he declared, believed that "GB will never address our wrongs." Coles knew the situation all too well. Madison's administration attempted to manage a delicate balance between war preparation and diplomacy. Indeed, Madison had hoped that Great Britain would see in American war preparations a reason to revise their foreign policy to avoid a military conflict. Coles was not as optimistic. Like Gerry, he increasingly believed that war was inevitable. As early as March 1812, he understood that unless England "change[d] her policy towards us, which is not to be expected . . . we must either have war or submission." While he acknowledged that "there are but few who do not revolt at the idea of the latter" and many who "hope[d] to avoid the former," he feared that "their wishes have got the better of their judgments."[22]

Two months later, the Madison administration awaited the arrival of diplomatic dispatches from Great Britain on the USS *Hornet*. Coles anticipated that the news aboard the *Hornet* would "unite all parties in the war against G.B." The ship also carried news of trade negotiations with France, and Coles arrogantly boasted that "if F. should not comply with our just expectations," Madison will wage "war against both" belligerent nations. He only got part of his wish when, in June 1812, the United States declared war on Great Britain.[23]

The War of 1812 lasted for three long years and plunged the nation into an international as well as a domestic political crisis. The opposition that greeted Madison's declaration of war fell almost entirely along sectional and party lines. Nearly all Republicans supported the call to arms, and the majority of the seventy-nine members of the House who voted in favor of the declaration hailed from the South and Pennsylvania. Similarly, nearly all Federalists and three-quarters of the members from New England and New York voted against the war measure. The results in the Senate were nearly identical. Despite the clear divisions within Congress, some Americans expressed relief that the government had finally made a decision. Years of economic embargos and slow communications across the Atlantic had produced fatigue and frustration throughout the country. A pessimistic Elbridge Gerry was glad his friend finally took action. "War is declared," he wrote Madison in July 1812, "God be praised, Our country is safe." Virginian William Wirt, who had long supported the idea of a military response to perceived British injustices, trumpeted to newly appointed secretary of state James Monroe that "we are beginning now to hold up our heads and boast that we are Americans. . . . There is not a man here," he continued, "who is not an inch taller since congress has done its duty." For those who opposed military action, this decision was troubling. Still, initially many Federalists were reluctant to voice their outright opposition. Abijah Bigelow attempted to place the situation in a positive light. He wrote his wife Hannah that he had little doubt that the war was "brought about by French intrigue [and] by ambitious and speculating individuals." He predicted, then, that the conflict would "be the means of putting down an administration unfit, both in talents and integrity," to remain in office. Bigelow closed the letter by declaring: "Let us do our duty and hope for the best."[24] From his perspective, a view shared by most Federalists, the demise of the Madison administration was the best they could hope for from the crisis.

"the pulsations of my heart"

Just as the nation braced itself for war, and Madison adjusted to the disappointment of rising opposition to his decision, Coles entered into a personal crisis. The promise of a marriage to the woman he loved disintegrated the same spring the United States marched toward war. Washington City had always served as a seasonal marriage market for many of the region's younger residents. Coles enthusiastically participated in these courtship adventures. "As to the girls," Coles reported in early 1810, "the City affords some pretty ones," and he noted that "12 or 15 . . . have come from a distance, as the saying is, to look for Husbands." When the congressional session opened again in December 1810, Coles once again noted the character of the women he encountered. "Some of the misses are pretty," he admitted. "So much so," he continued, "that with the dim light of the candles on my first interview with one of them I felt the pulsations of my heart much disturbed." Lest they think his heart was lost, however, Coles assured his siblings that "she proved defective by day light."[25]

Coles had become so practiced at the art of courting prospective spouses that he frequently encouraged others to join the competition. When he heard rumors that his brother John was spending a great deal of time in Richmond, Coles asked if "he is in love." Could it be, he teased, that his old bachelor brother thought he might capture "some sprightly little miss in her teens to light up the dark valley of old age." Such foolishness, he warned might snag a wife, but one who "will be very apt to act the part of an ignis-fatuus." Coles thought his brother would find better prospects in Washington. "What think you, Brother John," asked Coles, "of coming & courting our cousin the Widow [Lucy] W[ashington?]" He assured John that the woman would "suite you to a fraction," promising that "her natural gaity . . . would effectually prevent your propensity of biting off your thumb." Indeed, Coles declared that only "the great disparity of our ages has prevented my losing my heart."[26]

Coles may have joked with his siblings about the amorous adventures and marriage exploits he witnessed in the nation's capital, but underneath his wit and humor lay his own longing for companionship. Like many of his contemporaries, he understood marriage and family as a vital source of happiness as well as an outward sign of success. Coles, however, pursued the affections of the fairer sex quite differently from those around him. His sister, for example, teased him in April 1807 when rumors that he was courting a particular young woman made their way from Williamsburg to Enniscorthy. "Why Edward," Elisa Coles proclaimed, "you are quite a romantick lover! not to enquire whether the Lady is rich." She thought "that must certainly be the first question . . . your sex (yourself excepted) generally ask." She confessed that she had learned long ago "that wealth is more thought of than beauty, accomplishments, and everything else," and she could not help but be astonished that he had failed to ask "'is she rich' even *my* Brothers ask that question" first. Elisa was perhaps more correct in her assessment of her brothers than she thought. Like Edward, Isaac also frequently wrote home from Washington during his stint as Jefferson's private secretary with reports of eligible women in the city, but he focused on a particular set of qualities. "Miss Landsdale," he reported, was "a pretty little Girl with $20,000 in funds." Another young woman, "Miss Breckenridge," who was "as tall as I am & has red hair & is very pretty," also attracted the attention of many young men. "Her father you know," declared Isaac Coles, "is rich." While wealth as much as beauty signaled a young woman's eligibility for Isaac, Edward emphasized the potential for happiness that came from a marriage based on mutual love and affection.[27]

That Coles was decidedly more romantic than his older brother Isaac was supported by more than mere rumor. In a letter written to a college friend soon after he left Williamsburg, Coles explained his view of love. "I suppose love," he declared, "to be founded on esteem sustained by the acknowledgment of every amiable quality, refined by the most perfect delicacy of sentiment unsullied by the least idea unsympathetic and finally corroborated by the reciprocal confidence and unrestrained everflowing of two fond, chaste . . . hearts . . . melted into one." It was this view of love that led Coles to celebrate marriage as a "blissful state" and a wife as "the most agreeable & delightful of all worldly blessings." He believed, then, that a young man's courting habits should be guided by the pursuit of affection and happiness rather than financial gain or social standing. Just before he moved to Washington City, he congratulated a friend for finding "a 'help mate' so piously devoted" to her husband and confessed that "to my thirsting heart your condition is an endless source of new gratifications." In his friend's case, he found a happy marriage that confirmed what he had always suspected but had yet to experience, that a man's happiness could only be sustained by a companionate marriage based on love.[28]

That his idealistic views of love and marriage had remained unchanged during the years that followed was certain. In an entertaining tale involving his effort to unite his good friend Christopher Hughes with "his sweetheart," Laura Sophia Smith, Coles once again revealed his romantic tendencies. Apparently Hughes had arrived in the city unannounced in the winter of 1810 and appeared at a social gathering at the President's House, only to have "the whole of the . . . party abscond" and remain "incognito as long as he remained" in the city. The incident alienated him from Coles's social circle for the remainder of the week, causing a mortified Hughes to leave "the city in great trouble" and disappointed that he had failed to see the object of his affection more than once. Coles attempted to repair the situation by promoting his friend's prospects with Miss Smith. He reported to his family that he had engaged the young woman in "a long talk a few evenings ago about love, engagements, ones not being capable of loving more than once, [and the] frivolous objections on the part of parents." Though he never mentioned his friend's name directly, Coles hoped the young woman would take his advice and "overcome every impediment as a test of the warmth of her heart and sincerity of her affection" and confess her love for Hughes. Nor did he distribute this kind of advice to his friends alone. When his brother John refused to come a-courting to Washington, he tried to persuade him to be more confident in his social exploits closer to home. If "*It is possible for you* to find a woman that you can love *seriously & ardently*" in Richmond, declared Coles, "take my advice & marry her, if you can: for be assured as it is the most natural so it is the most happy state."[29]

Coles fell in love himself and proposed to Marie Antoinette Hay in late 1811. He had known Marie for many years, but their courtship had intensified during her most recent visit to Washington City. She was the daughter of George Hay, a prominent Republican and the U.S. district attorney for Virginia, son-in-law to James Monroe, and resident of Richmond. Marie Antoinette was Hay's beautiful and vibrant eldest daughter and a regular member of the Coles family social circle. In fact, Coles and Hay may have begun their flirtations as early as August 1807, when she stayed at Enniscorthy for several weeks following her mother's death. That the two continued to enjoy a playful acquaintance was clear when Coles wrote home from Washington for the first time in February 1810. In that letter he coyly asked his brothers and sisters to "give Miss A Hay & L. Carrington a kiss for me, if they will let you, & tell them I long to see them."[30]

Their attachment had grown more intimate and ardent a year and a half later, when she accepted his marriage proposal. Unfortunately, their attachment was not strong enough to keep the two young Virginians together. Apparently when she returned home to Richmond, Marie experienced a change of heart. Astonished and dejected, Coles wrote his brother in March to confirm "the change in my matrimonial prospects" and confessed that "her conduct is a perfect riddle and incomprehensible to me." Still, he did not "altogether despair" and remained hopeful that the situation might be resolved within the week. Marie was due to return to Washington City to attend a wedding scheduled for that weekend, and Coles intended to confront her then. The infamous "widow W" that Coles had tried to match with his older brother was no longer among the available belles of Washington. After rejecting him once, Washington had finally accepted Judge Thomas Todd's proposal of marriage, and the nuptials were to be held at the President's House. Coles, along with Dolley's brother John Payne and her son Payne Todd, served as grooms-men, while Marie Hay, Phoebe Morris, and Margaret Hamilton were the bridesmaids. It must have been an emotional day for both Coles and Hay as they watched another couple get married. He probably did his best to persuade his love to renew her promise to marry him. Evidently he was at least partially successful, for he extracted a promise from her that "she would unconditionally engage herself and also fix the time of our marriage" within four weeks' time.[31]

Marie's reluctance to commit herself to Coles may have been a reflection of the attitude of many southern women her age who avoided committing themselves to marriage because doing so marked the end of their already limited independence. Her hesitation might also have been encouraged by her father, who probably opposed the marriage on economic grounds. He had built a fairly prosperous life from a modest beginning as the son of a cabinet maker, but he still had a young family (the product of his second marriage, to James Monroe's daughter Elizabeth) to support. He knew that he had little to offer his daughter in the way of a dowry. If she wanted an economically secure future, Marie would have to marry well, and Coles was a man with uncertain future prospects. Coles recognized "the gloomy and melancholy fact" of his economic situation, "particularly connected with the idea of my being married, and that too to one who is poor and as proud as myself." Yet he remained optimistic. "I will not suf-fer myself to be dejected, I will not think of my bad luck." Instead, he pro-claimed that "if I cannot do better on Rockfish, *I must move elsewhere.*" The elder Hay may have objected to the match, as well, because of Coles's views on slavery. In just a few short years, Hay would emerge as one of the most ardent advocates for opening Missouri to slavery, a position Coles would just as adamantly oppose.[32]

Even if she had been immune to her father's likely objections, Marie may have changed her mind because she did not share Coles' willing-ness to leave Virginia for a new home in the West. Virginians had been leaving the state to resettle in the Ohio River Valley for many years and Marie undoubtedly knew of these experiences. Between 1790 and 1840, over one million Virginians left the Old Dominion to settle in the Ohio

River valley and the trans-Mississippi West. Many of these migrants wrote relatives who remained in Virginia describing their circumstances. These letters were full of tales of both hardship and economic success. For women, however, the opportunities presented by removal to the frontier often came at a high price. When they followed their husbands westward, wives sacrificed the emotional attachments to family and friends that had given meaning to their lives.[33] Perhaps she could not bring herself to sever her social connections for a life with Coles. In any case, the marriage between Marie and Edward was not to be, and Coles was heartbroken. Weakened and exhausted by the labors of the heart and mind, Coles returned home to Virginia in August 1812 and promptly fell ill with a severe case of hemorrhoids. The idealistic view of love he so romantically described in his letters to his friends had been tarnished by the practical reality of his unsuccessful amorous adventure. It would not be the last time Coles's experiences failed to match his ideals.

"no beginning or no end"

When Coles finally returned to Washington City in mid-October 1812, the sparkle and excitement so apparent in his letters home two years earlier was gone. "Everything goes on here as if there were no beginning or no end, as if everything were regulated by perpetual motion." The melancholy tone of his letters that fall could be attributed at least in part to disappointing war developments. After early optimistic predictions of success along the Canadian border at Detroit, in upstate New York, and on the high seas in July and August, the apparent ineptitude of the commanding officers (particularly William Hull and Henry Dearborn) raised serious questions about the ability of the Americans to prosecute the war. Massachusetts Federalist Abijah Bigelow complained that "The conduct of our armies is truly disgraceful." One report of a cowardly retreating commander was particularly disturbing and led him to declare: "What a deplorable situation. . . . Never were the affairs of a nation conducted worse than ours."[34]

On the home front, the situation had been frustrating and unstable from the beginning of the conflict. Federalist opposition to the war and vitriolic attacks on Madison quickly reached a fever pitch and showed little sign of abating. Within a few weeks of the war declaration, congressional Federalists issued a public statement, composed by ardent Massachusetts Federalist Josiah Quincy, claiming that the Madison had thrust the nation "into difficulties, with little calculation about the means, and little concern about the consequences." A Boston clergyman expressed his outrage when he roared from the pulpit that if "Mr. Madison has declared war, let Mr. Madison carry it on. . . . The Union has long since virtually dissolved," observed this Federalist. Let "the Disunited States take care of themselves." Even some of Madison's allies were beginning to question his leadership. Family friend William C. Preston complained that Madison's "judgment was not clear about the war or the mode of conducting it, nor had he about him friends whose pertinacity and firmness might supply his own defects in these qualities." Prosecuting the war would be much more difficult than Madison had imagined.[35]

The Madisons employed the same strategy to counter this contentious climate that had worked well for them in the past. Dolley opened the winter social season with her first Wednesday drawing room party on October 27 and immediately focused her energies on strengthening confidence in the administration. She also added additional social gatherings to the normal calendar of events. In fact, over the next few years, her social obligations, while certainly an essential component of the administration's political strategies, would exhaust her. In the middle of her husband's second term, she complained to Coles that she was so busy and "that the city is more crowded than ever with strangers" that "my head is dizzy." Her cousin did everything he could to help her in her efforts. In late November 1812, Coles organized and hosted a grand party on board the USS *Constellation*. Although he recognized the potential political value of an event that would bring together in one location Federalists and Republicans, administration officers and elites, and perhaps pressure Congress to approve the military appropriation bill under consideration at the time, Coles confessed that he looked forward most to encountering "some beauties that are said to exist" in the city. Yet the bitterness of his recent failed affair with Marie Hay clouded his perspective. "I do not however flatter myself with the hope of being much gratified in this way," he lamented to his brother, "for judging from my experience of the town belles" (by which he undoubtedly meant Miss Hay), "the more light that is thrown on their persons or characters the more hideous they appear." The celebration was indeed a grand affair. Hundreds of guests, including members of the cabinet and Congress as well as residents from the President's House and visitors in town, caroused late into the night. To his great relief, Miss Marie Hay was not among the guests, but clearly Coles had not recovered from the pain of their breakup. Washington was no longer the exciting cosmopolitan city that had lured him away from Virginia.[36]

The constant and monotonous demands of his position as well as his anxiety about Miss Hay eventually took their toll on Coles. The illness that had delayed his return to Washington a few months earlier resurfaced and intensified during the winter of 1812–1813. He had been complaining since his return that he did "not like my situation." His doctor had told him that he "should be well in a few days," yet it had been nearly a month "and my ulcer is not yet healed." He continued to limit his diet and tried to exercise more, but this strategy proved ineffective. By early December his health was deteriorating, and a second growth had appeared in the scar left by an operation he had endured in the summer. He was convinced "that all the suffering and privation I have endured has been for nothing" and concluded that "I shall have to undergo another operation before I shall be cured." Rather than return to Virginia to see Dr. Everett, who had failed to cure him the previous summer, Coles took Dolley's advice and traveled to Philadelphia, where he sought the attention of Dr. Philip Syng Physick, who performed another operation.[37]

Initially, it seemed as though Coles could not have chosen a worse time to leave the president's side. For months his opponents and supports alike had testified to the dire situation facing Madison. As early as December 1812, Massachusetts Federalist Abijah Bigelow confessed that "I envy not Madison his reelection. His situation must be truly wretched." As a member of the opposition, Bigelow knew all too well that the president would find little support in Congress, and he predicted that the president possessed little power to reverse the situation. Similarly, William A. Burwell, a Republican member of Congress from Virginia, recognized that "Mr. Madison is in a most perilous situation [and] unless he can impress more energy into the Army . . . disgust will prevail everywhere." Madison had attempted to alleviate the nation's anxiety by reorganizing his cabinet. He dismissed Secretary of the Navy Paul Hamilton and Secretary of War William Eustis and replaced them with William Jones and John Armstrong, respectively. The president also called for a special session of Congress and scheduled the opening day for the first of May. He hoped to use the special session to resolve the financial problems that had heretofore undermined his ability to prosecute the war. Simultaneously, Madison accepted an offer from the Russian government to mediate a peace conference, and he was eager to appoint a delegation to travel overseas. With so many priorities on the administration's agenda, Coles feared that his departure from the capital in March 1813 would hamper the president's ability to accomplish his goals.[38]

Little did Coles know that his temporary residence in Philadelphia would prove advantageous to the administration. As he had learned during his northern tour two years earlier, the social bonds Coles had forged during his day-to-day responsibilities in Washington City continued to hold wherever he traveled. After nearly a month recuperating in Philadelphia, Coles attended "a grand party at Mr. [Alexander] Dallas' in the company of Mr. Albert Gallatin & Mr. [James A.] Bayard," who were the most prominent members of the delegation charged with negotiating a peace settlement with Great Britain. By attending the gathering, Coles could inform Madison of the public reception of his decision to pursue a diplomatic resolution to the international conflict as well as the hopes and fears of the members of the delegation. He also regularly visited "with . . . Members of Congress who spent their recess" in Philadelphia, and thereby kept Madison abreast of the opinions and potential opposition of those who would be deciding the fate of the war effort during the upcoming congressional session.[39]

Despite his continued service to the president, Coles still worried that his absence would be burdensome. Accordingly, in May 1813 he resigned his position. Perhaps he still thought his stubbornly persistent health problems would prevent his return to Washington City indefinitely and did not want to leave the president without an assistant at such a crucial time. Or maybe he did not want to return to the capital city for emotional reasons. Miss Hay was a regular participant in the Washington social scene, and it was unlikely Coles was eager to be reminded repeatedly of her rejection.

Another explanation, however, may lie in his experiences in Philadelphia. His sojourn in the Quaker City was the first time he had lived for an extended period of time in a free state, and he may have gotten a taste of what his life would be like without enslaved laborers. His residence in Philadelphia also gave Coles the opportunity to form two important friendships that undoubtedly contributed to his decision to revisit his plan to liberate his slaves and move westward. Coles spent a great deal of his time with Nicholas Biddle, a rising Philadelphia lawyer of significant literary and political talents. The two men had a great deal in common. They were both very interested in politics and adamantly opposed to slavery. Like Coles, Biddle knew James Monroe quite well, a friendship that had begun six years earlier when he served as Monroe's secretary during the latter's stint as minister to Great Britain. They both were ardent supporters of the Madison administration and the war effort, and were nationalists at heart. After two months in Philadelphia, Coles explained just how important Biddle had become to him. "The attention and kindness of my friendship with Biddle I can never forget; he occupies the first place in my esteem," he confessed to his mother, and "scarcely a day passes without our being together." Significantly, Coles met Biddle just after the latter had completed work on a history of the Lewis and Clark expedition. It is not difficult, then, to imagine them discussing Coles's own journey through similar territory four years earlier, or the personal and national benefits of migrating westward.[40]

Coles also met and became close friends with Roberts Vaux, a philanthropist who was a regular attendee at the same city social functions Coles frequented during his year in Philadelphia. Vaux came from a prominent Quaker family and was involved in nearly every reform and humanitarian endeavor organized in the city. Perhaps most important for Coles, he was an active member of the Pennsylvania Society for Promoting the Abolition of Slavery and wrote several pamphlets arguing against the westward expansion of the institution. Although he was skeptical of the practical effectiveness of the national abolitionist movement, Vaux was committed to local efforts to end slavery, a view Coles would come to share in the near future. Coles certainly told Vaux of his plans to move west and liberate his enslaved laborers, a decision the Philadelphia philanthropist undoubtedly encouraged him to pursue.[41] Biddle and Vaux both remained intimate friends as well as personal and political advisors to Coles for the remainder of their lives. As each month in Philadelphia passed by, Coles grew increasingly impatient for both a cure to his disease and an opportunity to honor his antislavery ambitions.

James Madison, however, refused to accept Coles's letter of resignation. His cousin Dolley wrote him with the decision, explaining that she and Madison expected him to remain with them "to the last." She did admit that neither of them would want to "retard any plan for your prosperity" by refusing to accept his letter. By this she meant his plan to move westward. "I flatter myself," she declared, that "the Western country *may* be given up for something more consonant with your happiness & that of your connections." She assured him that no one among his family "feel a more affectionate interest for you than Mr. Madison & myself. I hope you will believe," she continued, "that such is our regard & esteem for you, that we should consider your leaving us a misfortune." Besides, she advised, "The winter is not a Season for emigration" and encouraged him to wait until next spring or summer "to make your election *to go, or not to go*." From her perspective, then, the issue was settled. "Mr. M can do very well without a Secry until your health is re-established." Coles decided to heed his cousin's advice and agreed to return, thereby delaying any decision about his future.[42]

"gangs of Negroes"

Despite his promise to defer again his antislavery ambitions, Coles made preparations to pursue a future in the West throughout the final years of Madison's administration. In the spring of 1813 he secured from his brother Walter a promise to purchase Rockfish plantation. "Tell Brother Walter," he instructed John, that "I hope there will be no difficulty in our bargain about the Land, as I foresee none." He acknowledged that both his poor health and the state of international affairs would compel him "to delay vesting my money in real estate," but he was eager to make the deal. Accordingly, he felt that there was no need for "prompt payments" and offered to settle their affairs "to our mutual satisfaction and advantage" when he returned home in a few months. In truth, Coles had been trying to sell his Rockfish estate ever since he took possession of the property. In the fall of 1810, for example, he had reminded his brothers of his intention to sell his plantation, but cautioned them that although he was "disposed to sell," he was "not so much bent on it as to make a sacrifice." He believed that Rockfish was worth at least $15,000, but revealed that he might seek as much as $17,000. By early 1811, however, he concluded that there was "little chance of making a sale of Rockfish in time to give possession this season." Still, Coles continued to try to "effect a sale as soon as possible" and was willing to "give possession whenever it can be done with convenience." Eighteen months later, his farm remained unsold, and by May 1812 he had become so frustrated with his financial situation that he could not help but complain to his brothers about his state of affairs. "I commenced my operations as a farmer more than four years ago," he observed, "with a debt of $500." Despite avoiding any additional investments in stock, furniture, "or indeed anything else," and living in Washington on a salary "sufficient to support me," Coles had not been able to pay off this debt or make the farm pay for itself.[43] So, when his brother Walter agreed to purchase the estate, Coles eagerly accepted the offer and saved the capital to invest in western land.

Coles had one more obstacle to overcome before he could move westward. He was still a slaveholder, and the issue of slavery remained an ever-present concern for him. In fact, during his tenure as Madison's private secretary he could not escape the issue. In the President's House he encountered numerous enslaved laborers who sustained the ordinary functions of the household. Bound laborers prepared and served the food, cleaned the rooms, greeted visitors, and always stood in the background ready to attend to every need of both the Madisons and their guests. Madison brought Paul Jennings, his personal valet, from Virginia, and he attended the president throughout his two terms in office. Mrs. Madison's primary housekeeper, Sucky, was likewise a fixture in the President's House, where she worked alongside dozens of others who were either brought from Montpelier or hired from area slaveholders to serve the crowded household.[44] Slaves, then, were everywhere around Coles.

Coles often discussed the issue with Madison. As he recalled many years later, he had frequently expressed to Madison "my surprise that just men, & long sighted politicians should not as well in reference to the acknowledged rights of man, as to the true & permanent interests of their Country, take the necessary steps to put in train its termination." According to Coles, Madison had privately acknowledged that slavery was wrong and, like many of his fellow-Virginians, he lamented the absence of an easy solution to the problem. As early as 1791, however, Madison had concluded that any public action against slavery was "likely to do harm rather than good." He feared that an unsuccessful bid to end the institution would only strengthen the forces that sought to preserve it. Madison believed that until popular sentiment for abolition increased, inaction remained the most prudent and practical course available. In the meantime, he treated his slaves well and sought to eliminate the harsher elements of the institution. He rarely employed corporal punishment and never made a display of one slave's punishment as a warning to others. His human property was well fed and clothed, and received generous (by the standards of the day) medical care when sick. Benevolence and paternalism, it seemed, was a compromise Madison hoped would make slavery tolerable for both the owner and the enslaved.[45]

Coles, however, remained unconvinced by Madison's rationalizations and continually criticized his mentor in subtle but potentially explosive ways. He felt that Madison's pragmatic approach to the slavery issue would produce the opposite of what the president intended; rather than preserve the "good," Madison's apathy, Coles believed, threatened to cause more "harm." No set of circumstances demonstrated his point more clearly than the brutal domestic slave trade that passed through the nation's capital. Coles recorded in his 1844 autobiography that he and Madison had frequently encountered "gangs of Negroes, some in irons, on their way to a Southern market." These enslaved men, women, and children had been torn from their families and sold by their masters to feed the insatiable demand for labor in the Southwest. He could not ignore the spectacle and took "the liberty to jeer" Madison "by congratulating him, as the chief of our great Republic," for having been "saved" from "the deep mortification of witnessing such a revolting sight in the presence of a representative of a Nation, less boastful perhaps of its regard for the rights of man, but more observant of them." As someone who hoped that the American republican experiment would serve as a model for the world, Madison surely felt the sting of this particular jibe. Even though many Washingtonians admitted that the District slave trade presented scenes of "wretchedness and human degradation disgraceful to our characters as citizens of a free government," the nation's congressional and executive leaders continually refused to discuss the issue. Far from setting the stage for the destruction of the institution, Coles reminded his mentor of his belief that inaction only increased the likelihood that slavery would spread unchallenged across the continent.[46]

The War of 1812 also ensured that the slavery issue would continue to occupy Coles's attention. Throughout the debates preceding the declaration of war and repeatedly during the conflict itself, Federalists deployed the politics of slavery, citing slave representation and Republican inconsistency on the issue, to cultivate opposition to Madison and the war effort. As a result, these antiwar northerners crafted a sectionalism that was built on a critique of slavery and the institution's impact on American politics.[47] At the same time, the spring of 1814 witnessed the emergence of a revitalized Great Britain. No longer preoccupied with Napoleon on the continent, the British military turned their attention and resources more directly to their conflict with the United States. American troop strength and skill were greatly improved by then, and the United States continued to have the advantage in the West, but the young Republic remained vulnerable along the Atlantic Coast. In fact, during much of the spring and summer of 1813, the British had raided the Chesapeake Bay area with relative ease. Dolley Madison described to Coles in May 1813 "the fears & alarms that circulate around me. For the last week," she explained, "the City & G. Toun [sic] . . . have expected a visit from the English & were not lacking in their expressions of terror & reproach." News of a British frigate positioned at the mouth of the Potomac River had reached Washington, inspiring everyone to make "considerable efforts for defence." The fort was under repair, and the militia had been called out and were drilling regularly. Although a Quaker, Dolley Madison was no pacifist "when assailed" and confessed to her cousin that she kept "the old Tunesian Sabre within my reach." By 1814, the British targeted both Maine (for its strategic significance in the Canadian campaign) and the Chesapeake Bay. They easily occupied eastern Maine by the summer. Simultaneously, British Admiral Alexander Cochrane plundered the Chesapeake coastline as he moved his forces toward the nation's capital and Baltimore.[48]

British movements along the Chesapeake Bay exposed a particularly southern weakness in the American defense. Just as had been the case during the American Revolution, residents of the Chesapeake region feared that slaves, a group many considered to be "an internal foe," would aid the British war effort.[49] As early as the spring of 1812, Virginia governor James Barbour warned that the residents of Norfolk "associate with an invasion a probable insurrection of their slaves, who," he believed, "take a deep interest in a rupture between England and this Country." A year later, Elbridge Gerry, Jr., who was visiting his father in Washington City, observed that "the blacks in some places refuse to work and say they shall soon be free, and then the white people must look out." Margaret Bayard Smith, a resident of Washington and the wife of the editor of the *National Intelligencer*, remarked that "as for our enemy at *home* I have no doubt they will if possible join the British," but she reassured her sister "that the few scatter'd slaves about our neighborhood, could not muster enough force to venture an attack." Still, her husband "procured pistols," and every precaution was taken to ensure their protection in the event of an insurrection.[50]

In the nation's capital, residents attempted to prevent slave misbehavior and threats of violence by encouraging men exempted from militia duty to form voluntary associations to patrol the city. Gerry observed that "should we be attacked" by the British, "there will be great danger of the blacks rising and to prevent this, patrols are very necessary to keep them in awe." Similarly, armed patrols constantly surveyed the coastal areas along the Chesapeake, shooting and arresting suspected escaped slaves wherever they appeared. In March 1813, Nathaniel Burwell reported that ten slaves suspected of plotting insurrection "have been apprehended and are in jail for examination." Four months later, another patrol in Hampton, Virginia, was greeted by the cheers of their neighbors when they shot at and retrieved twenty-two slaves who had commandeered a small boat in order to make their way to a British ship.[51] In general, most Americans, but especially southerners, responded to the persistent threat of slave insurrection during the war years by attempting to strengthen the slave system.

"to put into complete practice those hallowed principles"

Coles, however, concluded that the only way to rid the nation of such a dangerous internal enemy was to abolish the institution of slavery. Knowing that he lacked the authority and ability to accomplish the task himself, he wrote a letter to his friend and mentor Thomas Jefferson asking for help. Coles and Jefferson had been on intimate terms for many years, but he confessed that "I never took up my pen with more hesitation." He feared "appearing presumptuous" by calling the ex-president's attention to the persistence of slavery, an institution Coles knew Jefferson understood to be repugnant "to the principles of the revolution . . . [and] our free institutions." Still, Coles wrote "to entreat & beseech" Jefferson "to exert . . . your influence" in removing the contradiction by "devising & getting into operation some plan for the gradual emancipation of slavery." From Coles's perspective, such a "difficult task" could only be "successfully performed by the revered Fathers of all our political & societal blessings." More important, the young Virginian hoped to impress upon the Sage of Monticello that "it is a duty . . . that devolves particularly on you," as the man most responsible for championing "the rights of man, & the liberty & independence of your country." Only the father of freedom and equality, declared Coles, could mobilize the support required "to put into complete practice those hallowed principles contained in that renowned Declaration."[52]

Coles composed this letter as rumors of an impending British attack on the capital and reports of possible slave insurrections circulated among Washington's residents. He probably dismissed the rumors and reports as unlikely; similar threatening accounts had appeared a year earlier, but no attack or rebellion had materialized, allowing Coles and his fellow Washingtonians to feel secure. Even when the British increased their operations in the Chesapeake region in the early summer of 1814, fueling a revival of the reports of an assault, Coles most likely remained unconcerned. Many of his neighbors expressed little fear that the British would strike and wrote their family and friends outside of the city to reassure them that everyone was safe in the capital. This sense of security was reinforced by Secretary of War General John Armstrong's insistence that the British would never harm Washington. He claimed that the city offered little strategic advantage, and he was sure that the British

FIGURE 2.4. The taking of the city of Washington in America, 1814. (Courtesy of the Library of Congress, Prints & Photographs Division (LC-DIG-ppmsca-31113).)

would focus their assault on Baltimore, a place "of so much more consequence."[53] When Coles penned his note, then, his mind was undisturbed by his immediate surroundings and he focused his attention squarely on his future prospects.

The threat proved more real than anyone had imagined, and before Jefferson could respond to Coles's letter, the British attacked the nation's capital, forcing Madison to flee into the Maryland countryside as the enemy burned both the Capitol and the President's House. In his reply, then, Jefferson expressed his fear that emancipation would be the product, not of "the generous energies of our minds . . . [but] from the power of our present enemy." The British threat notwithstanding, the third president denied that he had any obligation to act, and confessed that "I had always hoped that the younger generation . . . would have sympathized with oppression where ever found, and prove[n] their love of liberty beyond their own share of it" by demanding the abolition of slavery. To his dismay, except for Coles's "solitary but welcome voice," he had encountered few aspiring leaders willing to pursue the cause. He "considered the general silence . . . on this subject," he informed his correspondent, "as indicating an apathy unfavorable to every hope." Still, Jefferson optimistically believed that "the hour of emancipation is advancing in the march of time," and insisted that it could only be achieved by the next generation of national leaders. In the meantime, he urged Coles not to liberate his enslaved property or abandon his native state. Instead, he instructed his young neighbor to "reconcile yourself to your country and its unfortunate condition . . . and when the phalanx is formed, bring on & press the proposition perseveringly until its accomplishment."[54]

Coles could not have been more surprised and dissatisfied with Jefferson's response. He ignored his correspondent's reference to the war and rejected Jefferson's advice that he wait patiently for a groundswell of support for emancipation to materialize. Jefferson was unwilling to act on behalf of emancipation and preferred to wait interminably, as he confessed just months before his death in 1826, until a "Revolution in public opinion" emerged naturally. Coles, however, insisted that "public sentiment . . . in matters of this kind ought not to be expected to lead, but to be led." He predicted that "there will always exist in society a kind of vis in ertia" when it came to slavery. Only a leader who possessed a "great weight of character," a man like "you, my dear sir," could "awaken our fellow Citizens from their infatuation" with economic and political self-interest and lead them "to a proper sense of justice & to the true interest of their country." As for his own efforts on behalf of abolition, Coles confessed that "if I had supposed myself capable of being instrumental in bringing about a liberation" of Virginia's enslaved laborers "it would afford me great happiness."[55]

Disappointed but no less committed to opposing slavery, Coles dismissed his mentor's counsel, ignored the objections of his family and friends, and in June 1815 embarked on a second tour of the Old Northwest. The timing of this trip could not have been better. Madison had little need of his services. The war had ended when the Treaty of Ghent was signed on December 24, 1814, and Congress adjourned in early March 1815 and would not begin a new session until December. More important, enthusiasm for western land and optimism about the nation's future revived following the War of 1812, and Coles joined a flood of Americans pouring into the trans-Appalachian West in search of economic opportunity. During his ten-month journey, he looked for a location that would both improve his economic circumstances and allow him to follow through with his convictions. With a portion of the cash from the sale of his farm to his brother Walter in hand, Coles purchased (along with his siblings Walter and Rebecca) a 6,000-acre tract of land of fertile land in Lincoln County, Missouri, called El Prado. His one-third portion of the land was most attractive, he declared, because "it offers immense inducements to men of enterprise. . . . I do not think I am extravagant in my calculations," he continued, "when I say that 10,000$ in the hands of only a tolerably judicious man will in five years be worth 100,000$." Soon after he returned to Virginia, however, he confessed to his friend Nicholas Biddle that "I was disappointed in the impressions I formed" of the frontier, but acknowledged that "it is probable I may yet make it the place of my residence."[56]

The despondency Coles expressed to Biddle probably reflected his continued reluctance to abandon his native state and the lifestyle he enjoyed. "Were I a married man I think I could set myself down and be very happy in the Illinois Territory, especially," he proclaimed, "if I could induce some clever sociable fellows to accompany and live near me." In reality, however, Coles was single and claimed "a partiality for society" that ensured that he "could not be happy" on the frontier "however much wealth and distinction I might acquire." Consequently, as had been the case when he returned home from college almost ten years earlier, Coles faced a difficult situation. His preference for high society frequently caused him to contemplate residing in a city like Philadelphia. Yet his conscience pushed him to consider resettling in the West where he could liberate his chattel property. "But then," he asked Biddle, "what should I do? A man must have some occupation, something to engage his attention or else he cannot be happy. On which of the remote horns of this dilemma I shall hang my destinies," he concluded, "is yet uncertain."[57]

"that blot of slavery"

Once again, the arrival of a letter from James Madison led Coles to defer his antislavery ambitions. Apparently, a breach of relations between the United States and Russia had occurred when the Russian consul general Nicholas Kosloff was arrested in Philadelphia for raping a twelve-year-old servant girl. Madison had refused to intervene on behalf of the Russian official, citing a lack of authority over state officials. André de Dashkoff, the Russian minister, expressed his outrage by informing the emperor that Madison's inactivity constituted a violation of diplomatic immunity. Emperor Alexander responded to the charge by banning the American chargé de affaires from St. Petersburg. Madison asked if Coles would be willing to present a collection of letters from the administration explaining the particulars of the situation to the Russian government. Unlike six years earlier, Coles did not hesitate to accept the president's request, informing Madison that without anything "at this time to engage my attention at home, and being desirous of seeing Europe, I have no objection to availing myself of this occasion to do so." In early August 1816, Coles boarded the United States brig of war *Prometheus* and once again headed east rather than west.[58]

Coles arrived in St. Petersburg two months later, only to discover that "the Emperor is now absent in Russian Poland" and was not expected to return for several weeks. Rather than pursue the Russian leader through the Polish countryside, as the American consul recommended, Coles "judged it more consistent with the dignity of the government he represented that he should await the emperor's return to St. Petersburg." As he waited, Coles traveled through the countryside comparing Russian and American society. Most striking to him were the significant differences between the labor systems of the two nations. As in the United States, "the VASSALS or slaves of Russia, are by law subject to the will and pleasure of their lords and masters." The law defined them as property "to be bought and sold . . . and [they could be] made to labor when, where and in the way" their masters demanded. Unlike the American South, however, in Russia vassals were "inseparably connected with the soil . . . and can only be disposed of along with it." Additionally, "they are not so much an object of traffic . . . nor are the duties they are required to perform or the treatment they receive," he explained, "anything like so severe or oppressive" as the enslaved laborers of America. Coles also noted that Russian vassals could own property, and rather than owing all of their labor to their masters, Russian serfs were only expected to spend a portion of their time cultivating crops for their owner, devoting the rest of their time to laboring for themselves. From these observations, Coles concluded that Russian serfdom was far less dehumanizing for both the laborer and the master than American slavery.[59]

According to Coles, the conditions vassals endured in Russia were also significantly better than those experienced by American slaves because "the situation of the vassals is gradually improving." Unlike America, where Coles found few southern men of his generation willing to promote abolition, he encountered in Russia a "young nobility" who were "more enlightened, and entertain[ed] more liberal sentiments than their fathers," and who were interested in ameliorating the condition of their country's bound laborers. More significantly, the emperor himself supported the eradication of vassalage. "It is hoped," Coles claimed, that

Emperor Alexander's "liberality and knowledge" would lead him to "follow up the goodly step he took last summer, when he issued his ukase [decree], for the gradual though speedy emancipation of all vassals of the province of Esthonia" with a more general proclamation. To his surprise and dismay, Coles had discovered that an autocratic society seemed more inclined to pursue emancipation than his own republican government, which unlike the former was founded on a belief in the inherent freedom of every individual.[60]

After he successfully concluded his official business in St. Petersburg in January 1817, Coles embarked on a ten-month tour of Europe and Great Britain. He visited Holland, France, England, and Ireland. As he moved from place to place, he attended court, dined with royalty, and formed acquaintances and friendships with General Lafayette and the Duke of Wellington. Although his trip abroad expanded his exposure to and increased his desire to remain part of elite society, Coles's experiences in Russia and Europe only confirmed his desire to emancipate his enslaved property. Throughout the tour, slavery remained foremost in his mind. During his two-month stay in Russia, he observed that "vassalage & treatment of the serfs . . . [was] infinitely a milder & less oppressive character" than American slavery. As he witnessed various instances of "oppression both political & religious" in the rest of Europe, Coles's own "conviction of the superiority of our political institutions" strengthened. He confessed that this "increased . . . admiration & pride" in his native country "did not reconcile me, or in the least abate my objections & feelings to[ward] the state of bondage" in the United States. Instead, "that blot of Slavery" on America's "otherwise enchanting escutcheon, was the more apparent & the more disfiguring." Consequently, he returned home in the fall of 1817 free of any official responsibilities in Washington City (the Madisons had returned to Montpelier and James Monroe had assumed the presidency) and more committed than ever before to "cheerfully hasten" his departure for Illinois where he intended to realize finally his antislavery ambitions.[61]

"to preserve my principles"

Thirty-one-year-old Edward Coles returned from his European tour still convinced that without the "talents & acquirements to become the champion of humanity" in Virginia, "all I can do is to preserve my principles & save my feelings by flying from the scene of . . . oppression." So, in the summer and fall of 1818, Coles journeyed to Illinois in search of land and employment in a free territory. In August he stayed in Kaskaskia and attended the territorial constitutional convention. Illinois was applying for statehood, and the delegates to the convention were drafting a proposed constitution. To Coles's delight, the document they submitted to Congress possessed a clause that appeared to prohibit slavery. During his exploration of the region, he also discovered that the position of Register of the Land Office at Edwardsville had become vacant. Rather than delay until he returned home, Coles immediately composed a letter to President James Monroe requesting consideration as a replacement. "You must be aware," wrote Coles, "that the life I have led for many years past, whilst it disqualifies me in many respects for the enjoyment of the dull pursuits of a Farmer, qualifies me in some degree, and has given me a taste, for the sedentary occupation of the desk and of the bustling routine duties of an office." Given his experience in Washington City, Coles expressed the hope that Monroe would agree that he was well suited for the post of Register of the Land Office at Edwardsville.[62]

To assure the president that he possessed the knowledge necessary to fulfill the duties of the office he requested, Coles also revealed that "I have been almost incessantly moving to and fro examining the different parts of the Illinois Territory." He was so delighted by what he observed that he purchased "4000 acres in small tracts" in the Military Bounty Tract and had decided "to settle . . . in the neighbourhood of Edwardsville." By investing in land and declaring his intention to reside in the region, Coles transformed himself from a visitor into a resident, a condition he intended to increase his attractiveness as a candidate for the land office post.[63] In January 1819, just three months after Coles returned from his western tour, Monroe informed his friend and neighbor that he had nominated him for the post and instructed Coles to "confer with the Senators" to ensure his success. Throughout the winter of 1819, Coles lobbied vigorously for the appointment. As Monroe had predicted nine years earlier, the personal and political connections established during his tenure as Madison's private secretary proved invaluable. By early March 1819, the Senate confirmed his nomination without hesitation, and Coles rejoiced in the fact that his long-deferred antislavery ambitions would finally be realized.[64]

3 / Pioneering Antislavery Politics

In early April 1819, thirty-two-year-old Edward Coles and his enslaved property journeyed from Pittsburgh to Harrod's Creek, a settlement just ten miles above Louisville, Kentucky, by floating down the beautiful Ohio River. Encountering a "good tide of water, and remarkably fine weather," they completed the second leg of their trip to Edwardsville, Illinois, in just over nine days. As Coles explained to his mother, the "voyage has been very agreeable . . . but for the sickness of Tom & Emanuel," two of the enslaved laborers he depended upon to direct the crowded flatboats down the river. Left with only Ralph and Robert to man the oars, he confessed that "I had to work hard the whole first week." Despite the inconvenience of laboring at the oars, however, Coles still accomplished the purpose of his journey, the emancipation of his human property. "Soon after getting on board the boat," he declared, "I called them all together, and told them . . . that they were . . . free." To Coles's surprise, Ralph, the leader of the group, "appeared to feel less than any of the others the value" of the right he had restored to them. Once he announced his intention to provide each individual over the age of twenty-three with 160 acres of land, however, Ralph "was more pleased." Relieved that he had finally followed through with his long-held determination to manumit his enslaved inheritance, Coles pledged to monitor "the recoiling effects of so . . . sudden a transition—from slavery and poverty, to freedom and independence."[1]

Like Coles, many of those who emigrated across the Appalachian Mountains in the early nineteenth century assumed that they would

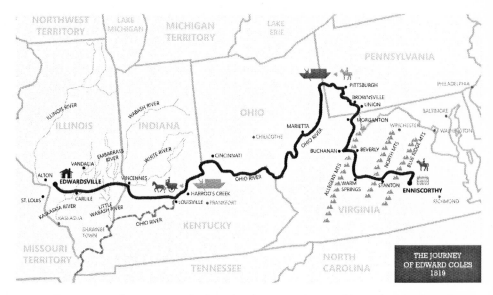

FIGURE 3.1. The Journey of Edward Coles, 1819. (Created by Mike Wirth and Suzanne Cooper Guasco, www.MikeWirthArt.com.)

preserve their freedom and independence in the West. William Newn-han Blane, an English gentleman who conducted a tour of western America in 1822, concluded that "in the United States a man, instead of renting a farm, can, for a small sum of money become a respectable landholder. . . . The emigrant," he proclaimed, "becomes here indepen-dent." Likewise, Elias Pym Fordham, an English-born surveyor who settled in Illinois in 1817, rhapsodized that "the wilds of Illinois . . . are the fields of enterprise, the cradle of freedom, [and] . . . the place of ref-uge to the oppressed." Significantly, many Americans envisioned a West that secured the freedom of its inhabitants by excluding slavery. As early as 1784, Philip Freneau, one of America's most noteworthy early poets, wrote: "While virtue warms the generous breast, There Heaven-born freedom shall reside. . . . When man shall no longer crush, when Reason shall enforce her sway, Nor these fair regions raise our blush, Where still the African complains, And mourns his yet unbroken chains." America's republican experiment, according to these observers, would be secured by a western region populated by a free and independent people.[2]

Illinois had a particularly strong reputation as an abundantly fertile region that promised economic prosperity to all who settled within its

FIGURE 3.2. Scene of the Emancipation, Mural by Phillipson Decorative
Company of Chicago, 1885. (Courtesy of Illinois Secretary of State.)

borders. Victor Collot, who visited the region in 1796, declared that "the
province of Illinois is perhaps the only spot respecting which travelers
have given no exaggerated accounts. . . . It is superior to any description," he continued, "for local beauty, fertility, climate, and the means
of every kind which nature has lavished upon it." Similarly, according to early emigrant Gershom Flagg, Illinois "is the Richest and most
handsomely situated of any I have ever seen." Not only was the land
fertile but the growing tide of immigration after 1815 seemed to guarantee that property values would increase. Two years after he settled
outside of Edwardsville, Flagg remarked that "land which was bought
two or three years ago for two dollars an acre is now selling at 10 to
12." Morris Birkbeck, a well-known British reformer and agriculturalist who bought thousands of acres of land and established a settlement
in eastern Illinois, likewise assured his friends in Great Britain that
"the working farmer, by the amount of capital required in England,

as a renter, may *own* and cultivate a much better farm" in Illinois. He attempted to encourage others to make their way to the Prairie State (and purchase land from him) by advertising that "our soil appears to be rich . . . so easy of tillage [and] profits on capital employed in this way in this country are marvelous."[3]

Edward Coles emigrated to Illinois expecting to experience this vision firsthand. The combination of enterprising but virtuous small farmers, free labor, and the abundant availability of inexpensive land was supposed to foster the development of a free, egalitarian society. As Register of the Land Office at Edwardsville, Coles intended to oversee the fair and systematic distribution of land to worthy settlers, to help construct the economic foundation and communal character that would ensure the expansion of this American ideal. As a liberator, he planned to demonstrate that emancipation was possible and indeed practical. Additionally, as an advocate of equality, Coles expected to help forge a community that was hospitable to free black settlers. In short, he hoped to realize the republican vision that had captivated so many travelers and emigrants during the early nineteenth century.

In many ways, however, Coles encountered a frontier community that was very different from that of his expectations. Rather than a region bubbling with economic prosperity, he found a state plagued by economic distress. Instead of an environment receptive to an experiment in black freedom, he encountered a population and legal structure decidedly hostile to free black settlement. And, perhaps most shocking, rather than a state populated by free laborers, he learned that Illinois allowed slavery to persist under the veil of indentured servitude. It was within this context, as well, that he discovered that a minority of his fellow Illinoisans intended to legalize slavery. Together, these conditions led him to conclude that his new home was far more similar to the Virginia he left behind than the free state he had imagined it to be. Unwilling to leave these circumstances unchallenged, Edward Coles entered the public arena and became an antislavery politician who worked to transform Illinois into a free, egalitarian community.

"make fortune enough"

The Illinois spring of 1819 was unusually wet. As he made his way from Louisville to Edwardsville, Edward Coles forded swollen rivers and slogged along muddy roads. He arrived in Edwardsville dirt-stained, wet, tired, and in a disagreeable mood. But he did reach his destination just in time for the opening of the next public land auction. As he strode into town, Coles encountered a small but thriving frontier community. Like Washington City, Edwardsville was a town in the midst of a transformation. What had once been a frontier outpost was quickly becoming an important trading center along the Mississippi River. The Reverend Thomas Lippincott, a longtime resident, thought that Edwardsville was "the most noted town . . . in Illinois." Along with a court house, land office, and Indian Agency, the town counted several taverns, at least two stores, a hotel, several boarding houses, a printing office and newspaper, a public bank, and a flour mill among its enterprises. Still, it was only a fraction of the size of the nation's capital and lacked the refined society and cosmopolitan characteristics that had made Coles's time with the Madisons so delightful. While Madison County was the most populated district in the state and Edwardsville (the county seat) was among the region's most developed towns, the town still only boasted a population of 166 and was surrounded by a sparsely settled hinterland.[4] It was impossible for Coles to ignore the fact that he had traded high society, friends, and refinement for a rustic, unpolished, frontier community of strangers in order to fulfill his dreams.

Coles immediately rented a room at Wiggins's Hotel, where he shared lodgings with another newly arrived emigrant, Hooper Warren. Like Coles, Warren had led a relatively peripatetic early life, moving from the state of his birth, New Hampshire, to Delaware, Kentucky, and then St. Louis before settling in Edwardsville in March 1819. He also shared Coles's opposition to slavery, and this fact more than anything else set the tone of his newspaper, the *Edwardsville Spectator*. They should have been great friends, but they were not. Instead, they developed a decidedly hostile relationship that remained bitter well into the 1850s. Over twenty-five years after their stint as roommates, Warren recalled with resentment what he understood to be Coles's anti-northern prejudices and aristocratic pretensions. "I found him to possess an inveterate and unconquerable prejudice against 'Yankees.'" He thought Coles only feigned friendship with northern-born residents because doing so might secure "the advancement of his purposes." Worse still, he found Coles uncritically supportive of "Southern statesmen." Warren complained that his roommate was so devoted to Jefferson, Madison, and their Republican followers that he believed that southerners alone had "a right to the management and control of public affairs." Warren's Coles also talked

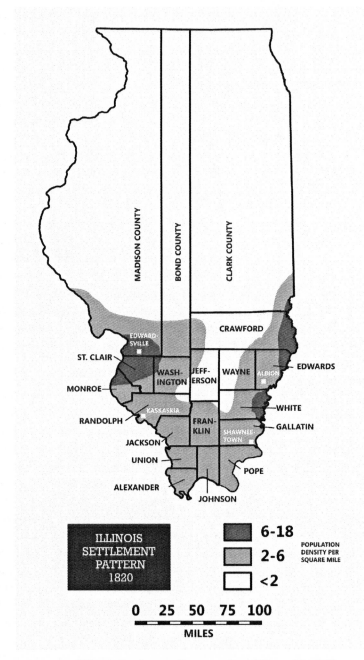

FIGURE 3.3. Illinois Settlement Pattern, 1820. (Created by Mike Wirth, www.MikeWirthArt.com.)

incessantly and always about himself. He claimed that he found Coles to be "exceedingly loquacious, and, although his conversations were generally interesting . . . he more than once talked me to sleep." He grew tired of Coles's repeated anecdotes of hobnobbing with the nation's leaders at the President's House and the "accounts of his dining and sporting with the Lords and Nobles . . . at London, Paris and St. Petersburg." As far as Warren was concerned, Coles was a close-minded nabob who was ill suited for frontier life and hardly deserved respect or admiration.[5]

Certainly, Warren's description of Coles contained more than a grain of truth. Coles had professed a deep distrust of northern politicians throughout Madison's administration. In early 1815, when peace was on the horizon and New Englanders were organizing the Hartford Convention, Coles was shocked by the "extraordinary and disgraceful course" pursued by the "*English* Federalists." From his perspective, these men had moved beyond "the very verge of treason" and were "boldly threatening the very salvation of our Country by striking at the cord of its Union." It should hardly be surprising, then, that Coles rejected northern political leadership. For him Federalists and New Englanders were all part of the same group of "deluded or base men" whose "prejudice, or infatuation, or wickedness" had led them to become "the most active and violent" supporters of disunion.[6]

Coles also saw himself as a dashing young man of refined manners who had traveled the world and who had moved amid the nation's most famous politicians and wealthiest families. Moreover, he had tried desperately to suppress his growing sense of dread and unease about settling in the West. As early as 1815, he confessed to his family and friends that he "anticipate[d] the many difficulties I shall have to encounter, not less from removing to a new country & into a society so differently organized from that in which I have been brought up," but also as a result of "the taste & habits I have acquired by the kind of life I have led for the last five or 6 years." Yet, only by venturing to the western frontier could he avoid the "utter derangement of my intended pursuits" as far as his slaves were concerned and promote "my pecuniary interests." Like his grandfather and father before him, he sought to accomplish the latter by investing in western land. Between 1815 and 1818, Coles purchased 5,890 acres in Missouri, nearly five acres of town lots in St. Louis, and an additional 3,680 acres of land in the Illinois Military Bounty Tract. The Missouri acreage was reputed to be among the best in the territory and the region. The Bounty Tract land he acquired contained rich prairies, abundant timber, and adequate access to water, all of which made it particularly desirable among new emigrants.[7]

By migrating to Illinois and assuming the position as Register of the Land Office there, Coles had found a way to improve his economic prospects and honor his antislavery ambition. Still, leaving Virginia for a new life in the western country did not necessarily mean he was entirely happy about ending up in Edwardsville. Indeed, toward the end of his westward journey, he had reassured his mother that "you must not conclude that I have made up my mind to spend the rest of my days in Illinois." He acknowledged that he could not bear to remain "far from you & all my beloved friends and out of that kind of society in which I have moved all my life. . . . No, my dear Mother," he declared, "My heart recoils at the idea." He had an entirely different plan. Instead of spending his life on the frontier, he hoped to "make fortune enough to enable me to live . . . in Phila or wherever else I may prefer." Illinois, then, was merely a temporary stop on a journey that would ultimately end east of the Appalachian Mountains amid the familiar society of his youth.[8] Warren's observations of his roommate undoubtedly reflected accurately the ambivalence about frontier society Coles had expressed to nearly all of his family and friends.

"leave the whole to my Negroes"

Forty-seven-year-old Ralph Crawford and the other ex-slaves Coles had left under his care concluded their long overland trek from Louisville to Edwardsville on May 16, 1819, two weeks after their ex-master. In total, eighteen souls followed Coles's one-time manservant. Ralph's wife Kate and their four children, sixteen-year-old Betsy, fourteen-year-old Thomas (who was sickly and weak), twelve-year-old Mary, and little William (who was nine) rode in one wagon. Emanuel and Suckey Logan drove a second wagon that carried their six small children. Thomas Cobb and Nancy Gaines, as well as Robert and Polly Crawford, who were probably Ralph's siblings, walked alongside the wagon train. Like Coles before them, they entered a crowded town, full of prospective settlers and land speculators. When they arrived, just over 16 percent of the town population was enslaved. Of the nine slaveholders who lived in the city limits, three were men Coles would associate with on a regular basis. Benjamin Stephenson, who served as Register of the Land Office before Coles and was the proprietor of one of the town's stores, owned eight chattel laborers and employed two free blacks. Robert Pogue, who owned and managed another town store, employed two slaves in his commercial enterprise. Similarly, the proprietor of the Edwardsville boarding house where Coles lodged owned two female slaves who probably cooked and cleaned for the guests. Edwardsville had a much smaller free black population, but together these residents ensured that the white inhabitants were accustomed to encountering black men and women during the course of their daily activities.[9] Still, the sight of eighteen black travelers arriving unaccompanied by a white patron must have grabbed the attention of the town's residents.

Although he had promised to employ his ex-slaves at least temporarily, Coles had yet to purchase a farm. So, when he was not managing the land auction, Coles collected supplies and scouted for a place to settle. The day after the group arrived, he sent Ralph Crawford to St. Louis to purchase more tools, wagons, and plough irons. Then, at the end of May and during the first weeks of June, Coles purchased a 394-acre farm called Prairieland. It was an ideal purchase because it already had "a deserted log cabin," a band mill, and several enclosed fields. He then purchased "6 weeding hoes . . . Geer [sic] for 2 horses," and $49 worth of tools for clearing and planting the prairie. On this farm he "employ[ed] no white person, but leave the whole to my Negroes," who had already "commenced ploughing up the Prairie, and splitting rails to fence it." They made rapid progress "breaking prairie, and planting corn until the first week in July." Indeed, using the four horses they brought with them, Ralph, Robert, Thomas, and Emanuel "planted between 12 and 15 acres in corn for each horse." The black laborers then turned their attention to "mowing hay from the prairie, and fallowing it to seed wheat" in the fall. By the end of the summer, Coles's laborers converted close to sixty acres of his farm to the cultivation of corn and may have produced as many as two thousand bushels of corn for the market.[10]

In general, Coles was pleased with their work. They "behave[d] themselves remarkably well since I have liberated them." Half of the men and women worked on his Prairieland farm, while everyone else hired themselves out "in this place and its neighbourhood." They worked hard to save enough money to invest in improvements on the quarter sections he gave to each man or woman over the age of twenty-three. He also made provisions for the children in the group. "To the young ones I have given books, promised to pay for teaching them, and premiums to those that learn to read and write." He was determined to implement his experiment in black freedom and demonstrate that free blacks could be productive members of society. Despite these successes, however, Coles

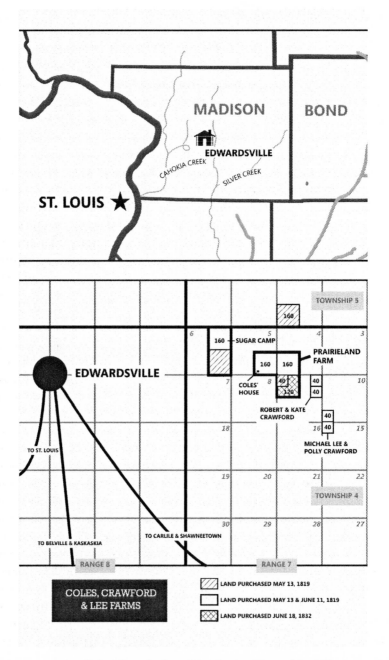

FIGURE 3.4. Coles, Crawford, and Lee farms. (Created by Mike Wirth and Suzanne Cooper Guasco, www.MikeWirthArt.com.)

remained unenthusiastic about his new life in Illinois. He was disappointed to discover that his official duties had failed to pay as well as he had anticipated. After the first land auction he earned a paltry $175.58, hardly a sufficient income to make up for the cost of his overland journey or starting his farm. In fact, he decided that "if it should not become soon much more valuable than it is at present, I shall certainly resign it this fall." In the meantime, he tried to alleviate his disappointment by focusing on his plans to return eastward for a visit. "I am already looking forward with impatience," he proclaimed, "to the time of my departure" and instructed his cousin Dolley "to assist me in getting a wife; for that I am more than ever convinced that it will not do to live in this solitary country without a helpmate."[11]

As much as he complained about his personal situation, Coles was a remarkably successful farmer. This was the case largely because he benefitted from several advantages few new landowners enjoyed. Unlike most new immigrants, Coles purchased his land outright, paying for the entire tract in one payment. The editor of the *Illinois Emigrant* noted in March 1819 that only "one fourth part" of Illinois' landowners "have paid for their possessions, and are able to purchase stock, tho' not to a great amount." These circumstances meant that most of Coles's neighbors lived in constant fear of losing their farms. This was true even though the government offered fairly liberal credit to prospective landowners between 1814 and 1820, and created conditions designed to ensure equal access to public land.[12]

Coles also bought an improved farm, whereas most new inhabitants purchased unimproved land. Consequently, settlers spent most of their initial months on the frontier building their lodgings, clearing enough land to feed their family, and constructing a fence to protect their fields from wild animals. Although a particularly industrious farmer with a large family might succeed in planting and fencing fields of corn or wheat on as many as thirty acres, most settlers managed to cultivate only "a small patch of corn for bread." As Elias Pym Fordham observed, most new inhabitants raised "a little Indian corn, pumpkins, hogs, and sometimes have a Cow or two. . . . but their rifle is their principle means of support." Indeed, as one new arrival commented, settlers struggled so much during their initial year that they "felt very rich" if they managed to construct a cabin, till a few acres, accumulate "an abundance of nuts— and [own] hogs . . . fat enough to kill."[13] Many new immigrants attempted to minimize the initial demands imposed by settling on unimproved land by relying on the generosity of neighbors who had arrived before them. Established residents often offered "every thing they possessed, in the way of tools, teams, wagons, provisions, and their own personal services" to aid their newest neighbor in establishing his farm. Neighborhood networks of mutuality, rather than the accumulation of cash, then, was the most common survival strategy on the frontier. Even with the aid of neighbors, however, most new arrivals managed to accomplish little more than what Morris Birkbeck described as "the *necessaries* of life," a roof over their head and enough food to last through the first winter.[14]

Perhaps most important, Coles's success during his first summer in Illinois resulted largely from the labor of the men and women he had emancipated. Kate Crawford maintained the house, cooked for those who worked on the farm, and cared for her children. Ralph and Robert Crawford as well as Thomas Cobb worked in the fields and, in the fall, managed the hogs Coles purchased for the farm. In exchange for working on his farm during the first year, Coles paid Kate, Thomas, Robert, and Ralph "wages in money" and covered their daily expenses. Throughout the year, for example, Coles bought corn meal, potatoes, beef, wine, and "bacon for my people." He also purchased "a dress for Kate," "cloth for Bob & Tom," "Linnen [*sic*] for my Negroes shirts," and paid them "for making their shoes." On several occasions he likewise paid their medical expenses. When Ralph became ill with "bilious fever" in the fall of 1819, Coles supplied the services of a doctor, the regular doses of wine the physician prescribed and, when he died in early October, he paid "for Ralph's coffin."[15]

Most new settlers, who rarely had the funds to buy their land, certainly lacked the extra cash required to hire laborers to work on their farms. In 1819, the average wage for a hired white farm laborer hovered around thirteen dollars a month for seasonal work and ranged between three and five dollars an acre for clearing land. Domestic help usually demanded five dollars a month as well as room and board. Additionally, Illinois suffered from a severe labor shortage. The availability of inexpensive government land as well as the ease with which settlers squatted on unsurveyed or unoccupied tracts discouraged most new arrivals from working for someone else. Even those who managed to find an individual willing to work constantly complained about the unreliability of the help. Christiana Holmes Tillson, a Massachusetts native who settled with her husband in Montgomery County soon after Coles arrived, hired five different women to help her maintain her house over a two-year period. But she complained that they often left without notice merely because they "longed for a change," and she was left exhausted by the daily demands of her household.[16]

Whereas the majority of Illinois's newest residents struggled to maintain ownership of their land and carve out a subsistence, Coles's wealth and access to labor ensured a degree of stability and a potential for improvement few newcomers enjoyed. During his first summer in Illinois, his Prairieland farm expenses, including the price of his property and the livestock he purchased during his westward journey, amounted to just over $2,300. By the end of the same period, the acreage converted to crops produced nearly 2,000 bushels of corn. Selling this at thirty cents a bushel, he earned roughly $600. Together with his income from the land office, which totaled $175, Coles's first few months in Illinois covered about half of his start-up costs. Fortunately for Coles, the public auction he conducted during the last two weeks of August proved lucrative, garnering him another $720. When combined with the proceeds from the sale of his wheat, Coles managed to break even after just ten months on the frontier, a feat the average settler accomplished only after at least two years of intense labor.[17]

In the fall of 1819, Madison congratulated Coles "on the various successes of your Western career." He celebrated his young protégé's successful overland journey and said he was astonished at the variety of roles the latter had fulfilled so effectively. The list of accomplishments mentioned by Madison included "a Ploughman, a rail splitter [and] a fence builder, a corn planter, a Hay maker, and soon to be a Wheat sower. To all these rural functions" he also added "the official dignity of Register of the Land Office." Perhaps more impressive to Madison was Coles's antislavery actions. "You are pursuing, I observe, the true course with your negroes in order to make their freedom a fair experiment for their happiness." He commended Coles for his generosity toward them; for "without the instruction, the property or the employments of a freeman, the manumitted blacks instead of deriving advantage from the partial benevolence of their Masters furnish arguments against the general efforts in their behalf." Like Coles, Madison believed that emancipation would only succeed if the newly freed blacks also possessed the tools and material goods necessary to prosper as free men and women. Madison only regretted that Coles could not change "their colour as well as their legal condition. Without this," he complained, "they seem destined to a privation of that moral rank & those social blessings, which give to freedom more than half its value."[18] Coles, of course, hoped to prove Madison's final point wrong and worked assiduously to help his ex-slaves achieve more than a mere subsistence.

"hard times"

The panic of 1819 conspired to thwart Coles's economic prosperity and made an already difficult situation for most western settlers even more dire. In the summer of 1818, officers of the Bank of the United States curtailed the expansion of banking and credit by demanding that all balances due from local branches be paid in full. Almost immediately, the value of paper currency everywhere dramatically depreciated. In Illinois "bank-bills soon fell to thirty-three and one-third cents on the dollar." Additionally, the region lacked a sufficient supply of eastern currency, the only money that retained its value. Coles revealed that throughout the land district, "all the notes of the Banks of the District of Columbia, and to the North and East of it . . . are immediately bought up by the merchants and sent to the Eastward to purchase goods; so that they are seldom in circulation" locally.[19]

Significantly for most settlers, the depreciation in state currency severely reduced their ability to retain or sell their land claims. The little cash they accumulated from the sale of surplus crops was no longer worth full value, forcing them to generate one-third to one-half again as much money to meet their land payments. Worse still, those who looked to sell their land before the next installment was due discovered that, like them, few individuals possessed the money necessary to buy. As Gershom Flagg observed, "there are many here who paid out all the money they had in first installments on land and depended on selling it before the other payments become due. And as the price of land is now reduced no body will buy it at the former price. It will of course revert to the United States," he continued, "unless some form of relief was offered." Without a stable currency, few residents, well-to-do or poor, could hope to purchase or keep land.[20]

A dramatic decrease in the price of agricultural commodities accompanied the devastating effects of the state's declining currency and contributed to the overall feeling that the people suffered from hard times. Prior to the recession, farmers sold their corn for between 33 and 75 cents and their wheat for as much as $1.45 a bushel. After the panic, most Illinois farmers were forced to accept prices as low as 15 and 25 cents a bushel for corn and wheat, respectively. Not only did the falling value of agricultural products diminish profits, but the low prices often prevented farmers from recouping the cost of transportation to market. As a result, many farmers avoided the market all together. At least one new resident concluded that "a farmer can no longer make his business . . . profitable."[21]

Coles's position as Register of the Land Office as well as his experiences as a farmer made him intimately familiar with the economic problems created by the panic of 1819. As he informed Josiah Meigs, the commissioner of the General Land Office in Washington City, "Little or no land . . . has sold above two dollars per acre; and," he continued, "much of the little that has been sold will be forfeited." Recognizing that reform was necessary, Congress revised the land laws in April 1820, reducing the price of land per acre from $2 to $1.25, as well as the minimum purchase requirement from 160 to 80 acres. Still, the scarcity of money, as Coles observed, continued to prevent prospective settlers from purchasing land and threatened the ability of those who already bought property to maintain ownership. Coles's land office account book dramatically reflected the decline in land sales. Between July and October 1819, he recorded collecting $30,762 for claims in his office. One year later, however, the revenue of his office had declined precipitously. From July to October 1820, he sold only $6,275 worth of land.[22]

Congress once again attempted to relieve the situation by passing new land regulations. The Relief Act of 1821 allowed landowners to relinquish portions of their earlier purchases and then rebuy smaller tracts of land at the new lower price without penalty. To the dismay of many settlers and land officers, the act required settlers to file their claims during such a short period of time that few landowners benefitted from the relief effort. Coles predicted that there "will not be sufficient time . . . to complete the business . . . in the time limited by law." Despite the efforts of national legislators, land sales continued to decline, and Coles's land office accounts reflected the trend. During the fall of 1820, he earned only $93, and the following year his commission fell to $31. Coles did attempt to collect $800 worth of fees "for filing Declarations and Relinquishments" in December 1821, but the commissioner of the General Land Office disallowed these fees, and Coles had to return the funds. After two years of working as Register, Coles had little income beyond his salary to show for his efforts.[23]

Coles's Prairieland farm accounts similarly reflected the economic devastation wrought by the 1819 recession. As already noted, he barely broke even after his first year in Illinois. When depression prices dominated the following year, it was a different story. In 1820 he garnered only 20 and 33 cents a bushel for his corn and wheat, respectively, sums that greatly reduced his income. Additionally, the illness and then death of Ralph in the fall of 1819 forced Coles to hire other laborers, who were paid in both cash and barter. Consequently, the income of his farm suffered from both the detrimental effects of the economic recession and the necessity of paying high wages in a constrained labor pool. Like his plantation in Virginia, Coles's Prairieland farm remained in debt the entire time he employed his ex-slaves. After 1824, he chose, like his neighbors, to rent his farm to local tenants rather than continue to operate it himself. Largely as a result of the economic problems of the 1820s, his goal of escaping debt by moving to the frontier proved elusive.[24]

"hold negroes in the utmost contempt"

Coles was surprised when the economic conditions occasioned by the 1819 recession exposed in sharp relief the strong antiblack prejudices of the region's residents. Fearful that the state's residents would have to compete for land and wages with free blacks coming into the region, the Illinois state legislature passed a series of laws that became known as the black code. Promulgated just a month before Coles arrived in the state, Illinois's black laws reimposed the measures included in the 1813 territorial law, which stipulated that new free black settlers had to leave the state within fifteen days or risk a public whipping. This restriction was not rigorously enforced, however, and the free black population grew significantly between 1818 and 1830; it increased 59 percent between 1818 and 1820 and a remarkable 228 percent between 1820 and 1830. While many of them were residents who gained their freedom after serving out the terms of their indenture contracts or as a result of emancipations, the vast majority of the state's growing free black population immigrated into the region. Indeed, in proportion to the state's total population, the number of free blacks increased by a higher percentage in Illinois than in any other state in the Old Northwest or in the northern states of New York, Pennsylvania, and Massachusetts.[25]

The persistence of free black immigration seemed only to heighten the desire among many white residents for stricter black laws. Consequently, as a further deterrent to the immigration of free people of color, the 1819 regulations also required all free blacks who already resided in the region to prove their status by presenting a certificate of freedom to the local county clerk. They also were compelled to register themselves and each member of their family. Anyone who failed to do so was "deemed a runaway slave or servant," arrested, and hired out to the highest bidder. In the spring of 1819, the state legislature also passed a statute declaring that black residents could not bear witness or bring suit against white inhabitants. Combined with the constitutional article restricting suffrage to white male inhabitants above the age of twenty-one, these laws severely restricted free black civil liberties.[26] These laws reflected the strong anti-black prejudices of many of Illinois's southern-born residents, white men and women who retained "many prejudices imbibed in infancy" and who continued to "hold negroes in the utmost contempt, . . . look[ing] on *negers*, as they called them, ...as an inferior race of beings." Coles, then, discovered that he had settled in a region that was very inhospitable to free black settlement.[27]

As he recorded in a narrative of his frontier experiences written in 1827, Coles and his ex-slaves experienced the force of this exclusionary culture firsthand. After working on Coles's farm for two years, Robert Crawford and Thomas Cobb, believing they could earn more money elsewhere, responded to a notice in the *Edwardsville Spectator* seeking laborers to work at an Edwardsville brick factory. Theophilus W. Smith, the proprietor of the enterprise, offered Crawford and Cobb each "$20 a month to labour . . . in making bricks." Coles, suspecting that the offer came from some "illdisposed and designing persons," advised the two men "to accept the offer [only] if they could be sure of being paid, and that such wages would be continued for any length of time." Confident that the proposal was legitimate, Crawford and Cobb left Coles's employ. Within a few months, however, the two men returned to Prairieland farm "very much out of temper, to complain that they had been deceived and cheated." Smith had refused to pay them in silver as promised and instead insisted on providing their wages in state money, which amounted to just one-third of the agreed-upon sum. Coles learned that neither man had secured a contract. Additionally, they possessed no evidence to support their claim other than the testimony "of coloured persons, which, by our unrighteous laws, [was] not . . . admissible against a white man." Unable to return to Coles's farm because he had hired replacements for them, Crawford and Cobb were forced to accept the reduced wages for their labor in the factory and find other employment in the neighborhood for the remainder of the year.[28]

Still, in the long run, Coles's ex-slaves fared far better than not only most Illinois free blacks but also many of the state's southern-born poor farmers. Unlike other free people of color in Illinois, Ralph and Kate Crawford, Thomas Cobb, Michael Lee (who married Polly Crawford in

1822), and Jessie Price (who married Betsy Crawford in 1826) owned land and enjoyed the patronage of a white person who was determined to help them overcome the obstacles imposed by an inhospitable frontier society. In 1822, for example, Robert, and possibly Thomas, returned to Coles's farm to resume their positions as hired laborers. Kate, widowed in October 1819, had remained at Prairieland farm, working as a house servant. Sometime after 1822, she married Robert, and for several years they worked "as tenant[s]" on his nearly four-hundred-acre farm, paying Coles "ten bushels of corn per man," a modest fee considering most tenants paid a bushel per four acres for rent.[29] After 1824, when Coles rented his farm to new tenants, the Crawfords moved to their own farm. By 1836 they had accumulated enough wealth to purchase eighty more acres of land. As Coles noted years later, the property they bought had "good dwelling houses, stables, barns, [and] fruit trees," in addition to "twenty or thirty acres . . . enclosed and in cultivation." Indeed, the Crawfords prospered as independent farmers, eventually accumulating "400 acres . . . several horses, oxen, many cows, cattle, sheep, [and] hogs." Their farm, proclaimed Coles, was "as large and as well stocked . . . and as neatly fixed as most of [their] . . . white neighbors."[30] Their experience, however, was the exception rather than the rule.

Coles likewise was surprised to learn that many residents attempted to avoid the economic distress of the period by employing enslaved laborers. For example, several months after their servant girl, Nelly, "had behaved badly," forcing them to "send her off," John and Christiana Holmes Tillson seized the opportunity to purchase the indenture contracts of two enslaved laborers from a close friend. Christiana claimed a "persistent feeling against slavery," but ultimately consented to retain Caleb and Lucy because "my kitchen labors were to be abated." The Tillsons were not the only Illinoisans who looked past their moral or ideological objections to slavery in order to benefit economically from the institution. Indeed, many residents agreed with an Englishman who settled in the region in 1817. "I would not have upon my conscience the moral guilt of extending Slavery over the countries now free from it. . . . But," he continued, "if it should take place, I do not see why I should not make use of it." Like many other new immigrants, he was finding it exceedingly difficult to succeed economically because without "servants I cannot farm, and there are *no* free labourers here."[31]

Although Illinois certainly counted among its residents far fewer enslaved men and women than the Old Dominion, slavery had existed in the Illinois Country from as early as the 1680s, when French settlers used enslaved labor to cultivate wheat on expansive farms. Even after the United States gained jurisdiction over the region and expressly prohibited slavery and involuntary servitude through Article VI of the Northwest Ordinance of 1787, French and American slaveholders continued to rely on enslaved labor, benefiting from local and national exemptions that allowed those who settled in the region before the act passed Congress to retain their chattel property. They maintained these exceptions by erecting an indentured servitude system that in theory was to be both voluntary and temporary, but that was in practice just as coercive and perpetual as southern slavery. Twenty years later, when Illinois joined the Union, slaveholding Illinoisans protected and perpetuated the territorial indentured servitude system, ensuring that the slave population would continue to grow. Indeed, they were so successful that both the number of slaveholders and the number of slaves increased by more than 24 percent during the first two years of statehood. As British emigrant George Flower observed, Illinois was "as much a slave state as any south of the Ohio River."[32]

"illy qualified to represent a just, free and independent state"

Coles also discovered that the slavery issue consistently occupied a central place in state politics. Within a few months of his arrival in Edwardsville, the national debate over Missouri statehood and the place of slavery in the nation had infiltrated local politics all over the country, and Illinois was certainly no exception.[33] In the 1819 congressional contest between Daniel Pope Cook and incumbent John McLean, slavery and Missouri statehood dominated the campaign. Chief among the concerns of Illinoisans was McLean's opposition to congressional efforts to prohibit the expansion of slavery into Missouri. The controversy began in January 1819, when James Tallmadge of New York greeted Missouri's petition for statehood with an amendment prohibiting slavery in the new state and providing for the gradual emancipation of all slaves born within its borders after statehood. Although the amendment repeatedly passed in the House of Representatives by slim margins, and did so despite McLean's opposition, the measure always failed in the Senate. In that chamber, southern senators were able to defeat the measure because they benefited from the allegiance of several conservative northern members, including Illinois's two senators Ninian Edwards and Jesse B. Thomas, who consistently voted against restriction. Angered by the behavior of their national representatives, some Illinois residents immediately voiced their displeasure by asking "Do you approve of the conduct of your members of congress?" If the answer was no, they insisted, then Illinoisans should "seize the first opportunity to discard from their service the men whose votes . . . have proved them illy qualified to represent a just, free, and independent state."[34]

Throughout the summer of 1819, Coles watched as residents flooded the state's newspapers with editorials and essays on slavery and Missouri. "An Elector" informed his readers that "the friends of Mr. McLean admit that he is in favor of the *extension of slavery*." Should anyone doubt the accuracy of this claim, he reminded them that "by his vote last winter," McLean declared "that he will not prohibit the introduction of slavery in Missouri. Mr. Cook," on the other hand, "has vowed his determination . . . to exclude it from that state. The alternative is now presented before you," the writer concluded. He hoped that the voters would cast their ballots for the candidate who would "vote the wishes and interests of *our* state" and not Missouri's.[35] Cook won the election easily, defeating incumbent John McLean with 58 percent of the popular vote. Residents throughout the state understood Cook's victory as a declarative statement that Illinoisans opposed the extension of slavery and hoped their other elected officials would take notice. "Our representatives must now be convinced from . . . the result of the late congressional election," thundered one resident, "that the vote they gave on the Missouri question is disapproved by a large majority of the people." How could they not understand, the author asked, "that we have been for a long time decidedly averse to slavery" and wish them to oppose Missouri's entrance into the Union as a slave state?[36]

A year later, when Cook ran for reelection, the slavery issue and Missouri statehood remained the most important issue. Senators Ninian Edwards and Jesse B. Thomas had not heeded the wishes of their constituents and continued to vote against any effort to restrict the extension of slavery into Missouri. Cook, however, had fulfilled his campaign pledge and consistently voted for restriction. Undeterred by Cook's voting record, Elias Kent Kane, Illinois's secretary of state, came forward to challenge the incumbent. Even more threatening than the prospect of another vote in favor of slavery in Missouri, warned Hooper Warren, the editor of the antislavery *Edwardsville Spectator*, was his discovery of a conspiracy among Edwards, Thomas, Kane, and their local supporters to legalize slavery in Illinois. Warren claimed that the offending group of state and national leaders, whom he labeled "The Old Slave Party," promoted Kane's candidacy because they intended to use his election as "an indirect expression" of the people's support for slavery and a justification for their movement to transform Illinois into a slave state. A vote against Kane in the 1820 congressional election, Hooper and other concerned columnists claimed, would not only signal Illinois's objection to Missouri statehood with slavery, but also proclaim the residents' opposition to any effort to legalize slavery within Illinois's borders. Cook easily survived Kane's challenge, earning 65 percent of the popular vote, but fears that a local party might successfully legalize slavery persisted.[37]

Although he never commented directly on the Missouri crisis or Illinois's congressional elections, Coles shared his neighbors' opposition to slavery. Indeed, his antislavery commitment was not a secret, for he publicly announced his opposition to slavery and inequality a mere three months after he arrived in Edwardsville. On July 4, 1819, Coles attended a public celebration and dinner in Edwardsville that included both pro- and anti-extension Illinoisans. Nicholas Hansen delivered a holiday oration in which he wondered aloud if he could "approve of your respect for the 'equal rights' of mankind? Is that liberty we boast of," he continued, "the enjoyment of all?" As his audience contemplated how they might answer these questions, he declared that "slavery is a foul stigma upon our nation's character" and admonished them to "be consistent and wipe it off." After the speech, Coles showed where he stood by offering a toast of his own: "*The rights of man*—They appertain equally to him, whether his complexion be white, red, or black."[38]

This was no idle statement for Coles; for just hours earlier he had composed the certificates of freedom for the enslaved men and women he had liberated on the Ohio River. In the document he declared that "whereas I do not believe that man can have of right a property, in his fellow man, but on the contrary that all mankind were endowed by nature with equal rights, I do therefore by these presents restore . . . that inalienable liberty to which they have been deprived."[39] Coles's opposition to slavery was grounded in the revolutionary principles of the founding generation and the preamble of the Declaration of Independence. As he became increasingly involved in local politics over the next several years, he intensified his effort to encourage others to base their opposition to slavery on his emerging antislavery nationalism, a nationalism that claimed for all Americans an antislavery past and demanded that everyone contribute to crafting the nation's antislavery future.[40]

Coles also undoubtedly identified with and supported the arguments offered by northern Republicans and reprinted in the state's papers during the Missouri crisis. As Coles would do throughout his long public career, northern restrictionists declared that slavery was a moral and political evil and that allowing the institution to expand westward not only violated America's founding principles but threatened the future welfare of the nation. Moreover, they indentified the Northwest Ordinance of 1787 as a precedent that established federal authority to prohibit the westward expansion of slavery. In their view, when it passed Article VI prohibiting slavery in the region north of the Ohio River, Congress had declared that they intended the future of the nation to be free of slavery. Coles and restrictionists, then, both argued that the founders, who had expressed their devotion to equality and freedom in 1776, had always intended the limitations they imposed on slavery's expansion to contribute to the eventual demise of the institution. Just as Coles had called on Jefferson in July 1814 to practice the principles he had professed, so too did northern Republicans call on their fellow Congressmen to fulfill the nation's antislavery legacy by opposing the expansion of slavery into Missouri, for doing so would ensure that the nation would become eventually a nonslaveholding republic.[41]

The emergence of a sectional antislavery consensus among northern Republicans during the crisis would have been both encouraging and disconcerting to Coles. He could embrace the rhetoric and mobilizing power of a campaign that reminded the public of the Revolution's antislavery legacy and his contemporaries' obligation to carry forward the founders' vision for the nation by opposing the westward expansion of slavery. It was gratifying to see and hear elements of his own developing antislavery nationalism proclaimed in newspapers, public pamphlets, and Congress. He was probably concerned, however, about the sectionalizing impact of the northern Republican campaign. Not only did their sectional antislavery threaten to divide the nation but the emerging sectional divide jeopardized the effectiveness of their antislavery efforts because emancipation could only succeed if leaders from all sections supported the enterprise. He could not ignore, for example, the fact that northern Republicans had provoked an intense response from southerners, particularly among Coles's Republican friends in Virginia, who saw in these northern pronouncements an attack on their economic well-being, future prosperity, and political position within the Union. Indeed, Coles's friend Thomas Ritchie, the editor of the *Richmond Enquirer*, predicted dire consequences for the South should the northern Republican proscription for Missouri prevail. Even his more moderate friends, Nicholas Biddle, Henry Clay, and James Monroe among them, voiced concern. Following a precedent set thirty years earlier, the nation's leaders chose to privilege the Union over their antislavery instincts, and brokered a compromise that allowed slavery in Missouri but prohibited the institution from all the territory north of the 36°30' parallel.[42]

Coles and his fellow Illinoisans were disappointed with the outcome, for the compromise signaled a defeat of restriction. By conceding ground to each side, the compromise failed to resolve the slavery issue and left in its wake a sectional legacy. Antislavery activism had become the province of the North and antagonized southerners to such a degree that a cross-sectional antislavery coalition appeared unlikely. Equally discouraging was the realization that the actions of the state's senators, as one editorialist declared, had "degraded" Illinois's "standing as a free state." Coles began to wonder if Illinois was a free state in name only. Still, he probably felt reassured because pro-restrictionists came out of the controversy with at least one encouraging result, for the acceptance of the compromise confirmed that Congress had the power to regulate slavery in the West.[43]

More generally, the Missouri Controversy had a lasting impact on local politics in Illinois. The prolonged national crisis over slavery and westward expansion revealed that a small but politically powerful proslavery faction existed in Illinois. The discussion of slavery and Missouri during the congressional campaigns of 1819 and 1820 also demonstrated that a majority of the state's residents opposed slavery and the westward expansion of the institution. The final outcome of the controversy likewise taught the residents of the state that they could not trust their elected officials, and as a result they became more deliberative and engaged in state politics. Rather than moving to a state without slaves, Coles had settled in a community where slavery was expanding and where it enjoyed the protection of state leaders who were determined to legalize the institution, even if the majority of the residents opposed such a reform.

"to become a candidate"

As the 1822 gubernatorial election approached, most of the residents of the state knew that slavery would be the central issue of the contest. Coles and his friends, however, feared that proslavery forces in the state might triumph if the voters behaved carelessly. One editorialist cautioned that "although a large majority of them are evidently opposed to slavery," voters "seem to think it no ways dangerous to place over themselves rulers who are of a quite opposite way of thinking—presuming, no doubt," he continued, "that these rulers were unwilling to dare to act contrary to the wishes of their constituents." He hoped they had learned their lesson during the Missouri crisis and would no longer "trust men without first testing their political principles." Joseph B. Phillips, the proslavery chief justice of the state Supreme Court, had already entered the race and was running unopposed when several "first citizens" of the state asked Coles "to become a candidate." He initially hesitated to accept the offer. "In the first place," he confessed to his niece, "I am doubtful whether I am not too poor, and in the next place" he wondered "whether it will not be productive of more trouble pain and vexation than of pleasure and happiness." Pressure from his friends as well as the pangs of his own conscience, however, led him to dismiss these apprehensions, and in October 1821 Coles announced his candidacy for the governorship in the *Edwardsville Spectator*, the state's only antislavery newspaper.[44]

From the outset, Coles viewed his extensive political experience in Washington City and abroad as an important qualification for office. His tenure as the president's private secretary in particular assured that he was familiar with the mechanics of running a government. This characteristic of Coles's reputation, however, hardly distinguished him from the other candidates. General James B. Moore, who joined the race in March 1822, never served in public office, but his military career furnished him with leadership experience. Both Thomas C. Browne, who declared his candidacy that same spring, and Joseph B. Phillips had served in the territorial government and on the state Supreme Court after 1818; so, they too could claim to possess the experience required to perform the responsibilities of the governorship effectively. Additionally, Coles's previous political experiences exposed a weakness in his candidacy. Unlike all the other candidates who had lived in Illinois for many years and boasted strong ties to the region, Coles had arrived relatively recently and, therefore, appeared more connected to national than local political leaders. He also continued to refer to Virginia, rather than Illinois, as his home. Together, these characteristics had the potential to lead voters to question his commitment to Illinois.

Coles's old roommate Hooper Warren exploited this apparent weakness early in the campaign. Under the guise of responding to an anonymous contributor's request for biographical information, Warren described Coles in ways that were hardly complimentary. He revealed, for example, that Coles was a native of Virginia, had served as President James Madison's private secretary, and moved to Illinois after his appointment to the land office. All of these details would become common components of any biographical sketch of Coles, but under Warren's pen these potentially favorable qualities became liabilities. According to

Warren, Coles acquired the post in the Edwardsville Land Office despite the objections of "one of our members of Congress," who argued against his selection because he believed "that our own state possessed citizens capable of filling the office." In this way, Warren portrayed Coles as an outsider who stole, through privilege and patronage, a lucrative position that rightly belonged to a local resident. From his perspective, Coles was a self-interested, ambitious man who lacked the "support of any individual in the state" and whose "pretensions" to office should be "candidly and dispassionately considered" by the voters.[45] Coles, he warned, was the antithesis of the type of political leader Illinois deserved or required.

In the next issue of the *Edwardsville Spectator*, a resident of the state challenged Warren's characterization of Coles, claiming that the editor had published "some extraordinary errors" in his biographical sketch of the candidate. Although he offered several alternative details regarding Coles's life before he immigrated to Illinois, and some of them inaccurate, "Justice" denied "that any personal, or interested motives, views, or circumstances, led to his appointment." More important, this editorialist maintained that Warren was "mistaken in supposing that Mr. Coles . . . had not the pledge of support from any individual." Instead, he assured his audience that although "He may not have received any pledge of support from either of the old parties . . . he had received assurances of support from the great mass of the people in this part of the state." Far from a designing and unpopular candidate, then, "Justice" described Coles as a model public servant who was not burdened by an affiliation with the political factions in the state and who enjoyed the affection of a significant segment of the state's population.[46]

Coles hoped that the voting public knew better than to believe Warren's characterizations of him. As Register of the Land, he had developed an extensive network of acquaintances among the region's farming community, making him familiar to the voting public. By contrast, General Moore, who entered the contest late, had "acquired some celebrity as a military man" during the War of 1812, but he remained unknown "beyond the Counties in his vicinity." The other two candidates, Browne and Phillips, both boasted a degree of popularity that rivaled that of Coles, but neither man was as intimately familiar with the economic problems average Illinoisans had endured over the previous two years. Not only did Coles experience similar financial woes but he also functioned as an advocate for those residents who attempted to take advantage of federal relief measures, even canceling his plans to visit his family and friends in Virginia and Philadelphia so he could remain in Edwardsville to oversee the administration of the relief program during the spring of 1821. Coles believed that these experiences made him a man of and not above the people.[47]

Coles also sought to increase his closeness to the people by touring the state canvassing for the public's support. He recognized, as Nathaniel Buckmaster, a stonemason and entrepreneur from Madison County, testified, that "the candidate . . . is obliged to ride over the whole state or district . . . attending every logrolling, petty muster, or barbecue, where he is expected to make . . . a stump speech." Accordingly, Coles journeyed to "the lower part of the state" and through the eastern counties, visiting prominent residents in various towns, delivering speeches before the public, and conversing with the region's inhabitants in local taverns. He concluded his loop around the state by stopping in Bond County to visit Horatio Newhall, a resident of Greenville, who observed in May 1822 that "electioneering is still going on at a great rate" and noted that "Coles . . . spent a day with us last week."[48] Determined to win the election, Coles used every tactic available to increase his popularity among the voters.

Warren could not resist mocking Coles's efforts to present himself as a man of the people. As the election drew closer, he informed the public that Coles had returned safely "to the bosom of his friends" in Edwardsville "after performing the arduous and fatiguing rounds of the state." Aware that many believed he was "personally hostile to" the candidate, the editor assured his readers that Coles had always treated him civilly. He scornfully proclaimed that the Virginian had "ever treated us, in our presence, with the most killing politeness . . . his incessant back-biting" he continued, "have never provoked us to break friendship with him." He then reminded his audience that his only source of information on Coles was "furnished by" the candidate himself, information often "confined to court-anecdotes, and incidents necessarily connected to them." Warren claimed that these subjects were his constant theme, and anyone who thought otherwise had only to recall that Coles "would frequently, at Wiggins's [Hotel] keep a barroom audience in profound silence," as they listened to the oft-told tales of his life experiences, stories that Warren assured his audience "would be amply sufficient to fill an octavo volume of 500 pages" even when limited to "the cream of them." In this editorial, Warren once again depicted Coles as an arrogant, bombastic pretender who was intensely self-absorbed and hardly deserving of the support of the voters.[49]

"the slavery question entered largely into the canvas"

Fortunately for Coles and possibly by his own design, several editorialists introduced slavery as a campaign issue at precisely the moment public criticisms of his elite pretentions were becoming most potent. Acknowledging that "it is pretty well known that a considerable ferment exists in some parts of the state, respecting the call of a new convention for the purpose of tolerating slavery," one editorialist called on each candidate "to give his opinion . . . on this all important subject." Another writer complained that "*some* [candidates] are *believed* to be favourable to slavery and a new convention; and that *any* are *unfavourable* is *uncertain.*" To remedy the situation, the author recommended that each candidate "do justice to himself," and the residents of the state, by "speedily and publicly declar[ing] his sentiment" on the issue.[50]

Prior to these requests, all four candidates pursued public support in similar ways. Each man toured the state, delivered speeches, and met with local inhabitants. Additionally, all four men boasted of their elite status and broad political experience, characteristics that defined them as members of the region's natural aristocracy. Consequently, voters possessed little, if any, way to distinguish one candidate from another and were left to rely on their personal knowledge or impression of the men as they considered whom to support. By the spring of 1822, however, the tone of the gubernatorial election changed dramatically and, more than anything, the slavery issue dominated the public discourse. Long-time resident and future Illinois governor John Reynolds observed that "the slavery question entered largely into the canvass, and governed the vote in many counties." Similarly, Horatio Newhall testified that "in the Choice of State & National officers the contest will be between those in favor of slavery, and those opposed to it."[51] To Coles's delight and advantage, the debate over which candidate deserved the support of the people focused less on political style and more on the slavery issue throughout the final months of the contest.

While he was widely recognized as an antislavery candidate because of his decision to emancipate his inherited bound laborers, all of Coles's opponents owned enslaved laborers, causing many voters to assume they supported slavery. Joseph B. Phillips, who resided in St. Clair County, owned several bound laborers in Tennessee, and, in July 1821 his defenders encouraged everyone "favorable to slavery to rally round" him because he was "a man through whom their objects can be accomplished." Thomas C. Brown, a Shawneetown lawyer who also owned 320 acres in the Saline district of Gallatin County, owned at least three slaves.

Although he consistently ignored the slavery issue, refusing to comment on his position publicly, most residents believed Browne was a proslavery candidate who would "receive a large vote" from the eastern portion of the state, where support for the institution was strongest. Moore was the only other potentially, though not confirmed, antislavery candidate. He lived in Monroe County, where he employed four enslaved laborers on his 160-acre farm and mill tract. As the election approached most voters concluded that they faced a choice among four men: one openly antislavery candidate, two apparent proslavery political aspirants, and one individual who refused to confirm or deny where he stood on the issue.[52]

Despite Coles's well-known antislavery credentials, the increasing visibility of the slavery issue hardly seemed to work to his advantage initially. Instead, like his refined manner and deportment, the emergence of the slavery issue provided Coles's critics with a new way to attack his candidacy. Hooper Warren, whose animosity toward Coles knew no bounds, warned voters that the public discussion of slavery "should not operate in favor of the pretensions of a candidate who may have *emancipated* half a dozen free negroes, with the sole view of thereby obtaining the votes of the Methodists and Yankees." Not only did he cast doubt on the sincerity of Coles's antislavery commitment, but the editor also challenged Coles's character as a leader when he informed his audience that no candidate "whose weight of character and influence are best calculated to defeat the [slavery] measure" was among the individuals vying for public support. Similarly, another anonymous author declared that Coles "had emancipated six or eight old and worthless negroes, and yet holds in bondage, in a neighboring state many young and valuable ones." From the perspective of both these critics, Coles's antislavery views were dubious at best. Worse still, the men implied, he had unleashed on Illinois society the very type of resident most white inhabitants despised, free people of color incapable of supporting themselves.[53]

Rather than idly stand by as his political enemies attempted to denigrate his character, deny the legitimacy of his claim to leadership, and manipulate the anti-black prejudices of the region's residents to his disadvantage, Coles explained his decision to emancipate his enslaved laborers in a public letter. Published in the *Illinois Intelligencer* and reprinted in the *Edwardsville Spectator*, Coles confirmed that "in accordance with my principles and feelings, which have, from an early period in my life, been very strongly opposed to slavery, I emancipated . . . all the slaves bequeathed to me." Although he acknowledged that several of the bound laborers he inherited remained under his care and lived in St. Louis, Coles declared that the circumstances were more complicated than they appeared. Among the chattels he inherited, he noted that "there was a woman who was the mother of five children . . . and knowing that it would be impossible for her to support herself when freed . . . I felt it my duty to assist her." To that end, he purchased her husband, who belonged to a neighboring planter, and provided for his freedom once he paid back the cost of his purchase. He also revealed that he had "executed her free papers to take effect when her husband should become free," which was to occur in August 1825. "In the meantime," Coles disclosed, "the support of her and her family devolved onto me." Of the ten enslaved laborers who had received their freedom in 1819, he continued, he had also given "a quarter section of land as a remuneration for their past services." Therefore, "far from holding in bondage many young and valuable negroes," he proclaimed, "I own none, but have liberated all, in the manner described."[54]

In this letter Coles attempted to negotiate carefully the narrow space between slavery and freedom that existed for most blacks in antebellum America. He counted those who remained in bondage as "free" because the mechanisms for their emancipation were already in place. He anticipated that such an arrangement would have been comforting to his readers. In a society that had promulgated laws prohibiting the settlement of free blacks amongst them as early as 1812, he hoped the residents of Illinois would cheer his efforts to avoid releasing into their midst blacks who were unable to support themselves. Yet, at the same time, by emancipating the other enslaved laborers he possessed and providing them with land, Coles unwittingly provided the very voters he courted with a reason to dislike him. Since many of them lacked the ability to purchase their own land and suffered financially from the severe depression sparked by the panic of 1819, most Illinoisans resented any competition from free black landowners. More important, poor whites often felt that successful free blacks threatened their independence and status among their white peers. As James Hall observed, "The blacks entertain a high respect for those whom they term 'gentlemen,' . . . but 'poor white folks' they cordially despise." Far from inspiring support for his candidacy, then, his explanation threatened to inspire many prejudiced residents to oppose his election.[55]

Still, through this public letter, Coles intended to portray himself as a principled man, who was rational, responsible, virtuous, and, most important, paternalistic. Far from being moved by unthinking passion or ambition, Coles freed his chattel property as a result of his "conviction of the impropriety of holding them." He accomplished his goal by executing a well-reasoned plan that acknowledged the utility and necessity of gradualism. Additionally, he maintained a paternalistic interest in his ex-slaves by supporting those who failed to support themselves and by providing the others with a secure future through land ownership. For those voters seeking to elect a responsible man who was willing to sacrifice his own private interest for the common good, Coles believed he posed a promising alternative to the other candidates. Unfortunately for him, Coles's representation of himself as a benevolent, paternalistic member of the elite clashed with the anti-black prejudices and egalitarianism, increasingly expressed as anti-elitism, exhibited by the state's residents.[56]

A month later, he continued his effort to defend his antislavery actions by submitting for publication in the *Illinois Intelligencer* a copy of Thomas Jefferson's response to his letter of July 1814 requesting that the Sage of Monticello come out of retirement to lead the fight against slavery in Virginia. His purpose here was twofold. First, he hoped that the state's democratically inclined residents would see his connection to Jefferson as evidence of his commitment to the interests of the people. Second, he sought to legitimize his own antislavery actions by associating them with the well-loved ex-president. In the publication, Jefferson expressed his regret that the revolutionary generation, "nursed and educated in the daily habit of seeing degradation," had been unable to carry their actions "the whole length of the principles they had invoked for themselves." He then concluded that the task of following through with these principles had been left to "the younger generation," whose knowledge and understanding of liberty he hoped would cause them to sympathize "with oppression wherever found." Perhaps most important, however, the letter clearly justified Coles's actions by demonstrating that Jefferson had provided him with a blueprint to follow. By liberating his chattel property, he had only accomplished one part of the program, and the implication was that if Illinoisans failed to elect him they would be going against the wishes of Jefferson, who had implored Coles to "come forward in public councils, become" an antislavery "Missionary . . . & press the proposition perseveringly until it is accomplished." By pursuing the governorship in Illinois, Coles was fulfilling the request of an honored mentor, and he hoped that after reading the letter the inhabitants of the Prairie State would be convinced that his leadership would expedite the arrival of that "hour of emancipation" that Jefferson claimed was "advancing in the march of time."[57]

On August 5, 1822, after a long and intense campaign, the residents of Illinois finally descended upon their courthouses to cast their ballots for a new governor. When the votes were tallied, Edward Coles, to everyone's surprise, including his own, was declared the winner, defeating Joseph B.

Phillips and Thomas C. Browne by a slim margin. Coles garnered 2,854, or 33 percent of the popular vote. Phillips received 2,687, or 31 percent, and Browne won 2,443, or 28 percent, while Moore gained only 622, or 7 percent, of the votes cast. Although the margins dividing the candidates were not great, Coles's victory, when examined at the county level, reveals that his 33 percent was probably stronger than it appeared. He won over 80 percent of the vote in five counties, while Browne could claim the same honor in only one county, and Phillips could not in any. Additionally, he claimed over 50 percent of the vote in eight counties. In the nine counties he won, then, Coles boasted a stronger showing than either Phillips or Browne could claim in the same situation.[58]

When considered from the perspective of the slavery issue, the election results demonstrated a significant pattern. Those counties farthest from the borders with the slave states and least dependent on enslaved labor supported Coles, the only openly antislavery candidate. But while he carried the northern counties with 69 percent of the vote, Coles failed to win a majority in any of the southern counties. Alternatively, either Phillips or Browne won majorities in every southern county except Monroe, where Moore resided. Those counties closest to the slave states and with the largest black population, enslaved and free combined, voted for either of the two recognized proslavery candidates. Additionally, although the election results seemed to imply that they favored slavery, many inhabitants in the southern part of the state may have voted against Coles not because they favored the extension of slavery but because they feared the consequences of his antislavery position. Rather than risk supporting a candidate who seemed to embrace social and economic equality for all men, black and white, they preferred to support a candidate who, like them, believed that blacks were inferior and should occupy a place at the bottom of the social order. Similarly, those voters in the north who supported Coles may have cared little about his antislavery credentials. Instead, they may have cast their votes for him because they thought it was the safest way to ensure that the black population in their midst remained small. The sectional division apparent in the election returns, then, was more complicated than a strict division between pro- and antislavery regions and everyone's concerns about race.

Hooper Warren immediately proclaimed his disappointment with the outcome of the election. In the August 31 issue of the *Edwardsville Spectator*, the editor declared that "we do believe that the circumstances of his election are degrading to the character of the state. The President can no longer hesitate, when he may wish to get rid of

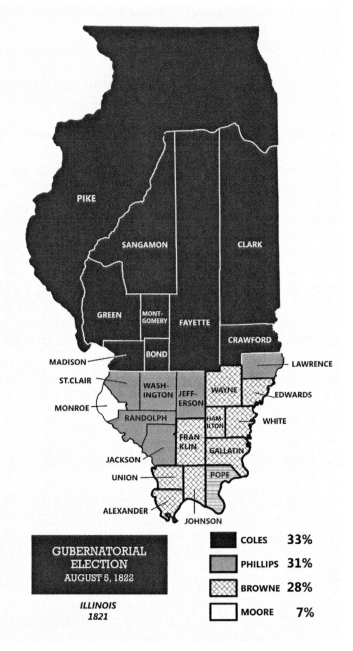

FIGURE 3.5. Gubernatorial Election, August 5, 1822. (Created by Mike Wirth, www.MikeWirthArt.com.)

a useless lackey," he continued, "to appoint him to a fat office in Illinois." Distrustful of Coles because he feared his political loyalties lay outside of the state, resentful of his elite pretentions, and convinced that he was politically inept, Warren refused to curtail his criticisms of the governor-elect. James Madison, on the other hand, was elated by Coles's victory. In a short note that accompanied a gift of a pedometer, Madison expressed his hope that Coles would "walk in a straight path and with measured steps" as he led the state over the next four years. Coles undoubtedly received this gift and note with great pride, as he had learned the art of politics by watching Madison steer the nation through its greatest crisis since the American Revolution.[59] Coles, however, had never been one to take measured steps, and he hardly intended to change his approach to the problem of slavery merely because he had been elected to office.

"for the abrogation of slavery"

On the afternoon of December 5, 1822, newly elected governor Edward Coles entered the small "wooden building . . . two stories high—not very high though," that housed Illinois's General Assembly. Inside, members from both houses of the state legislature, the lieutenant governor, secretary of state, and various clerks and secretaries from both chambers lined the walls and crowded onto the "long hard benches" that served as "seats for the members." Aware that few in the audience had predicted his victory and that many were skeptical of his political skills, Coles assumed a position "on a platform . . . a few inches high" and delivered his first speech as an elected official.[60]

As most of his audience anticipated, the new executive asked members to focus their attention on a variety of issues. Indeed, Coles used his inaugural address to outline his vision for the state, a program that he promised would "maintain the rights of individuals, and the common good of the community." To that end, he proposed to promote education, trade, and internal improvements, and encourage the development of local manufacturing, all improvements Coles assured his audience would advance the interests of both the state and the nation. He also promised those present that any differences of opinion that might emerge during his tenure as governor would be "an honest difference," and he vowed to do all he could to promote "harmony and kind feelings between the . . . branches of the government and between the individual members composing them."[61]

Such a vow, however, would prove difficult to fulfill, for Coles also used his inaugural address to bring the issue of slavery squarely before the legislature. He declared that it was "the intention of the framers" of the Northwest Ordinance of 1787 "that slavery and involuntary servitude should cease" in the region north of the Ohio River, but complained that "slavery still exists in the State." In order to honor those intentions as well as "our principles," Coles instructed the legislature to make "just and equitable provisions . . . for the abrogation of slavery in the state." Coles's speech immediately split the legislature into two factions, one in favor of and the other opposed to slavery. Both chambers appointed select committees to investigate the governor's recommendations. Within several weeks, each committee issued a report. Although they disagreed over whether or not the Northwest Ordinance of 1787 had abolished slavery, the committee members agreed that the only way to address the slavery issue was by calling for a constitutional convention.[62]

The division apparent in the reports reflected the conflicts and hostilities that had shaped Illinois society over the previous four years. The presence of four candidates who each possessed liabilities damaging to their candidacies resulted in a gubernatorial contest in which the outcome was nearly equally divided among the three strongest candidates. Unable to cultivate the support of a majority of the state's residents, thirty-five-year-old Edward Coles assumed the governorship well aware that he lacked the mandate to perform the reforms he desired. Still, Coles stepped forward boldly and devoted his tenure as governor to transforming Illinois into a prosperous free society of independent and enterprising farmers.

4 / Crafting an Antislavery Nationalism

On the cold, blustery evening of February 13, 1823, Edward Coles sat before a cozy fire in the governor's residence in Vandalia, Illinois, astonished by the recent turn of events. The day before, two-thirds of the state legislature had passed a resolution calling for a convention to revise the state's constitution, the first step in a scheme to legalize slavery. As he sat pondering the consequences of the vote, the sound of "shouts and yells . . . intermingled with loud blasts" disturbed his pensive mood. Peeking through his window, Coles spied Justice Joseph B. Phillips, Senator Theophilus W. Smith, and Senator William Kinney, "followed by the majority of the legislature and the hangers-on and rabble about the seat of government," assembled along the steps of the state house celebrating their victory. Armed with torches to light their way, the crowd formed "a noisy, disorderly and tumultuous procession" and marched through Vandalia's muddy streets "blowing . . . tin horns and . . . beating drums and tin pans," reportedly shouting "Convention or death!" They paused in front of Coles's residence and demonstrated their "contempt and displeasure" toward their antislavery governor by coupling their musical discharge with "a confused medley of groans, wailings, and lamentations." Drunk with the arrogance of triumph and undoubtedly a healthy dose of whiskey, the crowd sought to "intimidate and crush all opposition" to a constitutional convention. Despite this show of bravado, however, the contest had really only just begun.[1]

During the days immediately following the passage of the convention resolution, the members of the state legislature gathered together to support or oppose the convention. One "very large and respectable meeting of citizens" met in the legislative hall on February 15 to profess their "approbation" for a convention. They nominated a committee of seven men and instructed them to report "the sense of the meeting." Colonel Thomas Cox, a resident of Sangamon County and an ardent lobbyist on behalf of the convention resolution, invoked the preamble of the Declaration of Independence when he declared that those who supported the convention believed "the people are the only legitimate source of all political power, and that it is not only their right, but their duty, to amend, alter, or change their form of government" whenever they determined that it no longer served their best interests. Anyone who denied this "great and fundamental principle" of republican government, he charged, betrayed their own desire to sustain "the corrupt private interest of a few" over the "will of the majority."[2]

Undeterred by the riotous parade of convention supporters, Coles and several opponents of the convention likewise gathered a few days later in one of Vandalia's rooming houses to coordinate a strategy "to avert the tremendous curse that hangs over our State." As Rev. Thomas Lippincott later recalled, "never, probably, since our revolutionary fathers met to consider their rights and wrongs and dangers, has a meeting of free citizens, convened to consider a political question, been more completely under a sense of responsibility." Despite "a great deal of anxiety and some despondency," the men committed themselves "to keep out of our State the monster slavery" by signing an address explaining their opposition to the convention. Probably authored by Coles, the minority address acknowledged the "right of the people to alter, amend, and abolish . . . their constitution of government," but denied that constitutional reform was "the supreme object" of the proposed convention. Instead, the signers insisted that the real purpose was to repeal the clause prohibiting slavery, and, by doing so, "entail upon yourselves and your posterity the evils of slavery." They then implored the residents of the state not to be "deceived . . . [by] the song of the siren," which proclaimed that the council of revision, the judiciary, and the location of the seat of government required alteration, and declared that a vote for the convention was really a vote to legalize slavery.[3]

The pro- and anti-conventionists shared a common desire to promote the economic and social development of Illinois. From the perspective of the pro-conventionists, the constitution required revision, alterations that would eliminate aristocratic features they claimed violated the spirit of the nation's founding principles. Only by convening a convention, they claimed, could the state's leadership establish the social and political conditions necessary for the promotion of the interests of a free and independent people. The opponents of the convention, on the other hand, argued that the constitution was fine in its current form, and charged that the real object of the campaign for a convention was to legalize slavery, an institution they declared to be inherently incompatible with a free republican society. In the end, the convention contest became a competition between two incompatible visions of Illinois society. Although both groups envisioned a prosperous Illinois populated by a free and independent people, they disagreed over whether the legalization of slavery would facilitate or hinder the region's economic and social development and ensure its identity as a prosperous free state.

The convention contest also provided Coles with a forum to disseminate his antislavery views. Yet, with the memory of the sectional nature of the Northern Republican response to the Missouri Crisis fresh in his mind, he recognized the necessity of presenting his argument in a way that would resonate with the state's northern and southern-born residents. To that end, he repeatedly reminded Illinoisans that regardless of their place of birth they shared an antislavery past. The principles of liberty and equality first espoused by the founding generation had not only formed the bedrock of the nation, Coles insisted, but had also led most of America's revolutionary leaders to expect the republic they established to become eventually free of slavery. As members of the first American-born generation, Coles and his fellow Illinoisans, then, were obligated to ensure that the founders' antislavery vision for the nation was realized. As the convention contest played out over the next eighteen months, however, Coles realized that the revolutionary ideals he promoted might not persuade the majority of the state's residents to reject the convention and slavery. So, in the waning months of the contest, he combined his celebration of the nation's antislavery past with a free-labor critique of the institution. Together, these arguments became the central elements of an antislavery nationalism that would secure the triumph of the anti-convention forces in the state and safeguard Illinois' future as a free state.

"to do all in my power"

More than any other individual, Edward Coles emerged as the most recognized leader of the anti-convention cause, if for no other reason than his singular responsibility for precipitating the convention crisis. "Believing that my present office increases [my] . . . obligation . . . to enlighten the minds of my Fellow-Citizens," Coles revealed to his niece

Mary Carter, "I conceive myself bound, both as a Citizen and as an Officer, to do all in my power" to oppose the convention and slavery. From his perspective, the events of his first winter as governor were very disturbing. Although he had anticipated that the public discussion of the slavery issue would provoke a great deal of excitement, and possibly thrust the state into turmoil, he never imagined the extent of hostility his call for the abolition of slavery would generate. As John Reynolds, one of Illinois's earliest pioneers and a future governor of the state, noted, "Our country is in a great ferment on the Convention." Years later, he recalled that "men, women, and children entered the arena of party-warfare and strife, and the families and neighborhoods were so divided and furious and bitter against one another, that it seemed a regular civil war." Similarly, William H. Brown, future president of the Chicago Historical Society, declared that the convention question provoked so much tension and animosity that "old friendships were sundered, families divided, and neighborhoods arraigned in opposition to each other." Indeed, as Coles informed his family in Virginia, the convention crisis brought out the worst qualities in many residents of the state. "Party spirit raged with all the violence of a storm," reported Coles, "and against no object was its merciless pelting more severe than against the Executive."[4] Certainly, as he surveyed the publications in the newspapers and listened to the conversations of local residents, Coles came to doubt that his ambition to rid Illinois of slavery and transform it into a harmonious community of free and independent republicans would be successful.

With almost eighteen months to persuade voters to support or reject the convention resolution, both factions organized to influence the public. At the conclusion of the legislative session, Coles returned to Edwardsville to attend to his farm and help organize the anti-convention forces in the western part of the state. His journey was slow and labored. The road from Vandalia, although one of the more developed in the region, was marred by a thick, deep mud produced by the spring rains, forcing him to alternate between riding and walking his horse. Yet the lengthy trip was certainly worthwhile, for immediately upon his arrival a group of citizens cheered his return and announced their determination to celebrate his firm stand against slavery. As soon as Coles arrived in town, "a deputation on behalf of the Citizens of this town and County invited" him to participate in a public dinner. It was held on March 5, 1823, when many of the region's most prominent inhabitants gathered at New York native and Edwardsville pioneer Roland P. Allen's house to honor their governor. At the conclusion of the meal, Henry Starr, an attorney from

Sangamon County who was selected by the attendants to preside over the event, toasted "the occasion" by declaring that "Freemen delight in giving applause to faithful public servants." For the third toast, he proclaimed "Liberty. While we enjoy the blessings, may we not be willing to withhold it from others." Once the scripted toasts were completed, Coles stood to thank the audience for their show of support and offered a toast of his own: "The crisis: it is big with the fate of Illinois, and requires every friend of freedom to rally under the banner of the constitution."[5]

Coles recognized immediately that the success of the anti-conventionists rested on his ability build a coalition powerful enough to defeat the proslavery party. To that end, he and his allies organized a network of anti-convention societies. Coles led the "defenders of liberty" in Edwardsville, who were often referred to as "the Land Office clique" because they regularly held meetings in Coles's old office in the upper part of town. The Edwardsville anti-conventionists included many of Coles's close friends, among them Reverend Thomas Lippincott, Judge Samuel D. Lockwood, William P. M'Kee, Alexander Miller, and, whenever he was in town, Representative Daniel Pope Cook.[6] From their headquarters in Edwardsville, these men coordinated their strategies and then dispersed across the state to generate opposition to the convention. Coles traveled south to Bellville in St. Clair County within days of his reception in Edwardsville. There he personally recruited Rev. John Mason Peck, Risdon Moore, David Blackwell, and John Messinger, all of whom either affixed their names to or voiced their support for the anti-convention address published at the close of the legislative session. These men became the officers of the St. Clair Society and established a second headquarters for the cause. Coles likewise sent Lippincott and M'Kee to Monroe County, where they attended the inaugural anti-convention society meeting for that county in May. Throughout the spring, summer, and fall of 1823, Coles and his closest allies led their supporters as they formed societies across the state. Indeed, as Peck later recalled, no fewer than "fourteen societies had been organized in as many counties" by the winter of 1823.[7]

Coles also knew from his experiences in Washington City during Madison's presidency that organization mattered little if the public failed to understand the message offered. He understood, then, the power of the printed word, and set his sights on gaining control of a "newspaper establishment" and hiring an editor who was willing to "take a firm and manly stand against . . . slavery." Hooper Warren, the editor of the antislavery *Edwardsville Spectator*, emerged as the most logical choice.

Twenty-two anti-convention subscribers eventually raised one thousand dollars and delivered the sum to Warren by March 1823, ensuring that his paper would become the main anti-convention organ in the western part of the state.[8] To Coles's disappointment, however, Warren's commitment to the anti-convention cause hardly led the editor to suppress his personal animosity toward the governor. As Coles bitterly complained to his friend Nicholas Biddle, "four out of five of the newspapers printed in this State" supported the convention, and "the only press whose Editor is in favor of freedom has rendered himself unpopular with many by his foolish and passionate attacks upon many of the prominent men on his side of the question."[9] Coles feared that Warren lacked the republican sensibility necessary to elevate the anti-convention cause above his own personal interests and petty jealousies.

To resolve this problem, Coles recruited Richard Flower, a man who, like him, had immigrated to the state under "the firm belief that we should not be disturbed by the clanking . . . fetters of Slavery." Coles attempted to persuade Flower, a resident of the eastern part of the state, to establish a newspaper that could complement Warren's efforts and circulate anti-convention articles and essays. Albion was the ideal location, Coles reasoned, because "there . . . and [in] its vicinity, many persons [resided] who wield chaste and powerful pens, and who have the means" to subscribe to the new public print. If Flower chose to bypass the opportunity, Coles confessed that he also intended to "write and ask the same favor of Mr. Birkbeck," a man who shared their antislavery sensibility, but whom Flower detested.[10] When it became clear that neither man was willing to finance and manage a new newspaper on the eastern side of the state, Coles turned his attention to acquiring an interest in the *Illinois Intelligencer*, the state paper published in Vandalia. After pursuing the acquisition for "nearly twelve months," Coles finally secured ownership of the newspaper in early 1824. He removed pro-conventionists William C. Berry and Robert Blackwell from the editorship and replaced them with David Blackwell, the previous editor's brother, an officer of the St. Clair anti-convention society, and the newly appointed secretary of state. Installed in his new post by May 1824, David Blackwell provided the anti-convention forces with a second publishing resource during the last, and most crucial, months of the contest.[11]

Despite their organizational zeal, the anti-conventionist cause exhibited important internal divisions that threatened to undermine their effectiveness. From the outset, their forces contained two recognizable factions: abolitionists and exclusionists. Although a minority, the abolitionists hoped to use the convention crisis to eliminate all remnants of slavery in Illinois and revise the state's black codes. More than any other individual, Coles personified the abolitionist perspective. By the conclusion of his gubernatorial campaign, nearly every resident knew that he had emancipated his enslaved property. Additionally, most Illinoisans suspected that his republican sensibilities meant not only that he wanted to see slavery abolished but that he also believed the state's black residents should be treated as equals. As he had stated in his inaugural address and would repeat throughout the convention contest, "justice and humanity require . . . us" to reform Illinois laws so that they more accurately reflects the nation's republican principles.[12]

The second, and dominant, group of anti-convention supporters accepted the slave system that already existed in the state, but wanted to exclude any further immigration of black persons, enslaved or free. These exclusionists, to borrow a term from historian Lacy K. Ford, emphasized the negative consequences of a growing black population, which had increased by 34 percent during the first two years of statehood alone. One anonymous writer, for example, warned that if "the importation of slaves, and their constituent manumission" were legalized in Illinois, the population of the state would be "dark . . . in complexion, but infinitely darker in moral character!" Ultimately, exclusionists proposed to "whiten" their society by diminishing the size of the black population and marginalizing those who already lived in the state. By consistently portraying their adversaries as slave mongers and linking the spread of slavery to the threat of racial violence and social degradation, the anti-conventionists, both abolitionist and exclusionist, made a powerful appeal to the sensibilities of the state's southern-born nonslaveholding residents.[13]

Coles used the diversity of perspectives apparent among the anti-conventionists to his advantage. He insisted that, while remaining under the umbrella of a statewide leadership, each faction could present the public with a variety of arguments on behalf of the anti-convention cause. By targeting the feelings and interests of particular local audiences in this way, Coles and his colleagues hoped to generate broad opposition to the convention. They also intended their multilayered approach to forge a strong alliance between the state's political leaders and the general public. The end result, he hoped, would be the formation of a statewide coalition strong enough to defeat the pro-conventionists. Throughout the contest, the anti-conventionist leadership in the legislature and on the county level followed Coles's lead and attempted to consolidate support behind their cause by chanting "Convention and Slavery, No Convention and Freedom" at every opportunity.[14]

"dear lovers of Slavery"

The pro-conventionists, still basking in the euphoria of their legislative victory, initially saw little reason to organize their forces formally during the early months of the campaign. Slaveholders or proslavery men already controlled three of the state's four newspapers, and would eventually add a fifth to their arsenal. Further bolstering their confidence, a majority of Illinois's most prominent politicians supported the call for a convention. The state's proslavery residents also exercised political power well beyond their numbers. They elected slaveholders to nearly every top local and national office. In 1818, the governor, secretary of state, congressional representative, U.S. senator, and almost 30 percent of the state legislature either owned slaves or held proslavery views. By 1823, when the legislature passed the constitutional convention resolution, only Coles and Congressman Daniel Pope Cook opposed slavery among the state's top officials, while proslavery and slaveholding politicians expanded their control of the state legislature, increasing their presence there to 60 percent. "Our Governor is a plain good sort of man," observed one resident, "but many of our most influential public officers are dear lovers of Slavery and would gladly introduce into this state the same system which prevails at the South."[15]

Like their anti-convention antagonists, the pro-convention forces contained factions that competed for prominence. Most visible early in the campaign was a politically powerful contingent of proslavery men who unequivocally supported the expansion of slavery and the creation of a full-fledged slave system in Illinois. A second group of pro-convention men admitted that slavery was an evil, but believed that the subordination of black people was essential to the establishment of a stable social order. These subordinationists, then, viewed the legalization of slavery as the most efficient means of controlling the enslaved and free blacks who already lived in the region. A third band of pro-conventionists argued that if slavery spread westward, the horrors of the system, for both white masters and black slaves, would diminish and the institution would eventually disappear. Like the subordinationists, diffusionists acknowledged that slavery was an immoral institution, but, unlike their colleagues, they believed the expansion of slavery over a broader territory, when coupled with a colonization program, offered the only mechanism for the system's gradual demise.[16]

During the first few months of the contest, those who favored the convention had little reason to worry that their internal divisions would undermine their success. As Coles had discovered to his disappointment when he arrived in the state, the slave system had expanded by nearly 24 percent during the first two years of statehood. Moreover, the majority of the state's residents were southern-born yeomen farmers who migrated into the Old Northwest in pursuit of economic independence. Although some of these southerners may have immigrated to Illinois because of a moral or ideological opposition to slavery like Coles, the vast majority of them moved to the region to escape a hierarchical social order that placed the wealthy, educated, and propertied over the poor and land-less inhabitants of the South. Such distaste for the southern social order, however, rarely meant these residents supported the abolition of slavery. Instead, most white southern-born Illinoisans despised the presence of both the wealthy elites who controlled the political and social order from above and the black residents, enslaved and free, whom they viewed as an inferior class.[17]

Perhaps most encouraging for the pro-conventionists, the largely southern-born population had endured what many residents termed "hard times" during the first years of statehood. Subsistence farming dominated the state's early economy. Most farmers cultivated fields of corn, wheat, and occasionally cotton and tobacco. They also raised hogs and cattle, and produced much of what they needed at home, purchasing any other necessaries at a local store on credit. Few residents produced enough surplus to trade on the market. By the 1820s, however, market forces had infiltrated even the most distant western settlements and many residents aspired to achieve more than mere subsistence. Instead, they pursued a future in which they owned their own land and employed enough laborers to produce a surplus to sell on the market in New Orleans. They also hoped to sell their improved farms to the set-tlers who would follow them westward, making a nice profit in the process.[18] More than anything else, the pursuit of economic independence, whether secured through subsistence or market participation, shaped the way the settlers responded to the world around them.

The panic of 1819, however, stymied the ambitions of most Illinois farmers. Declining land values, a severe labor shortage, and a depreci-ated currency compromised even the most diligent farmer. Worse still, emigration into the state nearly halted, eliminating the promise of new land purchasers. The pro-conventionists offered slavery as the solution to the state's economic woes, promising that its legalization would provide residents with sorely needed laborers and induce wealthy slaveholding immigrants to settle in Illinois, where they would spend their money on improved farms. As one resident asked, "What is the only strong inducement held out to the voters for slavery? Inquire of every candid advocate for the measure," he responded, "and he will tell you, it is pecuniary interest—a relief from his distress, his embarrassments."[19] The apparent growth of the slave system, the regional character of the state's population, and declining economic conditions together led pro-conventionists to believe that the state's non-slaveholding majority would support the convention resolution.

The pro-conventionists, whose motto was "Convention or death," soon realized, however, that their failure to organize had allowed the opposition to gain public support. In May 1823, Coles and his supporters were "begin[ning] to think we shall be able to defeat the slave party." Similarly, Horatio Newhall, a resident of Greenville in Bond County, informed his brothers in Salem, Massachusetts, that although a majority of the people appeared to support the convention at the close of the legislative session, "The free party have been as industrious as possible." As a result, "a pretty considerable change has taken place in public sentiment." He boasted that "if the vote should be taken now, a majority of 2000 would oppose a convention." By September, Coles's confidence had increased. He enthusiastically informed his old friend Nicholas Biddle that "the advocates of a convention have been losing ground."[20]

Determined to counteract the organizational efforts of the "friends of freedom," the pro-conventionists met in Vandalia in December 1823. "Nearly all the friends of the convention," observed Coles, "have been here and held caucuses . . . adopted sundry resolutions, and made many arrangements." Like the anti-conventionists, those in favor of a convention "appointed committees for each county . . . [and] in each township" in order to influence public opinion. The residents of Fox River in White County, for example, met and passed a resolution denying that slavery had anything to do with the convention question. At a convention meeting in Fairfield, Wayne County, the inhabitants affirmed their right to revise or abolish the constitution. Similarly, over seventy residents of Pope County declared their support for the convention. With just eight months left in the convention contest, both sides rallied behind their leaders and settled in for a long, bitter contest. "The convention question," Newhall observed, "is a dish which is daily nay hourly served up.

It furnishes all our food for conversation, for reading and for newspaper scribbling."[21]

"giving vent to their spleen against me"

The pro-conventionists began their campaign by declaring that they were the true defenders of the people's interest, that they, and not the anti-conventionists, were true "republicans." They maintained that it was "the right of the people to modify" their government whenever they pleased, and accused their opponents of depriving the electorate "of their dearest rights." Those in favor of the convention portrayed themselves as "enterprising and republican supporters" of the people, and warned their audience not to be bullied by their "federalist" antagonists, men "so base, selfish, or aristocratical" that they viewed themselves to be "above the control of the people."[22] From their perspective, no individual embodied these qualities more than Governor Edward Coles. Accordingly, when he refused to sign a subscription to rebuild the statehouse after a fire, Coles's political opponents seized the opportunity to represent him as a haughty elite individual who willfully ignored the demands of the people. To protest his alleged elitist actions, a crowd of residents paraded "a man of straw" through the streets of Vandalia and then set it ablaze "amid the groans of the mob." As Coles explained to his philanthropic friend and Philadelphia resident Roberts Vaux, the mob was composed mostly of "the friends of a Convention," who "paraded the streets, nearly the whole night, giving vent to their spleen against me in the most noisy and disrespectful manner." Although they complained of his refusal "to rebuild the State House," he declared, their real "passions" had been ignited by "my opposition to a Convention." By reviving the charges of elitism that had colored the campaign for the governorship a year and a half earlier, Coles's political enemies hoped to render him, and the anti-convention cause generally, unpopular with the people.[23]

As he soon discovered, Coles's troubles were only beginning. Two weeks after the mob in Vandalia, he suffered a considerable personal loss when "about two thirds of all the buildings and enclosures on my Farm" outside of Edwardsville were consumed by fire. Not only was the small farmhouse occupied by Kate and Robert Crawford and their children destroyed, but so too were the extensive fruit orchards Coles had planted and nourished over the previous several years, as well as the fencing that protected his crops from the local wildlife. Anticipating the intense and time-consuming labor that would be required to repair a property that was already barely supporting itself financially, Coles was forced to contemplate renting out his farm. Whether the result of malicious pro-conventionists determined "not only to injure my standing with the people, but to break down my pecuniary resources," as he suspected, or the product of an unfortunate prairie fire so common in Illinois, the fire in Edwardsville appeared to be just one more incident among many aimed at discouraging Coles from continuing his opposition to the convention.[24]

The most unsettling assault on Coles, however, occurred in January 1824 when the pro-conventionists brought charges against him for illegally emancipating his slaves. According to a law passed in March 1819, but not published until October of that year, any individual who brought slaves into the state for the purpose of setting them at liberty was required to post a bond to ensure that they did not become a burden to the county. Because the slaves he emancipated entered Illinois as free individuals, Coles believed, and several lawyers confirmed, that the law did not apply to him. Nevertheless, at the behest of Theophilus W. Smith, the pro-convention state senator and editor of the *Illinois Republican*, a resident of Madison County issued a complaint to the County Commissioners in January 1824, demanding that they institute a suit against Coles to force him to pay a bond for each of his ex-slaves. The request remained tabled for most of the year, but was resurrected the following January at the urging of, as Coles later claimed, "a worthless and malignant partisan." Employing Henry Starr and Samuel D. Lockwood, two prominent anti-conventionists, as his lawyers, Coles attempted to defend himself and avoid paying a monetary penalty in a suit he believed was little more than a "party proceeding."[25]

The pro-conventionists hoped to accomplish several things by instituting the suit against Coles. He had already concluded that the contest would require so much of his attention that he would not be able to oversee his farm personally and had arranged for Robert and Kate Crawford to manage the property in his absence. In this way, Coles had prepared himself to focus exclusively on leading the anti-convention cause. By involving Coles in a legal battle, the pro-conventionists intended to distract him from his preferred occupation with a personal crisis. Coles had also pledged his entire annual salary of one thousand dollars to support the anti-convention cause. Several pro-conventionists hoped that the price of an attorney and legal fees would divert those funds away from the contest. Perhaps most important, the pro-conventionists attempted to manipulate the region's strong anti-black prejudice to their own benefit by encouraging residents to draw a connection between Coles's alleged unlawful act of emancipation and the growing free black population in the state. The suit, then, was part of a broader strategy designed to encourage voters to equate Coles in particular, but the anti-convention cause generally, with emancipation, free blacks, and lawlessness.

Coles assured his friends, however, that the "unrelenting and cruel persecution, which aims to destroy, not only my political influence, but my personal character and property," had failed to dissuade him "from promoting the cause of freedom." Instead, these recent experiences had caused him to reflect upon his actions "to see whether it has been correct." He concluded that "I have not given just cause of offense to any one; . . . the only complaint against me," he reasoned, "is that I am a friend to the equal rights of man, and am considered a barrier to my opponents acquiring the power of oppressing their fellow man." When viewed in this light, he concluded, "I am gratified that Providence has placed me in the van of this contest, and I am truly thankful that my system is so organized as to leave no room for doubt, fear or hesitation."[26] Coles's public stance contrasted sharply with the anxiety he expressed to his family. In the midst of the pro-convention assault on him, Coles confessed to his niece that he had spent most of "a very lonely and disagreeable winter . . . constantly . . . on the look out . . . watching the movements of my opponents" and had devoted his energy to "contradicting their secret machinations." Their efforts had only increased his determination "to enlighten the people on the question." While he willingly accepted the burden of absorbing most of the animosity of his political opponents when discussing them with his allies and friends, Coles reserved his true feelings for his family members. "There may be honor," he informed his niece, "but there is not pleasure in being governor to such a people at such a crisis."[27] Still, Coles predicted that the pro-convention assault would only strengthen his standing with the people of the state.

Coles countered their attack by publishing an essay of his own in the *Illinois Intelligencer*. Under the pseudonym "One of Many," he called the public's attention to the tone and character of the pro-conventionists' attack. He questioned why those who supported the call for a convention "expected" the residents of the state "to give their approbation to a call of a convention, without knowing its object." He similarly wondered why it was that the pro-conventionists seemed unwilling to allow the voters "to enquire into & discuss" the reasons for a convention. He warned his readers not to be "lull[ed] into acquiescence . . . by . . . the

Syren song of the peoples rights; the people are sovereign; the people cannot err." It was all a trick, he assured them, because the pro-conventionists knew that slavery was "not consonant with the interests or wishes of the people." Should anyone doubt the truth of his claim, he asked them to consider the efforts of his opponents to discredit him and prevent an open discussion of slavery and the convention. "Is this treating the people with respect?" Men so devoid of "political virtue and wisdom, of . . . stern Republican principle, [and] of that political and moral worth" so essential to republican government, concluded Coles, "should not be trusted" with the power to alter or amend the constitution.[28]

Echoing Coles's claims, other anti-conventionists reassured the public that they firmly believed that representatives were accountable to the people, a principle that they reminded their audience "will never be questioned." Encouraging the public "to rally round the banner of freedom," the anti-conventionists consistently identified themselves as the "defenders of liberty" and the "friends of freedom," and attempted to convince the electorate that opposing the convention really meant voting in favor of freedom and liberty. By rejecting the convention and slavery, they maintained, the residents of Illinois would prove "to the admiring world, that the principles which warmed the bosoms of their ancestors, still burns in theirs."[29]

Ironically, in their eagerness to muster public support by boasting of their accountability to the people, the pro- and anti-convention leadership contributed to a fundamental shift in political power in Illinois. Where the political elite initially controlled the contours of public debate, the unprecedented need for popular consent during the convention crisis provided the general electorate with an opportunity to determine the focus of the political discourse. By the summer of 1823, it mattered little which side was aristocratic or republican, for, after their experiences during the Missouri controversy and the gubernatorial contest of 1822, residents had become suspicious of any political leader who slung anti-republican insults at their opponents, a skill both sides had mastered equally. As a result, most of Illinois's small farming residents insisted that their political leaders abandon republican rhetoric and focus the debate on "*how* slavery is to do good to me, and the like of me—that is four citizens out of five in the State." For the remainder of the contest, both pro- and anti-conventionists were forced to explain the advantages and disadvantages of introducing slavery for the average small, and southern-born, farmer, and the result was that a comparison of free and slave labor and democratic and aristocratic society dominated the rhetoric of the convention campaign.[30]

"if slavery was admitted"

This was just the type of debate Coles wanted the convention contest to provoke. Throughout his residence in Illinois, he had worked tirelessly to promote the region's economic and political development. As Register of the Land Office, he oversaw the equitable distribution of land and when the panic of 1819 threatened to destroy Illinoisans' hope for economic independence, Coles vigorously administered the government's land policies and promoted the interests of the region's residents in his communications with Washington. Similarly, as founder and president of the Illinois Agricultural Society, he regularly published essays encouraging farmers to diversify their crops and supplement their agricultural pursuits with livestock management, while simultaneously promoting the development of local manufacturing and internal improvements. He repeated these desires in his 1822 inaugural address. Coles, then, had always envisioned Illinois as a society of free and independent men whose commitment to republican virtue required that they promote not only the agricultural development of the region but also the state's place within the nation's emerging market economy. From his perspective, the residents of Illinois had a duty to protect their political freedom and independence by promoting the economic development of the state, something he believed the legalization of slavery would prevent.[31]

Answering the demands of the electorate, the pro-conventionists attempted to garner public support by arguing that the expansion of slavery into Illinois would improve the state's prosperity. The small, but vocal, proslavery faction of convention supporters depicted slavery as a positive good for the community. "If slavery was admitted," they asserted, "our country would populate in abundance, wealth would be in our country, [and] money would circulate." They based this argument on two assumptions. First, the pro-conventionists declared that slave labor was essential for the continuation of the saline works, Illinois's main source of manufactured salt to preserve meat for local consumption and transportation to the market in New Orleans. "A Plain Man" argued that the rigors of saline production are "such as no white man . . . is willing to risk or able to endure." Black slaves possessed constitutions "better adapted to this climate . . . and [able to] endure heat and watching far better than whites." Besides, the author asked, "will any white man . . . take

[up] the slavish employments? . . . Would a white man for less than fifty cents a day make himself the veriest slave of the community?" He hoped not only to highlight the economic consequences of precluding the use of slave labor at the saline works but also to exploit his audience's proclivity to view any labor performed by blacks as best handled by slaves. The implication was that such work degraded any white man forced to perform it. Unlike their proslavery counterparts in the East, whose "positive good" arguments emphasized that slavery improved the condition of black people, these western defenders of slavery focused on the benefits slavery would bring to the white community. Where slavery existed, they proclaimed, white economic prosperity blossomed and equality among white people was guaranteed.[32]

Second, many pro-conventionists argued that Illinois suffered from a labor shortage. Introduce slavery, they announced, and all the residents of the state would have access to enough laborers "to raise [an] abundance of products . . . perhaps enough to commence some other manufactories [sic]." Confirming these claims, another editorialist complained that he could not hire laborers to work his farm. Admit slavery, he predicted, and even small farmers will be able to improve their own land. Whether they focused on the saline works or a reported labor shortage, these overtly proslavery pro-conventionists maintained that Illinois's economic prosperity depended upon the introduction of slavery. If anyone doubted the truth of their statements, they instructed the electorate to observe the prosperity of their slaveholding neighbor, Missouri. "Look," the pro-conventionists implored, "at those trains of wagons with their splendid teams, their carriages and their gangs of negroes. They are going over to fill up Missouri, and make it rich, while our State will stand still and dwindle, because you wont let them keep their slaves here."[33]

Pro-convention diffusionists offered another argument that echoed the positive good tenor of their proslavery colleagues with two important exceptions. Unlike their slavery-defending associates, diffusionists sought only the "qualified introduction" of slavery by proposing to couple the expansion of the institution with "a system of gradual emancipation." Conrad Will, a pro-convention member of the general assembly from Jackson County, promised that such a program would restore "thousands to their liberty, to whose bondage there is now no prospect of termination." Additionally, rather than highlight the advantages slavery brought to white residents of the state, these qualified supporters of slavery chose to emphasize the benefits the spread of the institution would bestow on black slaves. They argued that slaves "ought to be scattered over a wider space . . . in order that better profits to their master might procure better fare for them." Similarly, "A Friend to Liberty" predicted that extending slavery into Illinois "will better the condition of slaves, comport more with liberty and produce their general emancipation from bondage at an earlier day than if they are confined to a more limited district."[34]

Collectively, the pro-conventionists attempted to cast a comprehensive spectrum of arguments designed to generate support among the broadest electorate possible. They presented themselves as the true friends of the people, and attempted to discredit Coles and the opposition by describing them as haughty elites who would deny the people their right to govern themselves. Although probably attractive to only a fraction of the state's residents, the proslavery faction also sought to lure adherents to their cause by depicting slavery as a positive economic good for Illinois's struggling white farmers. Pro-convention diffusionists, on the other hand, claimed a more general middle ground, promising that while the temporary introduction of slavery would ensure economic prosperity, Illinoisans would be able to avoid the negative consequences of the slave system through the forced deportation of all slaves once they gained their freedom. Significantly, both pro-convention contingents pledged that the expansion of slavery would promote equality among all of the region's white residents by ensuring that only black people performed the degrading tasks associated with slavery. Ultimately, this diverse pro-convention strategy targeted the racial prejudices and economic ambitions of the state's predominately southern-born yeoman farmers. By doing so, they acknowledged that whoever was most successful at manipulating this particular constituency would win the convention contest.

"on the moral and political effects of slavery"

Coles and his anti-conventionist allies, who styled themselves the "friends of freedom," attempted to undermine the pro-convention strategy by crafting an antislavery appeal that would resonate with a majority of the state's voting residents. Coles claimed to "trust the good sense and virtue of the Citizens of Illinois" and was confident that they would never "sanction a measure . . . so directly opposite . . . those enlightened and liberal principles" espoused by the nation's founders. Unwilling to leave the outcome to chance, however, he maintained that "the public mind should be enlightened on the moral and political effects of

Slavery." Coles composed no fewer than thirteen essays and had them published in the *Illinois Intelligencer*. It was in these publications that he crafted and refined the central components of an antislavery nationalism that would become the hallmark of his public career. Throughout the contest, Coles claimed that slavery violated the nation's republican principles. "Filling the State with Slaves," he instructed, hardly "comports with the principles which gave birth to our independence, and forms the ... fundamental features of our Political and Religious Creed." Even the nation's revolutionary leaders recognized the contradiction inherent in a slaveholding republic. Quoting William Pinckney in a speech he delivered before the Maryland legislature, Coles found a lesson he hoped Illinoisans would take to heart. "We may talk of liberty in our public councils, and ... declaim with ... vehemence ... against oppression," Coles quoted, "but so long as we continue to cherish the poisonous weed of partial slavery among us, the world will doubt our sincerity." He likewise reprinted the words of St. George Tucker, who complained that Americans hypocritically "declared that *all men* are by nature *equally free and independent*," yet continued to countenance slavery "in defiance of so sacred a truth!" Few should doubt, Coles was demonstrating, that the nation's first generation of leaders recognized slavery to be a political and moral evil that violated the central principles for which the Revolution was fought.[35]

Coles acknowledged that, despite these pronouncements, many of the nation's founders had failed to abolish the institution they maintained was so deplorable. "It is certain," he confessed, "that they are much to blame for not having taken ... an effectual step for the gradual emancipation of their slaves." He claimed, however, that they had set "so noble an example" when they "proclaimed to the world the inherent & inalienable right of man to his liberty," that a broad movement against slavery and the slave trade had been born. Indeed, he boasted that although the founders did not legislate abolition for the nation, the first "fruits of our ... Revolution" had included a proscription against the slave trade and an ordinance prohibiting the extension of slavery into new territory. Local leaders likewise "abolished slavery in a majority of the States of the Union." Coles insisted, then, that "our fore fathers" had done everything they could "to prevent the importation & population of America with Slaves," as well as "to restrict & finally eradicate it from our soil."[36] The nation's revolutionaries, he concluded, were antislavery statesmen who set in motion developments that would lead ultimately to the demise of slavery.

By legalizing slavery, then, Illinoisans would not only violate the nation's founding principles, they would also flout the antislavery tide sweeping America and the world. The pro-conventionists, Coles assured his audience, "are endeavoring to introduce and legalize among us, an unnatural and unjust and anti-republican . . . system of oppression, which has been either eradicated or denounced by all the Govts . . . of the Civilized world." As Coles knew from personal experience, and frankly informed his audience, even the most despotic of nations like Russia had joined the march toward emancipation. Moreover, "in our own Country," he continued, "it has been abolished by a majority and reprobated by all." If Illinoisans legalized slavery, he warned his readers, "they will add an indelible stain on the character of the State, on the Union, and on free Governments." A vote for the convention and slavery, concluded Coles, would transform Illinois from "a free and happy community of citizens into an unnatural and miserable community consisting of Masters and Slaves." It would force the residents of the state to throw "down the mantle of freedom" they had inherited from the founders and put "on the armour of oppression."[37]

As he worked to cultivate opposition to the convention, Coles constructed the foundation of his antislavery nationalism. In his telling of the past, all of the founders, nonslaveholders and slaveholders alike, had confessed their belief that slavery was morally and ideologically wrong. They likewise had recognized that the institution violated the very principles they espoused and enshrined in the nation's governing institutions. In response, according to Coles, they had consistently (if in a limited way) endorsed laws intended to restrict and gradually destroy the institution. In some ways, Coles's use of the past was artful. The disagreements over slavery and how to deal with the institution during the Revolutionary era were certainly more contentious than his rendering of the past revealed. Perhaps, as well, they could have done more, both personally and politically, to orchestrate the demise of the institution. Still, he never falsely attributed antislavery sentiment to any individual or denied the limits of the post-revolutionary antislavery impulse. He carefully marshaled his evidence and displayed it boldly before his readers. He recognized in the nation's leaders men who had not allowed their personal failures to preclude public greatness, yet he called on Illinoisans both to be like and do more than their forefathers. He demanded that they reject slavery, and in doing so erase the "strange contradiction of our principles" and the "sinful difference between our professions and our practice."[38]

Many of Coles's anti-convention colleagues adopted this tactic, echoing his claim that slavery was inconsistent with the nation's founding principles. Publishing in the antislavery *Edwardsville Spectator*, one editorialist observed that "it is among the proudest recollections of the American patriot, that his country has been the first to assert and maintain the principles of self-government and equal rights. . . . Shall we," he asked the public, "arrest their noble career" by legalizing slavery? Doing so, he assured his readers, would be an "outrage upon the principles of free government and the rights of man." Another resident similarly wondered "why . . . we fought for liberty" if Illinoisans were willing to "strengthen the oppressor's chain? O," she lamented, "it is rank inconsistency!" James Deaton exploited his fellow residents' racial fears by insisting that "slavery tends to destroy not only the rights which all men are equally entitled to by the declaration of independence, but the equality which now exists between the *free whites*." Whether they valued the sacrifices their ancestors had made on their behalf or wished to protect their own right to equality, these authors implored Illinoisans to "prove yourselves true American patriots and republicans" by voting against the convention.[39]

"retarding the settlement and prosperity of the State"

Coles recognized that ideological arguments alone might not convince a majority of the state's residents to reject the convention resolution. Accordingly, he and his supporters adopted a strategy designed to persuade Illinoisans that slavery would also harm the prosperity of the state and demean honest white laborers. As early as April 1823, Coles enlisted the aid of his antislavery friends in Philadelphia when he asked Nicholas Biddle to help him "promote the virtuous cause" by obtaining pamphlets that would "elucidate the general character and effects of Slavery." In particular, he instructed his friend to obtain copies of material describing the "moral, political, & social effects" of slavery, "facts showing its effects" on emigration and economic development.[40]

Biddle immediately pledged to furnish "all the assistance which I can give or procure" and confessed that he had "already engaged two of our most active gentlemen familiar with the subject who will cheerfully & zealously contribute to your support." Additionally, he forwarded a pamphlet that "goes directly to the question of the superiority of free over slave labor." A week later, Coles received a letter from another friend, Philadelphia antislavery activist Roberts Vaux. Astonished "that any part of the inhabitants of your state should wish to introduce a system which is generally reprobated," Vaux offered "my own, and the services of a few of my friends, in this interesting cause." He proposed to make "judicious selections from writers whose purpose is to show the iniquity and impolicy of slavery," arrange for them "to be printed in the *Tract* form . . . and forwarded to Illinois for gratuitous distribution." Indeed, before the summer of 1824, when the contest was most intense, Coles had received at least two shipments of pamphlets, collections he distributed throughout the state.[41]

Armed with their own essays as well as publications from outside the state, Coles and his supporters combined his principled opposition to slavery with a Free-Soil critique that proved to be very effective. As Coles informed Roberts Vaux, they primarily sought to unveil slavery's "impolicy and injurious effects in retarding the settlement and prosperity of the State." One anti-convention author boasted that "the emigrants from the east will bring money, and industry—the very things we want." He warned, however, that "emigrants from the south will bring us idleness, luxury, and the slow but fatal disease of slavery—the things we do not want." Another editorialist predicted that encouraging slaveholders to migrate into the state would stifle the development of manufactures and invite unfair market competition. The writer signing himself "Democracy" claimed that slaveholders "are not men of manufacturing characters—they have seldom engaged in that business." Worse still, he decried, "they will raise grain and stock by the help of their servile labor, and . . . will undersell the poor man, who raises such things by the labor of his own hands." As Coles's good friend Morris Birkbeck assured his audience, "if we vote faithfully against a convention . . . true prosperity will begin to beam upon us." Clearly, most of those who opposed the convention believed that introducing slavery would diminish, not increase, the prosperity of the state.[42]

The exclusionist faction of the anti-conventionists were particularly interested in demonstrating both the "superiority of free over slave labor" and, as Coles declared, that slavery "would operate to the injury of the poor or laboring classes of society." One of the contest's more prolific writers, "Martus," claimed that "a white man in his own business, is more efficient than a black man in another's." He explained that "slavery destroys almost every inducement to action and to virtue; by withholding the rewards of industry and the virtues from the slave." From his perspective, only free white labor would improve the prosperity of the state. Exclusionist opponents of the convention also often recited statistics, comparing the productivity and prosperity of free and slave states to support their contentions. Coles's Edwardsville neighbor and political ally, Rev. Thomas Lippincott, who served as the corresponding secretary for the "Madison Association to oppose the introduction of Slavery in Illinois," compared Pennsylvania with Virginia. He found that both the property values and population increased more rapidly in Pennsylvania than in Virginia. He concluded that "the existence of slavery in one, and its non-existence in the other state, has caused the discrepancy."[43] The only way Illinois would prosper, Coles and his allies implied, was if slavery was excluded from the region.

Perhaps most appalling, many argued, was that slavery degraded white laborers. Citing an 1817 letter from Congressman R. G. Harper of South Carolina to the secretary of the American Colonization Society, Coles informed his audience that "when the laboring class is composed . . . of slaves distinguished from the free class by color, features, and origin," free men "are almost irresistibly led to consider labor as a badge of slavery, and, consequently, as a degradation." Harper had claimed that "in a country where slaves are generally employed . . . the mere circumstance of a freeman pursuing the same labour . . . [will] subject him to the contempt of the haughty master." Ultimately, the introduction of slavery, according to the "friends of freedom," threatened "to degrade honest but humble industry and sink the laborer." By glorifying the advantages of free labor, Coles and his contemporaries sought to convince the electorate to oppose the convention and, in doing so, celebrate a social order that rewarded efficiency and honest industry with economic independence and equality among white men.[44]

Both abolitionist and exclusionist opponents of the convention sought as well to demonstrate that slavery inevitably led to a hierarchical social order that oppressed nonslaveholding whites. "Martus," in the fifth installment of a series evocatively entitled "The Crisis," claimed that slavery "begets in its possessor a haughty, insolent, oppressive, overbearing temper dangerous to liberty." He feared that encouraging slaveholders to immigrate to Illinois would create a "practical aristocracy." Morris Birkbeck warned Illinois's small farmers that "the planters are great men, and will ride about, mighty grand, with their umbrellas over their head." After the deluge of anti-convention articles, pamphlets, and speeches, the enemies of the convention hoped that few small farmers would doubt that "all equality is destroyed" in a slave state because a slaveholding "community tends . . . to divide the citizens into different ranks and different castes or classes."[45] From the perspective of those who opposed the convention, the very nature of Illinois society was at stake. In August 1824, voters would not only choose between slave and free labor, but also between aristocracy and democracy.

All of these arguments proved most effective when the authors wove language laced with racial prejudice into their statements, betraying their preference not only for free labor but for free *white* labor in particular. Recognizing that the terms were interchangeable, several editorialists substituted "free" for "white" and "black" for "slave" in their essays. "The labor of a free man is always more productive than the labor of the slave," argued "Aristides," because "the white laborer has an interest in his toil" while the "miserable horde of blacks" only produced as much as the master demanded. This perspective also led many of these purported "friends of freedom" to denigrate free blacks, a population they thought "always to be dreaded." For example, one author warned that limiting slavery by coupling it with a gradual emancipation plan, as some of the pro-conventionists proposed, would leave Illinois "swarming with old free negroes, worn out in the service of their former master." These newly freed blacks, he continued, would stroll "about the country . . . begging and pilfering from house to house." Another author described a far more alarming fate in which an expanding free black population "would soon . . . [have] it in their power to contend . . . for supremacy with the whites." Although he did not believe blacks to be inferior, even abolitionist Edward Coles recognized the utility of making such arguments. If Illinoisans hoped to prosper, he convincingly argued, they would have to preserve "these beautiful and fertile prairies . . . [for] our kindred descendants of Europe, who are like ourselves enlightened," by excluding "the descendants of Africa, who are not only unlike us in person, but are to be a degraded race of slaves." By employing racial language that emphasized not only the inferiority of blacks but also characterized their presence in Illinois as a threat to white safety and prosperity, the anti-convention exclusionists attempted to exploit the strong aversion to blacks prevalent among the state's residents.[46]

Designed specifically to convince them to vote against the convention resolution, this multilayered discussion targeted the southern-born small farmer, who would easily recognize the world the writers described. As Abraham Carns informed his audience, "Many of us have been long accustomed to living in slave states, and we know the poor people in those states suffer." He reminded his readers that before they moved to Illinois, they "had to lock our cribs, meat houses, and milk houses, through fear of the negroes." He also warned that just as wealthy slaveholders watched "the poor white man . . . become the companion of slaves" when called upon to perform public works in the South, so too will "the haughty slaveholders . . . sit in the shade and drink their grog" as they observe their poor neighbors and slaves build roads across the prairie to facilitate the transportation of slave-produced goods to local markets. According to this author, few residents should doubt that the southern social order would be replicated in Illinois should slavery be legalized. Similarly, an editorialist, who called himself "A Friend to Illinois," confessed that "I was raised in a slave state," and recalled that those "who are not able to hold or own them [slaves], will be almost leveled with them. This," he declared, "I know from experience." By reminding the state's southern-born residents why they left their native states and the dangers that would accompany opening Illinois's borders to more black residents, enslaved and free, the anti-conventionists hoped to convince them to exclude slavery from the Prairie State by voting against the convention.[47]

As the convention vote neared, both sides publicly expressed their confidence, but privately feared their efforts would fail. For the anti-conventionists in particular, the fears were well founded. Not all of Illinois's southern-born small farmers opposed the convention or slavery. Although they were "despised and trampled on . . . by the aristocratic slaveholders, and contemned [sic] even by slaves," recalled Lippincott, many poor southern farmers "were found among the noisiest brawlers of the Convention." Asked why he supported the convention, one man replied that he "wasn't gwine to jine in with the darned Yankees." Others, who had left poverty behind when they moved to Illinois, believed that "their wealth might be enhanced and their ease promoted by owning one or more slaves." Slavery appealed to still others. According to Lippincott, men who had witnessed the "severe labor of their wives" and confronted "the difficulty of procuring domestic labor," viewed slavery as the only solution to their labor problems. Coles also recognized that the coalition of anti-conventionists was fragile because it consisted of the state's small number of abolitionists, exclusionists, slaveholders who opposed the introduction of new slaves but did not want their own property rights challenged, and many individuals "who profess to be opposed to Slavery and who rail much against it, but yet who are friendly to it." As the date of the final vote approached, it became increasingly difficult to predict if such a weak coalition could win the contest.[48]

"the decided voice of the people"

In the end, Coles's fears were unrealized. When the people of Illinois finally cast their ballots on August 2, 1824, they defeated the convention resolution by 1,688 votes. Eighteen counties, 6,640 individuals, or 57 percent of the voting population rejected slavery. Although the gap between the votes in favor and against the resolution appeared to be small, the strength of the anti-convention victory was significant. In eight of the eighteen counties that opposed the convention, more than 70 percent of the voters cast their ballots against the resolution. Only two pro-convention counties garnered a similar majority. In addition, in three of those eighteen anti-convention counties, more than 90 percent of the county's voting residents rejected holding a convention. Furthermore, voter turnout reached an all-time high of nearly 95 percent, with 11,612 residents casting their ballots on that warm summer day. This was a significant increase over popular participation in previous statewide elections. In the congressional campaign of 1820, only 6,944, or 54 percent, of the state's eligible voters had cast their ballots. By the gubernatorial race of 1822, the percentage of residents who participated in the election had increased to 67 percent, but still remained significantly lower than the 1824 total. Two years after the convention vote, when the population rose considerably but the visibility of the slavery issue practically disappeared, the number of voters only increased by 1,000, reflecting an overall decline in voter turnout. As the slavery issue had played an increasingly important role in Illinois's political culture, voter turnout correspondingly grew. Slavery, then, more than any other issue, served as the catalyst that motivated residents to participate in the political process.[49]

In August 1824, the anti-conventionists won a decisive victory by publicizing the evils of the slave system and drawing out more Illinois voters than ever before. By celebrating the merits of free labor, the benefits of a democratic social order, appealing to the residents' strong antiblack prejudices, and reminding the public that the founders had always intended the region to be free of slavery, they successfully articulated arguments that would resonate with the broadest possible coalition of voters. Exclusionists—those residents who did not want to see the size of the black population, both enslaved and free, increase under any circumstances—rejected the convention resolution in large numbers. Importantly, this group included slaveholders who wanted to retain their property but did not want to see more slaves imported into the state, and non-slaveholders

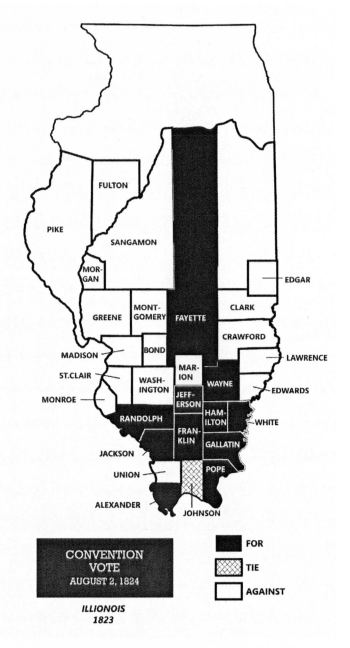

FIGURE 4.1. Convention Contest, August 2, 1824. (Created by Mike Wirth, www.MikeWirthArt.com.)

who left the South to escape a slave society that granted a disproportionate share of political power to slaveholders. Joining this portion of the
electorate was at least a small number of subordinationists, men who
believed that slavery offered the most efficient means of securing a social
order that elevated all whites above their black laborers. These men could
reject the convention while remaining proslavery because their vote did
not abolish slavery. On the contrary, it ensured that slave population
already present in Illinois would neither expand nor perish.

The final, and probably the smallest, group of voters to reject the convention resolution were the abolitionists: men like Edward Coles who
hoped that the defeat of the convention movement would be the first
step toward abolishing every form of slavery in Illinois. Unfortunately
for them, the coalition constructed by the anti-conventionists proved
too fragile to develop into an abolition movement. The central concern
that bound all of these anti-conventionists together was a shared understanding that the black population, whether enslaved or free, should not
increase if Illinois was to prosper economically. By rejecting the convention resolution, they confidently announced that they had prevented the
expansion of slavery and continued to maintain a firm commitment not
to interfere with slavery where it already existed, a position that would
emerge on the national level under the banners of the Free-Soil and
Republican parties. On that fateful day in August, the residents demonstrated their preference for a white egalitarian society, populated by
white independent yeomen farmers, by rejecting slavery and the hierarchical social order that placed the poor white farmer only slightly above
the black slave.

For Edward Coles, the conclusion of the convention contest was both
satisfying and disappointing. He was proud of his "instrumental [role] in
preventing a call of a Convention, and in making Illinois a Slave-holding
State." Additionally, his antislavery nationalism, when combined with a
Free-Soil and free-labor critique of slavery, had successfully persuaded
a majority of the state's southern-born residents to reject slavery. Antislavery sentiment, he concluded, need not be sectional in character, as
it had been during the Missouri crisis. Moreover, the rejection of slavery in 1824 represented a democratic affirmation of federal authority to
restrict slavery because it sustained the restrictive precedent established
by the Northwest Ordinance of 1787. But, he also learned that antiblack
prejudice was an essential motivating force, revealing that only an antislavery program that promoted the interests of free white men was likely
to succeed.[50]

The outcome was also discouraging because, despite their thorough defeat, the pro-conventionists continued to harass Coles. In 1825, Coles left the state for three months for a much-needed rest after a hard-fought contest. While he was visiting friends and family in the East, his rabidly pro-convention Lieutenant Governor Adolphus Hubbard staged a coup, claiming that Coles had relinquished the governorship by leaving the state. Although Hubbard's challenge failed, the effort exposed the deep resentment his convention opponents still held for him. The suit instituted against him in January 1824, once tangled in Illinois's court system, likewise reemerged after the convention vote to distract him from his official duties. According to Coles, the judges, John Reynolds and Samuel McRoberts, and the jury foreman, Hail Mason, were pro-convention men determined to ruin his reputation and financial standing. Not only was he forced to contend with antagonistic participants but the judge also refused to allow Coles to call witnesses, submit evidence, or testify on his own behalf. When he commented on the unfair proceedings of the court in the newspaper, McRoberts accused him of slander and filed a civil suit demanding $5,000 in damages. Eventually, both the original suit and the civil case were resolved, when in late 1825 the state legislature passed a law releasing from penalty any person, including Coles, who failed to post a bond for the slaves they emancipated during the previous six years. That same year, McRoberts's civil case failed to progress beyond the complaint stage, earning a dismissal because of an absence of sufficient grounds to proceed.[51] Rather than silence his opponents, then, Coles's anti-convention victory only increased their resentment.

Perhaps most dispiriting for Coles, slavery remained a very visible part of Illinois's social and economic structure after 1824. Coles attempted to use the popular mandate expressed in August to rid the state of the territorial remnants of slavery and improve the condition of the state's free black population, but he failed. As he had done two years earlier, Coles asked the legislature to "make just and equitable provision for . . . [the] abolition of . . . slavery." Naively, he expected the state's representatives to heed "the decided voice of the people" expressed in the convention vote. Of those who made up the anti-convention coalition, however, only a minority would have embraced abolition. By the end of his term, the situation had hardly changed. When he delivered his final address as governor, Coles renewed his call for abolition, and recommended that the legislature make provisions for the "amelioration of our code in relation to free Negroes." He reminded the state's leaders that they were "the Representatives of a people who love liberty," who had "resolved that their land shall be the land of the free." To his great dismay, the Illinois legislature ignored his advice. Enslaved labor remained a minor yet visible part of Illinois's agricultural and domestic economy until the 1840s, when the state Supreme Court finally declared the indenture system illegal. The state also retained a restrictive black code and thereby remained inhospitable to free blacks. Few Illinoisans shared Coles's disappointment. For them, the outcome of the convention contest and the laws perpetuating the inferiority of the state's black residents ensured that Illinois would remain an egalitarian society of white men.[52]

Still, when he reflected on "the abuse I endured, the labor I performed, [and] the anxiety I felt," Coles took comfort in the knowledge that he had never faltered from his principles. Indeed, his actions in Illinois had secured for him an antislavery reputation that spread up and down the Atlantic seaboard.[53] During his residence in Illinois, then, Coles learned a hard lesson that would shape his approach to the slavery issue for the remainder of his public career. To mobilize broad public support for any antislavery initiative, leaders had to remind voters of the nation's antislavery past, manipulate the antiblack prejudices of the public, and convince them that rejecting slavery served their pecuniary interests. Unfortunately, when confronted with the call for abolition, residents often privileged their antiblack prejudice over their antislavery sensibility, and the movement for abolition stalled. Unless he and other likeminded men could combine their antislavery nationalism with arguments that demonstrated the economic and political advantages of opposing slavery, there was little hope that local and national political leaders could be persuaded to enact emancipation.

5 / Antislavery Reform Denied

In late December 1827, just days before Christmas, Edward Coles sat alone in his boarding-house room in Edwardsville, Illinois. A week earlier he had turned forty-one, and in a few days the holiday would arrive. "The whole face of nature," he mournfully reported to his niece in Virginia, "has been covered with snow, . . . sleet, & ice." It was "as gloomy a winter," he continued, "as could be imagined." A year had elapsed since the end of his term as governor, and he felt acutely the pain of living "so far removed" from his friends, family, and "the scenes of . . . [his] youth." Without an occupation and few prospects locally, Coles was forced once again to contemplate "chang[ing] my course of life." As he looked back over his career in Illinois and forward to consider his future, he confessed that he was tempted "to cease, in despair, to labour to benefit others, and in [the] future . . . gratify more my predilection for the enjoyments of society." Certainly, he wanted "to sacrifice less of my personal comforts . . . and be content with more limited efforts to advance the cause of humanity." Yet he revealed that he was more often "impatient under the apprehension that I am wasting my life in idleness, instead of engaging more actively" in public life. The truth of the matter was, that over the past year he had constantly oscillated "between pleasure and duty" and which of these he would choose to indulge remained unclear.[1]

The year 1827 had proven to be a difficult one for Coles. Immediately following his farewell address to the Illinois legislature, he left for Virginia and a round of visits with friends in Washington, Philadelphia, and New York. As he traveled through the Old Dominion, he learned that the Madisons, who were surrogate parents to him, were in the midst of a family financial crisis. John Payne Todd, Dolley's untrustworthy son, had accumulated high debts during repeated gambling and drinking binges in New York and Philadelphia. The financial obligations that Madison had assumed on his stepson's behalf had come due, but, as the ex-president informed Coles, "I shall endeavor to provide for the demand, but I really fear it may be impossible." Coles spent much of the next several months negotiating with creditors and attempting to persuade Todd to return to Virginia. Indeed, he ultimately loaned his beloved mentor two thousand dollars, which relieved the Madisons of the most pressing debts.[2] During that same spring, Coles also learned that the political climate back in Illinois had devolved into chaos, with various members of the state's legislature accusing their colleagues of corruption. Apparently, several representatives had been buying and selling votes. Even Governor Ninian Edwards had been implicated and, as a result, was "on the defensive." Partisan politics had turned even more bitter than it had been during the Illinois convention contest, and Coles was happy to be beyond the reach of the political storm.[3]

Distance from the affairs of politics in Illinois, however, failed to shield him from the rancorous politics emerging as Andrew Jackson sought retribution for the political wrong he claimed had been perpetrated against him in 1824. In May 1827, Coles was pulled inadvertently into the vitriolic 1828 presidential contest when Lewis Williams, a congressman from North Carolina, produced a document claiming that Coles had announced at a Washington social event that Thomas Jefferson had always strongly disapproved of Andrew Jackson's popularity. "The disposition of the American people to elect General Jackson President," Coles's Jefferson allegedly declared, "was the single circumstance which had shaken his faith, and made him fear that the American republic was soon to follow the fate of all others and fall under military rule." News of Coles's rendering of Jefferson's views spread rapidly throughout the nation as editors eagerly reprinted the story. Fearful "that the bitterness of party feeling may lead to some ill-natured attack," Coles dispatched a letter to Thomas W. Gilmer, a close Virginia friend and ardent Jacksonian Democrat, asking him to corroborate his memory of Jefferson's opinion of Jackson. Privately, Gilmer confirmed Coles's representation, recalling that "Jefferson's opinion of General Jackson as a statesman was less favorable." Yet publicly Gilmer confessed that though Coles's account was accurate, the Sage of Monticello had also fervently disapproved of John Quincy Adams. Gilmer then chastised Coles for offering

Washington society and the nation a "very partial exposition," implying that his partisan preferences had led him to misrepresent the full extent of Jefferson's views.[4]

After months of declining to respond publicly to Gilmer or explain "the erroneous assertions" circulating in the papers, Coles could not stand the abuse any longer and finally agreed to set the record straight. In November 1827, he published a detailed explanation and declared that Jefferson had never trusted Andrew Jackson, a man he thought "had manifested an arbitrary and ungovernable disposition" and who he predicted would selfishly pursue "his own will" rather than serve the people. Coles concluded by declaring "that it is impossible for me to conceive, under any circumstances, that Mr. Jefferson could support . . . the election of General Jackson."[5] Despite his efforts to the contrary, the controversy over Jefferson's opinion of Jackson continued unabated and Coles's name was repeatedly disparaged and, from his perspective, misused in the public press.

Edward Coles's December 1827 lament to his niece, then, probably reflected his disenchantment with politics as well as the loneliness and sense isolation he felt, as much as any true crisis of purpose. The partisan character of local and national politics disgusted him, and he had little desire to reenter the political fray. He also desperately missed his family and friends. During a triumphal eastern tour in 1825, Coles had enjoyed an extended sojourn in Philadelphia, where he thanked Nicholas Biddle and Roberts Vaux for their invaluable help in the convention campaign. It was during this trip that he probably met Sally Logan Roberts, Vaux's beautiful eighteen-year-old niece. Although he had been wounded by love during his youth, Coles was smitten with her, his "feelings" often "impossible to control." It was only with "great difficulty" that he resisted the "inclination to go again" to visit her in "that charming City." Still, he remained preoccupied with a sense of duty to continue his fight against slavery. In February 1826, he and several of his antislavery associates had established the St. Louis Auxiliary Colonization Society. A year later, he had become a life member of the American Colonization Society when he attended the organization's annual meeting in Washington; founded in 1816, the American Colonization Society (ACS) pledged to promote emancipation by facilitating the voluntary emigration of the nation's free black residents and newly liberated southern slaves. This "herculean scheme of usefulness . . . engages much of my attention," Coles proclaimed that cold December, and he knew it offered a tantalizing way to remain actively involved "in useful & benevolent works."[6]

Indeed, in October 1827 Coles revealed just how committed he was to this new strategy in his struggle against slavery when he wrote a narrative proclaiming that colonization was the most effective means of achieving emancipation in America. As he justified this new element of his antislavery views, Coles insisted that the change did not reflect the inadequacies of the men and women he had liberated, for as far as he was concerned his experiment in black freedom had succeeded. The freed men and women lived "industrious, economical, and thrifty" lives and had been consistently "fair and honorable in their dealings; moral and religious in their lives; obedient to the laws; [and] civil and respectful to the white lordlings of the Land." In short, they had demonstrated their ability to be productive members of American society. Unfortunately, their very success made them (and Coles) a target of bitterness. White prejudice and discrimination, Coles concluded, was a powerful force that would always pose a formidable obstacle to emancipation. It was the white residents' "disposition to oppress and ill treat" blacks, then, that had led Coles to promote "the practicability of the removal of the blacks."[7]

Although he complained of being pulled in two directions, toward gratifying his personal desire to pursue a fuller relationship with Sally Logan Roberts and toward fulfilling his sense of obligation to continue fighting against slavery, he had already chosen the latter. Still, it would be two years before Coles would again work forcefully for the demise of slavery. Not until 1829, when the Virginia State Convention of 1829–1830, as well as the slavery debates in the Virginia General Assembly following Nat Turner's rebellion in 1831, did he encounter an opportunity to renew more publicly his campaign against slavery by promoting gradual emancipation and colonization. Armed with his antislavery nationalism, an appeal that combined an ideological opposition to the institution with a Free-Soil critique, a celebration of the nation's antislavery past, and colonization, Coles turned his attention to Virginia, where he intended to encourage Virginia's leaders to link emancipation and colonization to their demand for democratic reform and transform the Old Dominion into an egalitarian nonslaveholding state.

"to move in this great question"

Coles had cause to believe that popular support for colonization and emancipation among Virginia's residents might have increased since he left the Old Dominion in 1819. In November 1826, he learned from the

FIGURE 5.1. Portrait of Edward Coles, 1831, lithography by Albert Newsam after Henry Inman. (Courtesy of the Historical Society of Pennsylvania.)

pages of the *Richmond Enquirer* that the Richmond district had elected his brother-in-law, John Rutherfoord, to the Virginia legislature. Coles immediately dispatched a letter of congratulations. "I am greatly gratified at your election," wrote Coles, not only because of "the regard I have for you as a man," but also because "seeing men of your principles in relation to negro Slavery in the Councils of Virginia . . . cheers me with the hope that something will soon be done to repudiate the unnatural connection . . . between the freest of the free and the most slavish of slaves." The problem, as Coles understood it, was that Virginia's most recent history had been stained by the continued support for and protection of slavery. "Far from acting as if Slavery were an evil which ought to be gotten rid of," he complained, "every measure . . . has been taken to perpetuate it, as if it were a blessing." With the election of men like Rutherfoord, Coles hoped that this situation had changed. "It behooves Virginia," he declared, "to move in this great question; and it is a solemn duty," he continued, "which her politicians owe to their country, to themselves, and to their posterity." Now was the time to act, he instructed, "to look ahead and make provision for the future," a future Virginia without slavery.[8]

Rutherfoord had married Coles's youngest and most beloved sister Emily in April 1816. He had studied at Princeton and read the law with Richmond grandee George Hay (the father of Coles's doomed first love), before shifting his attention to a career in public service. As a member of the Richmond Colonization Society, Rutherfoord regularly defended the organization's "benevolent and philanthropic" as well as "politic and practicable" efforts to repatriate the state's free black population. "It is admitted on all hands, by the enemies and by the friends of this enterprise," he declared in a speech before the Richmond and Manchester Auxiliary meeting in January 1824, "that our country is cursed with an evil, which has 'grown with our growth, and strengthened with our strength.'" As a friend of colonization, he assured his listeners "that the scheme for colonizing the free people of colour upon the Coast of Africa" would bring "lasting benefits" to the nation, as well as "our slave population." His views had hardly changed by 1829. In that year, Rutherfoord continued to celebrate the "success which has attended . . . the experiment" and declared that the enterprise deserved the support of every true "patriot [and] . . . philanthropist."[9] Within his extended family, then, Coles found a potential ally in his crusade to rid Virginia and the nation of slavery.

The members of the American Colonization Society (ACS) acknowledged that "an infinite variety of opinions" existed among colonizationists, especially "as to the . . . slavery question." To preserve unity within their society, some members professed that their organization had no intention of interfering with slavery. Instead, they would seek to alleviate the deplorable position of free blacks throughout the nation, whose status was more like "a 'slave without a master'" than a free person, by organizing, financing, and managing the voluntary transport of the nation's free black population to a colony in Africa. Still, few members would deny the less visible, but equally important, goal of gradual emancipation. Who would complain, asked one advocate, if "in its progress, it . . . should convince the southern people and their legislatures, that emancipation might be both safe, practicable, replete with blessings, and full of honour." Though emancipation was rarely an explicit priority of the national organization, colonizationists saw themselves as liberators whose organization would contribute to the eventual demise of slavery.[10]

The members of the ACS also presented their program as consistent with the legacy of the founding generation. They characterized themselves as Christian reformers charged with a benevolent duty to correct the injustice of slavery. But they simultaneously insisted that the founders had bequeathed to their generation a responsibility to reconcile the nation's principles with practice, an argument Coles had been making for more than ten years. The genuine need for a national government in 1787, unanimously supported, led many of the nation's early leaders to support the Constitution even though "it recognized moral wrong in the laws of some of the States." They did so, wrote one author, "with [the] hope and expectation that this wrong [slavery] would be rectified." From the perspective of most colonizationists, "the opinion expressed in private by the first men of our country" condoned abolition and anticipated "that what on this subject was not demanded" during the founding of the nation "the states would accomplish" in due time. The author then asked, "Is it necessary to appeal to the testimony of Patrick Henry, or to the warning words of the venerable Jefferson?" Another supporter declared that "the benevolent enterprise" of colonization "has been formally recommended by the highest and most august assemblies in the land, both ecclesiastical and political."[11] The mission of the ACS was thus compatible with Coles's antislavery nationalism.

When Coles joined the organization, the ACS boasted a nationwide membership. As one supporter maintained, the organization "seems to captivate all classes of men," slaveholders and nonslaveholders, northerners, southerners, and westerners, and men from all political persuasions.

Citing the organization's 1825 annual report, one writer proclaimed that "a thousand powerful minds scattered throughout the Union, are at work for this Society." Indeed, men as diverse as Henry Clay, Daniel Webster, William Crawford, James Madison, James Monroe, Robert Finley, and Richard Rush were among the first life members of the society. Moreover, auxiliary organizations appeared in nearly every state, a testament to its appeal and growing popularity. Since the organization pursued a national rather than a sectional antislavery agenda, it should hardly be surprising that Coles was attracted to the movement.[12]

Philosophically, Coles could embrace much of the mission of the organization. He agreed that slavery was a moral evil that had to be eliminated because it violated the nation's founding principles. He also understood that in a nation of self-governing people, it was the responsibility of citizens "either by the sense of duty, the influence of example, the inducement of interest, or by all combined" to demand a change that would reconcile principle and practice. After his experiences in Illinois, he realized that slavery was a national problem that required a national solution. He maintained, then, that a private organization could not succeed without the support of state legislatures and Congress. He was likewise willing to use to his advantage those elements of the society's ideology he did not endorse. He did not believe, for example, that the nation's free blacks were "injurious in [their] . . . influence" on society and "degraded in character." Yet Coles knew from experience that free blacks would be "forever excluded by public sentiment [and] by law" from experiencing any real equality of condition. As a result, he felt he could overlook the strong anti-black rhetoric that polluted the pages of colonizationist literature, petitions, and memorials because he hoped that the eventual result of the society's efforts would be a national coalition opposed to and willing to eradicate slavery.[13]

By the mid-1820s, Coles's colonization ally, John Rutherfoord, had also emerged to lead the nascent Democratic forces in Richmond, forging a lasting friendship with Thomas Ritchie, the editor of the *Richmond Enquirer* and the leader of the Richmond Junto, a small group of eastern Tidewater elites who directed the politics of the state. In many respects, as a Jacksonian Democrat he represented the conservative eastern Tidewater elite in both his personal standing and familial background.[14] Rutherfoord differed from his conservative Old Republican constituents in at least one important way, however, and broke with the all-powerful Richmond Junto. As he had confessed to Coles in February 1826, Rutherfoord supported political reforms that would weaken the political power exercised by the eastern Tidewater grandees. During the winter before his election to the state legislature, he wrote to Coles predicting that "a convention certainly must & will take place before many years shall have elapsed. The 'powers that be,'" he continued, "may cause it to be deferred for a while, but their extraordinary & illiberal opposition to *the expression* of the popular will, must ultimately yield to the force of public sentiment." Indeed, a coalition of western Piedmont, Valley, and northern Piedmont reformers, along with a few Tidewater men like Rutherfoord, had sought constitutional reforms that would expand suffrage and reapportion the seats in the state legislature since the 1780s (when Thomas Jefferson and James Madison had issued the first call), but experienced little success. Virginia's Tidewater slaveholders, fearful such changes would render their enslaved property insecure, consistently prevented these efforts to, as one historian has described it, "democratize the Old Dominion." Public pressure for reform, however, continued to rise throughout the 1820s, and, as Rutherfoord had forecast, constitutional reform could not be avoided for long.[15]

It was in this context that Coles congratulated his brother-in-law on his political victory. Not only did his election bode well for broader democratic reforms in Virginia but Coles also hoped that the election of men like Rutherfoord might provide an occasion to tie emancipation to the long-denied political ambitions of the state's reform-minded residents. In the fall of 1829, Coles recognized in the 1829–1830 Virginia Constitutional Convention an opportunity to fasten his antislavery nationalism to the political and economic ambitions of the Old Dominion's western residents. After years of failed attempts, western reformers in Virginia finally succeeded in calling a convention to revise the state's constitution. Their goal was to expand the right of suffrage and reapportion representation to more accurately reflect the demographic changes that had transformed the state over the previous thirty years. Together, these changes would increase the political power of ordinary white men and enhance the authority of the predominately nonslaveholding western counties within the legislature. Likely to lose their political dominance if democratization succeeded, the eastern Tidewater elite objected to these political reforms. A majority of Virginia's freeholders, though, supported the movement, passed a referendum calling for a convention, and promptly elected delegates who would revise the constitution during the fall and winter months of 1829 and 1830.[16] It was in Richmond, at this event, that Coles intended to promote emancipation by advancing his antislavery nationalism among the ambitious representatives of Virginia's western residents.

At first glance, the sectional tensions that characterized the convention seemed to have little to do with the slavery issue. But Coles knew from personal experience as well as from frequent conversations with family still residing in the state that more and more Virginians seemed willing to embrace emancipation and colonization. Although he recognized that this transformation in public opinion probably had little to do with any principled opposition to the institution, Coles's experience in Illinois had taught him not to dismiss the antislavery possibilities that could be generated by antiblack prejudice and the desire for increased economic opportunity. Moreover, he hoped that a growing fear that slavery was causing the state's economic and political decline would swell support for emancipation. It was among Virginians of these views, men whom Coles recognized to be remarkably similar to the coalition that had rejected slavery in Illinois, that emancipation and colonization was becoming increasingly popular and whom he sought to mobilize against slavery. By the late 1820s, then, Coles hoped that political power, economic prosperity, and opposition to slavery had become intimately intertwined, transforming the long tradition of sectional tension in Virginia into a battle over the place of slavery in the Old Dominion. Coles believed he could not have designed a more perfect opportunity to press for emancipation.[17]

The chances of success in Virginia, however, were significantly less promising than they had been in Illinois. Virginia had the largest slave population in the country, and it was growing. The Old Dominion also contained a powerful but relatively insecure slaveholding elite who were determined to protect their own economic interests and quick to sound the alarm at the slightest hint of a challenge to slavery. The profound disappointment voiced by the likes of Thomas Ritchie, John Randolph, and Philip Barbour after the Missouri Controversy revealed the depth of many Virginian's commitment to slavery and foreshadowed the uncompromising posture Tidewater slaveholders would adopt during the convention.[18] Even in Illinois, where the number of slaves was a small fraction of the total population and the slaveholding population was correspondingly miniscule, Coles had not persuaded the states' leaders to abolish slavery, and in Virginia he faced an even more reluctant leadership. Still, he forged ahead determined to encourage westerners to call for the removal of the source of their oppression—slavery.

"a state of moral and political retrocession"

When Coles arrived in Richmond in October 1829, the city was crowded with spectators and residents eager to observe the convention proceedings. Among those elected as delegates were such Virginia luminaries as ex-presidents James Madison and James Monroe, Chief Justice John Marshall, and one-time senator John Randolph of Roanoke. Also present were future president and then senator John Tyler, Senator Littleton Waller Tazewell, and Governor William Branch Giles, as well as Benjamin Watkins Leigh, Chapman Johnson, and Philip Barbour. Although these were only some of the most prominent of the ninety-six delegates, they were all men Coles knew well, either through family connections or from his days as a student at the College of William and Mary. These social and familial connections gave Coles the confidence to insert himself into the debate and led him to expect that, even though he was only an interested observer, his views might influence the outcome of the convention.[19]

John Rutherfoord, Coles's most direct link to Virginia politics and his brother-in-law, was not among the convention delegates. Indeed, he refused to be a candidate. Although he ardently supported the call for a convention, and had eloquently defended the enabling legislation on the floor of the House of Delegates the year before, Rutherfoord refused to place himself before the people. As he confessed to Coles in April 1829, "so decidedly opposed were my own opinions and feelings to those of a majority of my constituents . . . that I wd not have been willing to represent the city during that session." Rutherfoord counted himself among the state's democratic reformers, men who sought to expand suffrage and increase the legislative power of the western counties in the state. Opposed to this position were Rutherfoord's constituents, Tidewater conservatives who feared that if the eastern slaveholding counties relinquished their authority, the state's slow but persistent economic and political decline would only intensify.[20]

The tensions Rutherfoord described between reformers and conservatives reflected long-standing divisions in the state, divisions that remained visible among the delegates elected to the convention. Three distinctive groups took their seats in the State House in Richmond and maintained coherence during the course of the debates over the crafting of a new constitution. John Randolph of Roanoke, Benjamin Watkins Leigh, and Abel P. Upshur emerged as the leading spokesmen of the eastern Tidewater conservatives. These men represented the state's oldest

FIGURE 5.2. Virginia Constitutional Convention, 1829–1830, by George Caitlin. (Courtesy of the Virginia Historical Society.)

slaveholding gentry families, men who nostalgically recalled Virginia's glorious past and sought to preserve a status quo that protected slave property as well as the authority of the Tidewater elite. Arrayed against them were western democratic reformers like John R. Cooke, Philip Doddridge, and Chapman Johnson. These men looked to the future of the Old Dominion and saw democratizing reform and economic diversity (which did not necessarily include a continued reliance on enslaved labor) as the key to Virginia's revival. Between these factions stood men like James Monroe and James Madison, renowned revolutionary leaders who favored compromise and consensus and hoped to preserve the unity of the state. Seasoned by decades of political battles shaped by these divisions, the delegates could hardly avoid resorting to these perspectives during the convention.[21]

Though he could not serve as a friend to Coles from inside the convention hall, Rutherfoord provided his brother-in-law with intimate access to several of the leading delegates. Coles was more than happy to take advantage of Rutherfoord's hospitality. Another brother-in-law, Andrew Stevenson, also resided in Richmond, where he and Coles's older sister Sally reigned over elite society. Coles stayed with this sister and brother-in-law in their Richmond home during the height of the convention. Each morning, Coles joined James Madison, who was also lodging with the Stevensons, to walk the few short blocks to observe the debates. During the evenings he socialized in the Rutherfoord and Stevenson parlors with various delegates, Madison, Monroe, Tyler, Giles, and Tazewell among them, as well as other friends in the city. To gain a sense of the public response, he also read daily reports in the *Richmond Enquirer*. Well positioned to observe the political developments on the convention floor and partake in more private discussions outside the statehouse walls, Coles searched intently for a way to shape the content of the discussions.[22]

In late October, barely two weeks into the proceedings, Coles boldly attempted to raise the slavery issue when he arranged for the publication of Thomas Jefferson's 1814 letter and, by doing so, expressed his hope that the deceased founder might yet lead Virginia toward emancipation. He included an editorial note revealing that he intended the communication to "enlighten the minds of those members of the Convention who have not sufficiently reflected on the evils of the system" of slavery. The most "expedient" means available to rid the state of the institution, Jefferson (and Coles) advised, was through a gradual program that also provided for the removal of the newly freed black population. Coles believed that he was addressing a sympathetic audience because so many of the delegates were colonizationists. Madison, Monroe, Marshall, and even Randolph, had been among the organization's founding members and first officers, admittedly for very different reasons. Moreover, these were all men who knew and respected Jefferson and should recognize in his voice a call to honor the nation's antislavery heritage.[23]

He was not alone in this effort. The residents of Augusta County, for example, published a "Memorial to the Honorable Convention of Virginia," during the early days of the convention, calling on the delegates to make "some constitutional provision for a system of emancipation." The author informed the delegates that the Augusta County reformers "wish for nothing that is unfair." From their perspective, "slavery [was] an evil greater than the aggregate of all the other evils which beset us." They insisted that any refusal to act on behalf of emancipation could only be the result of "heedless passion and uncompromising selfishness." The time to act had arrived, they declared, for "Virginia is in a state of moral and political retrocession" that only the elimination of slavery could forestall. Years of demands for democratic political reform had finally led to the convention, and few Virginians would deny that the place of slavery in the state was central to the apportionment and suffrage questions to be settled by the delegates.[24]

The Jefferson-Coles letter appeared on Friday, October 23, the day before the convention delegates opened their discussion of Madison's report on representation. The members of this committee proposed that "in the apportionment of representation in the House of Delegates, regard should be had to the white population exclusively." This would dramatically redistribute political power in Virginia by granting equal representation regardless of property ownership. The report elicited quite a few amendments, and no effort drew more attentive debate than John W. Green's proposal to strike the word "exclusively" from Madison's report and replace it with the words "and taxation combined," a move that would preserve the status quo. Although no one identified the issue directly, slave property was at the heart of this conflict. As long as property in slaves continued to determine the allotment of seats in the state legislature, eastern slaveholders would retain a disproportionate share of political power and Virginia would remain a fundamentally undemocratic society. By publishing the letter, Coles gambled that any discussion of the undemocratic distribution of political power would lead the state's western delegates to see emancipation as a means to achieve their political goals.[25]

Western reformers, who hoped to increase the political power of the predominantly nonslaveholding western counties, immediately objected to such a change in language. John R. Cooke, a delegate from Frederick County, argued that redesigning the constitution as Madison's report originally instructed would bring Virginia's government more in line with the state's renowned revolutionary heritage. Virginia's own Declaration of Rights, he reminded his audience, declared "that the principles of the *sovereignty of the people*, the *equality of men*, and the *right of the majority*" were the fundamental characteristics of a practical, legitimate government. Only the violent crisis of revolutionary war had prevented the framers from enacting these ideals more fully. The call for reform, he continued, "has never slept" and, as Jefferson himself demanded as early as 1781, the time had come to correct the "inconsistencies" of the old government by replacing it with a constitution that put these principles into practice.[26] Although he preferred to see the state's leaders embrace democratization by subtracting enslaved property from any representation calculations, Cooke never challenged the slave system directly. By focusing on equality for white Virginians, however, everyone knew his view indirectly challenged the political power based on slave property.

It was eastern Tidewater conservatives who raised the issue of slavery when Abel P. Upshur, a Tidewater conservative from Richmond, countered Cooke by repeating the long-held Old Republican view that only those who possessed a sufficient amount of property held an interest in society and should exercise governing authority. He warned that all who owned slaves would "feel it to be unsafe" if "the power of controlling" this property was put "into the hands of those who are not the owners." He acknowledged that "as a general proposition, in free Government, power ought to be given to a majority . . . of persons only," but only if everyone shared a common interest. In Virginia, however, "the several parts of the Commonwealth" had very distinct (and occasionally contradictory) interests, "and the difference between us," he submitted, "arises from [slave] property alone." In the government reformers envisioned, a government based on white persons only, he feared that the "peculiar" interests of the eastern Tidewater slaveholders would be "exposed to peculiar impositions, and . . . peculiar hazards." The only way to ensure the protection of their interests from "oppression" was to preserve the source of their political power, slavery. Accordingly, he defended the political power of the state's slaveholders by insisting that representation be calculated by "persons *and property*."[27]

Although they eagerly invoked the nation's revolutionary ideals to expose Virginia's political inconsistencies, reformers ignored Coles's implicit advice to link emancipation with the political interests of the state's nonslaveholding residents for fear such a move would destroy any prospect for success. It did them little good; for, despite three weeks of discussions, conservatives stubbornly refused to consider any of their opponents' demands, and the convention stalled. James Monroe, fearful that they would "go home without having agreed upon a constitution," instructed each side "to sacrifice a portion of their respective claims." To pave the way, he attempted to discard the one issue that seemed to provoke the most intransigence, slavery. "I am satisfied that if no such thing as slavery existed, that the people of our Atlantic border would meet their brethren of the west upon the basis of . . . free white population." Abolishing slavery, however, was out of the question, proclaimed Monroe, because such a move would only produce "disorganization . . . and perfect confusion." Even if they were liberated, the newly unshackled black population would be "separated from the rest of society by a different colour; . . . nor can you remove them," he continued. "The thing is impossible." After reassuring fearful conservatives that their slave property was safe, he then proposed a compromise he believed would honor everyone's commitment to the rights of "free and independent citizens." Why not achieve a balance of interests, asked Monroe, by allowing the House of Delegates to be apportioned according to the white population, while the seats in the Senate would be distributed by a "compound basis? . . . If you agree on this arrangement," promised the ex-president, all the delegates, as well as the residents of the state, "will, I think, be satisfied."[28]

Coles could hardly believe what he had heard. From his perspective, Monroe had mismanaged a golden opportunity to resolve the deadlock in a way that promoted emancipation. Although both sides seemed unwilling to concede an inch, Coles believed the discussions had inadvertently exposed a common ground. In one way or another during the debate, men on both sides of the issue had claimed that slavery was wrong and that, in the abstract, the principles espoused by the state's revolutionary leaders supported emancipation. As Philip Doddridge had pointed out just a few days earlier, even conservative Upshur had essentially admitted that "but for the possession of great masses" of slaves, "majority government would be safe." Although he did not necessarily endorse immediate abolition and expressed a common fear of a growing free black population, Philip Barbour acknowledged in his response to Doddridge that "if you give to the language" in the state's Declaration of Rights "all the force which the words literally import, what will they amount to but a declaration of universal emancipation to a class of our population . . . now in a state of slavery."[29] From Coles's perspective, these pronouncements provided Monroe with plenty of leverage to push the state's leaders to transform the Old Dominion into a more egalitarian nonslaveholding state. To his dismay, the ailing ex-president had failed to seize the moment and instead dismissed gradual emancipation and colonization as impractical.

Resolved not to let the moment pass, Coles immediately dispatched a letter over the signature "Jefferson" to the editor of the *Richmond Enquirer* declaring his "surprise" at the content of Monroe's speech. He chastised Monroe for "deprecating the effects of immediate emancipation" when, instead, he should "have taken a more enlarged view" of the issue. If he had thought more generously, Coles declared, then surely he would have realized that no "enthusiastic friend of . . . emancipation" had "ever entertained the idea of an immediate liberation of them. The only mode which has been suggested," continued Coles, "is a gradual emancipation." As for his claim "that it is impossible the slaves of Virginia can ever be removed out of it," Coles called Monroe's attention to "the plan suggested by Mr. Jefferson more than 40 years ago." Far from impossible or impracticable, as Jefferson's testimony revealed, gradual emancipation and colonization would be relatively easy.[30] Here, implied Coles, was the opportunity to link progressive democratic reform with emancipation. If eastern conservatives were reluctant to embrace democratization because it might threaten slavery, then eliminate the cause of their resistance. Implement a gradual emancipation and colonization program and, thereby, open the way to resolving the most visible obstacle to democracy in Virginia.

Coles's determination to promote emancipation as well as his long absence from the state led him to overestimate the popularity of gradual emancipation and colonization among Virginia's political leadership. As early as 1827, Virginia's leading colonizationists had become disturbed by the strategies of the national organization and warned the American Colonization Society leadership that petitioning for congressional support "may be considered a contempt of states' rights" by Virginia's political elites. Indeed, during the winter preceding the convention, Virginia's colonizationists demonstrated their opposition to seeking federal support by revoking their allegiance to the national organization. So, although many of the delegates were officers or members of colonization auxiliary organizations, few of them were willing to sacrifice the state's sovereignty by advocating colonization at the convention. Coles similarly failed to recognize (or chose to ignore) that Monroe had inadvertently resurrected these tensions when he claimed that emancipation and colonization could "never be done by the State itself" and that he would "look to the Union to aid in effecting it." Although Benjamin Watkins Leigh, the most vocal of the eastern Tidewater slaveholding delegates, agreed that slavery was "a moral and political evil," this view was overshadowed by his determination to guard Virginia's state authority. If they permitted "the interference of the General Government in this most delicate and peculiar interest of our own," he warned, "there will, there must be, an end of this Union."[31] Coles had underestimated the ways in which the colonization movement's national character provoked a defense of state sovereignty, and, thereby, pitted the political interests of all Virginians against emancipation.

Equally important was the broader debate on nullification then raging throughout Virginia and the country. As early as 1826, the Virginia General Assembly declared that tariff protection for northern manufacturing was unconstitutional and cited Thomas Jefferson, James Madison, and their "doctrines of '98" to bolster their position. Like Coles, John Tyler, William Branch Giles, and Littleton Waller Tazewell (all delegates at the convention and friends of Coles) marshaled the influence of the Jeffersonian name in their defense of state autonomy during the nullification crisis. These men insisted that the tariff represented an unlawful and dangerous consolidation of federal authority that states had the right to resist. To demonstrate the legitimacy of this claim, Giles published an extracted letter from Jefferson declaring "I see as you do . . . the rapid strides, with which the federal branch of our government is advancing towards the usurpation of all the rights reserved to the states, and the consolidation in itself." Although he counseled "patience," the Sage of Monticello that Giles presented to the public advised Virginians to "separate from our companions only when the sole alternatives left are the dissolution of our union . . . or the submission to a government without limitation of powers." In this way, Giles brought Jefferson back from the grave and clothed his own position on nullification in the armor of the founders. In 1826, 1827, and again in 1829, the Virginia Assembly passed resolutions and reports affirming their vigorous opposition to tariff protection and the use of federal funds to finance internal improvements.[32] The Tidewater elite then saw themselves as members of an embattled minority, victims on the national level of a usurpation of power that Jefferson, were he alive, would have been alarmed to witness.

Nullification became intimately linked to the debates at the constitutional convention because, although opposition to the tariff was strong in Virginia, it had declined as the presence and power of western delegates in the state legislature increased. Reapportionment, from the perspective of conservatives, then, threatened not only their "peculiar property" but also their ability to defend Virginia's sovereignty in the emerging national crisis. Few eastern Tidewater elites were willing to risk extending political power to men who did not share their view of the limited role of government in promoting economic development. One resident expressed his opposition to representation and apportionment on the white basis by highlighting this connection. He viewed the call for white-basis representation as dangerous because unlike the "odious tariffs," which "we may avoid" by declaring them null and void, any taxes imposed by a newly empowered western majority in the state legislature "we must pay, or our property must be dragged to the auction." In other words, in the reformed government westerners proposed, the slaveholding minority would become victims of an abusive authority against which they had no means of resistance. The author encouraged the state's leaders to pause and consider the consequences of enacting democratic reform and instructed them to create "a social compact" that would promote "mutual friendship and harmony" and not discord and hostility. Political reform, slavery, and government-supported economic development, then, were closely related to one another in Virginia. Just as Virginia's leaders led the movement against the tariff and Clay's American System, so too did they oppose political reform within the Old Dominion.[33] Coles made the fatal mistake of viewing the slavery issue as independent of the local and national political context shaping the actions of Virginia's leaders. As a result, he failed to recognize how acutely sensitive Virginia's leaders and the state's residents were to any reforms that might undermine their exercise of authority within Virginia or the position of the state in the national debate over nullification.

By early December, the convention remained deadlocked, and although new attempts at compromise emerged, none of them mentioned emancipation as part of the solution to the impasse. Instead, the delegates haggled over various combinations of several ideas, including counting slaves as three-fifths of a person and basing apportionment on the 1820 or 1830 census. None of these proved satisfactory to a majority of the delegates, and only after trading votes on several proposals did they finally reach an agreement. They apportioned both branches of the General Assembly by the 1820 census for the foreseeable future, a move that ignored the dramatic population growth in the nonslaveholding western region. In this way, "the political inferiority" of the western counties was guaranteed, as one delegate observed, "both for ourselves and our posterity." The reformers had lost, and a variation of the status quo was maintained. As Coles surely recognized, slavery remained unchallenged, and in 1830 Virginia was one of the most undemocratic slaveholding states in the Union.[34]

During his brief visit to his native state, then, Coles failed in his effort to link emancipation to democratic political reform. Instead, he witnessed in Virginia a disappointing transformation in the meaning of equality and freedom. As had been the case in Illinois, Virginians interpreted the principles of the revolutionary era as proclaiming freedom for white men only. Unlike Illinois, where the convention contest led residents to voice their preference for a free egalitarian white society, Virginia's elites protected and sustained a social order that denied political equality to a majority of the state's white nonslaveholding residents. Although the franchise expanded in subtle ways, suffrage remained tied

to individual wealth (and became more tightly linked to slavery), allowing Tidewater slaveholders to retain a disproportionate share of political
power. Coles left Richmond for Illinois disappointed that he had failed
to convince the delegates that emancipation and colonization would
enhance their chance for democratic reform, even when he and other
delegates linked reform and emancipation to the revolutionary legacy of
Thomas Jefferson.

"I will not be a creature of party"

In the year and a half following the close of Virginia's 1829–1830
constitutional convention, Coles led a nomadic life, traveling from
Richmond to Edwardsville, and through New York, Philadelphia, and
Baltimore. As had been the case in 1827, his attention continued to be
pulled in both private and public directions. His journey northward
certainly brought him great pleasure as he visited with his friends and
joined their festive social engagements. Despite these more pleasant
occupations, Coles still could not avoid politics. Nullification, which
had been so prominent in the state's newspapers during the convention, remained the dominant topic of discussion in Virginia as well as
among his friends and relatives. Since the opening of the nullification
controversy in 1828, Virginians had taken the lead in arguing for a
state's right to resist unconstitutional federal laws. By 1830, nullifiers in
both Virginia and South Carolina had adopted William Branch Giles's
position that secession was a legitimate response to the perceived consolidation of power in the federal government, a remedy he and others
regularly justified by citing the Virginia and Kentucky resolutions of
1798 and Madison's *Report of 1800*.[35]

Coles's frustration with the way the nullification issue sidetracked his
antislavery efforts in Richmond led him to monitor closely these developments, and he was eager to see Madison enter the political discussion to
counter the misuse of his name and the principles of '98. As early as 1828,
Coles's friends Joseph Cabell and James Barbour had beseeched Madison
to join the public debate, but he refused for fear his views would be misused within "the extravagances produced by the Presidential contest." In
December of that year, however, Madison had consented to publish two
letters he had written to Cabell. Appearing in the *National Intelligencer*,
Madison had declared emphatically that the anti-tariff movement's claim
of unconstitutionality was patently incorrect, and that the doctrine nullifiers proclaimed disregarded the fundamental republican principle of

majority rule. The irony of Madison occupying this position just one year before the Virginia constitutional convention, where he had failed to advocate for majority rule in the convention, probably did not escape Coles's notice. Despite Madison's efforts, the nullification crisis intensified as anti-tariff leaders continued to misrepresent the meaning of his activities during the 1790s.

Dismayed by the persistent popularity of nullification and, particularly, nullifiers' assumption that he would support the South Carolina position, Madison wrote another public letter in August 1830 insistently denouncing nullification, and arranged for it to be published in the *North American Review*. In this essay, Madison denied the right of a state to nullify a law and, once again, accused nullifiers of allowing their partisan ambitions to alter the true meaning of the past. Coles congratulated Madison on this publication, declaring that it was "among the best efforts of your pen and the clearest exposition of the Constitution I have ever read." Moreover, he reported that "with the exception of a few hot headed ultra State right men in Richmond, it was . . . highly extolled by all." To his mind, Madison's "publication has done much good in enlightening the community on constitutional doctrines, and correcting the political heresies of the day."[36]

Coles was a nationalist who, like Madison, understood that the federal nature of the nation's governing structure required a balanced distribution of sovereignty between the federal and state governments. As a result, Coles embraced the nationalist vision offered by John Quincy Adams and promoted by Henry Clay's American System. Throughout his tenure in Illinois, Coles had advocated for internal improvements, banking, and the development of local manufacturing as key elements of a prosperous economy. Also, like Madison, Coles believed that the Constitution rested on the will of the people and that sovereignty was divided between the federal and state levels. While he certainly worried that the nullification controversy might lead to disunion, Coles seemed confident that Madison's wisdom would prevail in the end. The slavery issue, however, was a different matter. The federal government under Andrew Jackson opposed federal aid for colonization, and as he learned from his attempts to influence Virginia's constitutional convention, partisan politics often overshadowed support for emancipation and colonization. As a result, Coles continued to be active in the American Colonization Society, raising funds to support the cause, while simultaneously surveying the political landscape for another opportunity to advance his antislavery agenda.[37]

Perhaps hoping to lend his voice to the opposition to nullification and promote a federal support for colonization, Coles decided to pursue national office. In April 1831, he announced that he "yielded to the wishes of a number of my friends" and agreed to become a candidate for the next election for a House of Representatives in the 1831 election. As he had done in the 1822 gubernatorial election, Coles cited his political experience as Register of the Land Office in Edwardsville and his service as President James Madison's private secretary as qualifying him for national public office. He also added that his position as "the People's Governor" made him more acquainted with the interests and concerns of the residents of Illinois than any of his opponents. Most significantly, Coles presented himself as a disinterested and virtuous candidate, informing the voters that "I will not be the creature of party, nor the humble follower of any man."[38]

Aware that the economic prosperity of the state was the dominant issue in Illinois politics, Coles tried to bolster his political prospects by establishing his nationalist approach to economic development. As we have seen, he sided with the nationalists in the nullification debate, confessing to Madison and his family members his commitment to the preeminent authority of the federal government in questions of political economy. He knew, however, that the debate over the tariff and nullification would have little meaning in Illinois, though he recognized that the state's residents cared a great deal about the more abstract issue of federal versus state authority. So when the Democratic-controlled legislatures of Illinois, Mississippi, and Indiana passed resolutions denying federal jurisdiction over public lands within their borders, Coles spied an opportunity to distinguish himself from his Jacksonian opponents and demonstrate his nationalist political perspective. He characterized this attempt to seize control of public lands as an assault on federal authority akin to nullification, a policy "calculated to excite [public] feeling and disturb the harmony of the Union." Fearful that this seemingly innocuous development might eventually evolve into a full-blown constitutional crisis, Coles asked Madison to compose an essay, like the "full and clear expose" he had published in August 1830, for only "the great weight of your opinions" could "put this sordid and fetting [disturbing] question to rest." Although he was unwilling to have his opinion published in the papers, Madison confirmed Coles's claim that "the lands were ceded to the Union," and as such the "title" to the lands belong to "the people" whose interests were served by the federal government and not to the individual states. Unlike Coles, who saw the resolutions as a dangerous precedent that might evolve into a crisis as threatening as nullification, Madison was confident that any conflict between state and national authority over land would be resolved easily by Congress.[39]

By the 1830s, however, Illinois's political culture, and indeed the politics of the nation as a whole, had undergone a dramatic transformation. The experience of participating in nominating committees and caucuses and identifying candidates with a particular issue during the convention contest laid the organizational groundwork for the emergence of party politics in Illinois. Once the convention vote resolved the slavery issue to the satisfaction of the state's residents, Illinois's voters placed increasing importance on a candidate's affiliation with national political figures. In the congressional campaign of 1826, for example, committees and caucuses throughout the state supported Joseph Duncan, a self-proclaimed Jackson supporter, over Daniel Pope Cook, who had cast his ballot for John Quincy Adams in 1824. Charged with ignoring the sentiments of the majority, Cook was ousted from political office for supporting the wrong national politician in that presidential race. Similarly, one resident observed that by 1826 "the political division" in Illinois "was between supporters of John Quincy Adams and General Andrew Jackson, the Yankees supporting Adams and the white people, Jackson." Gone were the days when personal reputation and name recognition alone translated into electoral victory. Coles recognized this emerging trend and associated himself with the National Republican platform. Indeed, he attended the party's convention in Baltimore in December 1831, where the chair invited him to take a seat at the bar next to Daniel Webster.[40]

When he aligned himself with the National Republicans, Coles fatefully misjudged the voters in Illinois and the strength of the emerging Jacksonian democratic political culture of the United States as a whole. He chose a party that promoted his nationalist vision, but that was also hampered by its adherence to a set of old-style political habits that celebrated the virtues of republican leadership epitomized by Coles's mentors, James Madison and Thomas Jefferson. As one editorialist complained, Coles's commitment to nonpartisanship led many to doubt his ability as a politician and question the degree of influence he would wield in Congress. Conversely, his most prominent political opponents in the race for Congress, Joseph Duncan and Sidney Breese, each identified their political interests with Andrew Jackson and Henry Clay, respectively.[41] Perhaps even more detrimental to his political chances, however, was Coles's frequent and prolonged absence from the state—he spent most of 1829 and 1830 traveling between family and friends in New

York, Philadelphia, Richmond, and Charlottesville. When the votes were finally tallied, Duncan, the Jacksonian incumbent, secured a landslide victory with 13,052 votes. His closest rivals, Breese and Coles, both Clay men, garnered the support of less than one-quarter of the eligible voters, earning 4,520 and 3,304 votes, respectively.[42]

Although he was certainly saddened by his showing, Coles's heart was likely elsewhere, for there was little to keep him in Illinois. Not only had the political developments in Virginia distracted him from his interests in Illinois, but so too did his expanding circle of associations in Philadelphia. Sally Logan Roberts, whom he had begun courting in 1825, probably monopolized his attention. In addition, the partisan politics of the state had distressed him, and he remained disappointed by the failure of Illinoisans to embrace the abolition of slavery or repeal the state's antiblack laws. He was uninterested in a career as a frontier farmer, especially if he was destined to manage his property without the help of a wife or the company of his friends and family. So, when the election concluded, Coles was inclined to turn eastward once again. When news of Nat Turner's slave insurrection reached Illinois, he immediately made plans to return to Virginia, where he hoped to contribute to the public debate over the place of slavery in the Old Dominion that had erupted in the wake of the violence.

"perpetuating the bondage of so many"

He arrived in Virginia in mid-September 1831, just as the public response to Nat Turner's rebellion began to appear in public print. During the aftermath of the insurrection, residents from all over the state produced editorials, petitions, and memorials demanding that their elected officials do something about the slave problem. Many of them advocated gradual emancipation and colonization programs, and the editors of the state's leading newspapers, the *Richmond Enquirer* and the *Richmond Constitutional Whig*, published them for public consideration. John Pleasants, the editor of the *Whig*, for example, published a memorial calling on the legislature to remove "the fatal, paralyzing, destroying" institution of slavery. Anticipating a future in which the black population, enslaved and free, outnumbered the white, the authors implored the legislature to devise a plan to promote emancipation and finance the removal of the black population. "Your memorialists are slave holders" whose sense of "humanity . . . patriotism, self-interest . . . call equally" for the removal of "this appalling and increasing evil." "A Freeholder of

HORRID MASSACRE IN VIRGINIA·

FIGURE 5.3. Horrid massacre in Virginia, Nat Turner's rebellion, from *An Authentic and Impartial Narrative of the Tragical Scene*, by Samuel Warren (New York: Warren West, 1831), 1. (Courtesy of the State Library of Virginia.)

Hanover County" called for the "gradual abolition of slavery" and recommended imposing a tax on slave property sufficient enough to raise the funds required to purchase and transport the state's enslaved population. Several editorialists in both newspapers avoided any discussion of the existing slave system and instead focused their attention on the elimination of the state's growing free black population. Whether they advocated emancipation, the removal of free blacks, or some combination of the two, everyone marveled at the openness of the public discussion, agreeing that something had to be done about slavery.[43]

As he did during every return visit to Virginia, Coles spent several days at Montpelier enjoying his friendship with the Madisons. With the discussion of the slavery issue swirling around them, Coles and Madison entered into an intense conversation on the retired president's plan for the "disposition" of his enslaved property. Coles acknowledged the delicacy of the subject, but insisted that "it is due to the finale of your character and career . . . that you should make provision in your Will for the emancipation of your Slaves." To refuse to do so, he declared "would be a blot and stigma on your otherwise spotless escutcheon." Indeed, "not to restore to your slaves that liberty and those rights which you have been through life so zealous & able a champion," Coles observed, would transform him from a man of "virtue . . . and pure principles" into a hypocrite. Although much difficulty would accompany emancipation, Coles warned his mentor that nothing would render the enterprise more difficult than "the example of your countenancing, and . . . perpetuating the bondage of so many unfortunate human beings." He implored Madison to consider how his actions would impact his fellow Virginians who consistently looked to him for guidance. Coles was sure that Madison's decision to embrace emancipation would "induce others to follow your example."[44]

He recommended that Madison put in place a plan that would gradually emancipate the enslaved labors and provide for their relocation in Africa. Echoing many of the articles published in Virginia's newspapers, Coles confessed that Turner's violent actions in August confirmed that it was "impossible for the two races ever to live harmoniously." Accordingly, colonization had to be part of any emancipation program the ailing ex-president designed. Anticipating Madison's objection that he could not afford to emancipate his human property without leaving his wife impoverished should she survive him, Coles recommended that "the estate should be kept together and the slaves retained in service, until they should have enabled the estate . . . to have fulfilled its other obligations." Once the financial stability of the estate was assured, Coles reasoned, the enslaved laborers could be required to earn "enough to transport" themselves to Africa.[45] Coles left Montpelier for Richmond convinced that he had persuaded Madison to liberate his enslaved property. More important for Coles, he believed that Madison's impending act of emancipation would serve eventually as yet another piece of evidence he might use to rally support for his antislavery nationalism.

Emboldened by his success at Montpelier, Coles arrived in Richmond determined to promote emancipation among the state's legislators. He recognized in the public enthusiasm for emancipation yet another opportunity to reform Virginia society. Other public leaders likewise recognized the call for action but were unsure how to solve the problem. Governor John Floyd, writing to his counterpart in Georgia, confessed his intention to demand more stringent laws restricting "Slaves to the estates of their masters," prohibiting "negroes from preaching," and "driv[ing] from this State all free negroes." He hoped to strengthen the slave system, create harsher laws, and prevent any future insurrections. He also wanted to use "the surplus revenue in our Treasury" to purchase "slaves, to work for a time" and then be "sent out of the country," a program he understood "as the first step to emancipation." Privately, Floyd repeated his modest antislavery intentions, declaring in his diary: "Before I leave this government, I will have a law passed gradually abolishing slavery in this State." When he delivered the opening address before the legislature in early December, however, Floyd avoided the issue of emancipation and called on the legislature to provide funds only for the removal of the state's free black population. Coles had seen himself in Floyd, hoping that, as he had done in Illinois, the governor would use his executive position to precipitate a public debate on the slavery issue, a discussion Coles was sure would end with a rejection of the institution and the promulgation of provisions mandating emancipation. In short, he expected to witness in Virginia a repeat of the events he had orchestrated in Illinois, but Floyd's disappointing performance hardly inspired Coles's confidence that such an outcome would emerge.[46]

Still, Coles forged ahead. He dispatched a letter to his friend, freshman legislator Thomas Jefferson Randolph. He called on his mentor's grandson "to bring forward & press . . . [the] absolute necessity" of enacting a program to rid the state of slavery. With Floyd's negligence fresh in his mind, Coles reminded Randolph "that it behooves the politician to look ahead," and he encouraged the young legislator to lead the effort "to arrest a state of things [that] . . . if left alone [would] inevitably produce ruin." Coles then instructed Randolph to promote a gradual emancipation and colonization program that might "satisfy [even] the most zealous advocate" of slavery. First, he recommended that the state impose "a small capitation tax" to raise enough revenue to fund the removal of free blacks. Second, he called on the state to assume guardianship of children born after a certain date, who would then be required to work to raise the cost of their transport to Africa. Third, he suggested that every slave born after January 1, 1840, be liberated at the age of twenty-one and required to work "for two years to earn enough to pay" for their emigration across the Atlantic. This program, concluded Coles, "would . . . by operating gradually give time for the two races to adapt themselves to the new order of things; & would almost imperceptibly withdraw the Slaves & substitute free labourers in their places. By fixing a period more remote," he assured Randolph, "you would [also] . . . render the measure more acceptable to" the state's slaveholders. Should the state's leaders prove reluctant to endorse such a program, Coles implored him to "submit such a Bill to the people at the next or succeeding election."[47] By placing the decision in the hands of the people, Coles intended to prevent the state's slaveholding political leaders from once again thwarting emancipation. More than anything, he hoped to avoid repeating what had happened in Illinois, where the voters clearly rejected slavery but the politicians refused to enact laws reflecting the popular will.

In early January 1832, Randolph introduced a resolution offering a gradual emancipation and colonization program that differed from Coles's recommendations in only one way. In a nod to slaveholder's property rights, Randolph allowed slaveholders to sell their property before the date of liberation. In every other particular, Randolph had accepted Coles's demand that he "step forward" and assume his grandfather's mantle. The motion immediately sparked a firestorm of discussion. Few of the members disputed "that slavery in Virginia is an evil," and most recognized that "the people demand[ed]" that "something should be done to alleviate or exterminate it." But some members thought the proposal was ill-timed. Thomas Marshall, Chief Justice John Marshall's son, objected to the proposal, declaring that such a "delicate question" could not be "freely discussed . . . without agitating the public mind." Dismissing the "numerous petitions and memorials . . . crowd[ing] . . . [the] table" because they "mistake the remedy," he maintained that he would not support such a measure until the "undeviating voice of a clear majority of the people shall say their happiness and security require gradual emancipation."[48]

Indeed, the role of the people in deciding the issue quickly emerged as the focus of discussion. Randolph had insisted that any emancipation law be issued only after "it is sanctioned by the people, . . . the best judges of their own interests." He did this not from the conviction that a majority of the state's residents would necessarily support the proposal, but because he was confident that, given the failure of democratic reform two years earlier, the politically powerful slaveholding representatives in the legislature would block any emancipation scheme. As Coles had warned, only a referendum could ensure that an emancipation law would be "irrevocable." Eastern slaveholding representatives immediately objected, reminding the members that allowing "those who own no slaves" to determine "whether those who hold them should give them up or not" would destroy all "security . . . for property." This doctrine,

William H. Brodnax, a representative from Greenville County, complained, would "bring upon us the principles of that celebrated *white basis,* against which we struggled so earnestly in the late convention." The only way to "secure to *minorities* their privileges and their property," he and his supporters maintained, was to let the legislature, not the people, determine how best to deal with Virginia's slave problem.[49] Virginia's slaveholding leaders jealously guarded their public power and refused to put the question before the people for fear democracy might destroy slavery.

Randolph attempted to strengthen his position by arguing that had his grandfather lived "to see this revolution in the public mind of Virginia . . . to see a majority of the house of delegates in favour of abolition in the abstract," he would have embraced the opportunity to debate the issue "without" risk of "insult." To prove that his grandfather's "opinions are . . . not against me," he read a portion of Jefferson's 1814 letter to Coles. "Come forward in the public councils," quoted Randolph, "become a missionary" of emancipation, "and when the phalanx is formed, bring on and press the proposition perseveringly until its accomplishment." In this way, Randolph intended to implore his fellow representatives to heed Jefferson's call to pass emancipation legislation. The phalanx had been formed, implied Randolph, and was populated by the majority of the people as well as most of the delegates, as evidenced by the petitions presented to and the pronouncements made before the legislature.[50]

Other delegates likewise deployed the legacy of the founders to generate support for emancipation. The nation's revolutionary leaders, declared Charles Faulkner, "had done enough for their day and generation." Their determination to achieve independence meant that they "could not, at that time, suffer the practical extension of their just and benevolent schemes" for emancipation. "*They* have, however, left their plan as a rich legacy . . . to *us* to say, whether we will carry it out or not." James McDowell, Jr. mockingly declared that he need not waste his listeners' time pointing out that "slavery . . . does not consist with the first and leading principles of a Republic." He was sure that his audience already knew that they were "a people resolutely violating towards others, that principle of absolute freedom on which they erected their own independence."[51] Echoing Coles's antislavery nationalism, those who supported emancipation attempted to generate support for their cause by investing their arguments with the moral authority of the nation's revolutionary principles, a strategy that had been successful in Illinois in 1824.

Ultimately, those who opposed emancipation prevailed. Despite all the declarations regarding the will of the people and championing of the nation's revolutionary past, Virginia's slaveholding minority success-fully prevented the slave question from being presented to the people at large. Instead, they kept the discussion within the legislature, where they focused the debate on the need to protect property rights and meet the demand for security. In doing so, they shifted the discussion from slavery to reducing the size of the free black population, a group many feared would inspire future insurrections. In the end, the members sup-ported an amendment declaring that it was "inexpedient . . . to make any legislative enactment for the abolition of slavery," but appeased emancipationists by approving Archibald Bryce's preamble promising that "further action for the removal of the slaves should await a more definite development of public opinion." Building on the antiblack com-mon ground exposed during the debates, the legislature also heeded Floyd's recommendations and passed laws restricting the movement of slaves and limiting the rights of the state's free black population. Again, to placate the emancipationists in the legislature, the House of Delegates also approved appropriations for the colonization of the state's free black population. For men like Coles, these small concessions eased the pain of disappointment over the failure of reform and left them with a small degree of hope that perhaps, someday, Virginia would become a free state. Their hopes proved misguided, however, for the failure to end slavery in 1832 turned out to be the last pre-Civil War moment when circumstances favorable to emancipation would exist in Virginia.[52]

Unlike Illinois, where Coles and his anti-conventionist support-ers effectively translated the popular belief that slavery was evil into a rejection of the institution, emancipationists in Virginia were unable to persuade enough of the state's slaveholding representatives to sacrifice their economic and political interests on the altar of their principles. In the end, the combination of economic, political, and ideological argu-ments proved too weak to overcome the increasingly ardent defense of property and power among Virginia's eastern slaveholders. Still, in many ways, the Virginia slavery debate foreshadowed the character of antislav-ery politics that would emerge after 1840. At that later date, southern slaveholders would again employ a states' rights rationale and declare that slavery was a positive good. Likewise, future antislavery westerners and northerners would celebrate once again the economic prosperity of a free egalitarian society supported by free labor and vociferously demand political equality. Not until that later period, however, would Coles's antislavery political tactics first attempted during the 1820s become strong enough to successfully challenge slavery.

Throughout his experiences in Illinois and Virginia, Edward Coles encountered a public eager to discuss the slavery issue. Indeed, although they rarely boasted the more ideological and moral motivations Coles claimed, the often less than virtuous paths many Americans traveled as they came to embrace restriction and emancipation did not lessen for him the significance of their decision to join him in his campaign to oppose slavery. It was not a general disinterest among the public that prevented the development of an effective movement against slavery before the early 1830s, then, as historians have claimed. Instead, it was the fragility of the antislavery coalition as well as the hesitancy of local political leaders, born of their pecuniary interest, partisan ambition, or antiblack prejudice (or some combination of the three) that thwarted progress toward abolition after the American Revolution.[53] Events in both Illinois and Virginia bore out this conclusion. It was state legislators in Illinois who refused to act on Coles's recommendation that the small number of slaves living in the state be liberated. It was, likewise, the state representatives in Virginia who refused to link their pursuit of democratic political reforms with emancipation. And, it was, once again, Virginia's slaveholding politicians who prevented the enactment of emancipation and colonization schemes so ardently requested by many of the Old Dominion's residents. By the early 1830s, slavery remained an elusive problem that Coles feared would remain unresolved.

On the evening of November 28, 1833, forty-six-year-old Edward Coles stood nervously in the parlor of Philadelphian Roberts Vaux, his good friend and antislavery ally from the Illinois convention contest. The room was crowded with guests, most of whom were prominent residents of the city. To Coles's delight, the company also included several southerners, among them his brother Tucker, sister-in-law Helen, and his younger sister, Betsy. His only regret was that James and Dolley Madison, not wishing to undertake a long journey in their advanced age, could not witness the events of the day. The candles illuminating the parlor cast a warm light across the room, making the atmosphere contrast sharply with the cold nervousness that caused him to anxiously survey his surroundings. While he remained stationed by the fireplace, everyone else moved through the room freely, pausing occasionally to chat amiably with one another as they awaited the start of the ceremony. Within minutes the guests settled into silence and Coles turned to the entryway only to gaze upon the beautiful Sally Logan Roberts. As she crossed the room and took his arm a calm feeling overtook him. Then, together, they turned to face the minster and took their vows.[1]

It should hardly be surprising that Coles found a bride and married in Philadelphia. Ever since his year-long sojourn in the city under the care of Dr. Philip S. Physick in 1813, he had felt a strong affection for Philadelphia and its cosmopolitan society. His removal to Illinois and the experience of living in a frontier community had failed to temper those feelings. Indeed, between 1825 and the year of his marriage, Coles spent

FIGURE 6.1. Mrs. Edward Coles (Sally Logan Roberts), 1836, by Thomas Sully. (Courtesy of Davidson College.)

nearly half of each year east of the Appalachian Mountains, and a significant portion of that time was spent visiting friends in Philadelphia. During these visits, Coles renewed his friendships with Nicholas Biddle, Roberts Vaux, William Short, Peter S. Du Ponceau, Richard Rush, and George Mifflin Dallas, as well as forging new relationships with John Vaughan, Charles J. and Joseph R. Ingersoll, George Cadwalader, George

Roberts Smith, Thomas Sully, Sidney George Fisher, and Dr. Nathaniel Chapman, all members of Philadelphia's most prominent social circle. As had been the case on the eve of his emigration westward, Coles had been continually haunted by the same dilemma during these years. Should he give in to his desire to enjoy "the pleasures of life" or honor his convictions and remain an "active & useful labourer in the great field of benevolence"? Although he was "ashamed of [his] . . . inclination to yield to such selfish considerations," Coles's experiences in the Prairie State and Virginia had led him to doubt his ability to serve the cause of humanity, much less succeed at eradicating the institution of slavery. Whenever he returned to the west, then, he continually experienced a crisis of purpose that led him to crave the company and polite society of Philadelphia.[2]

His marriage to the twenty-four-year-old Sally Roberts and their decision to reside in Philadelphia ultimately furnished Coles with an opportunity both to satisfy his yearning for society and fulfill his deeply felt sense of duty to fight against slavery. In Sally, Coles found a wife who connected him to one of the city's oldest and most prominent families. Her great grandfather was Hugh Roberts of Wales, a man of royal decent and a Quaker who immigrated to America with William Penn in the 1680s. Sally's father had maintained the family's status by establishing a lucrative iron business and was among the city's wealthiest residents. Throughout the Early National and Antebellum eras, nearly every Philadelphia social and cultural institution listed a Roberts as a member. When Coles was courting Sally, the family spent most of the year on an expansive estate called Pine Grove, just outside the city limits. Sally's two sisters, Elizabeth and Mary, were also connected to the city's refined elite. They were married to Dr. William Rush and George Roberts Smith, respectively, both of whom were friends with Coles and regular participants in the city's vibrant elite social life. Philadelphia was also the center of an emerging benevolent empire where reform-minded public and private elites created and joined organizations devoted to improving American society.[3] So with his marriage to Sally, Coles made more permanent his place in Philadelphia's cosmopolitan society and increased the likelihood that he would finally realize the personal happiness he had always craved.

Despite his newfound joy, Coles continued to struggle with the problem of slavery throughout his time in Philadelphia. He had spent years battling the institution at the local level, first in Illinois and then in Virginia. Undeterred by his limited success in the 1820s and early 1830s,

Coles became convinced that slavery remained a national problem that could only be solved by a national coalition. By the mid-1830s, Philadelphia boasted a variety of organizations whose goal it was to end slavery. The Pennsylvania Abolition Society, Pennsylvania Antislavery Society, and the Pennsylvania Colonization Society all competed for the support of the city's antislavery residents. These groups shared a commitment to the eradication of slavery but disagreed about tactics and, as he watched, the movement to end slavery became more divisive among Philadelphia's antislavery activists and the nation.[4] When combined with the lessons he had learned in Illinois and Virginia, this reality convinced Coles that his support for gradual emancipation and colonization was well placed, for only a program that included the removal of the nation's free blacks could destroy slavery and purge America of the one institution that contradicted the nation's founding principles.

"to try housekeeping in Phila"

Within a few days of their marriage, Coles and his new bride departed Philadelphia for a post-wedding trip to Virginia. As they journeyed to Albemarle County, they stopped in Baltimore and Washington City, where Coles introduced his wife to the broad network of friends he had developed over the previous twenty years. In the nation's capital, the couple stayed with his sister Sally Coles Stevenson and her husband Andrew, who was speaker of the House and awaited confirmation of his appointment as minister to Great Britain. They enjoyed all that the Washington social season had to offer. Coles undoubtedly took pleasure in conducting his new wife through the land of his previous heartbreak. As they made their way southward, Coles and his bride stopped for a brief visit with the Madisons. Dolley, who had long labored to find her cousin a wife, was surely delighted to see him finally happy. Indeed, she admired his wife's appearance and sense of fashion so much that she wanted her to "procure for me" at the spring clothing sales in Philadelphia anything that "suit[ed] her taste," because her choices "would be exactly [like] mine."[5] This was quite a compliment from a woman renowned for her trend-setting taste, and Coles was certainly pleased that the Madisons approved of his choice.

By late December they finally arrived in Albemarle County, and Sally Logan Roberts enjoyed her first glimpse of the genteel grandeur of the Coles family seat, Enniscorthy. Coles's mother Rebecca had passed away seven years earlier, but his older brother Isaac and his wife Julia lived at and maintained the family estate. Immediately after the couple's arrival at Green Mountain, the family invited their friends and neighbors to a variety of dinners and intimate parties so Ned (as they affectionately called him) could introduce Sally. As one Virginia chronicler nostalgically recalled, the Coles family "homes were [often] filled with guests and the round of hospitality carried us first to one house and then to another." This kind of conviviality was typical of the Coles family and, at least for this writer, "the society of that neighborhood and that time [was] the best that it was ever my privilege to know." At the close of their visit in early January, Coles took his bride to Richmond to meet the rest of his family. His youngest sister, Emily, lived there with her husband John Rutherfoord.[6] They made the social rounds, allowing Coles to reconnect with close friends and acquaintances. Even the persistent cold weather and snow could not dampen the pride Coles felt as Sally Logan Roberts was welcomed into the Coles clan.

Coles and his wife Sally journeyed back to Philadelphia in early January 1834. Initially, he had planned to return to Illinois and establish his family in the west. But news of a cholera epidemic in the region derailed their trip, and the young couple remained in Philadelphia for the time being. As they awaited better conditions in the Old Northwest, Coles took his young wife on a northern tour and spent most of the early summer months traveling in Canada, Niagara Falls, and Saratoga Springs. They then ventured southward again, fulfilling a promise made to Dolley Madison to return to Virginia when better weather prevailed so that Sally could see Green Mountain in all of its bountiful splendor. By late August 1834, Sally was pregnant, ending any likelihood that the couple would resettle in Illinois before the end of the year. So, the newlyweds returned to Philadelphia in October and began making arrangements for a more permanent residence. His wife was opposed "to being in a Boarding house this winter" and preferred instead to rent "a private & comfortable house" where her mother and sisters could assist her during her confinement. Anxious to please her, Coles secured a furnished house, "situated high up on Chestnut St. in a pleasant part of the City." He knew that he "gave more than I ought, but it was the only house with furniture that could be obtained" in the area. The lease lasted until June 1835, providing the young couple "an opportunity . . . to try housekeeping in Phila[delphia]." Although pleased to be settled in a city he enjoyed and to be among so many of his friends once again, Coles continued to doubt whether he had the financial means to maintain the lifestyle he and Sally craved or "whether I should be happy with so little to do."[7]

Cholera and a signed lease notwithstanding, Coles continued to contemplate establishing a permanent residence for his family in Illinois. Financially, he was firmly tied to the west. Throughout his life he had invested extensively in land, and by the mid-1830s he owned over twelve thousand acres of farm land in Illinois and Missouri as well as dozens of city lots in St. Louis, Edwardsville, Cincinnati, and Washington City. He employed agents in each of these cities to collect his rents and manage his affairs. He also purchased bank and railroad stock and loaned cash to enterprising farmers and merchants at 10 percent interest. Ironically, it was Jackson's fiscal policies and the resulting bank war that ensured the Whig-supporting Coles's economic security; for he made the lion's share of his income from loaning money to credit-hungry farmers, merchants, and developers. Robert Wash served as his agent in St. Louis, and in the summer and fall of 1835 Coles left as much as $5,000 in his care to loan on advantageous terms. He loaned just over $1,000 at 10 percent to an enterprising settler with ample security. Another $1,000 was invested in a dock-building project that promised to take advantage of the growing steamboat trade on the Mississippi River. The remainder Wash was holding until the spring, when "the tide of emigration & the kindling up of the spirit of improvements & speculation" meant that money will be "readily loaned out." Coles made a hefty income in this way. Whereas the average farmer and laborer rarely earned more than $250 to $500 annually, Coles earned a respectable $8,000 to $10,000 from these investments.[8] He was financially secure, but now that he was married he felt acutely the responsibility of providing for his new family.

Coles also worked to protect his financial interests in Illinois by exploiting his personal and political connections to the state. Soon after he settled into his Chestnut Street brownstone, he congratulated Joseph Duncan (who had defeated him in the congressional contest of 1831) on his election to the governorship of Illinois. Coles brashly advised Duncan on the proper course he should pursue to ensure Illinois's future prosperity. He reminded the staunchly Jacksonian governor of the dire economic conditions that had wracked Illinois during the panic of 1819 and expressed his hope that the state's legislators would "profit by the experience of the past" and be cautious in their financial policy making. "I fear many of the States will go to most injurious extreme in incorporating local Banks," he warned, because doing so would "flood the Country with a spurious paper currency." What Coles left unsaid was his more personal concern for this issue. He recognized that the proliferation of local banks would cut into his money-lending business; for enterprising farmers and speculators would turn to the state institutions for credit on better terms than he offered. When it came to his own financial security, Coles appeared more than willing to cast aside party loyalty.[9]

In this congratulatory epistle, Coles also addressed the issue of internal improvements. He informed Duncan that he thought it was particularly important to Illinois's economic future that the Illinois River be connected to Lake Michigan by a canal, a project that would be "so beneficial to the State & to the whole Union." He felt "a personal concern" in the enterprise as well, because he owned land in that part of the state and intended to reside there with his family. Echoing many of the claims made by advocates of Henry Clay's American System (which promoted economic prosperity through federal support for banking, internal improvements, and tariffs), Coles insisted that the completed project would facilitate emigration, increase agricultural production, and greatly augment the wealth of the region. None of this would come about, though, unless the governor "selected proper men to manage the business," men who do not have "selfish local or contracted views of the subject." Coles, of course, imagined himself to be just the sort of person Duncan should turn to for help. In fact, he apologized for his absence from the state, "as I intended . . . to give you such aid as was in my power in this long cherished & favorite work of mine." He then revealed that he intended to visit Illinois in the spring after his wife gave birth. "In the meantime" he offered to provide any "service to you or the State."[10] The letter achieved what Coles probably intended. In February 1835, Duncan appointed him president of the Board of the Illinois Canal Commission (a position he could fulfill while remaining in Philadelphia), and the responsibilities of this post occupied him for the next two years.[11]

Coles likewise spent much of his time engrossed in national politics. In August 1834, he tried to convince James Madison to enter the partisan public debate over President Andrew Jackson's decision to remove federal deposits. Coles saw in this action yet more evidence of the president's despotic tendencies and feared that his alleged abuse of executive authority would destroy the nation's political principles. He felt that only Madison, "the chief author and ablest expounder" of the Constitution, could save the country from ruin. Madison, however, refused to heed his protégé's call, citing a reluctance to provide fodder for the partisan disputes that already divided the country. Coles tried to persuade his mentor that his position "far above the motives & influences of the political parties" ensured that men on both sides of the question would respect him and listen to reason. His effort, however, was to no avail. Madison remained aloof of public affairs, concealed behind the doors of Montpelier, and the two men agreed to disagree on the issue.[12]

Several months later, Coles once again entered the political fray. His brother-in-law Andrew Stevenson, who had been denied the position a year earlier, was once again under consideration for minister to Great Britain. He deeply desired the post, but his rejection by the Senate the previous spring jeopardized his confirmation. Additionally, President Jackson, who detested the Senate's determination to thwart his authority at every turn, was considering robbing them of the privilege by refusing to nominate anyone for the position. Stevenson, however, wanted to forge ahead, and asked Coles to use his connections in Washington to promote his cause. Coles confessed that he could not "with propriety" contact Daniel Webster, who had voted against confirmation the previous spring despite a promise of support. Still, he was optimistic. He knew many other senators who might be worth consulting. Coles was willing to discuss his candidacy with senators Southard, Calhoun, Preston, Porter, Poindexter, Clay, and Roberts, all "gentlemen I have known a long time & most of them intimately." He also dispatched a letter to his old college friend and then senator John Tyler, hoping to enlist him in his efforts. Finally, Coles gathered intelligence from his Philadelphia contacts, Roberts Vaux and Joseph R. Ingersoll, as he tried to distinguish rumor from fact and keep Stevenson appraised of the changing political winds. In this fashion, Coles counted possible votes, wrote letters, and contemplated traveling to Washington to advocate on his brother-in-law's behalf in person. Ultimately, his efforts were unnecessary. Jackson followed the course anticipated and avoided any confrontation with Congress by choosing not to nominate anyone. Stevenson did eventually earn the post, but not until 1836, under the next administration.[13]

Then, in the spring of 1841, Coles was asked to serve as a commissioner investigating the Bank of the United States. Denied its charter renewal by President Andrew Jackson in 1832, the national bank had been struggling for years and was on the brink of bankruptcy by 1840. The stockholders and Board of Directors demanded to know why, and appointed a special commission to investigate the bank's lending and asset management policies. This must have been a difficult task for Coles. Nicholas Biddle, one of Coles's oldest and closest friends, had served as president of the bank for most of the period under examination, although he had resigned in March 1838. Coles had spent many pleasant evenings at Biddle's dinner table and enjoyed countless conversations with him in his parlor. Biddle had also helped Coles in his 1824 campaign against slavery in Illinois by connecting him with prominent antislavery writers in the city and facilitating the delivery of antislavery pamphlets to the Prairie State. Moreover, Coles was a long-time supporter of Henry Clay's American System and recognized the vital role the Bank of the United States played in fostering economic development. He had also adamantly opposed Jackson's assault on the bank five years earlier, when he called on Madison to chastise then President Jackson publicly. So, in both personal and political terms, Coles must have found his task as an investigator of the bank's practices uncomfortable.

But, as was always the case for Coles, principle was more important than personal and political concerns, and in this particular situation the integrity of the bank and the institution's obligation to serve the common good were at stake. Almost immediately the commissioners discovered that the bank's assets had been mismanaged. Biddle and his chief cashier had approved a variety of suspicious loans to individuals and organizations that would not be able to repay their debts. Additionally, they had authorized a series of foreign loans that left the Bank of the United States owing more abroad than the institution possessed in hand or was owed by domestic clients. Perhaps even worse, the committee discovered "that several of the officers of this Bank were themselves engaged in large operations in stocks and speculations." The result, they revealed, was that a few self-interested persons "monopolized the active means of the institution" and prevented "men engaged in business really productive and useful to the community" from benefiting from the institution.[14] Writing to his brother Isaac, a fellow Whig who had just been elected to the Virginia legislature, Coles warned that "you will find it a dark & appalling picture of Banking, & is disgraceful to the parties, & even to this community." Several members of the Board of Directors implored him to take over the directorship of the institution, but Coles knew better than to assume command of a sinking ship and politely refused. News of the investigation traveled across the Atlantic Ocean, as well. Coles's brother-in-law and devoted Democrat Andrew Stevenson, by then minister in London, wrote, "Mr. Biddle receives no quarter here." The general opinion, he reported, was "that of universal condemnation. . . . I rarely go into company without meeting some friend or acquaintance who has suffered deeply by the Bank." He then noted the irony of a states' rights, anti-Clay South Carolinian, Col. William Drayton, assuming the directorship of an institution so central to Clay's nationalist American System and "saving it from ruin."[15]

Coles approached all of his political dealings in this way. He communicated with equal candor to all of his family and personal associates regardless of their party affiliations. To his brothers-in-law Rutherfoord and Stevenson and many of his southern friends, he revealed his deepest anxieties about the spreading popularity of their party leader, Andrew Jackson. He was unapologetic about his views with James Madison, Joseph Duncan, Joseph Ingersoll, and Roberts Vaux, as well. Coles likewise expected his older brother Isaac, Daniel Webster, Henry Clay, John Tyler, and other national leaders to put aside their partisan commitments and honor his character as a friend by performing political favors when requested. For Coles, political principles and personal friendship, confirmed through intimate association, mattered more than partisan allegiances, and in an increasingly partisan political world he constantly challenged those around him to live by this creed. In essence, he saw himself as he had described Madison—a man above the influence of politics whose absence of partisan loyalties would lead others to respect him and heed his advice.

"much mutual advantage and instruction"

Edward Coles was not alone in this approach. He and Sally were part of a dynamic and cultivated elite society whose members likewise hoped that their carefully nurtured social relationships would temper, or even override, their political and sectional differences. Members of the Vaux, Ingersoll, Gilpin, Fisher, Cadwalader, Biddle, and Dallas families lived in refined neighborhoods, like the district where Coles settled, and belonged to exclusive clubs and organizations, such as the American Philosophical Society, Historical Society of Pennsylvania, the Philadelphia Club, the Athenian Institute, and the Athenaeum. Coles and his friends regularly attended concerts, lectures, and performances at the Academy of Music, Museum of Fine Arts, National Hall, and Congress Hall, all of which were located within walking distance of their neighborhood. Likewise, they hosted weekly private parties, balls, and "assemblies." It was through these networks of association that Philadelphia's elite remained involved in public and private affairs throughout the nineteenth century. Coles joined, as one foreign visitor described, an "agreeable and hospitable society" that was a "happy blending of the industrial habits of the north with the social usages of the south," qualities that made Philadelphia one of the most pleasant cities in America.[16]

Coles had a wide circle of friends in Philadelphia and, reflecting his belief that personal character and principle mattered more than partisan loyalties, he self-consciously cultivated associations that crossed partisan and sectional boundaries. He counted Democrats and Whigs among his friends and purposefully joined organizations (like the American Philosophical Society and the American Colonization Society) that exhibited a more national character. Among his Whig friends were Joseph R. Ingersoll, eminent lawyer and president of the Historical Society of Pennsylvania; Morton McMichael, editor of the *North American Review*; John Sergeant, congressman and one-time vice-presidential candidate; Henry C. Carey, publisher and prolific pamphleteer; Sidney George Fisher, lawyer and leisured gentleman; Thomas Sully, renowned portrait artist and fellow-colonizationist; and Moncure Robinson, railroad financier and engineer (and a Virginian by birth). Coles socialized with many of the city's Democrats, including Charles J. Ingersoll, brother to Joseph and a lawyer; George Mifflin Dallas, senator and vice president; Roberts Vaux, Quaker philanthropist; Richard Vaux, future mayor of Philadelphia; and Richard Rush, minister to France under Polk. As Coles's good friend Sidney George Fisher observed, the conversations at their social occasions almost always turned to politics. Occasionally they were "rather too warm," but he felt (and Coles surely agreed) that if "such topics could not be introduced & freely discussed in private circles . . . much mutual advantage and instruction would be . . . lost."[17]

Perhaps the most prestigious organization Coles and his friends belonged to was the American Philosophical Society. Founded in 1743, the organization became the premier American intellectual organization, promoting scientific learning in a fashion reminiscent of Great Britain's Royal Society. By the early nineteenth century, its treasurer and librarian John Vaughn, who was the lifeblood of the organization until his death in 1841, purposefully pursued a nationalist agenda, imagining in this society a mechanism for establishing America's national identity. To this end, he worked very hard to build a national membership. Men from North and South Carolina, Virginia, New York, Massachusetts, and Georgia were listed on the membership rolls, as were individuals from Great Britain, France, and Germany. In 1839, the year Coles was inducted as a new member, Bostonians Jared Sparks, Thomas L. Winthrop, William Jenkins, and William H. Prescott also became members, as did Massachusetts senator Daniel Webster. New members hailing from the South that year included Virginians George Tucker and John P. Emmet as well as South Carolinians Hugh S. Legaré and John Holbrook. Although initially confined to men of science, membership in the American Philosophical Society expanded to include planters, entrepreneurs, bankers, and politicians. Vaughn paid particular attention to forging connections with men from the South, a quality that was surely particularly pleasing to Coles; for, like Coles, Vaughn hoped that the shared qualities that made these men members of the American Philosophical Society would render them indifferent to any sectional differences they harbored.[18]

Membership in the organization alone was not enough to achieve Vaughn's nationalist goals. If a truly national leadership class was to be established, these men of wealth and influence had to establish and sustain relationships that were stronger than their regional and political loyalties. During the first third of the nineteenth century, the American Philosophical Society began sponsoring more formal social gatherings, known as Wistar parties, in order to tie the members to the organization and to one another. Modeled after the intimate social gatherings first hosted by Dr. Casper Wistar from 1811 until his death in 1818, these convivial assemblies provided attendees with the opportunity to cultivate "the social feelings" and "private friendships" that could bind the nation's most prominent men together. Held every Saturday evening from October to March, the Wistar parties were merely the most famous of a series of gentlemen's parties that were held each week. Many of Coles's closest friends hosted and attended these gatherings, and in the process became the national elite Vaughn had intended to create.[19]

Like Coles's immediate social circle, the members of the American Philosophical Society held a variety of political views. Some were Democrats and others were Whigs. Joel R. Poinsett, Langdon Cheves, William Meredith, Richard Vaux, Benjamin W. Richards, and Charles J. Ingersoll were among the Democrats, while Horace Binney, John Sergeant, and Joseph R. Ingersoll identified themselves as Whigs. Yet through their affiliation with the American Philosophical Society, these men recognized a shared commitment to the American nation and its founding principles that overshadowed their political differences. It is not too hard to imagine Coles exchanging anecdotes about Jefferson, Madison, and the other Founders with the likes of Robley Dunglison, William Short, and Peter S. Du Ponceau, all members who knew the Revolutionary leaders quite well. Du Ponceau, in particular, shared Coles's unassailable faith in the strength of the American Union. In 1831, when he delivered an address entitled "A Brief View of the Constitution of the United States" before the Law Academy of Philadelphia, Du Ponceau observed triumphantly that "the Union has already experienced severe trials, but has come off victorious from them all." As long as "the people remain virtuous, and true to themselves," he instructed, there can be no "real danger" to fear. It was true, he conceded, that it was impossible to know what "the increasing spirit of party" emerging in America would produce, but a "true patriot" could only forestall any dissolution of the Union by remaining true to the nation's original principles.[20]

In December 1840, Coles hosted one of the many Wistar parties that took place in his home. As he reported to his brother (and fellow Whig) Isaac, "I am so kindly invited to so many of the Wistar and other parties that I feel myself constrained every year or two to give one of those kinds of parties." The timing of this particular party was fortunate, for it came at the end of a turbulent election year. The Democratic Party had controlled the presidency since 1828, but by the late 1830s the Whigs were challenging their dominance. When he was in Washington the previous May, Coles witnessed firsthand just how nervous the Democrats had become. "The admin. & its friends," he observed, "are becoming . . . much alarmed. Calhoun not only looks depressed but badly." Among the Whigs, however, the enthusiasm for Harrison was striking. His friends from "the far West, who have come on to attend the grand Whig convention in Baltimore" had informed him that they had never witnessed "such enthusiasm" for the Whig Party. In his new home state of Pennsylvania, residents were divided evenly between Democrats and Whigs, and the contest remained too close to call for several weeks following the election. Coles's good friend Sidney George Fisher warned that "unless the Harrison majority" was large, the Democrats "will resort to any means however violent to retain power." He was hardly surprised, then, when reports that a Democratic mob had attacked the Whig headquarters on Chestnut Street circulated through his social circle. To Fisher's great relief, Whig candidate William Henry Harrison defeated Democrat Martin Van Buren, a triumph that marked the end of Democratic control of the executive office. Coles's soirée, which saw his "rooms full of very pleasant people," offered the perfect opportunity to heal the political wounds that had been opened during the campaign season.[21]

A similar idea governed all of Coles's social relations, even his most intimate connections. As his older (and Democratic-leaning) sister Sally expressed to him just weeks after the 1840 election, "I think and have always thought that friends may differ without quarelling and that political questions ought to have nothing to do with private friendships." Several months later, as she and her Democratic husband prepared to return home from London, she repeated the sentiment. "All men have a right to the exercise of their own opinions . . . friends & especially ourselves—ought to agree to disagree . . . after all, my dear Ned—Peace & love & good will are to be desired above all things." That Coles subscribed to this view was clear. In March 1840 he put aside his political loyalties and gave Democrat Richard Vaux and his bride, Mary Morris Waln, "a handsome wedding party," and entertained men and women vigorously supportive of Van Buren's candidacy even as he hoped for a Whig victory. Two years later, when his niece Angelica Singleton married Martin Van Buren's eldest son Abraham, he behaved similarly. In an 1842 letter to the ex-president, he admonished Van Buren that now that they were "so nearly connected" it was their "duty" to treat each other with kindness and respect. Politics, he insisted, should not interfere with their friendship. "You had no more right to be offended" by my politics, he announced, "than my own Brothers & brothers–in–law, & many other near & dear friends, who, like you, were supporters of Gen. Jackson's Admn." As he had maintained throughout his public and private life, personal affections and associations always took precedent over political obligations.[22]

"dangerous to the Union"

Coles thought the same approach should be applied to the issue of slavery. If so many Americans agreed that slavery was morally wrong and violated the nation's founding principles, then, Coles insisted, they should rise above their partisan differences, ignore their sectional loyalties, and promote the greater good by working to eliminate slavery. By the mid-1830s, however, the radical abolition movement had become a well-organized and potent association that alienated half the nation and appeared more skilled at provoking outrage than achieving emancipation. William Lloyd Garrison and his followers angered many southerners when they orchestrated a pamphlet campaign that filled southern post offices with essays denouncing slavery as a brutal institution administered and protected by cruel slavemasters. Coles's college friend John Tyler was typical among southerners when he spoke before a public meeting in Gloucester County, Virginia. He warned his audience that "a society has sprung up whose avowed object is to despoil us of our property at the hazard of all." This threat, he instructed, could only be met with a firm response. Tyler called on all the southern states to unite against this "fanatical" threat to their way of life. At the same time, antislavery activists bombarded Congress with petitions demanding an end to slavery in the District of Columbia. None other than Andrew Jackson characterized these petitions as the product of an incendiary tactic that abolitionists hoped would excite "the passions of the slaves" and "produce all the horrors of a servile war."[23] Coles would have recognized in this abolitionist tactic a strategy more inclined to incite southern anger and increase sectional animosity than an approach that might foster the cross-sectional cooperation he knew from experience was required to attack slavery with any success.

He also learned from the debate over slavery in Washington, D.C., that national politicians could not be relied upon to advance the cause of emancipation. South Carolinian John C. Calhoun greeted the arrival of the abolitionist petitions with the declaration that "Congress had no jurisdiction on the subject, no more in the District than in the State of South Carolina; it was a question," he continued, "not to be touched by Congress." He proposed, therefore, that Congress help prevent any future servile insurrections among the slaves and demands for disunion among beleaguered southerners by refusing to accept any antislavery petitions submitted for consideration. Calhoun's proposal was rejected, but in its place the Senate adopted a procedural mechanism that would table the question of whether or not to receive the petitions each time the topic emerged. In this way, the Senate imposed a gag rule that effectively prevented any debate on the content of the slave petitions, a gag that lasted for fifteen years.[24]

During the same congressional session, House members simultaneously debated a similar proposal from Henry L. Pinckney, another South Carolinian, who suggested sending every petition regarding slavery in the nation's capital to a committee with instructions echoing Calhoun's provision. He also argued that Congress should not interfere with slavery because "it would be a violation of the public faith, unwise, impolitic, and dangerous to the Union." As had occurred in the Senate, the House made a procedural decision that effectively prevented any discussion of the slavery issue on the House floor. Unlike in the Senate, however, the House rule had to be renewed each year, and with each ensuing debate the likelihood of renewal diminished. Although this procedural requirement was finally defeated in 1844, the gag rule stifled debate for six years.[25]

From Coles's perspective, the unwillingness of Congress to acknowledge the constitutional authority of the government to abolish slavery in the District of Columbia resulted from an ignorance of "historical facts." In a letter addressed to the editors of the *National Intelligencer*, Coles declared "that Congress would not only conceive itself possessed of the power, but that it would exercise it, and even before this have abolished slavery." As proof of his assertion, Coles argued that the land cessions to the Federal government by Virginia and various other states, as well as the Land Ordinance of 1785, bequeathed to Congress the power to regulate the institutions established in those regions. More important, he claimed that the Northwest Ordinance of 1787, which he maintained was authored by Thomas Jefferson, prohibited slavery north of the Ohio River, and was, therefore, an example of Congress exercising powers equivalent to abolishing slavery in the District of Columbia.[26] In direct contradiction to Calhoun, Coles insisted that it not only had the power to eliminate slavery in the nation's capital, but that Congress should use it.

In many ways, Coles had moved ahead too quickly. While he launched into a debate about the authority of the federal government, the men in Congress did everything they could to avoid the issue altogether. No one in Congress was willing to risk the political consequences they feared would accompany an open debate about slavery on the floor of Congress. With the nullification crisis still fresh in their minds, few leaders were willing to reignite the sectional tensions that might lead to disunion. Perhaps more important, Democratic and Whig party leaders were unwilling to risk losing southern support in an election year. It was hardly surprising, for example, that it was presidential aspirant Henry Clay who devised the procedural mechanism that resulted in a fifteen-year gag rule in the Senate, or that Martin Van Buren declared in the spring of 1836 that Congress should not interfere with slavery in the District.[27] Certainly, Coles was disappointed in both the forestalled debate on the slavery issue on the floor of Congress and the apparent conspiracy among the nation's political leaders to avoid any discussion of the issue whatsoever. He could not avoid the suspicion that national politics might not be the best venue to advance his brand of antislavery nationalism.

Still, he harbored great hope that what the nation's elected officials refused to pursue officially might be achieved more symbolically by the last remaining Founding Father; for it was James Madison who had promised Coles in 1831 that he would emancipate his enslaved property in his will. This act of benevolence, Coles remained confident, would prove his claim—that the Founders had envisioned a future for the nation that did not include slavery.

When in July 1836 he learned that the venerable and much-loved James Madison had died, Coles was personally distraught. Since his father's untimely death in 1808, he had recognized in Madison a father and a mentor. In every way, Coles looked up to the ex-president and was devoted to him. He knew that Madison's health had been declining for some time, but even though he was "somewhat prepared . . . for the event," it was still "painful to lose a beloved friend." His pain, of course, paled in comparison to his cousin Dolley's, whose anguish was born of so many years of "devoted and reciprocal attachment." He took comfort as he wrote her, in the knowledge that they (and the world) had enjoyed such a long connection to a man "not less distinguished for greatness than goodness, who was as preeminent for his private and domestic virtues, as for his great abilities & useful services as a benefactor of the human race." He tried to console her by reminding her that she "had done every thing which the most amiable & affectionate of Wives could do to render him happy, & that you made him supremely so," he continued, "must be to you a most soothing & healing balm to your wounded heart." He beseeched her to rely upon him for anything she needed. "Next to your son, Brother, & Sister, I claim to be your nearest & dearest friend." Nothing, he concluded, could make him happier than to do all "in my power to serve you in any way."[28]

A week later, Coles received the information he had been most eager to learn—news of Madison's disposition of his slaves in the will. As he looked over the description of the will provided by John C. Payne, Dolley's brother, Coles was shocked and disappointed to discover that Madison had not outlined any plans for emancipation. Just over five years earlier, Coles had (he thought) extracted a promise from Madison to liberate his enslaved property. Together they had designed a gradual emancipation plan that would have ensured Dolley's financial security while simultaneously providing for the liberty of his bound laborers. Coles was stunned. Madison had failed to follow through with their agreement.[29]

In late July, a steaming-mad Coles wrote his sister to vent his frustration. "His slaves not emancipated! For this," he howled, "Mr. S[tevenson, his brother-in-law] will have much to answer." Coles believed that Andrew Stevenson, who visited Madison soon after Coles did in 1831, had "presented such difficulties . . . as to make him doubt the utility of the contemplated provision." In some ways, Coles blamed himself. He had shared the news of these plans in the mistaken belief that Stevenson agreed "that the emancipation of his Slaves was necessary to a perfect finale of his life & character." What an "unfortunate communication!," Coles grumbled. Angered by his brother-in-law's interference, Coles accused him of "defacing his [Madison's] character with its greatest if not only stain." Still disappointed, he arranged to visit Montpelier, hoping to rectify the situation. Coles was glad to see his cousin and eager to comfort her in her grief. He had missed the funeral and probably asked her to relate in detail everything that had happened since Madison's death two months earlier. But the visit turned out to be more disturbing than comforting. As news of Madison's failure to emancipate his slaves and the resulting economic burden imposed on his widow spread beyond Montpelier, slave traders called on the president's widow with startling regularity. "It was like a hawk among the pigeons," he told his sister. As the traders appeared at the plantation, "the poor creatures wd run to the house & protest agt being sold," claiming that their deceased master had promised that none of them would be sold without their consent. Rather than confirm Madison's emancipatory wishes, Coles watched helplessly as Dolley sold a woman and two children during his visit. He could not help but conclude that "Mr. Madison's course has been unfortunate for his memory." More significant for Coles, Madison's inaction robbed him of a potent example proving the legitimacy of a central feature of his antislavery nationalism—that the Founders were antislavery statesmen.[30]

Over and over again, the men of the founding generation, Coles's mentors, had failed to live up to his expectations when it came to slavery. His first disappointment had been directed toward Bishop James Madison. When asked how he could allow a wrong to continue just because it had been done in the past, Madison had justified his inaction with the claim that emancipation was too difficult. Coles was frustrated again in 1814 when Thomas Jefferson refused to heed his call to act against slavery in Virginia, preferring instead to wait until some undetermined future date when more Virginians would share his antislavery view. On a third occasion, he had called James Monroe to task for failing to seize an opportunity to promote emancipation when he offered compromise rather than bold reform during the 1829–1830 Virginia Constitutional Convention. When his most cherished of mentors, James Madison, had failed to be the exception to this disturbing trend, Coles was devastated.

"there is a prejudice in narrow minds"

Nearly six months after Madison's death, Coles received a letter that somewhat alleviated his feelings of disappointment. Kate and Robert Crawford, two of the slaves he had liberated in 1819, sent news from Illinois. Coles had consistently kept track of them as well as of all the enslaved men and women he had emancipated. Robert Wash provided regular updates on Suckey and Emanuel Logan and their children, Alfred, Franky, Elizabeth, Wilson, Lucinda, and Emily. This family had settled in St. Louis in the early 1820s and lived rent-free in a house Coles owned in that city. They also regularly borrowed money from Coles to cover their medical expenses and to protect them from sliding into poverty during difficult economic times. Coles monitored Robert and Kate Crawford through regular correspondence and their mutual association with Isaac Prickett, an Edwardsville storeowner. Coles helped them purchase an additional eighty acres of land near his Prairieland farm and relied on them to manage his nearby property. He also paid their land taxes throughout his lifetime and offered security for a line of credit in Edwardsville. Polly Crawford, Robert's younger sister, married a free black man named Michael Lee in 1822, and by the mid-1830s they lived on an eighty-acre farm a quarter of a mile southeast of the Crawford's property.[31] Coles always felt a keen interest in everyone's progress and did everything he could to ensure their success.

In his response to their note, Coles declared his "respect" for their "honorable, correct, & piously virtuous conduct" and assured them he was glad to hear from them. He reminded them (and perhaps himself) why he had emancipated them in 1819. "Prompted by feelings which respected the rights of my fellow beings & yielded to the dictates of justice, & of that rule which emanates from Heaven, of doing to others as you wish to be done by," he declared, "I restored to you that which was mine by the Laws of man, but yours by the inherent principles of right, & the immutable Laws of God." He then revealed that he had pursued this course over the objections of those who claimed "that the African race were incapable from their natures to enjoy" their rights "& are happier as slaves than they would be as freemen." He was delighted to observe that they had conducted themselves "as to sustain my conduct & confirm my opinions of the unity & equality of man, & of his capacity to govern himself, & best promote his own happiness." From his perspective, their success was all the more important because it demonstrated that African Americans could "in every respect" maintain "as fair a character under your brown faces, as the fairest of your fair faced neighbours." They had done this, he declared, despite the fact that "there is a prejudice in narrow minds agt you, because your God & their God has seen fit to give your skin a darker hue."[32]

The exchange with the Crawfords could not have happened at a better time. Disappointed with Madison's failure to follow through with his promise, this correspondence was just what Coles needed to rejuvenate his work for emancipation. As he had acknowledged repeatedly since the convention contest in Illinois, the prejudices of white Americans were too great for emancipation to proceed without colonization. That white prejudices about African Americans had failed to diminish in the intervening ten years was certain. Just two weeks after he mailed the letter to the Crawfords, Coles's cousin John Payne announced that Dolley no longer required his help with her husband's estate and that he was contemplating seeking his fortune in the west. Payne was intrigued by the region north of the Ohio River and wondered if Coles might offer some advice. He was hesitant to commit to a move, however, if he could not be confident settling there would improve his economic situation, and he had doubts because of some travelers' reports that were worrisome. "The annoyances of insects and free blacks," he revealed, "is very objectionable. Tho' a thorough disciple of the principles proclaimed in our declaration," he continued, "the southern prejudice is strong with us all in regard to the social position of these people." Payne confessed that he preferred, then, to "avoid the vicinity of any assemblage from this class."[33]

John Payne was not alone in his view of free blacks. Even in Coles's Philadelphia the racial climate was hardly more hospitable to free blacks than in Illinois and Virginia. During the middle third of the nineteenth century, Philadelphia was a city in the midst of a dramatic transformation. The city's population had increased by nearly 38 percent, largely as a result of an influx of immigrants, but also because rural Americans increasingly sought advancement in an expanding urban economy. Merchants and aspiring businessmen tore down older and abandoned buildings and replaced them with imposing new business structures. Popular promenades and shopping districts as well as elegant hotels transformed many neighborhoods into busy cosmopolitan districts. As one foreign visitor commented, Philadelphia was "a remarkably animated city, with streets crowded with as fashionable a set of people as you could wish to see."[34] It was precisely these qualities that attracted men like Coles to the city.

The economic expansion and prosperity so many visitors celebrated, however, elevated the cost of living, making many of the advantages of city living beyond the reach of ordinary residents. Immigrants, free blacks, and the lower sort, who worked in the factories and households of the well-to-do, shared the anticipation of improvement but regularly experienced only the disappointment of a market economy with unpredictable peaks and valleys. As a result, many of these Philadelphians witnessed the underside of economic change. They lived in the poorly constructed shacks, boarding houses, tenements, and houses abandoned by the better sort as they moved to newer neighborhoods near the Schuylkill River.

For the less-well-to-do, the city had become overcrowded, dirty, and unhealthy. Frequent economic recessions exacerbated these conditions, exposing a dramatic gap between the wealthy and the poor. The panic of 1837, for example, developed into a recession that remained potent until 1842. In April 1837, Coles complained to his brother-in-law John Rutherfoord that his "money matters have been very much out of sorts of late." While he certainly voiced an anxiety shared by most Americans, he hardly risked losing his livelihood, and he weathered the downturn with relative ease. Others were not so fortunate. Indeed, as one of his friends exclaimed: "Never before, in the history of our country have ruin & embarrassment been so extensive & so deeply felt."[35]

Not surprisingly, the anxiety and frustration that accompanied these and other disruptive conditions caused a variety of problems in the city, the most visible of which was racial violence. Throughout the 1830s and 1840s, race riots, the product of a pervasive antiblack prejudice and resentment over competition for employment, broke out with startling frequency all over the country. New York, Cincinnati, Baltimore, and Philadelphia all experienced racial violence. While Coles visited family in Virginia in August 1834, a white mob that included several hundred people marched through one of Philadelphia's black neighborhoods, destroying houses and businesses and intimidating and attacking free black residents. The violence lasted for nearly three nights and only ended when a mounted militia subdued the rioters. A year later, another mob brutally attacked the city's free black residents again. This second mob seized a collection of antislavery pamphlets and dumped them into the Delaware River to prevent their distribution. Perhaps the most spectacular act of violence happened in 1838, when a mob of allegedly respectable white citizens burned to the ground Pennsylvania Hall, a meeting house built by Philadelphia abolitionists. Their anger had rumbled to the surface as they witnessed a racially mixed group of antislavery activists attend lectures condemning the institution. Four years later, a white mob attacked an African American procession commemorating emancipation in the British West Indies. The violence was transformed into a full-scale riot that lasted several days and brought destruction to countless African American residences and businesses. Robert Purvis, one the city's most prominent free blacks, complained about the utter "apathy and inhumanity" of Philadelphia's "whole community." Everyone, "the press, church, magistrates, [and] clergymen . . . are against us."[36] Antiblack and anti-abolition sentiment were as strong in Philadelphia as in the Virginia and Illinois communities Coles had previously called home.

"enjoy not partial liberty but its full power"

In this context, Coles concluded that colonization was the only pragmatic means of promoting emancipation. Like him, many colonizationists saw themselves as liberators, abolitionists of a different stripe. They
shared with Garrison and his followers the desire to bring about an end
to slavery. Property rights, political concerns, and apprehensions about
security convinced them that gradual and voluntary rather than immediate and forced emancipation was more likely to succeed. As one observer
noted, the goal of the organization was to create a middle ground where
the "jarring interests and feelings of the North and the South" could
"meet together in harmonious action." And this was the feature of the
organization that attracted Coles. Unlike abolition, which alienated and
insulted southerners and their way of life, Coles recognized in the colonization movement a national approach with cross-sectional and bipartisan appeal.[37]

This approach, however, made the organization vulnerable to attacks
from all sides. As William A. Duer, a New York colonizationist, complained, some opponents tried to discredit the organization by associating it with radical abolitionists. Others claimed that it was really "a
device to interfere with the question of slave property in the South." Each
of these misrepresentations, Duer claimed, could be easily corrected.
The more difficult criticism to counter, however, was the charge "that
the society was constituted to perpetuate slavery." No matter how long
the list "of slaves emancipated to be colonized," the organization's most
ardent opponents continued to declare that the American Colonization
Society "riveted closer the chains of the slave." In his *Thoughts on African Colonization* (1832) William Lloyd Garrison issued a scathing attack
on colonization, claiming that the program only served to buttress the
institution of slavery because it facilitated the removal of the weakest
and most difficult slaves while leaving behind the most profitable and
useful bound laborers. In this way, Garrison effectively set up abolition
and colonization as diametrically opposed to one another, erasing the
middle ground colonizationists attempted to occupy.[38]

Colonizationists met Garrison's challenge directly by claiming the
moderate and national character of their society. The biracial community
of equals envisioned by Garrison and his followers, insisted most colonizationists, was foolish and unrealistic. As R. R. Gurley claimed at the
annual meeting of the Pennsylvania Colonization Society in November
1839, America's free black population was "denied everywhere, by law,

custom, circumstance, or all combined, many of the richest blessings of freedom." Antiblack prejudice, he insisted, was strong and unlikely to change. Anyone interested in improving their condition, then, should support the effort to establish and maintain a colony where America's free blacks "will enjoy not partial liberty but its full power." In a not-so-subtle reference to the abolition movement, Gurley complained that the entire enterprise of emancipation had been hindered by "the direct and fierce attacks" of "societies exclusively northern in their origin and action." Any public discussion of slavery over the past six years, he grumbled, had "alienate[d] . . . the affections of one half the country from the other, and excited, in the minds of sober patriots and able statesmen, a sense and apprehension of danger." Only an organization like the Pennsylvania Colonization Society, he maintained, could furnish "a bond of union between the south and the north; a channel in which their mutual sympathies, opinions, and charities may comingle; a broad and lofty ground on which the citizens of both may cooperate."[39]

Coles joined the Pennsylvania Colonization Society in 1836. Two years later he was elected to the Board of Managers and joined an executive leadership composed of many of his friends and associates. Joseph R. Ingersoll, who may have attended his wedding, was president of the organization. Like Coles, he was an ardent anti-Jackson man and was a fixture at Philadelphia social events. Among the vice presidents from Philadelphia were Dr. John Bell, William Short (Thomas Jefferson's protégé and a prominent American diplomat), John Breckenridge, and Mathew Carey. Also among the membership were many of the men he knew from the American Philosophical Society and the Athenaeum, including Peter S. Du Ponceau, Moncure Robinson, Thomas Sully, John Vaughn, Dr. Nathaniel Chapman, and others. Southerners John Own and John McDonough were also among the vice presidents. These men adopted a revised constitution in 1837 that emphasized the society's antislavery ideals, pledging their commitment to "the gradual and peaceful demise of slavery" in Article II. As they defended their organization from abolitionist attacks, then, they emphasized their commitment to emancipation. In less than twenty years, they boasted in their publication, the *Colonization Herald*, that colonizationists had helped hundreds of slaveholders liberate thousands of bond persons. "How many have abolitionists emancipated during the same period?," they asked. Coles was uncomfortable with the organization's antiblack rhetoric, for he did not believe that blacks were inherently inferior. He did agree, though, that white prejudice was an immutable characteristic of American society.

So he chose to ignore their prejudicial pronouncements because it was their commitment to emancipation that made him an ardent advocate and fundraiser for the organization. Accordingly, when he was elected to serve as a delegate to the annual American Colonization Society meeting in Washington, Coles accepted the post and traveled to the nation's capital to represent his local auxiliary.[40]

Over the next several years, Coles served on the Board of Managers, attended several annual meetings in Washington, D.C., subscribed to the *Colonization Herald* and the *African Repository*, and made regular financial contributions to the Pennsylvania Colonization Society. He also helped the organization collect and distribute copies of pamphlets promoting their cause. In October 1839 the organization purchased 150 copies of *An Inquiry into the Condition and Prospects of the African Race* (1839) and distributed them to Philadelphia residents. Like Coles, this anonymous author claimed that he had "early imbibed a strong prejudice against slavery, as incompatible with the freedom of our government." Although he regretted that "the rancor of bitter political strife has for a time withdrawn public attention from" the slavery issue, the writer believed that the nation was in the midst of a crisis that demanded a full and free discussion of the slavery issue. He then proceeded to denounce immediate abolition as misguided in its condemnation of southerners and slaveholders. Colonization, the author argued, was the only option with any hope of succeeding because northerners and southerners alike could embrace the organization's gradual and voluntary program. He closed his treatise by declaring what Coles already believed—that it was time to make colonization and emancipation a national issue.[41]

"dust in the balance"

In the spring of 1844, Edward Coles seized an opportunity to present his own experience with emancipation as a model for others to follow when he received a request that he explain "the causes which led me to emancipate my slaves." He responded with a narrative for public consumption that championed the antislavery nationalism he had fashioned twenty years earlier. He reviewed many of the components of his biography that were already familiar to the public. After chronicling the history of his family's emigration and settlement in Virginia, Coles described how, while attending Bishop James Madison's moral philosophy course at the College of William and Mary, he had concluded that he "could not consent to hold as property what I had no right to, & which was not, and could not be property, according to my understanding of the rights & duties of man." When he informed his family that he planned to emancipate his inherited property and resettle in the west, every one of them objected and worked hard to discourage him. He revealed that although the execution of his plan to liberate his enslaved property was delayed by his service as President James Madison's private secretary and a brief journey abroad, his conviction that slavery was incompatible with the nation's political principles never wavered. Indeed, his determination to free the enslaved property he inherited from his father only grew stronger during these early years.[42]

Coles situated this information, familiar in its details, in a broader narrative structure that was designed to offer some important lessons to the public. By his telling, following through with his convictions had required great personal sacrifice. When his siblings objected to his chosen course, he recalled explaining to them that "I am as fully sensible as any one can be of the inconveniences & privations I shall subject myself to by pursuing" emancipation. He had likewise acknowledged that not only would he have to abandon his family and friends and live among strangers, but he would also have to forfeit the greatest source of his wealth. "But all this is as dust in the balance," he proclaimed, "when weighing the consolation & happiness of doing what you believe right, with the corroding of feelings, & the upbraiding of conscience, at doing what you believe wrong." The lesson here was not only that principle should always prevail over pecuniary and personal interests but that following such a path need not lead to financial ruin. Emancipation was difficult, and it could not be done without great sacrifice, but it was possible to thrive afterward.[43]

Coles also wanted his readers to understand that the Founders had bequeathed to them the responsibility of eliminating slavery from the American landscape. The Madison he described in this autobiography was an antislavery statesman. Coles presented him as a man whose "principles were sound, pure, & conscientious, & his feelings were sensitive, & tender in the extreme. . . . No man," he insisted, "had a more instinctive repugnance to doing wrong to another than he had." He then claimed that Madison had "never justified or approved" of slaveholding, but continued to own slaves "from the force of early impression, the influence of habit & association, & a certain train of reasoning, which lulled in some degree his conscience." As proof of Madison's antislavery sensibility, Coles cited their November 1831 conversation about "what he ought to do with his Slaves at his death." He confessed that Madison had been reluctant, fearful that liberating his slaves in his will would leave his wife destitute. Coles recalled that Madison had agreed to adopt a plan that would remedy his objections and still "carry essentially into effect his wishes." He then described "my astonishment to learn . . . that he had not freed his slaves. . . . It is to me," he proclaimed, "inexplicable."[44]

He also presented Thomas Jefferson, a man whose "views were more in accordance with mine than those entertained by Mr. Madison," as an ardent supporter of emancipation. He cited Jefferson's August 1814 response to his request that he put into operation a gradual emancipation program in Virginia, as proof of Jefferson's antislavery sensibility. In the letter, Jefferson claimed that his age and infirmity prevented him from acting, but he instructed Coles to "come forward in the public councils, become the missionary of this doctrine . . . and press the proposition . . . until its accomplishment." Coles also claimed that Jefferson showed this letter and the instructions it contained to "a number of young & talented men" and called on them to "'associate' & form a 'phalanx' to eradicate, what he called, the 'mortal reproach to us.'" Once he established Jefferson's support for emancipation, Coles then explained that nothing had come of his efforts because he was "unable . . . to recruit volunteers in the cause." The failure of emancipation in Virginia, then, was not the fault of its most famous "champion of human rights," but the result of the younger generation's failure to accept the torch of liberty when it was passed to them.[45]

In Coles's narrative, then, the Founding Fathers, his mentors, were in principle opposed to slavery and recognized that the institution contradicted the nation's core political values. Although they had failed to transform their beliefs into action, Coles insisted that they had envisioned a future for the nation that did not include slavery. The message Coles hoped to convey was that it was the responsibility of the next generation, his own generation, to promote and implement an emancipation scheme that would finally rid the nation of the institution. Should any of his readers doubt the plausibility of Jefferson's instructions, they had only to read the rest of Coles's narrative. The remainder of the letter described how he followed Jefferson's advice. He severed "the manacles of bondage" and let "loose on the buoyant wings of liberty the long pent up spirit of man." The effect of this transformation from slavery to freedom on his unsuspecting slaves, he testified, "was electrical." At first they were silent with disbelief, but once "they began to see the truth of what they had heard & to realize their situation," he exclaimed, "there came on a kind of hysterical giggling laugh . . . [and] they gave vent to their gratitude."

According to Coles, he then instructed his newly liberated slaves that the future of any emancipation enterprise depended upon their success; for if they did well, he claimed, their prosperity would prove "that the descendants of Africa were competent to take care of & govern themselves, & enjoy all the blessings of liberty, & all the other birthrights of man." By their example, he recalled telling them, they would "promote the universal emancipation of that unfortunate & outraged race of the human family." He was happy to report that they had acquitted themselves very well and continued to live prosperously in Illinois.[46]

Although he certainly intended this portion of his narrative to counter the argument that blacks "were incompetent to take care of themselves, & that liberty would be to them a curse rather than a blessing," Coles also wanted to provide ample evidence of the unassailable nature of white prejudice. He recalled witnessing, for example, several instances of "the most flagrant & outrageous cases of kidnapping." Sober, industrious, and prosperous free blacks, he testified, were routinely captured and sold back into slavery. Unable to seek the protection of the law, these free black residents of Illinois lived in constant fear of their white neighbors, men and women who were willing to pursue their pecuniary interests with little regard for human rights. He, too, had been subjected to the prejudices of his neighbors, who did everything they could to discredit him before the public. As he led a movement to prevent Illinois from becoming a slave state, a group of men filed suit against him "to punish me . . . for giving freedom to my fellow man." He ultimately prevailed, but only "after several years of trouble & expense."[47]

It was the pervasive white prejudice encountered by his ex-slaves and the partisan attacks on his character that led Coles to add colonization to his antislavery nationalism. Although the enslaved laborers he liberated "have succeeded well, enjoyed their freedom, & led happy lives," he declared, he had come to believe that they would be happier and better off if they "removed to a country exclusively occupied by the people of their own colour." More than anything else, Coles's observations of and confrontation with white prejudice in Illinois inspired his determination to promote colonization. And his residence in Philadelphia only confirmed his commitment. "Races of men that differ so much in appearance as the White & Black man," he concluded, "will never . . . associate as equals, & live in harmony & social intercourse." Such a prospect was even more unlikely, he continued, "when one of these races has . . . been held in bondage & looked upon as a degraded race by the other." Intimately familiar with the "disadvantages & indignities" his ex-slaves regularly endured, Coles repeatedly encouraged them to emigrate across the Atlantic. He even offered to pay for Robert Crawford, now a prosperous farmer and minister, to journey to Liberia. Coles hoped that Crawford would "write a full & faithful account" of the colony that could be published "for the information of his black brethren generally." But, like many free blacks in America, Crawford consistently refused to leave the United States. As he informed Coles, Crawford was "so fully engrossed & happily occupied in attending to his Family, his Farm, & his Congregation," that he had no desire to leave Illinois.[48]

As he lay down his pen, Coles must have been simultaneously proud and disappointed by the narrative he had crafted—proud that he had followed through with his convictions, proud that he had overcome the hardships that resulted from the sacrifices he had made on the altar of his principles, and proud that his experiment in black freedom on the Illinois frontier had succeeded. If he had any doubts about this last element, Coles had only to peruse one of the many letters he had received from Robert and Kate Crawford to affirm the correctness of the course he had pursued. Just three years earlier, they had written to express their sorrow at learning of the death of Isaac A. Coles. They took the occasion, as well, to declare: "We are truly thankfull that our old Master John Caules and his wife Rebechah ever had a son born by the name of Edward we believe that God have made him the means of doing us this Great Good." Ultimately, Coles's life experience sustained his commitment to the antislavery nationalism he had spent a lifetime crafting, and he hoped others would see in his experiences a model worth emulating.[49]

Coles was probably disappointed, however, by the clear limits of colonization as a program to end slavery. Like Robert Crawford, most free blacks refused to leave a nation they and their ancestors had helped to build. Moreover, both the American Colonization Society and the Pennsylvania Colonization Society were constantly plagued by financial problems that inhibited the execution of their programs. In fact, the national organization experienced such dire economic circumstances that Coles's Pennsylvania auxiliary pursued an independent route, raising their own funds and directly recruiting free blacks for their own settlement at Bassa Cove in West Africa. Perhaps most disappointing of all was the reality that the Pennsylvania organization's efforts met with only partial success. By the mid-1840s, they had only facilitated the emancipation of a few hundred slaves and transported a few hundred more free blacks to their colony. At the same time, they could read any census report and see the truth of their ineffectiveness. Throughout the South and Southwest, the slave population grew by tens of thousands, a number that greatly outstripped their emancipation record. The gap between their ambitions and the reality of their experience was difficult for Coles to ignore.[50] But, as had always been his habit, Coles persevered and never abandoned his cause.

"dull details of my Family matters"

In the summer of 1845, after nearly twelve years in Philadelphia, Edward Coles finally established a permanent residence in the city when he bought a large four-story brownstone on Spruce Street, just west of Thirteenth. The lot also included a three-story back building that would house his carriage and horses, as well as provide lodging for his servants. The house itself contained a handsome parlor set off from the main entryway by two large, elegant white pillars. Along the walls he planned to hang his portraits of Thomas Jefferson, James Madison, and James Monroe. There was also a large dining room for entertaining and a well-appointed kitchen. The upper floors contained sitting rooms, bed chambers, a fancy bath, and several water closets. By November he had nearly finished refurbishing the house. He informed his brother-in-law Richard Singleton that "we have completed all the essential furniture for our new house." The workers, he continued, were due to finish installing "fixtures for the use of Gas" in a few days. He only regretted that "the Chandeliers . . . will not be done" and installed at the same time. Coles had moved into the "fashionable quarter," a neighborhood one observer described as "thronged with spacious and elegant residences . . . giving abundant evidence of affluence, taste, and luxurious ease and comfort."[51]

His family was thriving. Over the previous decade he and Sally had welcomed into their family three children, Mary, Edward, and Roberts. As was the case with most young families, the Coleses spent a great deal of time nursing their children through bouts of illness. The year 1839 was a particularly hard one. Young Edward barely survived a dangerous eye infection. In a fit of anxiety, Coles woefully declared to his brother Isaac: "My heart bleeds when I think of his suffering, not only from his eye, but from the severe & torturing remedies that have been resorted to." In May 1845, his youngest son Roberts caught the measles and the disease spread to the other children. The episode was more frightening than usual because a six-year old nephew on Sally's side of the family had recently died from the illness. His children, however, survived the experience. Despite these periodic scares, Coles's family was generally healthy and flourishing. In 1840, Coles wrote his cousin Dolley with an update on the "dull details of my Family matters. . . . My dear little Mary," he revealed, "still continues the most devoted child to me I ever saw, & still often reminds me of you." Apparently, Edward resembled Sally and her family "& is the handsomest child of all three." Roberts, Coles confessed, "is said to be like me. All three," he concluded, "I am happy to say are promising," bright children. Coles was devoted to his family and boasted that "I seldom move without having one & more frequently all three with me."[52]

This blissfully mundane domestic routine was frequently interrupted by visits from Coles's extended family. It was not uncommon to find Tucker and Helen Coles staying with them for weeks at a time. Betsy Coles and John and Emily Coles Rutherfoord also visited often. Their brother-in-law (and South Carolinian) Richard Singleton stayed with them intermittently when visiting his sister, who was a resident at an insane asylum in the city. Andrew and Sally Coles Stevenson likewise stopped to see Coles whenever they were in town. A retinue of nieces and nephews similarly passed through Philadelphia regularly and stopped for a meal or an evening's entertainment with their uncle. Only Dolley Madison, hindered by poor health, failed to make a regular pilgrimage to Philadelphia. Coles also occasionally took his young family southward for visits with his older brother Isaac and his wife Juliana at their summer retreat in Baltimore. At least once every few years, Coles likewise took his family to Enniscorthy and the other family estates in Albemarle County, Virginia. As had been the case throughout his childhood, the Coles clan cared deeply for one another. Although they lived far apart from everyone else, Coles's children came of age with a strong attachment to their southern family members and the Coles family homestead in Virginia.[53] In many ways, his extended family exhibited the very national qualities he cultivated among his friends and associates in Philadelphia. His children and his extended relations were comfortable among both northerners and southerners and were, he hoped, developing a more national (as opposed to sectional) identity.

By the late 1840s, however, Coles found that national political developments conspired against these nationalist efforts and threatened to disrupt his peaceful family life. In early November 1847, he composed his weekly letter to his Democratic and states' rights–advocating brother-in-law John Rutherford. The two men enjoyed a long and affectionate friendship and corresponded and visited regularly throughout their lives. Although few private events escaped their attention, they respected each other's political views and only occasionally discussed public affairs or slavery in their correspondence. When news reached Coles that Rutherfoord intended to let his "daughter Emily . . . spend the winter in Charleston," however, Coles could not hide his disapproval. "The result," he warned, "will be she will marry and spend her life there." Too many of his close relations, he complained, already resided in South Carolina, "a State which considers Slavery a blessing." How could he consent to send "a Niece I am more attached to" than any other, to a place where the most prominent men unapologetically exert "every human effort to increase" slavery "& prevent [it] from harmlessly passing away."[54] With this, Coles revealed how the intensifying national political debate over slavery and westward expansion had pierced the carefully maintained bubble of social and political harmony he lived within in Philadelphia. As he would soon discover, the whole nation would be pulled into a discussion of the slavery issue, and he and his extended family would find themselves on opposite sides of the debate. Only the hope that his extended network of cross-sectional and bipartisan social relations as well as his antislavery nationalism might quell the rising sectional hostilities and repair the potential breach in his family relations preserved his optimism about the future.

7 / Antislavery Nationalism Resurrected

In early September 1848, Edward Coles received an interesting letter from Philadelphia's ex-mayor Benjamin W. Richards. "You cannot fail to observe with lively interest," declared the Free-Soil Democrat, "the rapid progress . . . of the Free Soil party, who have come forward to resist the extension of slavery." Richards's observation was timely; for the nation was embroiled in a bitter presidential contest that pitted three candidates against one another in a fractured political climate. Disagreements over slavery and westward expansion in the aftermath of the Mexican-American War threatened to divide the nation along sectional lines, and in a month Americans would be choosing between Whig Zachary Taylor, Democrat Lewis Cass, and Free-Soil candidate Martin Van Buren. Richards wrote to Coles with the intention of luring him into the presidential contest. Coles had known Richards for many years and had developed a close friendship with him, cultivated during the public and private gatherings that populated Philadelphia's crowded social calendar. Emboldened by this sense of familiarity, Richards asked his friend to provide a record "of the views . . . entertained by those great fathers of the republic" on the subject of "the extension of slavery" to new territories.[1]

Coles eagerly crafted a response to Richards's inquiry and forwarded it to the editors of the *National Intelligencer*, who published it. He tried to avoid any appearance of taking sides in the contentious presidential election by offering what he thought was an objective assessment of the political situation facing the nation. "Every friend of freedom and lover of his country," he declared, "must look with pain and mortification on the present state of parties in the United States." How could a nation "where all should cherish and prize liberty . . . and wish it extended to all nations and races of the human family," he asked, be so violently "agitated throughout its whole length and breadth, by the advocates and opponents of slavery!" He could hardly believe that so many of his fellow citizens were "willing to risk, certainly to weaken, the ties of our blessed Union, and to jepordise [sic] their own peace, if not their liberty, for the purposes of extending to the utmost limit . . . the slavery of their fellow beings."[2]

Coles blamed this state of affairs on a dramatic shift in the attitude of the nation's leaders toward slavery, a change he believed threatened to destroy the Union. During America's early years, he observed, nearly every national leader was "opposed to slavery," and freely admitted that "it was a great moral, social, and political evil." Moreover, they all shared the conviction that the institution "would soon cease to exist." To Coles's great dismay, this post-revolutionary denunciation of slavery had been replaced by a celebration of the institution. Now, he lamented, the "new partisans of slavery" sought in their speeches and actions to "glorify slavery, declare it ordained of heaven, and more to be patronized and cherished than anything in our political system." Rather than imagine a future without slavery as their predecessors had, these new leaders insisted on the perpetuation of the institution, arguing that "without [it] . . . they could not exist." For those who wondered what Jefferson would think of this transformation, Coles had a simple, unequivocal response. No "language would be sufficiently strong," he declared, "to express the disapprobation of the great apostle of liberty, were he alive to witness" the southern-born movement "to extend and perpetuate human bondage." He would be astonished by their determination "to claim it as a right, and to deny the existence of any power in Congress or elsewhere, to prevent Slavery from spreading over all the territories of this greatly extended republic."[3]

Coles believed that this transformation had emerged because the nation's leaders "are so blinded by local and partizan zeal" that they advocated the extension of slavery and demanded that the national government protect the institution even though it violates "every principle they profess." All too often public leaders proved willing to pervert the nation's ideals to serve their own political interests and to perpetuate their party's claim to power. Coles turned to the nation's history to demonstrate the truth of his claim. He reminded his audience that Jefferson and all the founders had always proclaimed equality and freedom to be "the corner stone of our political edifice." Moreover, they had enshrined these "great fundamental truths" in the Declaration of Independence, an "immortal instrument" universally cherished by all Americans. The leaders "of the new school of slavery," however, have publicly "taunted and ridiculed and pronounced" them "false and absurd." Jefferson's devoted disciple complained that they have "unblushingly denied that all men were born equal, and possessed an inherent right to liberty." Instead, these "new school politicians [have] proclaimed Slavery, and not Liberty and Equality, as the cornerstone of our free institutions."[4] Although he avoided endorsing the Free-Soil platform, as Richards had hoped, Coles offered in both tone and substance an indictment of party politics and the failure of the nation's leaders to build upon the antislavery sensibility first expressed by the nation's founders.

From Coles's perspective, the controversy over slavery and westward expansion did threaten to divide the nation, but it also provided anti-slavery nationalists with an opportunity to promote change. For years, national politicians had avoided the issue by honoring a gag rule that prevented any open discussion of slavery on the floor of Congress. Now, however, the issue was squarely before the people, and the only way to move forward was to elect a moderate leader who was inclined to rise above partisan and sectional divisions to pursue a policy that would both end slavery and preserve the Union.[5] Coles recommended, then, that Americans renew their faith in "the natural and invigorating principles of liberty." More important, he advised "every good citizen not to lend himself even indirectly to one side or the other." Residents of both sections should "refrain from violence on the subject," but southerners in particular should "reject the counsels and influences of the ultra slavery men of the new school." In his response, Coles simultaneously, if not explicitly, supported the Free-Soil platform and promoted his antislavery nationalism as a middle ground voters should eagerly endorse in the upcoming presidential election.[6]

In the fall of 1848, the American public elected General Zachary Taylor, a Whig candidate who promised to promote national harmony by returning to the nation's original principles. These promises notwithstanding, the territorial controversy that shaped the election endured beyond 1848 and marked the beginning of a decade-long struggle over the place of slavery in the American nation. Edward Coles embraced this controversy, and throughout the 1850s he repeatedly reminded politicians and the public that they had inherited an antislavery legacy that demanded decisive action on behalf of emancipation. He insisted that the founders had always intended to restrict the westward expansion of slavery and recognized in such a policy the first step in a process that would eventually lead to the total eradication of the institution. He also argued that the founders had endorsed gradual emancipation coupled with colonization as the most reasonable program for achieving this outcome. Coles, then, recognized in the chaotic and hostile political world of the 1850s an opportunity to resurrect what he understood to be the antislavery nationalism of the post-revolutionary generation and, in doing so, finally transform a slaveholding America into the free republic he insisted the founders had always intended to create.

"ultra politicians of the day"

As Zachary Taylor prepared to take office, the political crisis over how to organize the lands acquired in the Mexican-American War intensified. The newly elected president attempted to alleviate the tensions by proclaiming in his inauguration address his hope that "the enlightened patriotism" of the nation's congressional leaders would lead "that body to adopt such measures of conciliation as may harmonize the conflicting interests and tend to perpetuate . . . [the] Union." Harmony and Union, the themes of his election campaign, he instructed, would direct his administration's national policy.[7] But his efforts met with little success. When he assumed office, the Senate was in disarray as Whig party leaders competed with one another in the crisis. No fewer than three possible proposals lay before the Senate, but Henry Clay's approach was gaining support. He called for admitting California as a free state, permitting the territories of New Mexico and Utah to decide the slavery issue for themselves, prohibiting the slave trade in the District of Columbia, and strengthening the Fugitive Slave Law. In this mixture of ideas, Clay attempted to appease everyone and achieve a Union-saving compromise.[8]

As he monitored the congressional debate on the compromise measures from his home in Philadelphia, Coles wrote Clay warning that "the conduct of the ultra politicians of the day," if left unchecked, would "destroy our hallowed Union." Southern extremists objected to the idea of compromise because slavery would be excluded from California, and they continued to believe that residents of the southern portion of the territory wanted to divide the region and legalize the institution. Moderate Democrats opposed compromise because they contended that the federal government lacked the authority to legislate on the slavery issue. Coles's own brother-in-law Andrew Stevenson angrily predicted that "I should not be surprised if we have to *fight* yet for our *Property & Rights!* . . . There is a greater *evil* than *disunion*," he continued, and warned that the time would soon arrive "when *Southern men must arm & women pray to God!*" William Bigler, a Democratic Pennsylvania state senator who aspired to the governorship, thought that Congress was wasting its time haggling over the issue. He maintained, like many Democrats, that "whatever the action of Congress on the subject may be, the question of slavery in the territories will be *contested* and in the end *settled* by the people of such territories themselves." Throughout the debate, it remained unclear whether popular sovereignty or federal authority would prevail.[9]

As he had done in 1848, Coles once again entered the political fray with purpose. Along with the letter to Clay, he transcribed and dispatched a copy of James Madison's "Advice to My Country." Clay's central role in the controversy as well as his reputation for compromise made him the ideal person to contact if Coles wanted to shape the national agreement brokered in Washington, D.C. In his "Advice," Madison declared that his fondest wish was that the Union should be preserved and bequeathed to the next generation intact. Madison implored his readers to "Let the open enemy of it [the Union] be regarded as a Pandora with her box opened; and the disguised one as the Serpent rising with his deadly [venom] into Paradise." Coles understood the metaphor to imply that disunionists were an enemy that threatened to bring untold suffering to the nation, and he hoped that Clay would recognize in the serpent the partisan fanatics who offered a false devotion to the Union to disguise their real commitment to their own self-interest. The document, he informed Clay, contained sentiments that "might be used to good effect during the present diseased state of the public mind," a condition he claimed had been "brought about by political quacks & madmen."[10] Coles feared that partisan interests would not only disrupt national harmony but also prevent the nation's leaders from seizing an opportunity to resolve the slavery issue. He hoped that with the aid of Madison, Clay might prevail against Democrats, states' rights advocates, and popular sovereignty.

Coles was not alone in his assessment of the situation. Francis E. Brewster, a prominent Philadelphia Democrat, declared that "the continuance of the Union is the primary object of patriotic desire" and cautioned his readers "to distrust the patriotism of those who . . . may endeavor to weaken its bonds." Echoing Coles, he insisted that the current crisis "should not be left to party men and politicians," because "they . . . cannot be trusted." Instead, he implored his audience to "save our country" by investigating "the covenants of your national compact" for themselves. They will discover, he contended, that the Declaration of Independence proclaims equality for all men, that the Constitution does not define slaves as property, but instead, "they are called persons." Brewster also maintained that the present agitation was for naught because the "whole question was settled by the ordinance of 1787." To remind Philadelphians of their proper revolutionary heritage, another resident voiced his agreement with Coles when he asked attendees at a local Fourth of July celebration: how could it be "that slavery is 'a blessing' instead of a curse, as it was held to be by Washington, Jefferson, Madison, and most if not all of their contemporaries"?[11] Rational men who surveyed the nation's past, who investigated the place of slavery in a free society for themselves, these authors implied, could not help but conclude that the institution threatened the Union and contradicted the ideals it was founded upon.

With the help of Illinois Democrat Stephen A. Douglas, Clay's compromise measures eventually passed the Senate and seemed to resolve the crisis. Coles, however, feared that the proposals laid only a thin veneer over the slavery conflicts that had threatened the Union for nearly five years. As developments in South Carolina revealed, the compromise measures did not necessarily appease the South's most ardent defenders. Even before Congress passed the compromise, William Gilmore Simms, a poet, novelist and unflinching southern loyalist from South Carolina, declared that he had "no hope, and no faith in compromise of any kind, and am not willing to be gulled by them any longer." From his perspective, any compromise measure accepted by southerners "must originate in cowardice and a mean spirit of evasion on the part of the South." Unwilling to follow such a course of action, Simms continued to believe that "the separation" of the sections was "now inevitable." Simms's declaration was more than mere hyperbole; for in the wake of the compromise South Carolina fire-eaters called on their sister states to send delegates to a secession convention in Nashville on two occasions, first in June and then again in November. Although the delegate turnout was disappointing on each occasion, the secession movement did not collapse, and the idea of a separate southern confederacy became firmly planted in the southern imagination. Indeed, in November 1850 Simms predicted that in "five years at the utmost . . . [we] will see the dissolution of the Union," an event provoked by abolitionist northerners who "in their insolence . . . will push the South to extremes." At least among the South's most radical leaders, loyalty to the Union had been severely weakened by the territorial controversy.[12]

Coles and his fellow moderates throughout the North sought to counteract these developments immediately by organizing public meetings that celebrated Clay's compromise, the peaceful resolution of the slavery controversy, and the perpetuity of the Union. In an announcement of Philadelphia's Grand Union Meeting published in the *Pennsylvania Inquirer*, Coles and other event managers implored the residents of the city to put aside "the bitterness of party feeling." Philadelphians "who differ widely, and sometimes harshly," the sponsors proclaimed, "may now unite . . . not as Whigs or as Democrats, but as Americans." Only in this way could the residents of the city demonstrate that they "appreciate the noble legacy of liberty and free institutions bequeathed by our fathers." As Coles had claimed all along, unity and harmony among the sections would only be maintained if everyone cast aside their partisan ambitions to revive the founders' commitment to the success of the revolutionary experiment.[13]

The call for support drew thousands of Philadelphians to the grand saloon of the Chinese Museum at Ninth and Chestnut Streets. Six men who Coles dined or socialized with each week presided over the event, and he, along with Robert Tyler, Samuel Beck, Charles J. Ingersoll, and many other close friends, were among the vice presidents who stood prominently before the crowd. General George Patterson opened the event by declaring that they had gathered together to declare publicly their "respect [for] the rights of our sister States." Each of the speakers celebrated the Union and called on the residents of Pennsylvania to honor the Constitution and the laws of the nation by sustaining the compromise measures, and in particular, the new Fugitive Slave Law. They argued that by emphasizing their proslavery sympathies they could "rekindle the almost extinguished confidence and friendship of our Southern brethren" and show "that we deeply and sincerely sympathize in the sufferings and wrongs to which they have been subjected." They also pledged themselves to avoid any "further agitation of the subject of slavery which has . . . promoted neither the welfare of the slave nor the cause of emancipation and can be productive of nothing but evil." Partly because of the large population of southern-born transplants who had made the city their home after 1830, but also because so many of the city and state's political leaders harbored southern sympathies, many Philadelphians were determined to bind the nation together by supporting the compromise even if it meant protecting slavery.[14]

Coles embraced many of the positions espoused by the event's speakers. He was a devoted supporter of the Union. He agreed that they had a solemn responsibility to assume the "guardianship of Liberty and Union" and that they had "inherited an obligation to preserve them untarnished together." He had great difficulty, however, condoning a policy that perpetuated the political domination of southern fanatics and allowed slavery to persist indefinitely. Perhaps more important, he could not support his friend Josiah Randall's claim that "slavery is the subject of domestic policy, and each State, old or new, has the right to admit or exclude it, as the people . . . may determine." For Coles, the federal government possessed the authority to restrict slavery in new territories and had always held that power. When Randall insisted that "the admission or exclusion of slavery . . . rests with the people" and that "neither the Ordinance of 1787 nor the . . . Missouri" settlement affects it, Coles had to withhold his approbation, and he refused to place his name on the published proceedings. Although the slavery issue appeared to have been laid to rest, Coles saw in the Philadelphia Union Meeting clear evidence that the potentially volatile ingredients for a future conflict over slavery remained, ready to be revived at the slightest provocation.[15]

Only a minority of anti-compromise northern Whigs and Free-Soil Democrats shared Coles's fears. In the years to come, however, they would be an important disgruntled minority whose antislavery views exacerbated an already weakened party system by perpetuating increasingly sectionalized divisions among party regulars. Most Americans enthusiastically embraced the idea of compromise and the devotion to the Union embodied in the measures Congress finally finished passing in early September 1850.[16] Along with the constitutional concessions agreed to in 1787 and the Missouri Compromise of 1820, the Compromise of 1850 came to embody for them the spirit of conciliation and unity that had held the Union together throughout its existence. If nothing else, Americans hoped that by coming together in this moment of crisis they could demonstrate to the world that they possessed the ability to "sacrifice . . . local ambition, prejudices and interests . . . and exercise [the] . . . disinterested virtue" necessary to preserve the founders' great experiment in freedom and self-government. Indeed, five thousand other Philadelphians, as well as all but one of the vice presidents (Coles) and presiding officers at the Philadelphia Union Meeting, affixed their signatures to the proceedings to show their support for the spirit of compromise. They recognized, as Abraham Lincoln later declared, that on this particular occasion a "devotion to the Union rightfully inclined men to yield somewhat, in points where nothing else could have so inclined them."[17]

"to lull the blind & reckless passions of the day"

Coles knew, however, that a willingness to yield on principles was not shared by everyone. Soon after the compromise measures passed, he received a letter from his brother-in-law Richard Singleton, a wealthy South Carolina planter who had married his older sister Rebecca in 1812, alluding to the ongoing political crisis in the Palmetto State. Singleton and Coles communicated regularly about family news throughout their lives. Singleton's granddaughter attended school in Philadelphia, and Coles served as a guardian for her, paying her tuition and offering his household as a second home whenever she craved the affection of family. He also managed the affairs of Singleton's sister, a patient at a local insane asylum. Coles paid her hospital fees, visited her regularly, and reported to Singleton on her condition. Coles's niece and Singleton's favorite daughter, Angelica, lived nearby in New York with her husband (and Martin Van Buren's oldest son) Abraham Van Buren. In short, Coles served as Singleton's primary link to the members of his family who settled in the North. As was the case with his communications with all of his brothers-in-law, Coles recognized that they possessed very different political views and, as a result, he generally avoided political topics. But in January 1851, sectional tensions remained so intense that Coles could not avoid giving vent to his frustrations. He confessed that "I have lost my patience. From all I can see & learn of her proceedings," he declared "I am forced to the reluctant & painful conclusion that nothing will satisfy the *leading politicians*" of South Carolina "but the separation of the Union." In fact, he complained, "Their great grievance is the Union."[18]

Indeed, Coles was so dismayed by the persistence of such extreme views in the South that he dispatched another copy of Madison's "Advice to My Country" to the editors of the *National Intelligencer* and asked them, once again, to publish the piece.[19] In doing so, he joined a chorus of other Pennsylvanians who likewise counseled moderation. Democrat James Buchanan declared that "the Fugitive Slave law must be sustained because I believe it is right in principle & in sustaining it we sustain the Union." He lamented, however, that "in the present excited condition of the extreme Southern States, Heaven alone can predict the consequences."[20] Similarly, an anonymous Pennsylvania Whig proclaimed, "We are friends of the Union . . . loyal to the Constitution . . . and in favor of the compromise measures." Any refusal to honor them, he warned, would "rekindle the fires of discord," a development he claimed Whigs heartily wished to avoid. Unfortunately, "disaffection ... is spreading widely and rapidly" among southerners who feared the North would refuse to enforce the Fugitive Slave Law and among northerners who spied in the Compromise evidence of a slave power conspiracy. The Whig author implored his audience to remain true to their moderate view by cautioning them not to "act in such a manner as to add fuel to the flame which threatens to consume the edifice of the Union."[21] All of these men, and Coles in particular, continued to fear that neither the spirit of compromise nor a loyalty to the founders would assuage southern sectional hostilities.

So when he discovered as he read a New York newspaper that South Carolinian J. R. Poinsett was likewise attempting to establish a middle ground that would preserve the Union, Coles wanted to be sure this southerner's moderate approach was based on accurate information. Accordingly, he quickly dispatched a letter correcting Poinsett's essay to the editors of the *Philadelphia Inquirer* for publication. Poinsett had erroneously offered Illinois as proof that the fate of slavery could be decided by local authorities, claiming that the Prairie State's residents had employed the principle of popular sovereignty in their dealings with the slavery issue. Although he appreciated the South Carolinians' "patriotic efforts to lull the blind & reckless passions of the day," Coles insisted that Poinsett had misconstrued the significance of the events in Illinois. He informed Poinsett that the state legislature "had no constitutional right" to legalize slavery and declared that the institution "had been abolished ... by the Ordinance of 1787, originally drafted," he noted, "by Jefferson." Rather than an act of local authority, he argued, it was laws passed by the federal government that had ensured that Illinois would be a free state. Coles then suggested that perhaps Poinsett was confused by the efforts of a nefarious proslavery minority that had attempted to subvert the national government's prescription by calling a convention; a contest in which he had "exerted all my powers" to support the anti-convention force. "Greatly to my gratification, the people concurred with me in opinion" and sustained the Ordinance of 1787 by rejecting the legalization of slavery. In the example of Illinois, then, Coles hoped the nation would recognize the legitimate authority of the federal government to regulate slavery in western territories, as well as the peoples' confirmation of that power.[22]

Coles also reminded Poinsett and the newspapers' readers of the founder's antislavery sensibilities. Although he recognized that his opposition to slavery "is not popular in your state," Coles informed Poinsett that "such was the opinion of Washington, Jefferson, Madison, & all the great & good men of my native State of Virginia, without a single exception." The current state of affairs, he was sure, "has been produced by political considerations . . . and will be of short duration." Quoting Jefferson's prophecy "that 'the hour of emancipation is advancing in the march of time,'" Coles predicted "that the time is not very remote when the people will see the propriety of . . . getting rid of slavery."[23]

Poinsett, who was decidedly opposed to southern extremism, responded by informing Coles that he had invoked the events in Illinois to demonstrate "that a majority of the people of [the] Sovereign State of California possessed the power and might exercise it under the Constitution to introduce slavery." For him, the moderate approach to resolving the slavery problem lay somewhere between Coles's antislavery nationalism and southern demands for secession. He advocated the doctrine of popular sovereignty, hoping the middle course first advocated by Lewis Cass, sustained by Clay and Webster in some of the compromise measures, and increasingly articulated by Stephen A. Douglas, would help extinguish the passions exhibited by leaders on both sides of the controversy. This was precisely what alarmed Coles about Poinsett's publication, for he recognized in the South Carolinian's effort an attempt to divest popular sovereignty and federal nonintervention of its proslavery quality. Yet, as Coles knew all too well, proslavery southerners and congressmen had consistently offered nonintervention to challenge the antislavery Northwest Ordinance of 1787, and whenever territories retained the possibility of allowing slavery, emigrants arrived with slaves and secured the region's slave status. Coles would have nothing of it.[24] The only moderate plan he could accept had to guarantee the containment of slavery.

"to correct an error"

When another member of Congress misappropriated the Northwest Ordinance of 1787 again two years later, Coles was quick to offer another correction. In a speech honoring his predecessor, Robert Rantoul, Jr., Massachusetts senator Charles Sumner had inaccurately credited Massachusetts native Nathan Dane with the authorship of the Northwest Ordinance of 1787. Coles immediately recognized in the moment an opportunity to remind the antislavery freshman senator, and the nation as a whole, of America's cross-sectional antislavery past.[25] Identifying himself as "the friend of Mr. Jefferson," Coles wrote to the senator from Massachusetts "to correct an error . . . by which you take from him [Jefferson], & give to another, one of the noblest & most consistent acts of his life," the authorship of the Northwest Ordinance of 1787. Although he admitted that Jefferson was in France at the time of the Ordinance's final passage, Coles maintained that the final instrument "retained . . . in the identical words used by Mr. Jefferson" the language prohibiting the extension of slavery into the new territories. Accordingly, Jefferson, not Nathan Dane, was the true author of the clause prohibiting slavery in the region north of the Ohio River. "However zealous & influential he [Dane] may have been in effecting the final passage" of the Ordinance, Coles assured Sumner that "it gives him no claim to the Authorship . . . & certainly no credit for the applauded clause . . . which, in the words of Jefferson, . . . provided for the prohibition of slaves in all Territory" in the Old Northwest. Coles closed the letter expressing the hope that "you will properly appreciate my motives for troubling you with this letter" and implored Sumner to "correct [the] mistake . . . in a manner equally public as it was made."[26]

At first glance, Coles's decision to call the senator's attention to this alleged mistake could be described as an effort to promote his own fame through his personal ties to Jefferson. It could also be offered as evidence of an overzealous devotion to the memory of the Sage of Monticello. It might likewise be characterized as a misguided attempt to glorify the South generally or more particularly his native state of Virginia, whose national reputation and prominence had greatly diminished since the Old Dominion last controlled the presidency. Yet, Coles's motives were much more disinterested and national than these explanations allow; for the same motivation that had animated his public antislavery activities since the 1820s likewise compelled him to rectify Sumner's public statement. As had been the case throughout his public career, Coles strove to promote a brand of antislavery nationalism grounded in the idea that all of the founders, northern and southern alike, shared an opposition to slavery. Moreover, he had consistently maintained that the Ordinance of 1787 confirmed their desire to see the institution eventually disappear from the American landscape, as well as the federal government's right to regulate slavery in the territories. Such a view had been silenced during the 1830s and 1840s, a victim of the gag rule in Congress and the prominence of a more radical and vociferous abolition movement. But, to his great delight, Coles and those who shared his vision had successfully resurrected his antislavery nationalism during the Mexican-American

War. He was not going to allow Sumner's seemingly insignificant statement misrepresenting the true origins of the Ordinance undermine the delicate middle ground he had been working his whole life to sustain, a middle ground that offered federal authority to regulate slavery as an alternative to both unimpeded expansion of the institution and immediate abolition.

In his letter to Sumner, and through the correction he hoped to elicit, Coles also sought to defend Jefferson's authorship because doing so reinforced the antislavery reputation of the founding generation. Long the central component of Coles's antislavery nationalism, the Ordinance of 1787 reflected the antislavery heritage Coles hoped to see fulfilled. He thought it was equally, if not more, important that Jefferson be understood as the author of the document because he was a southern slaveholder. In the climate of the 1850s, Coles hoped that Jefferson's southern identity would prove that many of the region's most prominent leaders had long opposed slavery. If southern leaders had done so in the past, Coles seemed to be saying, so too could they in the present and future. As far as Coles was concerned, Jefferson's status as the author of the antislavery clause in the Northwest Ordinance of 1787 was important for both national and sectional reasons. It was evidence that the founders intended their republic to be a nation without slavery, and it established the role of the federal government in achieving that goal. It also demonstrated that a southern slaveholder could possess an antislavery sensibility and, even if only in a limited way, work to oppose the expansion of the institution. In other words, Coles argued that a southern identity need not be synonymous with the radical proslavery perspective seeking to dominate the public discussion of the issue after 1830. A southerner could oppose slavery, and in doing so they would be following in the footsteps of one of the region's most renowned public leaders.

Sumner's response to Coles's letter could not have been more disappointing. Sumner assured Coles that he "would not take from this great patriot one of his many titles of regard." While he certainly recognized that Jefferson was responsible for "the early though unsuccessful effort" to prohibit slavery, he insisted, however, that ample proof existed demonstrating "that the Ordinance of 1787, as finally adopted, was from the pen of Nathan Dane." Should Coles doubt his claim, he offered Dane's own testimony in "his great work on American Law, published in 1824" as evidence. He also cited Daniel Webster's defense of Dane "in his remarkable reply to Mr. Hayne" in 1830. In his speech, Sumner declared, Webster argued convincingly that "it is no derogation from the credit" due

Dane "that its principles had before been prepared and discussed." As far as Sumner was concerned, the "question had already been" settled. "To Jefferson belongs the honor of the first effort to prohibit Slavery in the Territories," concluded Sumner, and "to Dane belongs the honor of finally embodying this Prohibition in the Ordinance drawn by his hand in 1787."[27]

Coles's dissatisfaction with this reply reflected the unavoidable conclusion that Sumner did not share his nationalist antislavery vision as much as it resulted from the senator's failure to acknowledge that his own view of the past was incorrect. From Coles's perspective, he and Sumner should have had a great deal in common when it came to the slavery issue. They shared, for example, a similar antislavery sensibility. They held in common the Whig view that slavery was a sin and morally wrong, and they both regretted their party's frequent decision to compromise their antislavery ideals to retain southern support and secure political success on the national stage. They agreed, as well, that the more radical abolitionist demand for immediate abolition was untenable. Instead, they both claimed to advocate a more moderate approach, a view that conceded that slavery was a product of "the *local* laws of each State," but also "a *national* evil, for which . . . the *nation* and all its parts are responsible." Accordingly, they displayed a mutual determination to prevent the westward expansion of the institution, but to do so in a way that preserved the Union and left unprovoked the more extreme elements of both sections. Coles recognized in Sumner a potentially powerful voice in Congress for his antislavery nationalism. But the senator's determination to emphasize the northern origins of the post-revolutionary antislavery sensibility was sure to alienate most southerners and, thereby, undermine the national character of their antislavery vision. Coles believed Sumner was squandering an opportunity to highlight the southern role in constructing the nation's antislavery legacy, because as Coles had learned in Illinois, opposition to the extension of slavery would remain ineffective without southern support.[28]

"the truth of history"

Determined to combat Sumner's sectionalism and sustain the national character of his antislavery nationalism, Coles spent most of the fall of 1852 researching and writing an article designed to prove that the southern-born Thomas Jefferson was the original author of the antislavery provision of the Northwest Ordinance of 1787. In late December, he

FIGURE 7.1. Portrait of Edward Coles, 1852, by John Henry Brown. (Courtesy of Winterthur Museum.)

submitted to the editors of the *National Intelligencer* an essay entitled, "Who was the Author of the Ordinance of 1787?," which they published in the January 4, 1853, issue of the paper. After citing Sumner's evidence specifically, Coles explained that "the truth of history" required that he correctly state the facts so that "credit [is] given to whom credit is justly due." Coles, however, published the essay for more than historical accuracy. Even more important for him was the influence the document might exert in the present political crisis over slavery. He argued that Jefferson's authorship had to be sustained, because failing to do so "would diminish . . . [the] weight and influence" of the Ordinance. Perhaps most important, "as a Southern man" Jefferson's authorship would bestow on the Ordinance "an influence . . . where it is chiefly wanted," among southerners. Additionally, as a slaveholder, Jefferson's objections to the extension of the institution gained credibility and authority in the South. For, unlike Dane, Jefferson knew from firsthand experience the cultural and economic cost of his dependence on slave labor. Together, Jefferson's reputation as "one of the most distinguished political founders of liberty" as well as his status as a southern slaveholder imbued the Ordinance with the power to deliver "the national blow" to slavery the author had intended.[29]

Coles then proceeded to demonstrate, using the *Journals of Congress*, that "the ordinance, conceived, draughted [*sic*], and introduced by Mr. Jefferson, was the instrument that ultimately became . . . the great fundamental statute" for the region north of the Ohio River. As had been the case in August 1852, Coles's near obsession with Jefferson's authorship sprang from his lifelong desire the see slavery eradicated. As early as 1814, when he wrote Jefferson soliciting his aid on behalf of emancipation, Coles confessed his belief that slavery could be destroyed most effectively and peacefully by the nation's founders. Although he greatly regretted his mentor's failure to heed his call, Coles enthusiastically assumed the role of an oracle, proclaiming the antislavery will of the nation's founding fathers. He did so by consistently emphasizing that "the sound political orthodoxy of the ordinance . . . was the work of a preeminently enlightened and distinguished *Southern* statesman," a man revered in "every part of the country."[30] In this essay, Coles attempted to accomplish the correction Sumner refused to provide, and in the process, preserve for the South a claim to the post-revolutionary antislavery sensibility that was the centerpiece of his antislavery nationalism.

Within a week of the publication of the essay, Coles received a complimentary note from Martin Van Buren, the 1848 Free-Soil Party presidential candidate and father-in-law of Coles's niece. The ex-president and reformed antislavery politician wrote to inform Coles of "the satisfaction" he felt upon reading the essay. "Is it not painful to see," he lamented, the "unequalled political merits of the great Father of American Democracy are not only unnoticed, but constantly & clandestinely deprecated." In his response, Coles likewise complained of "the want of attachment and veneration for the memory of their great founders." Worse still, grumbled Coles, were the actions of the "Calhoun school of politicians," who claim to be disciples of "the Jefferson school," yet "denounce him" by "proclaim[ing] as a fundamental creed . . . the revolting doctrine that Slavery is a blessing, and Freedom, unaccompanied by slavery, a curse." Coles also received a letter from his old college friend, Virginia native and fellow Whig Joseph C. Cabell. He thanked Cabell for the "flattering commendation of my publication," and confessed that his "approbation" was even more satisfying because of the nearly universal condemnation he had received from many "of my Southern friends," who complained that "it did not add to the reputation of Mr. Jefferson to prove he was the originator" of the Ordinance and its antislavery provision.[31] Coles should have seen in the more general southern response a warning that his nationalism was far more sectional than he allowed. But, as had been the case throughout his life, he charged ahead hoping that his opponents would cast aside their self-interest and partisan loyalties and embrace his more principled approach.

Published in the early 1850s, Coles's essay appeared when most Americans preferred to believe the slavery issue had been made irrelevant by the Compromise of 1850. As the Coles-Sumner exchange revealed, however, the place of slavery in the nation and the legacy of the founders remained contested terrain. To be sure, on the surface, the sectional controversy of the early 1850s was about whether or not slavery should remain part of the nation. But, more deeply for Coles and many antislavery nationalists, the public discussion of slavery was really a battle over the construction of an acceptable and effective middle ground, a middle ground Coles insisted should include the antislavery legacy of the founding generation. On one side of the contest was Coles, and eventually Lincoln's Republican followers, who believed that the federal government possessed the authority to limit the expansion of slavery. These antislavery nationalists also insisted that the principles of equality and liberty proclaimed by Jefferson in the Declaration of Independence were the foundation of American political society and should be applied generally to everyone. Moreover, they insisted that the founding generation had always opposed slavery, recognizing it as a social and moral evil that should not be allowed to spread westward. Although these forefathers had recognized that any public discussion of the issue threatened the Union during their lifetime, they had faith that the contradiction between slavery and democracy could be eventually resolved peacefully.[32]

On the other side of the conflict were men like Jefferson Davis, James Henry Hammond, and Edmund Ruffin, who claimed that the fate of slavery in the western territories should be determined by the residents themselves. They also insisted that slavery was the foundation of American liberty and freedom, denying that the institution was a moral or political evil and instead celebrating it as good for the slave and the master. Moreover, these men declared that any obstacle preventing slaveholders from carrying their enslaved property into new territories violated their inherent property rights as protected by the Constitution, and they were willing to sacrifice the Union to sustain them. Coles envisioned a revolutionary legacy that celebrated universal equality and freedom, while his opponents imagined an inheritance that championed property and individual rights. One vision demanded the gradual elimination of slavery while the other insisted on its perpetuation. By 1853, the moderate middle ground Coles had been trying to sustain had become contested terrain. The political controversies of the 1850s that culminated in the election of Abraham Lincoln and the secession crisis soon thereafter, then, were really a series of contests over the meaning of American nationalism, a nationalism that would become associated exclusively with the North.[33]

"a most ridiculous and false delusion"

The apparent consensus on the slavery issue exhibited during the immediate aftermath of the Compromise of 1850 began to fade in 1854, when Illinois senator Stephen A. Douglas introduced before Congress a bill to organize the Nebraska territory that rekindled the public conflict over slavery. At the heart of the controversy was Douglas's perceived capitulation to southern members of Congress to gain support for his measure. He had revised his original proposal to adopt the idea of popular sovereignty (a doctrine he supported in principle), but many southern leaders still refused to favor it unless he included an explicit repeal of the Missouri Compromise, the 1820 law that established the 36°30' parallel as the line above which slavery could not exist. Anticipating northern outrage over his decision to appease the South, he split the region into two territories, Kansas and Nebraska. In this way, he attempted to mimic the precedent established by the Compromise of 1850. He intended to offer a measure that contained something for everyone and that he hoped could generate the consensus necessary to pass through Congress. The measure immediately provoked a firestorm of opposition that spread throughout the nation, severely undermined the fragile sense of unity and harmony that had emerged a few years earlier, and reignited the debate over the nation's identity.[34]

Several senators publicly rebuked Douglas in an open appeal published in the *National Era* on January 19, 1854. Salmon P. Chase, an antislavery senator from Ohio, crafted a document designed to warn the nation's elected officials as well as its residents of an "imminent danger" that threatened "the freedom of our institutions" and the "permanency of the Union." Echoing Coles's antislavery nationalism, he claimed that Douglas's Nebraska bill represented a "gross violation of a sacred pledge" made by the founders to reserve the "vast unoccupied region" for "free laborers" because failing to do so would "convert it into a dreary region of despotism, inhabited by masters and slaves." Citing Jefferson's Ordinance of 1787, Chase and the other signees, which included Charles Sumner, Joshua R. Giddings, Edward Wade, Gerrit Smith, and Alexander DeWitt, maintained that the "sound policy and sacred faith" of the founders had always promoted the "non-extension of slavery." The Nebraska bill violated this policy and also repealed the Missouri Compromise of 1820, a "compact . . . universally regarded . . . as inviolable American law." This action, they insisted, threatened to destroy the Union by allowing "slavery in all the yet unorganized territory." From Chase's perspective, the threat to the Union was not an impending civil war or disunion, but instead the destruction of the nation's core principles of liberty and equality. "The Union was formed to establish justice and secure the blessings of liberty. When it fails to accomplish these ends," he concluded, "it will be worthless, and when it becomes worthless it cannot long endure." For these men, as well as for many Americans, the meaning of American nationhood was at stake.[35]

Outraged by the attack, Douglas defended the Nebraska bill by claiming that it comported more fully with the revolutionary ideal of self-governance than any previous legislation on the slavery issue. He denied "the assumption that the policy of the fathers of the republic was to prohibit slavery in all the territory ceded by the old States." Although he conceded that the Northwest Ordinance of 1787 excluded slavery from the region north of the Ohio River, Douglas maintained that it "permitted and protected" slavery in the region south of the river. "The only conclusion that can be fairly and honestly drawn," Douglas declared, was that the founders intended "to prescribe a line of demarcation between free . . . and slaveholding territories." The Missouri Compromise, he maintained, continued this precedent, by confirming, if at the same time slightly redefining, the boundary between slave and free territory. As he understood the nation's legislative past, then, a dividing line and not nonextension was the true legacy of the founding generation when it came to slavery and the territories.[36]

He also insisted that he had not repealed the Missouri Compromise. Instead, those who supported the Wilmot Proviso and thereby provoked the need for the Compromise of 1850 had replaced the idea of a geographic boundary with the idea of "congressional non-intervention" and recognized "that the people of the Territories . . . were to be allowed to do as they pleased upon the subject of slavery." Accordingly, the principle of popular sovereignty advanced in the Nebraska bill conformed to the most recent treatment of the slavery issue. Even if his audience disagreed with his assessment of the nation's legislative history, he insisted that his new program was justified because all previous congressional instruction on the issue had been wholly ineffective. To prove his claim, he cited the case of Illinois, where slavery was "prohibited . . . by law" but persisted "in fact." According to Douglas, wherever the national government attempted to restrict slavery, the institution expanded "because the people there regarded" any federal instruction as a "usurpation on the part of the federal government." Only when liberated from the authority of the national government, argued Douglas, did Illinoisans reject slavery and "of their own free will and accord," construct and implement "a system of emancipation." Far from violating the nation's sacred political principles, Douglas insisted that his proposal sustained the ideal of democratic self-governance by entrusting "the people with the great, sacred, fundamental right of prescribing their own institutions."[37]

Sixty-eight-year-old Coles joined the growing number of individuals who voiced their opposition to the Nebraska bill. After reading Douglas's speech in the *National Intelligencer,* he immediately penned an open letter to the Democratic senator from Illinois expressing his shock and surprise that such a gross misrepresentation of both the founders' views and events in early Illinois history could come from such a "high source." From his perspective, Douglas's claim that his doctrine of popular sovereignty represented a moderate approach to the territorial issue was dubious at best. The precedent had been set long ago and consistently sustained throughout the nation's history that moderation required the continued support for federal prevention of extension. If Douglas's claim that the founders never intended to prevent the westward extension of slavery were true, Coles caustically assured his readers, then "our greatest men and highest functionaries have been for seventy years under a most ridiculous and false delusion." Here Coles referred to both the Northwest Ordinance of 1787 and the Missouri Compromise. The latter, in Coles's view, was "an act by Congress" that "prohibit[ed] slavery" in all of "the new territory" north of the 36°30' parallel. If the Illinois Senator's assertion that "the want of power in Congress to pass" such prohibitions was true, asked Coles, then imagine "how much time and excitement would have been saved!"[38]

Perhaps most important, Coles knew from personal experience that Douglas's representation of Illinois history was inaccurate. Far from a state that consciously repudiated the slavery restriction in the Ordinance of 1787, Illinois had adopted almost verbatim the prohibitory language of that document in its constitution. Although some faint remnants of slavery remained in the state, Coles insisted that such was the case not from an absence of law, but because of the lack of vigilance on the part of federal and state authorities. The truth of the matter was, he concluded, that the Ordinance of 1787 implied that the last vestiges of slavery in the region "should be abolished." From Coles's perspective, few should doubt either "the validity" or the effectiveness "of the ordinance." Far from demonstrating the limits of federal authority, Illinois (and the entire Old Northwest for that matter) proved that the founders intended to contain slavery, and that only through such prohibitions could the principles of freedom and equality be extended to all the nation's citizens.[39]

At stake here for Coles were the essential elements of the middle ground in a contentious political terrain. Douglas sought to occupy familiar territory. He crafted legislation that harkened back to the compromises of the past. Like the Missouri Compromise of 1820, his proposal preserved the balance of power in Congress by admitting one slave and one free state. Like the Compromise of 1850, he also sustained the practice of local self-determination, and he included provisions that would make everyone happy. Northerners and southerners alike could be reassured that slavery would persist and the balance of power would remain intact. For Coles and other antislavery nationalists, however, this middle ground had lost its appeal. In the new environment of the 1850s, they insisted, the place of slavery in the Union was increasingly challenged, and more and more Americans agreed that the institution was incompatible with the nation's revolutionary legacy. Accordingly, the new middle ground offered by Coles was one in which slavery would gradually and through the auspices of federal policy disappear from the American landscape. Containment was the first step in this process, and to achieve this antislavery goal moderate leadership was needed.

"the most virtuous, calm & amiable of men"

When he received an inquiry from Hugh Blair Grigsby, an old Virginia friend who was writing a history of the founding era, in December 1854, Coles welcomed the opportunity to present the founders as an example of moderate antislavery leadership. Grigsby was an ardent Democrat who despised the Whig Party and the sectional character of the emerging Republican Party. Yet, as had always been the case for Coles, personal ties forged during multiple social engagements and a shared determination to promote political moderation in a partisan climate eclipsed their political differences.[40] Coles enthusiastically responded with a long letter narrating the events of the late 1770s as he knew them "from the lips of Jefferson, Madison, Monroe, [and] the 2 Adams." Coles proceeded to describe James Madison as the ideal statesman, a leader who was both moderate in his temperament and politics and antislavery. He described his mentor as "the most virtuous, calm & amiable of men; possessed of one of the purest hearts & best tempers with which man was ever blessed. Nothing," he concluded, "could excite or ruffle him." In contrast to the political leaders of their time, Madison "was always cool collected, & self-possessed. . . . He looked upon all the troubles & disasters, passion & prejudice as temporary & that triumph was certain." Whenever confronted with the passions of partisan conflict, Coles recalled, the fourth president relied on his "confidence in . . . the intelligence & virtue of his Fellow Citizens." By relying on the good sense of the people, Coles's Madison remained confident that "his deluded countrymen would see their error[s]" and change course. The lesson for the nation's political leaders, Coles seemed to be saying, was to confront the passions of the day and the sectional divisions emerging everywhere with calmness and moderation, for doing so would ensure the survival of the Union.[41]

Although Grigsby had not inquired after Madison's views on slavery, Coles also included in his letter an extended section describing Madison's "wish to provide in his will for the emancipation of his slaves at the death of his wife." Like his Jefferson, Coles's Madison had always opposed slavery, but had worried that delaying emancipation until his wife's death might endanger her welfare. As a result, according to Coles, he omitted the emancipatory provision from his will and had relied on her to implement his wishes. That his final wishes were never realized, he declared, reflected the inaction of his wife and not the limits of Madison's antislavery commitment. Clearly, Coles intended Grigsby to conclude that Madison was committed to liberating his enslaved property, and he hoped that any history of the Revolutionary era would project forward the antislavery sensibilities of the father of the Constitution.[42]

For Coles, the founders' intentions regarding slavery more than their actions were important. As he had learned in his moral philosophy courses at the College of William and Mary more than fifty years before, human frailty often prevented individuals from enacting their principles. He had also witnessed this firsthand. Both of his mentors, Jefferson and Madison, had failed to follow through with their commitment to freedom and equality by liberating their enslaved property. Similarly, state leaders in both Illinois and Virginia had refused to enact laws reflecting growing popular opposition to slavery. During the 1830s, the nation's leaders refused to address the issue even as petitions arrived on the floor of Congress demanding that they do so. On every occasion, the actions of public leaders bitterly disappointed him. For Coles, however, these failures hardly negated the intrinsic value of pursuing the principles they neglected to fulfill. He hoped others would do more than these past leaders had done by translating principle into practice.

In Madison's case, however, Coles was incapable of accepting the limits of his mentor's antislavery sensibility. In fact, he was so determined to prove that his understanding of Madison was correct that he desperately clung to even the slimmest of circumstantial evidence to sustain his claims. In December 1855, he wrote a letter to Nellie Willis "to enquire what you know, or have good reason to believe, was your Uncle Madison's wishes and intentions as to freeing his Slaves, and the reason why he did not do it in his Will." Her son John responded confirming that "it was strongly his [Madison's] wish to emancipate" his bound laborers and that he had not freed them in his will because he expected his wife, Dolley Madison, "would emancipate them at her death." Furthermore, his mother recalled that Madison had left written instructions on the subject. On the day of his burial, John revealed, his mother witnessed Dolley Madison retrieve "from a drawer two sealed papers," one containing Madison's will and the other addressed to her. Apparently, the latter, "which nothing more was ever seen of" again, was thought to have contained written directions regarding his human property. Coles's investigations, then, confirmed that Madison had intended to liberate his slaves and had failed to do so, not because of any hesitation on his own part but because his wife had neglected to honor his wishes. As far as Coles was concerned, this at best anecdotal evidence demonstrated that James Madison had consistently expressed his opposition to slavery and preserved his mentor's reputation as an antislavery statesman.[43]

Two years later, William Cabell Rives contacted Coles for information on Madison for the biography he was preparing. Coles immediately dispatched a copy of John Willis's December 1855 letter suggesting the existence of a codicil to the late president's will emancipating his slaves. Furthermore, Coles felt that, as his biographer, Rives had a special obligation to present the fullest portrait of his subject. "However painful it may be to you to make such a disclosure, or encounter for a time the prejudice which may be created in certain quarters against you, for stating the fact of Mr. Madison's intentions to free his slaves," Coles assured his correspondent that the censure "by posterity" he would endure for "omit[ting] to mention so important a fact" would be even more painful. Coles already had to correct a mistake made by his fellow Philadelphian Charles J. Ingersoll, who had claimed that Madison had concluded "his slaves [were] unprofitable, [and] directed by his last Will that they be sold." He suggested to Rives that his biography, if it contained a true representation of Madison's "feelings & principles," could prevent such misrepresentations from appearing during this period of "fever[ed] . . . partisanship."[44] Even more important, by sustaining Madison's antislavery credentials, Rives would remind the public that even the most moderate of statesmen expected the nation to eventually be free of slavery.

"the endearing ties of blood"

Although the nation's political troubles occupied a great deal of his time, Coles remained equally involved in the ordinary affairs of his family. Although he frequently complained about his own well-being, Coles's wife and children were the picture of health. All three of his children attended schools in their neighborhood, and he boasted regularly that they were "nearly all the time at the head of their respective classes." They studied Latin, French, as well as the other standard subjects. He had also hired a music and dance teacher who came to their house to instruct his children and several other boys and girls from the neighborhood. At midcentury, Mary was fifteen and had grown into a beautiful young women who was a devoted companion to her mother. Edward, Jr. and

Roberts were thirteen and twelve, respectively, and accompanied their father everywhere he went in the city. His home was a bustling jumble of children and activities that kept him very content. As his abundant surviving correspondence reveals, he also communicated regularly with his extended family in Virginia and South Carolina. Indeed, they exchanged so much family news and commentary on their mutual friends and neighbors that the correspondence nearly erased the geographic distance that separated them from one another.[45]

The Coles clan also maintained their familial bonds by traveling to visit one another regularly. In the summer of 1847, for example, the Coles family enjoyed an informal reunion of sorts at White Sulphur Springs, Virginia. Coles took his family away from Philadelphia every summer to escape the heat and disease associated with city life. Normally they journeyed to Schooley's Mountain, New Jersey, or Saratoga Springs, New York, the favorite summertime resorts of Philadelphia's elite residents. But, he also occasionally took his family south to renew their attachments to his extended family. As he reported to his brother-in-law Richard Singleton, his children were counting "the days of their departure for Va—preferring a visit to their Uncles to a trip to any other place." During this southern trip, they reconnected with his "Brother Walters Daughters & their families from Carolina" as well as the extended Singleton family. Several Singleton children had returned to Virginia from Missouri and Ohio for the gathering. He also stopped in Albemarle County, where he intended to "make our friends there a visit for several weeks." During this part of the journey, they enjoyed the company of his brother Tucker and his sisters Sally, Emily, and Betsy and their families. He took his family south again in 1852, 1855, and 1858 for extended visits that took him to each of his brother's estates in Albemarle County and to see the Rutherfoords in Richmond.[46]

His siblings and their families also regularly visited him in Philadelphia. His niece Isaetta, Isaac's daughter, stayed with him for a month in 1848 and occupied her time with singing lessons and sightseeing. Many of them even accompanied Coles to his northern summer retreats. Tucker and Helen as well as several of his nephews traveled to Niagara Falls and Saratoga Springs in 1848. In 1851, his brother John's widow Selina Skipwith Coles brought her son Peyton to Philadelphia. Similarly, Tucker and Helen visited regularly, as did Andrew Stevenson. Coles encouraged his nephew John Coles Rutherfoord to bring his new wife north on a honeymoon "ramble" in December 1856.[47] As had been the case when he was a young man, all the members of the Coles family remained very close to one another. His affection for his extended family and their affection for him remained unimpaired by his political views as well as his opposition to slavery. Indeed, they had been remarkably successful at keeping their political and private worlds separate.

Yet, in an increasingly contentious political climate, Coles found it hard to maintain this separation. In the spring of 1856, Coles confessed to his nephew John Coles Rutherfoord, a delegate in the Virginia legislature since 1853, that "my heart is painfully burthened" by a recent turn of events in the winter legislative session of his native state. Over the previous year, Pennsylvania and Virginia had become locked in a political battle over a fugitive slave case. Jake Green, a slave from the northwestern part of Virginia had escaped into Pennsylvania, only to be successfully pursued by his owner, Colonel Isaac Parsons and his nephew, James Parsons, Jr. The nephew apprehended Green on a train to Pittsburgh, but a crowd formed and in the confusion that followed, Green escaped and the younger Parsons was arrested for kidnapping. To Coles's "pain & mortification," the Virginia legislature passed a series of resolutions demanding the return of Parsons and, in retaliation for the perceived insult, authorizing the governor to arrest any Pennsylvanians who dared to travel through the Old Dominion and confiscate their property.[48]

For Coles, Virginia's response, and particularly his nephew's "eagerness" to facilitate the passage of so offensive and unjust an act, was disturbing because he "considered [it] to be a frivolous ground to make war upon," especially when such a move threatened "to put an end to the Union." Virginia's actions were particularly "unkind and offensive," insisted Coles, because "Pennsylvania, though entertaining different feelings and principles on the subject of slavery has uniformly stood by Virginia." Although he recognized that the current political climate might account for the heightened political tensions, Coles was especially upset that his nephew's familial connections had not influenced his actions. Ever since his decision to settle in Philadelphia in 1834, Coles had painstakingly cultivated cross-sectional social and familial ties he hoped would reinforce the patriotic bonds of Union. He was greatly disappointed, then, when "the endearing ties of blood" had failed to restrain his nephew's "zeal if not your vote for a law to imprison your fair Cousin," who would depart for a visit in Virginia in a few weeks.[49]

Coles was also disappointed because the episode exposed the ineffectiveness of the politics of moderation. For much of the 1850s, Coles had struggled to forge a middle ground and convince the public to reject the extremists in both sections. Only by pursuing the politics of moderation, Coles had insisted, could the Union be preserved and the antislavery legacy of the founders be fulfilled. In Virginia's response to the Parsons case, however, Coles recognized an event that would only sustain the perspectives of the nation's extremists. "The Nullifiers and their allies the Abolitionists, in the war they are now carrying on against the Union," complained Coles, "will be much cheered & encouraged by the late proceedings of the House of Delegates of the . . . influential state of VA." Even moderate men in the North would be hard pressed, he cautioned, to dismiss Virginia's actions as unimportant. "You may rely upon it," he insisted, "your late proceedings will be counted as evidence of the violent and provoking hostility of the South against the North and as a provocative of disunion." The failure to pursue a more moderate course, and the passionately extreme politics of his nephew, Coles chided, had done nothing to stem the tide of disunion.[50]

Perhaps most dispiriting for Coles was how the event contributed to the growing sectionalization and diminishing power of his antislavery nationalism. As his nephew knew all too well, Coles had vigorously and openly argued that "Washington, Henry, Jefferson, Madison, and all the great men of their day" had opposed "the extension and perpetuation of Slavery." During a visit with the younger Rutherfoord in 1855, Coles had regaled him with tales of his experiences with these men, detailing the founders' views on a wide range of topics. But his nephew seemed to have ignored the central lesson of his storytelling. For his generation, Coles feared, the founders' perspective, once celebrated and revered, had been transformed into a quality that made even the mildest of antislavery men "unfit for any public trust." Coles admonished his errant nephew that "If Jefferson were now living, his opinions on Slavery would have prevent[ed] his election . . . to any office in the South. Should not this," declared Coles, "make you Southern men more forebearing [sic], and less given to follow the example of your intolerant opponents?" Coles maintained that by behaving in such a provocative way, Rutherfoord and the Virginia legislature had weakened the very heart of antislavery nationalism and exacerbated the already intense sectional tensions threatening the Union. "I have but a little time to remain in this world," concluded the seventy-year-old Coles, "but the pleasures of the remnant will be greatly lessened by the mortification produced . . . when I contemplate the horrors of civil war attendant on the dissolution of our blessed Union."[51]

Coles had only to pause and consider the political divisions in his own family to see the limits of the middle ground he sought to promote. No one in his family shared his antislavery nationalism or his approach to the politics of the day. Each of his brothers-in law had, like him, become increasingly alarmed by the events of the 1850s. But unlike Coles, they came to embrace more fully the southern states' rights approach to the slavery problem. The only brother who had a chance of agreeing with him was Isaac, but his early death in 1841 had robbed Coles of his only Whig ally in the family. Moreover, it was unlikely that even had he lived into the 1850s, Isaac would have shared Coles's antislavery nationalism, for he remained a slaveholder throughout his life and never expressed any reservations about the system. Indeed, he had followed his younger brother westward in search of economic opportunity in 1819, but had avoided free territory and chosen to transplant some of his slaves and establish a plantation in the slave state of Missouri. The bonds of family affection, then, were not enough to gain converts to his antislavery nationalism. If he could not count on his family to see the wisdom of his vision, the prospect of the nation's leaders heeding his call seemed unlikely.

"a curtailment of slave territory"

Undaunted, Coles redoubled his efforts to promote the central components of his antislavery nationalism. In early June 1856, Coles delivered a speech at the Pennsylvania Historical Society before an audience of many of Philadelphia's most prominent residents and his close friends. As had become the custom in the city's elite social circles, these intellectual and cultural events offered the participants a way to engage in politics without becoming directly involved in partisan skirmishes. Coles, who had become particularly adept at using these kinds of events to achieve broader political goals, used the occasion to launch a vigorous defense of the antislavery character of the founding generation. He claimed again that the Ordinance of 1787 proved the anti-slavery and anti-extension credentials of the founding generation, and he argued that Jefferson expected this law to abolish slavery and prevent the further introduction of bound laborers into all the western territories.[52]

In case anyone should doubt the truth of his assessment of the past, Coles demonstrated that Congress and the American people had repeatedly sustained the antislavery provisions of the law. When petitions requesting a repeal of the antislavery clause arrived in Congress, the nation's political leaders consistently refused to honor their requests. "To these applications," Coles reported, "Congress uniformly and decidedly refused its assent, and sustained the prohibitory clause of the Ordinance." In Illinois, where a small group of designing partisans attempted to subvert the Ordinance by revising the state constitution so as to legalize the institution, the Ordinance was "sustained by a major- ity . . . of the people . . . thus terminat[ing] the last struggle . . . to defeat the wise and philanthropic purposes of the Ordinance of 1787." All of these actions, declared Coles, confirmed that the law had been intended to result in "a curtailment of slave territory—in fact, its actual abolition" in the region.[53]

Coles also supported his claim by reciting for his listeners a long list of legislation that confirmed the uninterrupted application of the revo- lutionary generation's opposition to slavery and its extension westward. Over and over again, Congressional leaders had turned to the antislavery provision of the Ordinance as a resource as they sought to absorb new states into the Union. Indeed, the anti-slavery article became a template for all subsequent legislation. In 1820, as legislators crafted the Missouri Compromise, they adopted the same language, declaring that in the region north of the 36°30' latitude "slavery and involuntary servitude, otherwise than in punishment of crimes . . . is hereby forever prohib- ited." Fifteen years later, the congressional resolution annexing Texas likewise contained language first written in the Ordinance. The enabling legislation for the Oregon Territory confirmed the nation's commitment to the principles of the Ordinance, as well. Congress legislated that the residents of that region "shall be entitled to enjoy all and singular rights, privileges and advantages . . . contained in the ordinance" of 1787. Even as recently as 1850, maintained Coles, when the territory of California was organized, the "peculiar language" of the Ordinance's proscrip- tion against slavery was adopted. For "a period of sixty-seven years," emphasized Coles, "eight different Congresses passed and six different individuals acting as Presidents . . . approved eight laws . . . enacting and re-enacting, sanctioning and confirming and extending, . . . the ordi- nance of 1787." From Coles's perspective, the Ordinance established a precedent that slavery should not spread westward.[54]

Throughout the 1850s, Edward Coles repeatedly championed the central components of an antislavery nationalism he first articulated in Illinois during the 1820s. According to his view, he and his generation had inherited an antislavery legacy from the founding fathers, men who had always intended (indeed, expected) slavery to disappear from the American landscape. According to Coles's telling, these men had always recognized the dangers of immediate and unconditional emancipation and, as a result, they all advocated gradual emancipation coupled with colonization as essential to the success of any abolition program. They also had consistently claimed that the national government possessed the power to limit the geographic expansion of the institution. Importantly, their unqualified support for the Northwest Ordinance of 1787 had established a precedent repeated by the Missouri Compromise and the Compromise of 1850. In each case, the federal government had determined the place of slavery in western territories. Coles was often gratified to find elements of his antislavery ideology expressed by others throughout the nation. As he read through newspapers and pamphlets during his almost daily trips to the Philadelphia Athenaeum, Coles encountered support for his view of the past as well as his understanding of federal authority in the West. But, he had yet to see all of these elements brought together and promoted by a national leader. Instead, the instinct to compromise, to appease the South, seemed to prevail among party leaders and he wondered if he would ever see his antislavery nationalism prevail.

"As those fathers marked it"

As the 1860 presidential election approached, any doubts seventy-three-year-old Edward Coles felt about the utility of his antislavery program must have faded, for the Republican Party platform contained nearly every element of his antislavery nationalism. When they met in Chicago to select their candidate, the party members declared their commitment to maintaining the principles embodied in both the Declaration of Independence and the Constitution. They denounced all threats of disunion and pledged to honor each states' right to regulate its own domestic institutions. The document adopted at the convention also declared that the ordinary condition of American territory was free and that any effort to claim that the Constitution allowed for the extension of slavery into any U.S. territory defied all precedent. Here Coles would have recognized his own antislavery views and the position he had been promoting for more than forty years.[55]

Abraham Lincoln, who had long supported colonization and seemed to share his reverence for the nation's revolutionary past, must have inspired Coles's confidence, as well. Lincoln had gained the attention of Republican leaders after his February 1860 speech at New York's Cooper Institute, where he responded directly to Douglas's claim that the federal government lacked the authority to prohibit the extension of slavery. In this address, he refocused the public's attention on how the nation's founders would have viewed the problem of slavery. Echoing

Coles, Lincoln challenged every claim denying the nation's antislavery heritage. From 1787, when Congress confirmed the Northwest Ordinance, through to the Missouri Compromise of 1820, "no line dividing local from federal authority . . . forbade the federal government . . . . control . . . [of] slavery in federal territory." Republicans, declared Lincoln, aspired to do no more than the founding fathers had before them. "As those fathers marked it," he insisted, "so let it be again marked, as an evil not to be extended, but to be tolerated and protected only because of and so far as its actual presence among us makes that toleration and protection a necessity." He then assured his audience that Republicans only wished to act consistently with the approach originally crafted by the nation's founding fathers. "We stick to, contend for," he maintained, "the identical old policy" toward slavery, a policy that prohibited the westward extension of a destructive institution. Democrats, on the other hand, proposed a new policy that required northerners to recognize that "slavery is morally right and socially elevating," concessions that would lead inevitably to "a full national recognition" of slavery. True Americans, declared Lincoln, believed "in common with our fathers . . . that slavery is wrong" and as a result were duty-bound to reject such an extreme position. "Neither let us be slandered from our duty by false accusations against us, nor frightened from it by menaces of destruction to the Government," he instructed his audience, but instead "let us have faith that right makes might, and . . . dare to do our duty as we understand it."[56] In Lincoln, Coles and anyone who shared his antislavery nationalism had found a candidate worth supporting.

When news of Lincoln's nomination reached Philadelphia, a crowd of supporters gathered outside Coles's Spruce Street brownstone and "serenaded" the ex-governor of Illinois. They did so to celebrate the hope that, like Coles, Lincoln would make a "decided & effectual stand against the extension of slavery." Despite this show of support for Coles and the Republican Party, broad support for Lincoln in Philadelphia was far from certain. The city's old-time Whigs, men like Joseph R. Ingersoll and Henry C. Carey (both close friends with Coles), possessed strong southern and conservative sympathies that led them to see the Republican Party as dangerously radical. They sought a middle ground by joining the Constitutional Union Party, an organization pledged to "the Constitution and country, the Union of the States, and the enforcement of the laws," because they hoped to alleviate "the troubles and dangers of the country" through "the protection and preservation of our institutions." Union-loving men from both the North and the South saw in the Constitutional Union Party an opportunity to avoid "sectionalism and disunion." Their candidate, John Bell of Tennessee, was "known to be moderate" and attracted those who saw in the two other parties only "extreme opinions."[57]

Coles's friends elsewhere were equally attracted to this third party. William Cabell Rives, Coles's longtime friend and collaborator in sustaining and promoting Madison's reputation, professed his support for the Constitutional Union ticket, believing "that the true interest of all the States . . . will ever be found in the maintenance of our Constitutional Union." Although he was inclined to insist that Virginia resist any attempt "at interference with her domestic institutions or the reserved states rights of the States," Rives remained convinced that the only way to do so was by "maintain[ing] the integrity of the Union against every attempt to weaken or subvert it, whether from the north or the south."[58] Similarly, Coles's good friend in Boston, Robert C. Winthrop, pledged his support for the Constitutional Union Party. He and likeminded men from Boston met as the election approached, hoping to secure a victory for the moderate and conservative position espoused by John Bell.[59] The rising popularity of the Constitutional Union Party among his friends, men who had shared his hope for a nation without slavery, as he supposed, must have been disturbing, for in choosing Bell, he thought they had rejected the middle ground of his antislavery nationalism. For Coles, the election presented a choice between Bell and a conciliation that allowed slavery to continue and expand indefinitely, or Lincoln and the promise that through containment and colonization slavery would eventually disappear as the founders had expected. On Election Day, then, Coles cast his ballot for Abraham Lincoln and, with his victory, witnessed the resurrection of his antislavery nationalism.[60]

Despite his excitement about the Republican ascendancy, Coles was surely conflicted as he watched the political changes around him. On the one hand, he welcomed the party's electoral success. Finally, the message he had been projecting since the 1820s had become a central part of a national party's political platform. His determination to infuse the politics of slavery with a healthy dose of historical perspective had succeeded. Lincoln's rise as well as the emergence of the Republican Party revealed just how much his eighteenth-century emphasis on principle above partisanship could shape democratic politics. On the other hand, he must have been equally concerned about these developments. It was only when his views were absorbed into the party system that they gained popularity. The price of this turn of events was the institutionalization of two competing understandings of the legacy of the American Revolution. Rather than bringing all Americans together in support of one common view, the legacy of liberty and equality he offered contributed to the very sectional divisions he hoped to avoid.[61] Indeed, the vision Coles had spent his whole life trying to identify with southern founders had become associated exclusively with the North. He had both failed and succeeded at the same time. He failed to promote a nationalism that would bind the sections together, yet he had succeeded in persuading political leaders to adopt his vision for the nation. In the end, his antislavery nationalism was unable to overcome the rising sectionalism of the late 1850s, the sectional character of the presidential election, or prevent the secession of the southern states.

"the hour of national peril"

In the months following Lincoln's election, Philadelphians and northerners generally watched in disbelief as one state after another seceded from the Union. Morton McMichael, editor of the *North American*, optimistically proclaimed that the "restless" behavior in the deep South did "not disturb or diminish our confidence in free institutions." He then naively predicted that, with "a little firmness and patience," the nation will survive the "ill grained resistance" exhibited by the South. He promised that secession was not embraced by "the body of the southern people," but was instead the product of extreme and radical leaders.[62] Not willing to leave anything to chance, Philadelphia's most prominent leaders organized and hosted a Union Meeting. Edward Coles, along with his friends Charles J. Ingersoll, George Cadwalader, Samuel Breck, Moncure Robinson, Robert Patterson—all men who had held the Union Meeting after the Compromise of 1850—joined the meeting as vice presidents. After a procession that wound through the city, a large crowd of people met at Independence Square, where they demonstrated their "devotion to the Federal Union" and their determination "to maintain unbroken the great national compact."[63] A month later, Coles joined Philadelphia's prominent residents once again. On January 3, 1861, a meeting to decide "what measures should be adopted in the present condition of our national affairs" gathered at the Board of Trade Rooms. The assembled men unanimously declared their "devotion to the Union."[64] Few should doubt, if they ever had, that Philadelphia's residents ascribed to a moderate view, they declared— a view that rejected the extremes pronounced from both sections.

Instead, they supported the nation that had been established within the walls of Independence Hall.

On the bitterly cold afternoon of February 21, 1861, president-elect Abraham Lincoln disembarked from his train in Philadelphia and was greeted by a huge crowd of residents. As one editorialist observed, "People of all parties turned out to welcome" him, forgetting "all party in their patriotic demonstration." Lincoln pushed his way through the crowd and boarded an "open barouche drawn by four white horses" for the ride to the Continental Hotel. All along the procession route he was greeted by throngs of supporters. From nearly "every piazza, balcony, and window," declared one witness, spectators hung American flags and waved handkerchiefs as they shouted their support. Some residents tossed "beautiful bouquets of exotics . . . into his carriage. One of these" carried the inscription "'Preserve the Union.'"[65] As Lincoln arrived at the hotel, Edward Coles pushed his way through "a solid wave of human-ity," caught the attention of the nation's new leader, and extended his hand. Lincoln warmly accepted the greeting and, as Coles later recalled, the president-elect "expressed great delight to see him, and said that he was held in universal reverence throughout the state of Illinois."[66] In this fleeting moment, Coles finally became the physical link he had always aspired to be, connecting the nation's rapidly fading revolutionary past to its emerging, yet still unfulfilled, antislavery future.

Lincoln released his grasp and then reappeared on the hotel's balcony and pledged his determination "to restore peace, harmony and prosper-ity to the nation, and the liberty of these States and all these people" and promised to "do nothing inconsistent with the teachings of" the nation's founding fathers. [67] The next morning, Lincoln made his way to Indepen-dence Hall to participate in a ceremony to honor George Washington's birthday and raise a new flag containing thirty-four stars, one each for all the states, including those that had seceded from the Union and nation's newest member, Kansas. Those present recognized the significance of the president-elect addressing the crowd from within such "venerable walls" during "the hour of national peril and distress," during a time "when the great work achieved by the wisdom and patriotism of our Fathers seemed threatened with instant ruin." Declaring the "deep emotion" he felt "at standing here in this place," Lincoln acknowledged the grave responsibility he had assumed. He promised the audience that "all his political sentiments" and actions would continue to be "drawn . . . from the sentiments which originated and were given to the world from this hall." It was here, he reminded the crowd, that the founders composed and approved the sacred Declaration of Independence. He suggested that the political leaders and soldiers of that earlier time had fought to ensure "that in due time the weights would be lifted from the shoulders of all men," and it was on this ideal, he maintained, that the country must stand.[68]

Although he may not have attended the second day of events during Abraham Lincoln's visit to Philadelphia, Coles surely read the detailed descriptions that appeared in the city's newspapers the next day. Much of what Lincoln said during his visit would have resonated with Coles, a man who had always championed the ideals that Lincoln proclaimed. Although he spent most of his time during the 1850s reminding the public of the importance of the Northwest Ordinance of 1787, Coles was no less dedicated to the principles presented in the Declaration of Independence. In many ways he saw the two documents as part of the same antislavery spirit. He could not have been more delighted to witness in the ascendancy of Lincoln the moment when the ideals of liberty and equality became once again the guiding principles of the nation. He hoped that such a turn of events would likewise translate into the final defeat of slavery, the removal of the long-deplorable contradiction inherent in a democracy of slaveholders. Like the other residents of Philadelphia, Coles probably also hoped that Lincoln's visit to the nation's birthplace would inspire the new president to do everything in his power to keep the Union whole.[69]

Afterword

In the summer of 1864, more than three years after the beginning of armed hostilities between the North and South, fifteen thousand Philadelphians attended the opening ceremonies for the Great Central Fair. For more than six months, the members of the executive committee and thousands of volunteers on hundreds of specialized committees had organized and advertised the event. By the spring of that year, the fair buildings engulfed Logan Square. Several individual structures as well as an elaborate central hall offered attendees a wide variety of items to purchase as well as wonders to see. Flags and banners lined the walls and hung from the ceilings. For one dollar, fairgoers entered through one of three gates and strolled by tables showcasing everyday items and luxury goods produced by local and regional artisans. They lingered before exhibits displaying art, horticultural marvels, home furnishings, and modern household amenities. The three-week event was designed to raise funds for the United States Sanitary Commission, an organization that provided much-needed care to wounded soldiers and support to an often undersupplied Union Army. Mayor Alexander Henry opened Philadelphia's fair on June 7 by declaring that "all that can gratify the senses and gladden the heart has been stored in this spacious temple dedicated to loyal benevolence."[1]

Among the hundreds of Philadelphia residents to devote their time and labor to this enterprise was Mary Coles, the twenty-nine-year-old daughter of Edward Coles. She served on the Committee of Useful and Fancy Articles (Home-made). Along with nearly a dozen other prominent Philadelphia women, she answered the call directing "every true hearted patriot in Pennsylvania" to demonstrate their loyalty by "work[ing] in a good cause, even at the cost of great personal exertions and sacrifice." Sidney George Fisher, a Coles family friend, was amazed by the accomplishments of so many volunteers. "All the immense labor of superintending the arrangement of the innumerable things of this fair, of managing its myriad details & of selling the articles is performed by volunteers, ladies & gentlemen many of them, all of them highly respectable people." From his perspective, there was no better demonstration of the "prosperity, . . . wealth, . . . intelligence, public spirit, right feeling & good taste" of the city's Union supporters. Even more astonishing to him was the success of the whole affair. The Sanitary Commission spent millions of dollars each year caring for sick and wounded soldiers and did so entirely through voluntary subscriptions, donations "from all classes of the people, rich & poor." On the day he attended, the fair raised nearly $500,000—impressive indeed.[2]

Perhaps still weary with grief after his son Roberts's death in February 1862, or beaten down by old age, seventy-seven-year-old Edward Coles did not attend the fair. Instead, he remained sequestered in the quiet of his home for most of the war. The only evidence that he ventured beyond the walls of his Spruce Street brownstone appeared in the August 4, 1862 issue of the *Philadelphia Inquirer*. In a brief notice entitled "Citizen's Voluntary Bounty." he was listed among many of the city's most prominent men who gathered at the Board of Trade Rooms and Independence Hall. They assembled to express their "attachment to the Union" and demonstrate the "patriotic liberality of the people of Philadelphia." With his gift of $500, Coles offered the largest single donation by an individual that day. But this was probably the extent of his public activities during the war. When most of his friends met a few months later to establish the Union League of Philadelphia, Coles was not among the founders or listed on the membership rolls. One of his close friends attended the organizing meeting and found a room full of men who "denounced with great bitterness" anyone who sympathized with the rebellion. Before the night was done, everyone present agreed to support the "vigorous prosecution of the war" and boasted "an uncompromising determination to crush the rebellion and reduce the South to absolute submission, at any sacrifice."[3] Perhaps the idea that the enemy should be pounded into "absolute submission" was too much for the Virginia-born Coles, whose beloved son had died defending the Confederacy. An even more likely explanation for his absence, however, lay in his ever-declining health.

FIGURE A.1. Portrait of Edward Coles, ca. 1864–1868, by John Henry Brown. (Courtesy of Winterthur Museum.)

Despite the disruptions of war and the discomfort caused by neuralgia, Coles did try to maintain some sense of normalcy in his life during the conflict. He continued to write to his southern family members, even though nearly all of his siblings and their spouses had died before the war. Isaac had passed away unexpectedly in 1841. John, Sally, Mary, Rebecca, and Walter had perished between 1848 and 1856. His brothers-in-law, Richard Singleton and Andrew Stevenson, died before the war, as well. Tucker, who visited him most often among his family members, passed on just a month before the opening salvoes of the war struck Fort Sumter. Only two sisters, Betsy and Emily, and a brother-in-law, John Rutherfoord, still lived in Virginia. The difficulties of getting letters across enemy lines, however, severely limited their communications. In 1863, for example, Emily's husband John Rutherfoord complained that they had not received his latest letter. Even when correspondence could be exchanged, the wartime conditions inhibited their communications. In one note that did make it to Philadelphia, Rutherfoord confessed his regret that "we are under such restraint in our correspondence, otherwise," he continued, "we should have much to say." The war also hampered Coles's ability to monitor his financial affairs. As early as 1860, he turned over management of his investments and western properties to his son, Edward, Jr. The unstable nature of the western theater, particularly in Missouri, during the war, prevented the younger Coles from visiting the region or communicating with their agents with any regularity. So by the summer of 1864, the Civil War had robbed Coles of his youngest son, essentially cut him off from his extended family, and threatened to destroy his financial well-being.[4] As he had predicted three years earlier, Coles seemed destined to be unhappy for all of his remaining days.

Still, he surely found encouragement in the news that the war might bring about an end to slavery, an outcome he had always hoped could be achieved peacefully. From the very beginning of the war, African Americans recognized in the conflict an opportunity to seize their own freedom. Thousands fled their master's plantations and sought refuge in Union camps. This created quite a dilemma for the military as well as President Lincoln's administration. Most famously, General Benjamin F. Butler labeled the escaped slaves that appeared at Fortress Monroe in Norfolk, Virginia, in the summer of 1861 contrabands of war. In this way, he transformed the Federal Army into a liberating force and, from this modest and localized beginning eventually emerged a fully developed emancipation policy. To be sure, Abraham Lincoln remained ever mindful of the fragile support for the Union in the Border States and only haltingly embraced the idea of emancipation as a goal of the war. He had, after all, quickly rescinded the liberating decrees of Generals John C. Frémont and David Hunter. Yet he did explore simultaneously the possibility of devising an emancipation policy. He initially described it as a military necessity and offered to compensate slaveholders in the Border States. When they declined his offer, Lincoln warned that regardless of their objection, emancipation would come. By the end of the summer of 1862, he had composed the Emancipation Proclamation and only awaited a military victory to announce the wartime policy. The battlefield triumph finally came at Antietam in September, and Lincoln released a preliminary proclamation just days later.[5]

Throughout the late summer and fall months of 1862, Philadelphia's newspapers were filled with articles and letters commenting on the president's proclamation. Some articles described in detail the panic spreading through parts of the South. Apparently, southerners were outraged that Lincoln would incite insurrection among their laborers. Predictions of murder and mayhem filled these reprinted southern newspaper columns. Other authors celebrated the president's decision, gratified that the war had become finally a contest to preserve both "Liberty and Union." Many writers predicted that Lincoln's new policy would improve the nation's relationship with foreign countries and make impotent all charges that the North fought out of ambition more than principle. In Philadelphia, the wartime policy of emancipation remained controversial throughout the war.[6]

It is hard to imagine that Coles would have been anything but delighted with the Emancipation Proclamation. As a young man in Virginia, he had concluded that slavery was morally and ideologically wrong. Once he became a resident of Illinois, Coles had transformed his principled opposition to the institution into a broader antislavery appeal that included a free-labor critique of slavery and a demand that Americans fulfill the antislavery legacy of the nation's founders. When he successfully prevented the expansion of slavery into Illinois during the 1820s, he became convinced that this antislavery nationalism could prevail on the national political stage. Even his failure to persuade Virginia's leaders to promote emancipation and democratic political reform in the late 1820s and early 1830s did not dissuade him from pursuing his antislavery goals. Nor did his disappointment in James Madison's failure to emancipate his enslaved property discourage Coles from demanding that the nation's leaders do more than those who came before them by orchestrating the gradual demise of slavery. In the rise of the Republican Party and the

FIGURE A.2. Emancipation, ca. 1865, lithography by Thomas Nast.
(Courtesy of the Library of Congress, Prints & Photographs Division
(LC-DIG-pga-03898).)

electoral victory of Abraham Lincoln, Coles found a national leader who
shared his antislavery perspective and who on January 1, 1863, enacted
a policy that liberated millions (though not all) of the nation's enslaved
men and women. When Congress passed the Thirteenth Amendment
two years later, Coles witnessed the triumph of the antislavery nationalism he had first articulated more than forty years earlier.

The destruction of slavery during the Civil War, however, was tarnished by strong prejudices against free blacks. Decades earlier, Coles
had begun his campaign against slavery convinced that, if given the same
opportunities as their white neighbors, blacks could prosper and live as
equals in American society. The success of Robert and Kate Crawford as
well as the life experiences of the other enslaved men and women he had
liberated demonstrated the accuracy of his claim. Coles abandoned this
idealistic vision when he witnessed firsthand the prejudice of Illinois's
white community. He joined the American Colonization Society and
came to believe that this institution offered the most pragmatic solution
to the problem of slavery. Not only did the organization address the antiblack prejudice so pervasive among white Americans, but it also offered

a solution that residents in every section of the country could support. In the American Colonization Society, he hoped he had found a national rather than a sectional solution to the slavery issue and, as a result, colonization became an essential component of the antislavery nationalism he promoted after 1830.

During the war, the experiences of Philadelphia's free blacks confirmed that little had changed since Coles's time in Illinois. Even as black men enlisted in the Union Army, white Philadelphians refused to desegregate the city's street cars, and African Americans continued to live as second-class citizens. Emancipation and the Thirteenth Amendment hardly changed these circumstances. Not surprisingly, then, Coles included in his last will, written in July 1865, a substantial donation to the American Colonization Society. When he died three years later, Edward Coles bequeathed to his children a nation much more reflective of the republic first imagined by the founders, but one whose citizens continued to struggle with the persistent problem of racial prejudice in a society ostensibly committed to equality.[7]

Abbreviations

CHS	Chicago Historical Society
HSP	Historical Society of Pennsylvania
ISHL	Illinois State Historical Library
ISHS	Illinois State Historical Survey
JER	*Journal of the Early Republic*
PU	Firestone Library, Princeton University
SLWM	Earl Greg Swem Library, College of William and Mary
UVA	Alderman Library, University of Virginia
VHS	Virginia Historical Society
VMHB	*Virginia Magazine of History and Biography*
WMQ	*William and Mary Quarterly*

NOTES

Introduction

1. "The Great Victory at Roanoke Island: Extracts from Rebel Papers"; "The Great Victory!," *Philadelphia Inquirer*, February 14 and 15, 1862; Darrell L. Collins, *46th Virginia Infantry* (Lynchburg, Va.: Howard, 1992), 12; William B. Coles, *The Coles Family of Virginia and Its Numerous Connections* (New York: n.p., 1931), 701.

2. Roberts Coles to John Rutherfoord, October 13, 1861, Rutherfoord Family Papers, VHS and Roberts Coles to Jenny Cary Fairfax, February 7, 1862, Roberts Coles Letters, VHS; Edward Coles to John Rutherfoord, October 15, 1861, Edward Coles Collection, HSP.

3. Judkin Browning, *Shifting Loyalties: The Union Occupation of Eastern North Carolina* (Chapel Hill: University of North Carolina Press, 2011), 27–54; Kevin Dougherty, *Strangling the Confederacy: Coastal Operations in the American Civil War* (Philadelphia: Casemate, 2010), 69–80; John G. Barrett, *The Civil War in North Carolina* (Chapel Hill: University of North Carolina Press, 1963), 66–85. See also Drew Gilpin Faust, *This Republic of Suffering: Death and the American Civil War* (New York: Vintage, 2008).

4. Ralph L. Ketcham, "The Dictates of Conscience: Edward Coles and Slavery," *Virginia Quarterly Review* 26 (Winter 1966), 46–62; Elizabeth Langhorne, "Edward Coles, Thomas Jefferson, and the Rights of Man," *Virginia Cavalcade* 23 (Summer 1973), 30–36. Coles is also mentioned in a number of broader studies. See Annette Gordon-Reed, *The Hemingses of Monticello: An American Family* (New York: W. W. Norton, 2008), 538; Louis P. Masur, *1831, Year of Eclipse* (New York: Hill and Wang, 2001), 58–61; Don E. Fehrenbacher, *The Slaveholding Republic: An Account of the United States Government's Relations to Slavery* (New York: Oxford University Press, 2001), 67; William W. Freehling, *Road to Disunion: Secessionists at Bay, 1776–1854* (New York: Oxford University Press, 1990), 140–41.

5. John Thomas Cassidy, "The Issue of Freedom in Illinois under Governor Coles,"

Journal of Illinois State Historical Society 57 (Autumn 1964), 284–88; Donald S. Spencer, "Edward Coles: Virginia Gentleman in Frontier Politics," *Journal of Illinois State Historical Society* 61 (1968), 150–51; Robert M. Sutton, "Edward Coles and the Constitutional Crisis in Illinois, 1822–1824," *Illinois Historical Journal* 82 (Spring 1989), 33; Kurt E. Leichtle and Bruce G. Carveth, *Crusade against Slavery: Edward Coles, Pioneer of Freedom* (Carbondale: Southern Illinois University Press, 2011), 2–4, 130, and 207–10. For an exception to this scholarly trend, see David Ress, *Governor Edward Coles and the Vote to Forbid Slavery in Illinois, 1823–1824* (Jefferson, N.C.: McFarland, 2006). Ress argues that Coles was a remarkable man worth celebrating because he not only followed through with his convictions but also led a populist antislavery campaign against powerful proslavery elites, and emerged victorious.

6. Paul Finkelman, *Slavery and the Founders: Race and Liberty in the Age of Jefferson* (London.: M. E. Sharpe, 1996); Gary B. Nash, *Race and Revolution* (Madison: Madison House, 1990) and Gary B. Nash, *The Forgotten Fifth: African Americans in the Age of Revolution* (Cambridge: Cambridge University Press, 2006).

7. Don E. Fehrenbacher, *The Slaveholding Republic: An Account of the United States Government's Relations with Slavery* (New York: Oxford University Press, 2001); Adam Rothman, *Slave Country: American Expansion and the Origins of the Deep South* (Cambridge: Harvard University Press, 2005); David Waldstreicher, *Slavery's Constitution: From Revolution to Ratification* (New York: Hill and Wang, 2009); Gary Kornblith, *Slavery and Sectional Strife in the Early American Republic, 1776–1821* (Lanham, Md.: Rowman and Littlefield, 2010); George William Van Cleve, *A Slaveholder's Union: Slavery, Politics, and the Constitution in the Early American Republic* (Chicago: University of Chicago Press, 2010).

8. Richard Newman, *The Transformation of American Abolitionism: Fighting Slavery in the Early Republic* (Chapel Hill: University of North Carolina Press, 2002); Matthew Mason, *Slavery and Politics in the Early American Republic* (Chapel Hill: University of North Carolina Press, 2006); John Craig Hammond, *Slavery, Freedom and Expansion in the Early American West* (Charlottesville: University of Virginia Press, 2007); Eva Sheppard Wolf, *Race and Liberty in the New Nation: Emancipation in Virginia from the Revolution to Nat Turner's Rebellion* (Baton Rouge: Louisiana State University Press, 2006); John Craig Hammond and Matthew Mason, eds., *Contesting Slavery: The Politics of Bondage and Freedom in the New American Nation* (Charlottesville: University of Virginia Press, 2011). For a study of the Southern view of this issue, see Lacy K. Ford, *Deliver Us from Evil: The Slavery Question in the Old South* (New York: Oxford University Press, 2009). For an exception, see Robert Pierce Forbes, *The Missouri Compromise and Its Aftermath: Slavery and the Meaning of America* (Chapel Hill: University of North Carolina Press, 2007).

9. James Brewer Stewart, *Abolitionist Politics and the Coming of the Civil War* (Amherst: University of Massachusetts Press, 2008); Paul Goodman, *Of One Blood: Abolitionism and the Origins of Racial Equality* (Berkeley: University of California Press, 1998); John Stauffer, *The Black Hearts of Men: Radical Abolitionists and the Transformation of Race* (Cambridge: Harvard University Press, 2002).

10. Jonathan Earle, *Jacksonian Antislavery and the Politics of Free Soil* (Chapel Hill: University of North Carolina Press, 2004); Reinhard O. Johnson, *The Liberty Party, 1840–1848: Antislavery Third Party Politics in the United States* (Baton Rouge: Louisiana State University Press, 2009).

11. Beverly C. Tomek, *Colonization and Its Discontents: Emancipation, Emigration, and Antislavery in Antebellum Pennsylvania* (New York: New York University Press, 2011); Sean Wilentz, *The Rise of American Democracy: From Jefferson to Lincoln* (New York: W. W. Norton, 2005), and William Freehling, *The Road to Disunion: Secessionists at Bay, 1776–1854* (New York: Oxford University Press, 1990), and Freehling, *The Road to Disunion: Secessionists Triumphant, 1854–1861* (New York: Oxford University Press, 2009).

1 / Becoming Antislavery

1. Edward Coles to Papa, December 6, 1805, Edward Coles Collection, HSP. On the college, see Susan H. Godson et al., *The College of William and Mary: A History, Volume 1, 1693–1888* (Williamsburg: King and Queen Press, 1993). On Williamsburg, see Lyon Gardiner Tyler, *Williamsburg, The Old Colonial Capital* (Richmond: Whittet and Shepperon, 1907).

2. Thomas Jefferson to Richard Price, August 7, 1785 in *The Papers of Thomas Jefferson*, edited by Julian P. Boyd (Princeton: Princeton University Press, 1950–1997), 8: 357; Thomas Todd to Charles S. Todd, March 9, 1808, "Letters of Judge Thomas Todd, of Kentucky, to His Son at College," *WMQ* 1st Ser. 22 (July 1913), 21; Carter Henry Harrison to David Watson, June 11, 1797, "Letters from William and Mary," *VMHB* 30 (July 1922), 277; Isaac A. Coles to Henry St. George Tucker, July 20, 1799, "Glimpses of Old College Life," *WMQ* 1st Ser. 8 (January 1900), 158.

3. Edward Coles to John Coles, December 6, 1805, Edward Coles Collection, HSP.

4. Edward Coles, "Autobiography," April 1844, Edward Coles Collections, HSP. On the Coles family generally, see Elizabeth Coles Langhorne, K. Edward Clay, and William D. Rieley, *A Virginia Family: Its Plantation Houses* (Charlottesville: University Press of Virginia, 1987); and William B. Coles, *The Coles Family of Virginia: Its Numerous Connections, from the Emigration to America to the Year 1915* (New York, 1931). See also John Hammond Moore, *Albemarle, Jefferson's County, 1727–1976* (Charlottesville: University Press of Virginia, 1976).

5. "'City in the Air': William Byrd Founds Richmond," in *Richmond, A Reader, 1733–1983*, edited by Maurice Duke and Daniel P. Jordon (Chapel Hill: University of North Carolina Press, 1983); Langhorne et al., *A Virginia Family*, 5–9; Coles, *The Coles Family of Virginia*, 36–39; Virginius Dabney, *Richmond: The Story of a City* (New York: Doubleday, 1976), 12–22.

6. Langhorne et al., *A Virginia Family*, 7–9, 11–16; Coles, *The Coles Family of Virginia*, 17–18; Moore, *Albemarle*, 16–18. On land, slaves, and the limits of Tidewater prosperity on the eve of the Revolution, see Allan Kulikoff, *Tobacco and Slaves: The Development of Southern Cultures in the Chesapeake, 1680–1800* (Chapel Hill: University of North Carolina Press, 1985), and T. H. Breen, *Tobacco Culture: The Decline of the Great Tidewater Planters on the Eve of the Revolution* (Princeton: Princeton University Press, 1985).

7. Henrico County Deed Book, 1744–1748, 345–47, Library of Virginia; Coles, *The Coles Family of Virginia*, 39–43; Langhorne et al., *A Virginia Family*, 7–9.

8. Coles, *The Coles Family of Virginia*, 18–27.

9. Col. John Coles of Enniscorthy—Account Book, 1774–1780, Carter-Smith Collection, Box 1, UVA; Ledger of John Coles, 1770–1807, 1: 95–195, UVA.

10. Col. John Coles of Enniscorthy—Account Book, 1774–1780; and John Coles to

Rebecca Coles, ca. 1775, Carter-Smith Collection, Box 1, UVA; Ledger of John Coles, 1770–1807, 1: 121 and 2: 260, UVA; John Coles to Edward Coles, December 14, 1805, Edward Coles Collection, HSP; Mrs. Drummond to Thomas Jefferson, March 21, 1771, in *Papers of Thomas Jefferson*, edited by Julian Boyd (Princeton: Princeton University Press, 1950), 1: 65. For the description of John Coles II, see Anne Hollingsworth Wharton, *Social Life in the Early Republic* (Philadelphia: J. B. Lippincott, 1902), 139. See also Langhorne et al., *A Virginia Family*, 18–27; Moore, *Albemarle*, 35–44.

11. Ledger of John Coles, 1770–1807, 1: 69 and 121, and 2: 96–201, UVA; Andrew Drummond to Col. John Coles, March 15, 1780; Andrew Drummond to Col. John Coles and Mrs. Coles, April 5, 1780, Box 1, Carter-Smith Collection, UVA; Langhorne et al., *A Virginia Family*, 16–28; Coles, *The Coles Family of Virginia*, 51–52.

12. Michael L. Nicholls, "Piedmont Plantations and Farms: Transplanting Tidewater Traditions?," *Magazine of Albemarle County History* 49 (1991), 1–17; Michael A. McDonnell, *The Politics of War: Race, Class and Conflict in Revolutionary Virginia* (Chapel Hill: University of North Carolina Press, 2007), 24–33; Bruce A. Ragsdale, *A Planter's Republic: The Search for Economic Independence in Revolutionary Virginia* (Madison: Madison House, 1996), 1–47; Moore, *Albemarle*, 16–18, 31–44. See also Phillip Hamilton, *The Making and Unmaking of a Revolutionary Family: The Tuckers of Virginia, 1752–1830* (Charlottesville: University of Virginia Press, 2003); Robert Dawidorff, *The Education of John Randolph* (New York: W. W. Norton, 1979); Emory Evans, *Thomas Nelson of Yorktown: Revolutionary Virginian* (Williamsburg: Colonial Williamsburg Foundation, 1975), 124–38; Robert Brugger, *Beverley Tucker: Heart over Head in the Old South* (Baltimore: Johns Hopkins University Press, 1978).

13. John Banister to St. George Tucker, August 1786, cited in Hamilton, *The Making and Unmaking of a Revolutionary Family*, 73. On Virginia's postwar economic troubles, see McDonnell, *The Politics of War*, 515–27; Ragsdale, *A Planter's Republic*, 258–82; Herbert E. Sloan, *Principle and Interest: Thomas Jefferson and the Problem of Debt* (New York: Oxford University Press, 1995); Emory G. Evans, "Private Indebtedness and the Revolution in Virginia, 1776 to 1796," *WMQ* 3rd Ser. 28 (July 1971), 349–74. On soil problems, see John R. Wennersten, "Soil Miners Redux: The Chesapeake Environment, 1680–1810," *Maryland Historical Magazine* 91 (June 2001), 156–79. For two examples of agricultural innovation, see Lynn A. Nelson, *Phrasalia: An Environmental Biography of a Nineteenth-Century Plantation* (Athens: University of Georgia Press, 2007), introduction and chapter 1; and A. Glenn Crothers, "Agricultural Improvement and Technological Innovation in a Slave Society: The Case of Early National Northern Virginia," *Agricultural History* 75 (Spring 2001), 135–67. On the generational perception of decline, see Hamilton, *The Making and Unmaking of a Revolutionary Family*, 132–64; Cynthia A. Kierner, "'The Dark and Dense Cloud Perpetually Lowering over Us': Gender and the Decline of the Gentry in Post-Revolutionary Virginia, *Journal of the Early Republic* 20 (Summer 2000), 15–99; and Robert P. Sutton, "Nostalgia, Pessimism, and Malaise: The Doomed Aristocrat in Late-Jeffersonian Virginia," *VMHB* 76 (January 1968), 41–46. See also Susan Dunn, *Dominion of Memories: Jefferson, Madison and the Decline of Virginia* (New York: Perseus Books, 2007). St. George Tucker married widow Frances Bland Randolph in 1778. John Randolph of Roanoke was her youngest child from her first marriage and, therefore, Tucker was his stepfather. Tucker and Frances Randolph had two sons together: Henry St. George (who was close friends with Edward's older brother Isaac) and Nathaniel Beverley, who was among

Edward's circle of friends in the early nineteenth century. Tucker, then, was father to both John Randolph and Nathaniel Beverley, and Coles would have been intimately familiar with their economic struggles.

14. Ledger of John Coles, 1770–1807, volume 2, especially 192, Carter-Smith Collection, UVA; Coles, *Coles Family of Virginia*, 11–37. On slavery, tobacco, and the economics of being a planter in the South, see Brenda E. Stevenson, *Life in Black and White: Family and Community in the Slave South* (Oxford: Oxford University Press, 1996).

15. Coles, *Coles Family of Virginia*, 45–65. On the increasing emphasis on emotion and affection within planter families at the turn of the century, see Hamilton, *The Making and Unmaking of a Revolutionary Family*, 40–97; Anya Jabour, *Marriage in the Early Republic: Elizabeth and William Wirt and the Companionate Ideal* (Baltimore: Johns Hopkins University Press, 1998); Jane Turner Censer, *North Carolina Planters and Their Children, 1800–1860* (Baton Rouge: Louisiana State University Press, 1984); Jan Lewis, *The Pursuit of Happiness: Family and Values in Jefferson's Virginia* (New York: Cambridge University Press, 1983); Daniel Blake Smith, *Inside the Great House: Planter Family Life in Eighteenth Century Society* (Ithaca: Cornell University Press, 1980); Melinda S. Buza, "'Pledges of Our Love': Friendship, Love, and Marriage among the Virginia Gentry, 1800–1825," in *The Edge of the South: Life in Nineteenth-Century Virginia*, edited by Edward L. Ayers and John C. Willis (Charlottesville: University Press of Virginia, 1991), 9–36.

16. William H. Runge, "Isaac A. Coles," *Magazine of Albemarle County History* 14 (1954–1955), 50–57; Coles, *The Coles Family of Virginia*, 103–105.

17. Edward Coles to Papa, December 6, 1805, Edward Coles Collection, HSP.

18. John Coles to Edward Coles, December 14, 1805, Edward Coles Collection, HSP. For the prevalence of student socializing, see "Letters from William and Mary, 1795–1799," "Letters of William T. Barry," and "Glimpses of Old College Life," in the 1922, 1921, and 1900 volumes of the *William and Mary Quarterly*.

19. Garrett Minor to David Watson, April 28, 1798, "Letters from William and Mary, 1795–1799," *VMHB* 30 (July 1922), 244; William T. Barry to Brother, February 6, 1804, "Letters of William T. Barry," *WMQ* 1st Ser. 9 (July 1904), 110–111.

20. Isaac A. Coles to Henry St. George Tucker, July 20, 1799, "Glimpses of Old College Life," *WMQ* 1st Ser. 8 (January 1900), 159.

21. Edward Coles to Papa, November 21, 1806, Edward Coles Collection, HSP; Joseph C. Cabell to David Watson, June 17, 1799, "Letters to David Watson," *VMHB* 29 (July 1921), 262. For Coles's school friends, see W. H. Hurlurt, *The History of the College of William and Mary, From Its Foundation, 1660, to 1874* (Richmond: J. W. Randolph and English, 1874), 105–107.

22. Edward Coles to Papa, November 21, 1806, and "Autobiographical Notes," 1863, Edward Coles Collection, HSP; Benjamin Howard to David Watson, January 30, 1799, "Letters from William and Mary," *VMHB* 30 (July 1922), 249; Joseph Carrington Cabell to David Watson, April 6, 1801, "Letters to David Watson," *VMHB* 29 (April 1921), 276–79.

23. John Coles to Edward Coles, December 14, 1805, and Edward Coles to Papa, November 21, 1806, Edward Coles Collection, HSP. On Ambler, Travis, and Tyler, see Louise Pecquet Du Bellet, *Some Prominent Virginia Families*, volumes 1–2 (Lynchburg, Va., J. P. Bell, 1907), 1: 25–37; Lyon Gardiner Tyler, *Williamsburg, The Old Colonial*

Capital (Richmond: Whittet and Shepperon, 1907), 271; and "The Cocke Family of Virginia (Henrico)," *VMHB* 5 (July 1897), 83; Thomas Todd to Charles S. Todd, June 4, 1808, "Letters of Judge Thomas Todd," *WMQ* 1st Ser. 22 (July 1900), 23. On prominent families in Virginia generally, see Jackson T. Main, "The One Hundred," *WMQ* 3rd Ser. 11 (April 1954), 354–84.

24. Edward Coles to Papa, November 21, 1806, Edward Coles Collection, HSP.

25. James Madison to Thomas Jefferson, December 28, 1786, "Letters of Rev. James Madison , President of the College of William and Mary, to Thomas Jefferson," *WMQ* 2nd Ser. 5 (April 1925), 87; Charles Crowe, "Bishop James Madison and the Republic of Virtue," *Journal of Southern History* 30 (February 1964), 59–64.

26. Bishop James Madison, *Manifestations of the Beneficence of Divine Providence towards America* (Richmond, 1795), in Ellis Sandoz, *Political Sermons of the American Founding Era: 1730–1805*, 2nd ed. (Indianapolis: Liberty Fund, 1998), volume 2, http://oll.libertyfund.org/title/817/69446. See Godson et al., *The College of William and Mary*, 190–92. On post-revolutionary education, see David W. Robson, *Educating Republicans: The College in the Era of the American Revolution, 1750–1800* (Westport, Conn: Greenwood, 1985), and Mark A. Noll, *Princeton and the Republic, 1788–1822: The Search for Christian Enlightenment in the Era of Samuel Stanhope Smith* (Princeton: Princeton University Press, 1989). See also David J. Hoeveler, *Creating the American Mind: Intellect and Politics in the Colonial Colleges* (Lanham, Md.: Rowman and Littlefield, 2002); and Henry F. May, *The Enlightenment in America* (New York: Oxford University Press, 1976).

27. Joseph Shelton Watson to David Watson, November 4, 1799, "Letters from William and Mary College," *VMHB* 29 (April 1921), 147; Adam Smith, *An Inquiry into the Nature and Causes of the Wealth of Nations, Representative Selections* (Indianapolis: Bobbs-Merrill, 1961); May, *The Enlightenment in America*, 155–57 and 282; Robson, *Educating Republicans*, 170.

28. Robson, *Educating Republicans*, 162–65. See also May, *Enlightenment in America*, 164–67, and D. L. Le Mahieu, *The Mind of William Paley: A Philosopher and His Age* (Lincoln: University of Nebraska Press, 1976).

29. May, *Enlightenment in America*, 164–76; Robson, *Educating Republicans*, 170–71.

30. " J. C. [James Madison] to Mr. Dwight, Author of an Oration," *National Intelligencer*, November 20, 1800; Joseph C. Cabell to David Watson, March 4 and July 8, 1798, Joseph Carrington Cabell Papers, SLWM; Joseph C. Cabell to David Watson, April 6, 1801, "Letters to David Watson," *VMHB* 29 (April 1921), 278. See also Robson, *Educating Republicans*, 170–77; and May, *Enlightenment in America*, 137–39, 164–76, and 344–48.

31. *Address of the Students of William and Mary College*, signed John B. Johnson, Chairman, and John Tayloe Lomax, Secretary, June 8, 1798, Chronology File, 1781–1815, SLWM. See also *Philadelphia Aurora*, June 18, 1798. Joseph Carrington Cabell to David Watson, July 8, 1798, Joseph Carrington Cabell Papers, SLWM; and Robert J. Morrison, ed., "Memoranda Relating to the College," *WMQ* 1st Ser. 27 (July 1918), 232. On the Federalist agenda generally, see Doron Ben-Atar and Barbara B. Oberg, eds., *Federalists Reconsidered* (Charlottesville: University Press of Virginia, 1998); Marshall Foletta, *Coming to Terms with Democracy: Federalists Intellectuals and the Shaping of American Culture* (Charlottesville: University Press of Virginia, 2001); David Hackett

Fischer, *The Revolution in American Conservatism: The Federalists in the Age of Jeffersonian Democracy* (New York: Harper and Row, 1965).

32. Joseph Shelton Watson to David Watson, December 24, 1799, and March 2, 1801, "Letters from William and Mary," *VMHB* 29 (April 1921), 161; Chapman Johnson to David Watson, May 18, 1800, and Joseph C. Cabell to David Watson, April 6, 1801," Letters of David Watson," *VMHB* 29 (April 1921), 271 and 279; Thomas L. Preston to Andrew Reid, Jr., January 7, 1802, "Glimpses of Old College Life," *WMQ* 1st Ser. 8 (April 1900), 216. On Jeffersonian democracy, see Sean Wilentz, *The Rise of American Democracy: Jefferson to Lincoln* (New York: W. W. Norton, 2005), especially part I.

33. Bishop James Madison to Thomas Jefferson, December 28, 1786, "Letters of Rev. James Madison, President of William and Mary College, to Thomas Jefferson," *WMQ* 2nd Ser. 5 (April 1925), 87; I. A. Coles to Henry St. George Tucker, July 20, 1799, "Glimpses of Old College Life," *WMQ* 2nd Ser. 8 (January 1900), 159; David Yancey to David Watson, June 6, 1795, "Letters from William and Mary, 1795–1799," *VMHB* 30 (July 1921), 224.

34. Edward Coles, "Notes on Rousseau," Edward Coles Collection, HSP.

35. Class notes, Edward Coles Collection, HSP.

36. Ledger of John Coles, 1770–1807, volume 2, especially 192, UVA; John Coles to Edward Coles, December 14, 1805, Edward Coles Collection, HSP. See also Stevenson, *Life in Black and White.*

37. John Coles to Edward Coles, December 17, 1806 (emphasis added), Edward Coles Collection, HSP. On the Coles family prominence in Albemarle County, see Moore, *Albemarle*, 151.

38. Catherine Allgor, *A Perfect Union: Dolley Madison and the Creation of the American Nation* (New York: Henry Holt, 2006), 15–19.

39. Stephen B. Weeks, *Southern Quakers and Slavery: A Study in Institutional History* (Baltimore: Johns Hopkins University Press, 1896), 214–15; Louis Morton, *Robert Carter of Nomini Hall: A Virginia Tobacco Planter in the Eighteenth Century* (Williamsburg: Colonial Williamsburg, 1945); John Randolph Barden, "'Flushed with Notions of Freedom': The Growth and Emancipation of a Virginia Slave Community, 1762–1812," Ph. D. dissertation, Duke University, 1993; Melvin Patrick Ely, "Richard and Judith Randolph, St. George Tucker, George Wythe, Syphax Brown, and Hercules White: Racial Equity and the Snares of Prejudice," in *Revolutionary Founders: Rebels, Radicals, and Reformers in the Making of the Nation*, edited by Alfred F. Young et al. (New York: A. A. Knopf, 2011), 323; Melvin Patrick Ely, *Israel on the Appomattox* (New York: A. A. Knopf, 2004); Anthony Iaccarino, "Virginia and the National Contest over Slavery in the Early Republic, 1780–1833," Ph. D. dissertation, University of California, Los Angeles, 1999, 9 and 103–109; François Furstenberg, *In the Name of the Father: Washington, Slavery and the Making of a Nation* (New York: Penguin, 2007); James Sidbury, *Ploughshares into Swords: Race, Rebellion and Identity in Gabriel's Virginia, 1730–1810* (Cambridge: Cambridge University Press, 1997), 184–85.

40. Eva Sheppard Wolf, *Race and Liberty in the New Nation: Emancipation in Virginia from the Revolution to Nat Turner's Rebellion* (Baton Rouge: Louisiana State University Press, 2006), 39–84, see especially Table 1 (43) and Table 2 (46).

41. On the prevalence of antislavery thought at the College of William and Mary,

see Terry L. Meyers, "Reconstructing Anti-Slavery Thinking at William and Mary," unpublished paper, shared with the author December 16, 2011.

42. Coles, "Autobiography," April 1844, Edward Coles Collection, HSP.

43. William Brockenbrough to Joseph C. Cabell, April 29, 1798, Cabell Papers, UVA, cited in May, *Enlightenment in America*, 249. See also Meyers, "Reconstructing Anti-Slavery Thinking."

44. Chapman Johnson to David Watson, January 24, 1802, "Letters of David Watson," *VMHB* 29 (July 1921), 280.

45. Gary Kornblith, *Slavery and Sectional Strife in the Early American Republic, 1776–1821* (Lanham, Md.: Rowan and Littlefield, 2010); Don E. Fehrenbacher, *The Slaveholding Republic: An Account of the United States Government's Relations to Slavery* (New York: Oxford University Press, 2001); Paul Finkelman, *Slavery and the Founders: Race and Liberty in the Age of Jefferson* (London: M. E. Sharpe, 1996).

46. Wolf, *Race and Liberty in the New Nation*; Gary B. Nash, *Race and Revolution* (Madison: Madison House, 1990); William H. Freehling, *Road to Disunion: Secessionists at Bay, 1776–1854* (New York: Oxford University Press, 1990), 121–43; Alison Goodyear Freehling, *Drift toward Dissolution: The Virginia Slavery Debate of 1831–32* (Baton Rouge: Louisiana State University Press, 1982); and Iaccarino, "Virginia and the National Contest over Slavery."

47. Thomas Jefferson, *Notes on the State of Virginia*, edited by William Peden (New York: W. W. Norton, 1954), 138–40. See also Wolf, *Race and Liberty in the New Nation*; Andrew Burstein, *Sentimental Democracy: The Evolution of America's Romantic Self-image* (New York: Hill and Wang, 1999), 160–62; Joseph J. Ellis, *American Sphinx: The Character of Thomas Jefferson* (New York: A. A. Knopf, 1997); John Chester Miller, *The Wolf by the Ears: Thomas Jefferson and Slavery* (Charlottesville: University Press of Virginia, 1991); Paul Finkelman, *Slavery and the Founders: Race and Liberty in the Age of Jefferson* ; and Iaccarino, "Virginia and the National Contest over Slavery," 89–92.

48. Coles, "Autobiography," April 1844, Edward Coles Collection, HSP.

49. John Coles to Edward Coles, June 10, 1807, Edward Coles Collection, HSP.

50. Edward Coles to John Coles, December 6, 1805; John Coles to Edward Coles, November 11, 1806; Edward Coles to John Coles, November 21, 1806; John Tucker to John Coles, May 20, 1808, Edward Coles Collection, HSP.

51. Will of John Coles, Albemarle County Will Book 4, 1798–1809, 298, Library of Virginia. For Isaac's nostalgic longings for Enniscorthy during college, see Isaac A. Coles to Mary Eliza Coles, June 4, 1797, Carter-Smith Collection, Box 1, UVA.

52. Will of John Coles, Albemarle County Will Book 4, 1798–1809, 298, Library of Virginia; Edward Coles to Campbell, [May] 12, 1808; Edward Coles to Hawkins, March 1, 1809, Papers of Edward Coles, 1786–1868, PU; Rebecca Coles, "Almanac Memorandum," undated, Edward Coles Collection, HSP; Langhorne, *A Virginia Family*, 133.

53. Coles, "Autobiography," Edward Coles Collection, HSP.

54. Coles, "Autobiography," Edward Coles Collection, HSP.

55. Coles, "Autobiography," Edward Coles Collections, HSP.

56. Coles, "Autobiography"; "Autobiographical Notes"; Travis Tucker to Edward Coles, [May] 10, 1809; and Rebecca Coles, "Almanac Memorandum," undated, Edward Coles Collection, HSP. For the plantation rental, see Ledger of John Coles, 1770–1807, 2: 278, UVA.

2 / Antislavery Ambition Deferred

1. Edward Coles to James Madison, January 8, 1810, Papers of Edward Coles, 1786–1868, PU; Edward Coles, "Autobiography," April 1844, Edward Coles Collection, HSP.

2. Coles, "Autobiography," April 1844, Edward Coles Collection, HSP.

3. Harriet Martineau, *Retrospect of Western Travel, in Two Volumes* (New York: Harper and Brothers, 1838), 143. For recent literature on the politicization of social space, see Catherine Allgor, *Parlor Politics: In Which the Ladies of Washington Help Build a City and a Government* (Charlottesville: University Press of Virginia, 2000); Fredrika J. Teute, "Roman Matron on the Banks of the Tiber Creek: Margaret Bayard Smith and the Politicization of Spheres in the Nation's Capital," in *A Republic for the Ages: The United States Capitol and the Political Culture of the Early Republic*, edited by Donald R. Kennon (Charlottesville: University Press of Virginia, 1999), 89–121; Rubil Morales Vasquez, "Monuments, Markets, and Manners: The Making of the City of Washington, 1783–1837," Ph. D. dissertation, Rutgers, 1999; Holly Cowan Shulman, "Dolley (Payne Todd) Madison," in *American First Ladies: Their Lives and Their Legacy*, edited by Lewis L. Gould (New York: Routledge, 2001), 21–36; and Cynthia D. Earman, "Boardinghouses, Parties, and the Creation of a Political Society: Washington City, 1800–1830," Masters thesis, Louisiana State University, 1992.

4. *Census of the United States, Third, 1810* (Washington, D.C., 1812), 1. Mary Beth Corrigan, "A Social Union of Heart and Effort: The African-American Family in the District of Columbia on the Eve of Emancipation," Ph.D. dissertation, University of Maryland, 1995); Stephanie Coles, "Servants and Slaves: Domestic Service in the Border Cities, 1800–1850," Ph.D. dissertation, University of Florida, 1994; Mary Beth Corrigan, "Making the Most of an Opportunity: Slaves and the Catholic Church in Early Washington," *Washington History* 12 (Spring/Summer 2000), 90–101; Fredrika J. Teute, "'A Wild, Desolate Place': Life on the Margins in Early Washington," in *Southern City, National Ambition: The Growth or Early Washington, D.C., 1800–1860*, edited by Howard Gilette, Jr. (Washington, D.C.: George Washington University Center for Washington Area Studies, 1995), 47–68; Laura Croghan Kamoie, *Irons in the Fire: The Business History of the Tayloe Family and Virginia's Gentry, 1700–1860* (Charlottesville: University of Virginia Press, 2007); Constance McLaughlin Green, *The Secret City: A History of Race Relations in the Nation's Capital* (Princeton: Princeton University Press, 1967); Mary Tremain, *Slavery in the District of Columbia: The Policy of Congress and the Struggle for Abolition* [1892] (New York: Negro University Press, 1969).

5. Don E. Fehrenbacher, *The Slaveholding Republic: An Account of the United States Government's Relations to Slavery* (New York: Oxford University Press, 2001), 49–88; Mary Beth Corrigan, "Imaginary Cruelties?: A History of the Slave Trade in Washington, D.C.," *Washington History* 13 (Fall/Winter 2001–2002), 5–25; William T. Laprade, "The Domestic Slave Trade in the District of Columbia," *Journal of Negro History* 11(January 1926), 29; Walter C. Clephane, "The Local Aspect of Slavery in the District of Columbia," *Records of the Columbia Historical Society* 3 (1900), 24–25. See also Tremain, *Slavery in the District of Columbia*, 58–60; Green, *The Secret City*, 20–21; and Matthew Mason, *Slavery and Politics in the Early American Republic* (Chapel Hill: University of North Carolina Press, 2006), especially chapter 2.

6. Rebecca Coles's Almanac and Edward Coles to Mama, January 13, 1810, Edward Coles Collection, HSP; Catherine Allgor, *A Perfect Union: Dolley Madison and the*

Creation of the American Nation (New York: Henry Holt, 2006), 45, 180–81, 211–15; David B. Mattern and Holly C. Shulman, eds., *The Selected Letters of Dolley Payne Madison* (Charlottesville: University of Virginia Press, 2003), 97–99; Ralph Ketcham, *James Madison, A Biography* (Charlottesville: University Press of Virginia, 1990), 477.

7. Edward Coles to Brothers and Sisters, February 3, 1810, Edward Coles Collection, HSP. On elite society and the Madisons in Washington, see Allgor, *A Perfect Union*, 232–55; Allgor, *Parlor Politics*, 48–101; Mattern and Shulman, eds., *Selected Letters*, 90–105, and James Sterling Young, *The Washington Community, 1800–1825* (New York: Columbia University Press, 1966).

8. Augustus John Foster, *Jeffersonian America: Notes on the United States of America Collected in the Years 1805, -6-7 and 11–12*, edited by Richard Beale Davis (San Marino, Cal.: Huntington Library, 1954), 155; Margaret Bayard Smith, *The First Forty Years of Washington Society*, edited by Gaillard Hunt (New York: C. Scribher's Sons, 1906), 29.

9. Alexander Dick, quoted in Mattern and Shulman, eds., *Selected Letters*, 96. On Dolley Madison during her Washington years, see Allgor, *A Perfect Union*, 41–62, and Mattern and Shulman, eds., *Selected Letters*, 38–48 and 90–105.

10. J.C.S. Stagg, *Mr. Madison's War: Politics, Diplomacy, and Warfare in the Early Republic, 1783–1830* (Princeton: Princeton University Press, 1983); Bradford Perkins, *Prologue to War: England and the United States, 1805–1812* (Berkeley: University of California Press, 1968); Clifford L. Egan, *Neither Peace nor War: Franco-American Relations, 1803–1812* (Baton Rouge: Louisiana State University Press, 1983); Donald R. Hickey, *The War of 1812: A Forgotten Conflict* (Urbana: University of Illinois Press, 1989). See also Ralph Ketcham, *James Madison, A Biography* (Charlottesville: University Press of Virginia, 1990), 441–73.

11. Edward Coles to Brothers and Sisters, February 3, 1810, Edward Coles Collections, HSP. On War Hawks, see Thomas Kanon, "'Mr. Madison, Felix Grundy, and the Devil': A Western War Hawk in Congress," *Filson Historical Quarterly* 75 (Fall 2001), 433–68; Harry W. Fritz, "The War Hawks of 1812: Party Leadership in the Twelfth Congress," *Capital Studies* 5 (Spring 1977), 25–42; Ronald L. Hatenbuehler, "The War Hawks and the Question of Congressional Leadership in 1812," *Pacific Historical Review* 14 (Winter 1976), 1–22; and Clifford Egan, "The Path to War in 1812 through the Eyes of a New Hampshire 'War Hawk,'" *Historical New Hampshire* 30 (Summer 1975), 147–77. On Henry Clay, see Robert V. Remini, *Henry Clay: Statesman for the Union* (New York: W. W. Norton, 1991), 55–71. See also Steven Watts, *The Republic Reborn: War and the Making of Liberal America, 1790–1815* (Baltimore: Johns Hopkins University Press, 1987).

12. William Plumer, diary entry, March 5, 1806, in William Plumer, Jr., *Life of William Plumer*, edited by A. P. Peabody [1857] (New York: DeCapo Press, 1969), 340–41; Abijah Bigelow to Hannah Bigelow, December 29, 1810, "Letters of Abijah Bigelow, Member of Congress, to His Wife," *Proceedings of the American Antiquarian Society* New Series 40 (April 16–October 15, 1930), 313; William Plumer, *Memorandum of Proceedings in the United States Senate, 1803–1807* (New York: E. S. Brown, 1923), 478; and Bigelow to Bigelow, December 23, 1810, "Letters of Abijah Bigelow," 311.

13. Edward Coles to Mother and Sisters, February 4, 1810, Edward Coles Collection, HSP. See also Edward Coles to Brother [John], February 3, 1810, Edward Coles Collections, HSP. On the circumstances surrounding Isaac Coles's resignation, see

Isaac A. Coles to James Madison, December 29, 1809, Edward Coles Papers, CHS; Isaac A. Coles to Brother [John], January 8, 1810, Edward Coles Collection, HSP. See also editorial note in J.C.A. Stagg et al., eds., *The Papers of James Madison*, Presidential Series (Charlottesville: University Press of Virginia, 1992), 2: 151. For contemporary reports of the investigation of the incident, see *Annals of Congress* 11 Congress, 2nd Session, 685, 705, 987–88.

14. Edward Coles to Mother and Sisters, February 4, 1810, Edward Coles Collections, HSP; William Plumer, Jr., *Life of William Plumer*; "Memoirs of a Senator from Pennsylvania, IV," *Pennsylvania Magazine of History and Biography* 62 (April 1938), 235–36.

15. Minnie Clare Yarborough, ed., *The Reminiscences of William C. Preston* (Chapel Hill: University of North Carolina Press, 1933), 8–9.

16. Edward Coles to Brother [John], November 30, 1810, Edward Coles Collection, HSP; Foster, *Jeffersonian America*, 86. See also Allgor, *Parlor Politics*, 48–101.

17. Seaton diary, November 12, 1812, in Josephine Seaton, *William Winston Seaton of the National Intelligencer* [1871] (New York: Arno Press, 1970), 86.

18. Edward Coles to Brother [John], January 28, 1811, Papers of Edward Coles, 1786–1868, PU; Edward Coles to Brother [John], March 18, 1811, Edward Coles Collection, HSP. See also "Autobiographical Notes," 1863, Edward Coles Collection, HSP. On American relations with Great Britain and France during this period, see Perkins, *Prologue to War*; Egan, *Neither Peace nor War*; and Stagg, *Mr. Madison's War*.

19. On Robert Smith's intrigues, see James A. Rutland, *Presidency of James Madison* (Lawrence: University Press of Kansas, 1990), 74; Ketcham, *James Madison*, 484–87; and Thom M. Armstrong, *Politics, Diplomacy and Intrigue in the Early Republic: The Cabinet Career of Robert Smith, 1801–1811* (Dubuque, Iowa: Kendall/Hunt, 1991). For the newspaper battle, see *National Intelligencer*, April 25, 1811; Robert Smith, *Address to the People of the United States* (n.p., 1811); *National Intelligencer*, July 4, 6, and 9, August 13 and 15, 1811; and Joseph Gales, "Recollections of the Civil History of the War of 1812," *Daily National Intelligencer*, August 8, 1857. See also Stagg, *Mr. Madison's War*, 68–74.

20. Edward Coles to Dolley Payne Todd Madison, June 10, 1811, Papers of Edward Coles, 1786–1868, PU. See also Dolley Payne Todd Madison to Edward Coles, June 15, 1811, in Mattern and Shulman, eds., *Selected Letters*, 144. Samuel Smith had campaigned vigorously for Madison's election in 1808, but adamantly opposed the appointment of Albert Gallatin as secretary of state, and, together with Virginians Wilson Cary Nicholas and William Branch Giles, blocked Gallatin's nomination. In an effort to appease Smith and repair this division within the Republican Party, Madison appointed Smith's brother, Robert, to the post of Secretary of State and reserved the Treasury for Gallatin. Although temporarily appeased, Smith, Nicholas, and Giles formed the nucleus of the "Invisibles," a group of senators who routinely thwarted administration policy initiatives throughout Madison's presidency. On opposition to Gallatin and the rise of the "Invisibles," see Frank A. Cassell, *Merchant Congressman in the Young Republic: Samuel Smith of Maryland, 1752–1832* (Madison: University of Wisconsin Press, 1971), 144–47; Dice Robins Anderson, *William Branch Giles: A Study in the Politics of Virginia and the Nation, 1790–1839* (Menasha, Wisc.: George Banta, 1914), 146–49; John S. Pancake, *Samuel Smith and the Politics of Business, 1752–1832* (Tuscaloosa: University of Alabama Press, 1972), 71–91; and Irving Brant, *James*

Madison: The President, 1809–1812 (New York: Bobbs-Merrill, 1956), 22–33. See also John S. Pancake, "The 'Invisibles': A Chapter in the Opposition to President Madison," *Journal of Southern History* 21 (February 1955), 17–37.

21. Regarding who and where Coles visited, see James Monroe to Edward Coles, May 19 and 25, 1811, Papers of Edward Coles, 1786–1868, PU; "Autobiographical Notes," 1863, Edward Coles Collection, HSP. On Republican disunity in Pennsylvania, New York, and Maryland, see J.C.A. Stagg, "James Madison and the 'Malcontents': The Political Origins of the War of 1812," *WMQ* 3rd Ser. 33 (October 1976), 61–63; Stagg, *Mr. Madison's War*, 48–53.

22. Elbridge Gerry to Edward Coles, March 17, 1812, Papers of Edward Coles, 1786–1868, PU ; Edward Coles to Brother, March 26, 1812, Edward Coles Collection, HSP.

23. Edward Coles to Brother, May 6, 1812, Edward Coles Collection, HSP; Stagg, *Mr. Madison's War*, 100–108.

24. Elbridge Gerry to James Madison, July 5, 1812, in Robert A. Rutland and Thomas A. Mason, eds., *The Papers of James Madison, Presidential Series* (Charlottesville: University Press of Virginia, 1999), 4: 560; William Wirt to James Monroe, quoted in Norman K. Risjord, *Jefferson's America, 1760–1815* (Madison: Madison House, 1991), 282; Abijah Bigelow to Hannah Bigelow, June 16, 1812, "Letters of Abijah Bigelow," 339–40. See Hickey, *The War of 1812*, 52–53.

25. Edward Coles to Brothers and Sisters, February 3, 1810, Edward Coles to Mother and Sisters, February 4, 1810, Edward Coles Collection, HSP.

26. Edward Coles to Brother [John], February 27, and December 17, 1810 Edward Coles Collection, HSP.

27. Elisa Coles to Edward Coles, April 1, 1807; Isaac A. Coles to John Coles, January 8, 1810, Edward Coles Collection, HSP.

28. Edward Coles to William Madison, December 23, 1807; Edward Coles to Hawkins, March 1, 1809, Papers of Edward Coles, 1786–1868, PU. The idea that young people might marry for affection rather than economic interest was gaining popularity during the early nineteenth century. See Anya Jabour, *Marriage in the Early Republic: Elizabeth and William Wirt and the Companionate Ideal* (Baltimore: Johns Hopkins University Press, 1998).

29. Edward Coles to Mother and Sisters, February 4, 1810; Edward Coles to Brothers, February 27, 1810, Edward Coles Collection, HSP.

30. Edward Coles to Brothers and Sisters, February 3, 1810, Edward Coles Collection, HSP. For the earlier possible reference to Miss Hay, see Eliza Coles to Edward Coles, April 1, 1807, Edward Coles Collection, HSP. For Miss Hay's presence at Enniscorthy, see William Cabell Rives to Edward Coles, August 4, 1807, Edward Coles Collection, HSP. On George Hay, see E. Lee Shepard, "George Hay," *American National Biography Online* http://www.anb.org/articles/11/11-00396.html.

31. Edward Coles to Brother [John], March 26, 1812, and May 6, 1812, Edward Coles Collection, HSP. See also Dolley Madison to Anna Cutts, March 20, 1812, in Mattern and Shulman, eds., *Selected Letters*, 157; and Ketcham, *James Madison*, 519–20. On Marie's reluctance, see Anya Jabour, *Scarlett's Sisters: Young Women of the Old South* (Chapel Hill: University of North Carolina Press, 2007), 113–149.

32. Shepard, "George Hay," *American National Biography Online*, http://www.anb.org/articles/11/11-00396.html. On Hay and Missouri, see Robert Pierce Forbes, *The*

Missouri Compromise and Its Aftermath: Slavery and the Meaning of America (Chapel Hill: University of North Carolina Press, 2007), 64–65 and 98.

33. Jabour, *Scarlet's Sisters*, 177–180; David Hackett Fisher and James C. Kelly, *Bound Away: Virginia and the Westward Movement* (Charlottesville: University of Virginia Press, 2000), 135–80; Philip J. Schwarz, *Migrants against Slavery: Virginians and the Nation* (Charlottesville: University Press of Virginia, 2000); Joan E. Cashin, *A Family Venture: Men and Women on the Southern Frontier* (Baltimore: Johns Hopkins University Press, 1991); and Melinda S. Buza, "'Pledges of Our Love'": Friendship Love, and Marriage among the Virginia Gentry, 1800–1825," in *The Edge of the South: Life in Nineteenth-Century Virginia*, edited by Edward L. Ayers and John C. Willis (Charlottesville: University of Virginia Press, 1991), 9–36.

34. Abijah Bigelow to Hannah Bigelow, December 18, 1812, "Letters of Abijah Bigelow," 346.

35. [Josiah Quincy], "Address of the Minority to Their Constituents," *Annals of Congress*, July 1, 1812; sermon by David Osgood quoted in Ketcham, *James Madison*, 537; Yarborough, ed., *The Reminiscences*, 9. See also Hickey, *The War of 1812*, 54–56; Allgor, *A Perfect Union*, 289–293 and Ketcham, *James Madison*, 534–53.

36. Edward Coles to Brother [John], November 25, 1812, Papers of Edward Coles, 1786–1868, PU; Dolley Madison to Edward Coles, June 10, 1813, Dolley Payne Todd Madison Papers, UVA; Edward Coles to Mother [Rebecca Tucker Coles], December 2 and 9, 1812, Edward Coles Collection, HSP. See also Ketcham, *James Madison*, 553; Allgor, *A Perfect Union*, 291–93. The event was at least a partial success politically. The next day the naval committee approved a much needed appropriation bill.

37. Edward Coles to Brother, November 25, 1812, Papers of Edward Coles, 1786–1868, PU; Edward Coles to Mother, December 9, 1812, Edward Coles Collection, HSP. Dr. Everett had attempted to cut off the offending sac in July 1812, but during the fall Coles experienced a second attack. The operations left him confined to his bed for long periods as he waited for the incisions to heal. See also Edward Coles to John Coles March 28, 1813, Edward Coles Collection, HSP.

38. Abijah Bigelow to Hannah Bigelow, December 18, 1812, "Letters of Abijah Bigelow," 346; William Burwell to Letitia Burwell, January 19, 1813, quoted in Allgor, *A Perfect Union*, 293. See also Ketcham, *James Madison*, 558–62; Allgor, *A Perfect Union*, 296–99; Stagg, *Mr. Madison's War*; Hickey, *The War of 1812*, 107–58.

39. Edward Coles to Mother, May 3, 1813, Edward Coles Collection, HSP.

40. Edward Coles to Mother, May 26, 1813, Edward Coles Collection, HSP. See also Peter J. Kastor, "'What Are the Advantages of Acquisition': Inventing Expansion in the Early American Republic," *American Quarterly* 60 (December 2008), 1003–35. See also Fisher and Kelly, *Bound Away*, 135–80. On Nicholas Biddle, see William G. Shade, "Nicholas Biddle," *American National Biography Online*, http://www.anb.org/articles/03/03-00039.html; and Thomas P. Govan, *Nicholas Biddle: Nationalist and Public Banker, 1786–1844* (Chicago: University of Chicago Press, 1959).

41. Roderick N. Ryon, "Moral Reform and Democratic Politics: The Dilemma of Roberts Vaux," *Quaker History* (Winter 1970), 3–14; and Donald Brooks Kelley, "Roberts Vaux," *American National Biography Online*, http://www.anb.org/articles/15/15-01249.html.

42. Dolley Payne Madison to Edward Coles, May 13, 1813, in Mattern and Shulman, eds., *Selected Letters*, 176–77. Madison confirmed this decision himself in a letter

written a week later. See James Madison to Edward Coles, May 17, 1813, Papers of Edward Coles, 1786–1868, PU. For Coles's reaction, see Edward Coles to Mother, May 19, 1813, Edward Coles Collection, HSP.

43. Edward Coles to Brother [John], June 2, 1813; Edward Coles to Brother [John], November 30, 1810, Edward Coles Collection, HSP; Edward Coles to Brother [John], January 28, 1811, Papers of Edward Coles, 1786–1868, PU; Edward Coles to Brother [John], March 26, 1812, Edward Coles Collection, HSP. In fact, Coles never lived on the plantation. He rented it in 1809 and then hired Mr. Weathered, his father's trusted overseer, to manage the estate while he was in Washington City. See Ledger of John Coles, 1770–1807, 2: 278, and "List of Clothing Issued in the Fall, 1810–1811," Box 2, Carter-Smith Collection, UVA.

44. Allgor, A Perfect Union, 213–15.

45. James Madison to Robert Pleasants, October 30, 1791, in Robert A. Rutland and Thomas A. Mason, eds., The Papers of James Madison, Presidential Series (Charlottesville: University Press of Virginia, 1983), 14: 91–92. On Madison's benevolence, see Allgor, A Perfect Union, 211–13. For an insightful discussion of Madison's views on the slavery issue, see Drew R. McCoy, The Last of the Fathers: James Madison and the Republican Legacy (Cambridge: Cambridge University Press, 1989), 260–76.

46. Coles, "Autobiography," April 1844, Edward Coles Collection, HSP; James Madison to Robert Pleasants, October 30, 1791, in Rutland and Mason, eds., The Papers of James Madison, 14: 92. On the domestic slave trade in Washington City, see works cited in note 5 above. On Madison's concern for the influence of the persistence of slavery on the American image abroad, see McCoy, Last of the Fathers, 262–72. On the expansion of slavery into the Southwest, see Seth Rothman, Slave Country: Expansion and the Origins of the Deep South (Cambridge: Harvard University Press, 2007).

47. Mason, Slavery and Politics, 42–74. See also Rachel Hope Cleves, "'Hurtful to the State': The Political Morality of Federalist Antislavery," in Contesting Slavery: The Politics of Bondage and Freedom in the New American Nation, edited by John Craig Hammond and Matthew Mason (Charlottesville: University of Virginia Press, 2011), 207–26.

48. Dolley Madison to Edward Coles, May 13, 1813, in Mattern and Shulman, eds., Selected Letters, 176; for a general description of the British strategy in 1813–1814, see Hickey, The War of 1812, 182–95.

49. John Randolph to Josiah Quincy, July 4, 1813, in Edmund Quincy, Life of Josiah Quincy of Massachusetts (Boston: Ticknor and Fields, 1868), 333. Christopher T. George, "Mirage of Freedom: African Americans in the War of 1812," Maryland Historical Magazine 91 (Winter 1996), 433–34, and Frank A. Cassell, "Slaves of the Chesapeake Bay Area and the War of 1812," Journal of Negro History 57 (April 1972), 144–55.

50. "Report of His Excellency Governor Barbour to the Council of State, May 12, 1812," in H. W. Flournoy, ed., Calendar of Virginia State Papers and Other Manuscripts from January 1, 1808 to December 31, 1833 (Richmond, 1892), 10: 137; Elbridge Gerry, Jr., The Diary of Elbridge Gerry, Jr. (New York: Brentano's, 1927), 199; and Margaret Bayard Smith to Mrs. Kirkpatrick, July 20, 1813, in Smith, The First Forty Years, 90.

51. Diary of Elbridge Gerry, 198–99; Nathaniel Burwell to Governor of Virginia, March 30, 1813, in Flournoy, ed., Calendar of Virginia State Papers, 10: 217; and Richmond Enquirer, July 30, 1813. On slave patrols generally, see Sally E. Hadden, Slave

Patrols: Law and Violence in Virginia and the Carolinas (Cambridge: Harvard University Press, 2001).

52. Edward Coles to Thomas Jefferson, 31 July 1814, Papers of Edward Coles, 1786–1868, PU.

53. Allgor, *A Perfect Union*, 303–11 (quote on 310); Hickey, *The War of 1812*, 195–201; Anthony S. Pitch, *The Burning of Washington: The British Invasion of 1814* (Annapolis: Naval Institute Press, 2000), 17–21; Andrew Tully, *When They Burned the White House* (New York: Simon and Schuster, 1961), 108; George, "Mirage of Freedom," 433–34; Cassell, "Slaves of the Chesapeake Bay Area," 144–55.

54. Thomas Jefferson to Edward Coles, 25 August 1814, Papers of Edward Coles, 1786–1868, PU. On Jefferson and war with Britain, see Christa Dierksheide, "'The great improvement and civilization of that race': Jefferson and the 'Amelioration' of Slavery ca: 1770–1826," *Early American Studies: An Interdisciplinary Journal* 6 (Spring 2008), 174–75. On the British attack, see Allgor, *Perfect Union*, 312–19; Hickey, *The War of 1812*, 197–201; and Pitch, *The Burning of Washington*, 99–129.

55. Thomas Jefferson to James Heaton, 20 May 1826, in Merrill D. Peterson, ed., *Writings: Autobiography/ Notes on the State of Virginia/ Public and Private Papers/ Addresses/ Letters* (New York: Library of America, 1984), 1345; Edward Coles to Thomas Jefferson, 26 September 1814, Papers of Edward Coles, PU. On Jefferson and slavery's natural death, see François Furstenberg, *In the Name of the Father: Washington, Slavery and the Making of a Nation* (New York: Penguin, 2007), 89–92; Paul Finkelman, *Slavery and the Founders: Race and Liberty in the Age of Jefferson* (London: M. E. Sharpe, 1996)," 181–212.

56. For his 1815 western tour, see Edward Coles to Mother, June 27, 1815, Edward Coles Collection, HSP; Edward Coles to James Madison, July 25, 1815, Edward Coles Papers, CHS; Edward Coles to Brother [John], July 28, 1815 and September 11, 1815, Edward Coles Collection, HSP; Edward Coles to James Madison, November 6 and 24, 1815, Edward Coles Papers, CHS. See also Rebecca Coles, "Almanac Memorandum," undated, Edward Coles Collection, HSP. On the sale of Rockfish farm, see Edward Coles to Brother [John], November 30, 1810 and June 2, 1813. For his western land purchase, see "Elprado," November 9, 1815, deed recorded May 1, 1816, recorded in Edward Coles, "Ledger: Land Transactions, 1818–1869; Some Accounts of Hugh Roberts Estate, 1836–66," volume 5, Edward Coles Collection, HSP. For the final quote, see Edward Coles to Nicholas Biddle, May 15, 1816, Edward Coles Papers, ISHL.

57. Edward Coles to Nicholas Biddle, May 15, 1816, Edward Coles Papers, ISHL.

58. James Madison to Edward Coles, July 7, 1816, Papers of Edward Coles, 1786–1868, PU; Edward Coles to James Madison, July 11, 1816, Edward Coles Papers, CHS; Rebecca Coles, "Almanac Memorandum," undated, Edward Coles Collection, HSP. For a discussion of the diplomatic problem Coles was dispatched to resolve, see Harry Ammon, *James Monroe: The Quest for National Identity* (Charlottesville: University Press of Virginia, 1990), 350.

59. "Memoir of Edward Coles," undated, ISHL; Edward Coles to Brother [John], October 4, 1816, Edward Coles Collection, HSP; Edward Coles to James Monroe, December 14, 1816, Papers of Edward Coles, 1786–1868, PU. For Coles's observations on Russian society, see "Interesting Views of the Russian Empire" [by Edward Coles], *Richmond Enquirer*, December 13 and 16, 1817. On American slavery and Russian

serfdom generally, see Peter Kolchin, *Unfree Labor: American Slavery and Russian Serfdom* (Cambridge: Harvard University Press, 1987).

60. [Coles], "Interesting Views of the Russian Empire."

61. "Memoir of Edward Coles," undated, ISHL; and Coles, "Autobiography," April 1844, Edward Coles Collection, HSP. See also Yarborough, ed., *The Reminiscences*, 28.

62. Ninian Edwards to Edward Coles, January 18, 1818, Edward Coles Papers, CHS; Edward Coles to James Monroe, October 11, 1818, Edward Coles Collection, HSP.

63. Edward Coles to James Monroe, October 11, 1818, Edward Coles Collection, HSP.

64. Edward Coles to James Monroe, October 11, 1818, Edward Coles Collection, HSP; James Monroe to Edward Coles, January 31, 1819, Papers of Edward Coles, 1786–1868, PU. Coles received his appointment on March 5, 1819. See E. B. Washburne, *Sketch of Edward Coles, Second Governor of Illinois, and of the Slavery Struggle of 1823–24* [1882] (New York: Negro University Press, 1969), 54.

3 / Pioneering Antislavery Politics

1. Edward Coles to Mother [Rebecca Tucker Coles], April 24, 1819, Edward Coles Collection, HSP. For a more romantic rendering of the emancipation scene, see Edward Coles, "Autobiography," April 1844, and Edward Coles "The Emancipation of His Slaves, as Told by Him," October 1827, Edward Coles Collection, HSP. Coles and his slaves left Virginia on March 30 and arrived at Pittsburgh on April 11. See Rebecca Coles, Almanac Memorandum, Edward Coles Collection, HSP.

2. William Newnham Blane, *An Excursion through the United States and Canada during the Years 1822–23* (London: Baldwin, Cradock, and Joy, 1824), 167; Elias Pym Fordham, *Personal Narrative of Travels in Virginia, Maryland, Pennsylvania, Ohio, Indiana, Kentucky and of a Residence in Illinois Country, 1817–1818*, edited by Frederic A. Ogg (Cleveland: A. H. Clark, 190), 187–88; Philip Freneau, "On the Emigration to America" (1784), in Giles Gunn, ed., *Early American Writing* (New York: Penguin Books, 1994), 560–61.

3. Victor Collot, *A Journey in North America*, 2 volumes. [1826] (New York: AMS Press, 1974), 1: 233; Gershom Flagg to Azariah C. Flagg, December 7, 1817, and June 12, 1819, in Barbara Lawrence and Nedra Branz, eds., *The Flagg Correspondence: Selected Letters, 1816–1854* (Carbondale: Southern Illinois University Press, 1986), 12–13 and 24–25; Morris Birkbeck, *Notes on a Journey in America* (Ann Arbor: University Microforms, 1966), 55; Morris Birkbeck to [unknown], November 30, 1817, in Morris Birkbeck, *Letters from Illinois* [1818] (Ann Arbor: University Microforms, 1968), 17–18.

4. Reverend Thomas Lippincott, "Early Days in Madison County, No. 10," 35–36, Thomas Lippincott Papers, transcripts, ISHS. See also Ellen Nore and Dick Norrish, *Edwardsville, Illinois, An Illustrated History* (St. Louis: G. Bradley Publishing, 1996), 8–34; W. T. Norton, *Centennial History of Madison County, Illinois and Its People, 1812–1912* (Chicago: Lewis Publishing, 1912), 497–502.

5. "Replication by Warren," *Free West*, May 3, 1855, reprinted in *Governor Edward Coles*, edited by Clarence Alvord (Springfield: Illinois Historical Society, 1920), 339.

6. Edward Coles to Payne Todd, January 3, 1815, Papers of Edward Coles, 1786–1868, PU.

7. Edward Coles to Nicholas Biddle, April 8, 1815, and Edward Coles to R.S.M., March 31, 1815; Edward Coles to Payne Todd, January 3, 1815, Papers of Edward Coles,

1786–1868, PU. "Elprado," 2,000 acres, November 9, 1815, $3000.00; St. Louis, 6 arpents (about 5 acres), September 7, 1818, $2,500.00; "Soldier Bounty Lands," 3,680 acres, August 15, 1818, $2,300.00; and "Bryants Creek Tract," 2,250 acres, November 25, 1818, $3500.00, Edward Coles, "Ledger: Land Transactions, 1818–1839; Some Accounts of Hugh Roberts Estate, 1836–66," volume 5, Edward Coles Collections, HSP. On the Military Bounty Tact, see Siyong Park, "Perceptions of Land Quality and the Settlement of Northern Pike County, 1821–1836," *Western Regional Studies* 3 (Winter 1980), 5–21; and Theodore L. Carlson, *The Illinois Military Tract: A Study of Land Occupation Utilization and Tenure* (Urbana: University of Illinois Press, 1951).

8. Edward Coles to Mother, April 24, 1819, Edward Coles Collection, HSP.

9. Phyllis J. Bauer, ed., *Madison County, Illinois 1820 Federal Census* (McHenry, Ill.: Phyllis J. Bauer, undated), ISHL; "Tax List, 1820," in Theodore Calvin Pease, *The County Archives of the State of Illinois*, Collection of Illinois State Historical Library, volume 12, Bibliographical Series, volume 3 (Springfield: Illinois State Historical Library, 1915), 410 n2; Margaret Cross Norton, ed., *Illinois Census Returns, 1810, 1818* (Springfield: Illinois State Historical Library, 1935) ; Norton, ed., *Illinois Census Returns, 1820* (Springfield: Illinois State Historical Library, 1934); Nore and Norrish, *Edwardsville, Illinois*, 8–34; Norton, *Centennial History*, 497–506; and Solon J. Buck, *Illinois in 1818* (Springfield: Illinois Centennial Commission, 1917), 90.

10. Edward Coles to James Madison, July 20, 1819, Edward Coles Papers, CHS; Edward Coles "Prairieland Farm," 394 acres, May 20 and June 11, 1819, $1,800.00, "Ledger: Land Transactions, 1818–1839," and "Account Book, 1818–1839," volume 4, Edward Coles Collection, HSP. See also *History of Madison County, Illinois, with Biographical Sketches of Many Prominent Men and Pioneers* (Edwardsville, Ill.: W. R. Brink, 1882), 97.

11. Edward Coles to James Madison, July 20, 1819, Edward Coles Papers, CHS.

12. *Illinois Emigrant*, March 20, 1819, cited in Buck, *Illinois in 1818*, 152. See also James Simeone, *Democracy and Slavery in Frontier Illinois, The Bottomland Republic* (Dekalb: Northern Illinois University Press, 2000), 46; and D. W. Meinig, *The Shaping of America: A Geographical Perspective on 500 Years of History*, vol. 2, *Continental America, 1800–1867* (New Haven: Yale University Press, 1993), 236–45.

13. Daniel M. Parkison, "Pioneer Life in Wisconsin" [1855], *Collection of the Historical Society of Wisconsin* (Madison: University of Wisconsin Press, 1984), 326–27; Fordham, *Personal Narrative*, 125; and Christiana Homes Tillson, *A Woman's Story of Pioneer Illinois*, edited by Milo Milton Quaife (Carbondale: Southern Illinois University Press, 1995), 81–82. See also Simeone, *Democracy and Slavery*, 42–46.

14. Parkison, "Pioneer Life in Wisconsin," 327; Fordham, *Personal Narrative*, 125; and Birkbeck, *Notes on a Journey in America*, 57–58, 112, and 131–32. On frontier mutuality, see John Mack Faragher, *Sugar Creek: Life on the Illinois Frontier* (New Haven: Yale University Press, 1987), 130–36, and Arthur Clinton Boggess, *The Settlement of Illinois, 1778–1830* (Chicago: Chicago Historical Society, 1908), 169–70.

15. Coles, "Account Book, 1818–1839," volume 4, Edward Coles Collection, HSP. During their second year of employment, Coles paid them in "stock, tools, [and] food" and allowed them to keep "half of all they made" on the farm, which they then sold on the market for a profit. He also continued to purchase "Beef for my Negroes," clothing for Robert, Thomas, Kate, and the children, and once again covered their accounts with the local physician. Nancy Gains and Polly Crawford found employment as domestic

servants in Edwardsville and the immediate countryside. Suckey and Emanuel, along with their children, moved to St. Louis, where they lived in one of Coles's rental units and worked as hired hands and domestic servants. See Dana O. Jensen, ed., "The Diary of a Yankee Farmer in Missouri, 1819: 'I At Home: Part IV,' by Stephen Hempstead, Sr.," *The Bulletin—Missouri Historical Society* (April 1958), 285–87.

16. Tillson, *A Woman's Story of Pioneer Illinois*, 108; Buck, *Illinois in 1818*, 137–41; and Boggess, *Settlement of Illinois*, 169–71.

17. Coles, "Account Book, 1818–1839," volume 4, Edward Coles Collection, HSP.

18. James Madison to Edward Coles, September 3, 1819, Papers of Edward Coles, 1786–1868, PU.

19. Edward Coles to Josiah Meigs, August 5, 1819, cited in Malcolm J. Rohrbough, *The Land Office Business: The Settlement and Administration of American Public Lands, 1789–1837* (New York: Oxford University Press, 1968), 139. On the panic of 1819, see John Lauritz Larson, *The Market Revolution in America: Liberty, Ambition, and the Eclipse of the Common Good* (New York: Cambridge University Press, 2010), 39–45; Daniel Dupre, "The Panic of 1819 and the Political Economy of Sectionalism," in *The Economy of Early America: Historical Perspectives and New Directions*, edited by Cathy Matson (University Park: Pennsylvania State University Press, 2006), 263–93; and Edwin J. Perkins, "Langdon Cheves and the Panic of 1819: A Reassessment," *Journal of Economic History* 44 (June 1984), 455–61.

20. Gershom Flagg to Azariah C. Flagg, December 20, 1820, in Solon J. Buck, ed., "Pioneer Letters of Gershom Flagg," *Transactions of Illinois State Historical Society* (1910), 167.

21. Gershom Flagg to Artemas Flagg, October 6, 1820, in Buck ed., "Pioneer Letters of Gershom Flagg," 166; Horatio Newhall to [J. and J.] Newhall, March 22, 1823, Horatio Newhall Papers, Folder 1, ISHL.

22. Edward Coles to Josiah Meigs, August 5, 1819, cited in Rohrbough, *Land Office Business*, 139; Coles, "Account Book, 1818–1839," volume 4, Edward Coles Collections, HSP.

23. Edward Coles to Josiah Meigs, August 6, 1821, cited in Rohrbough, *Land Office Business*, 146; Coles, "Account Book, 1818–1839," volume 4, Edward Coles Collections, HSP.

24. Coles, "Account Book, 1818–1839," volume 4, Edward Coles Collections, HSP.

25. "An Act to Prevent the Migration of Free Negroes and Mulattoes into this Territory and for other purposes," in *The Laws of the Illinois Territory, 1809–1818*, edited by Francis S. Philbrick (Springfield: Illinois State Historical Library, 1950), 91–92; Norton, ed., *Illinois Census Returns, 1810, 1818*, and *Illinois Census Returns, 1820*; *Fifth Census (1830), Illinois*, M-19, roll 22, Western Reserve Historical Society, Cleveland.

26. "An Act Respecting Free Negroes, Mulattoes, Servants and Slaves," March 30, 1819, reprinted in Helen Cox Tregillis, *River Roads to Freedom: Fugitive Slave Notices and Sheriff Notices Found in Illinois Sources* (Bowie, Md.: Heritage Books, 1988), 2–12; *An Act Regulating the Practices of the Supreme and Circuit Courts of Illinois, at their Second Session, Held at Kaskaskia, 1819* (Kaskaskia, Ill.: Blackwell and Berry, 1819), 143; Emile J. Verlie, ed., *Illinois Constitutions* (Springfield: Illinois State Historical Library, 1919), 27. See also Charles N. Zucker, "The Free Negro Question: Race Relations in Ante-Bellum Illinois, 1801–1860," Ph. D. dissertation, Northwestern University, 1972, 164.

27. Thomas Lippincott, "The Conflict of the Century," transcript, Thomas Lippincott Papers, ISHS; John Woods, *Two Years' Residence in the Settlement on the English Prairie, in the Illinois Country, United States* (London: Longman, Hurst, Rees, Orme, and Brown, 1822), 175. For the southern origin of Illinois's early American settlers, see John D. Barnhart, "The Southern Influence in the Formation of Illinois," *Journal of the Illinois State Historical Society* 32 (September 1939), 348–78; James E. Davis, *Frontier Illinois* (Bloomington: Indiana University Press, 1998), 159–69; Nicole Etcheson, *The Emerging Midwest: Upland Southerners and the Political Culture of the Old Northwest, 1787–1861* (Bloomington: Indiana University Press, 1996), 306; Faragher, *Sugar Creek*, 45–46; Boggess, *Settlement of Illinois*, 91–92; and Buck, *Illinois in 1818*, 95–98. This is not to say that no northerners immigrated to Illinois during this period. While a fairly sizable number immigrated into the region during the first decades of the nineteenth century, the majority of the state's northern-born immigrants settled in the northern portion of the state after 1830. See Solon J. Buck, *The New England Element in Illinois Politics before 1833* (Davenport, Iowa: n.p., 1912).

28. Coles, "Sketch of the Emancipation," October 1827, Edward Coles Collection, HSP. For the job advertisement, see *Edwardsville Spectator*, June 26, 1821, and "Replication by Warren, June 29, 1855," *Free West*, July 5, 1855, in Alvord, *Governor Edward Coles*, 363–64.

29. Thomas Cobb appears in Coles's account book for the last time on June 2, 1821, when Coles noted purchasing "9 yards of Linen for Tom." See Coles, "Account Book, 1818–1839," volume 4, Edward Coles Collection, HSP. On rent, see Boggess, *Settlement in Illinois*, 166. He notes that the average rent was one peck of corn per acre per year. Four pecks equals a bushel. If Coles's ex-slaves had paid by the acre, their rent should have been 73.5 bushels of corn. Instead, they paid 30 bushels.

30. Coles, "Sketch of the Emancipation," October 27, Edward Coles Collection, HSP.

31. Tillson, *A Woman's Story of Pioneer Illinois*, 138–41; Fordham, *Personal Narrative*, 210–12.

32. Norton, ed., *Illinois Census Returns 1810, 1818* and *Illinois Census Returns 1820*; George Flower, *History of the English Settlement in Edwards County, Illinois: Founded in 1817 and 1818, by Morris Birkbeck and George Flower* (Chicago: Fergus Printing, 1882), 199. See also John Craig Hammond, *Slavery, Freedom, and Expansion in the Early American West* (Charlottesville: University of Virginia Press, 2007), 96–123; and N. Dwight Harris, *The History of Negro Servitude in Illinois and of the Slavery Agitation in that State, 1719–1864* (New York: Negro University Press, 1969), 12–14.

33. The fervor over the Missouri controversy in Illinois contradicts Glover Moore's contention that few Americans were interested in the issue. See Glover Moore, *The Missouri Controversy, 1819–1821* (Lexington: University of Kentucky Press, 1953), 269–70. A number of more recent studies have likewise challenged Moore's assessment of the Missouri crisis. See Robert P. Forbes, *Missouri Compromise and Its Aftermath: Slavery and the Meaning of America* (Chapel Hill: University of North Carolina Press, 2007); Matthew Mason, *Slavery and Politics in the Early American Republic* (Chapel Hill: University of North Carolina Press, 2007), 177–212; Hammond, *Slavery, Freedom and Expansion*, 150–68.

34. *Edwardsville Spectator*, June 5, 1819.

35. *Illinois Intelligencer*, June 30, 1819.

36. Theodore Calvin Pease, *Illinois Election Returns, 1818–1848* (Springfield: Illinois State Historical Library, 1923), 4; *Illinois Intelligencer*, June 30, 1819; *Edwardsville Spectator*, August 28, 1819.

37. *Edwardsville Spectator*, July 4 and 11, 1820; Pease, ed., *Illinois Election Returns*, 5.

38. *Edwardsville Spectator*, July 10 and 31, 1819. Coles did own a significant amount of land in Missouri (see note 7 above), and at the time of the Missouri crisis he owned 3,000 acres of farmland in Missouri and was a major investor in St. Louis. See Coles, "Ledger: Land Transactions," Edward Coles Collection, HSP.

39. "Deed of Emancipation," in Patricia L. Sapp, ed., *Illinois, Madison County Court Records, 1813–1818 and Indenture Records, 1803–1826* (Springfield, Ill.: Folk Works Research, 1993), 101–104.

40. For the prevalence of this antislavery view, see Sean Wilentz, "Jeffersonian Democracy and the Origins of Political Antislavery in the United States: The Missouri Crisis Revisited," *Journal of the Historical Society* 4 (Fall 2004), 387–88.

41. Hammond, *Slavery, Freedom and Expansion*, 150–168; Wilentz, "Jeffersonian Democracy," 386–389; Joshua M. Zeitz, "The Missouri Compromise Reconsidered: Antislavery Rhetoric and the Emergence of Free Labor," *JER* 20 (Fall 2000), 451–53; Mason, *Slavery and Politics*, 188–192; Forbes, *Missouri Compromise*, 35–68.

42. Mason, *Slavery and Politics*, 155– 212; Forbes, *Missouri Compromise*, 106–110.

43. *Edwardsville Spectator*, April 17, 1821. See also Wilentz, "Jeffersonian Democracy," 391.

44. *Edwardsville Spectator*, April 17, 1821; Edward Coles to Mary Carter, April 18, 1821, Carter-Smith Family Collection, UVA; Announcement, *Edwardsville Spectator*, October 30, 1821.

45. Editorial Response, by Hooper Warren, *Edwardsville Spectator*, November 27, 1821.

46. To Mr. Warren, signed "Justice," *Edwardsville Spectator*, December 4, 1821.

47. John Reynolds, *My Own Times: Embracing also the History of My Life* (Chicago: Fergus Printing, 1879), 158; Reynolds, *Pioneer History of Illinois, Containing the Discovery, in 1673, and the History of the Country to the Year Eighteen Hundred and Eighteen, When the State Government was Organized* (Chicago: Fergus Printing, 1887), 112–14 and 194; William H. Brown, *Historical Sketch of the Early Movement in Illinois for the Legalization of Slavery* (Chicago: Steam Press of Church, Goodman and Donnelley, 1865), 19.

48. Nathaniel Buckmaster to John Buckmaster, April 14, 1822, Buckmaster-Curran Papers, Box 1, Folder 3, ISHL; Horatio Newhall to [J. and J.] Newhall, May 11, 1822, Horatio Newhall Papers, Folder 1, ISHL.

49. "Hon. Edward Coles, Esq.," by Hooper Warren, *Edwardsville Spectator*, April 9, 1822.

50. "For the Spectator, *To the various candidates who offer their services to the people of Illinois, to fill the office of Governor*," signed "The People of Illinois"; "For the Spectator. *To the Candidates for the next Legislature*," signed "A majority of the People," *Edwardsville Spectator*, April 2 and 13, 1822.

51. Reynolds, *My Own Times*, 159; Horatio Newhall to [J. and J.] Newhall, May 11, 1822, Horatio Newhall Papers, Folder 1, ISHL. For an opposing characterization of the election, see Kurt E. Leichtle and Bruce G. Carveth, *Crusade against Slavery: Edward Coles, Pioneer of Freedom* (Carbondale: Southern Illinois University Press,

2011), 92–98. Leichtle argues that "more important than slavery was banking, with internal improvements as a strong minor theme" (97).

52. "From the Intelligencer, No. 2," signed "Another One of the People," *Edwardsville Spectator*, July 10, 1821 (original in the *Illinois Intelligencer*, July 3, 1821). Phillips never denied that he held proslavery views. In December 1821, he did, however, confide to Thomas Sloo, Jr., a future representative from Jefferson County, that he thought the slavery issue was irrelevant. See Joseph B. Philips to Thomas Sloo, Jr., December 31, 1821, in Isaac J. Cox, ed., "Selections from the Torrence Papers," Historical and Philosophical Society of Ohio, *Quarterly* 6 (1911), 52. For Browne, see Norton, ed., *Illinois Census Returns, 1820*, 81; and Thomas Browne, Town lot, Gallatin County, March 8, 1815, and 320 acres, Saline, February 1, 1817, March 16, 1818, and August 31, 1818, Illinois Public Domain Land Tract Sales, ISA. For Moore, see Norton., ed. *Illinois Census Returns, 1820*, 201; James B. Moore, 160 acres Monroe County, December 3, 1814, Illinois Public Domain Land Tract Sales, ISA. Moore has been identified as an antislavery candidate by historians of early Illinois. See Theodore Calvin Pease, *The Frontier State, 1818–1848* (Chicago: McClurg, 1922), 74; R. Carlyle Buley, *The Old Northwest, Pioneer Period, 1815–1840* (Bloomington: Indiana University Press, 1962), 2: 21–22; and Boggess, *Settlement of Illinois*, 181–82.

53. Editorial by Hooper Warren, and "From the Illinois Intelligencer, June 29," *Edwardsville Spectator*, April 2 and July 6, 1822.

54. "From the Illinois Intelligencer, Extract of a letter dated, June 4, 1822," signed Edward Coles, *Edwardsville Spectator*, July 6, 1822. The original appeared in the *Illinois Intelligencer* on June 29, 1822.

55. "From the Intelligencer," *Edwardsville Spectator*, July 6, 1822; James Hall, *Letters from the West, containing sketches of scenery, manners, and customs and anecdotes connected to the first settlements of the western section of the United States* (London: Henry Colburn, 1828), 142.

56. "From the Intelligencer," *Edwardsville Spectator*, July 6, 1822.

57. "For the Intelligencer, Thomas Jefferson to Edward Coles, August 25, 1814," *Illinois Intelligencer*, July 2, 1822.

58. Pease, *Illinois Election Returns*, 14–18.

59. Editorial by Hooper Warren, *Edwardsville Spectator*, August 31, 1822; James Madison to Edward Coles, October 19, 1822, Papers of Edward Coles, 1786–1868, PU.

60. Mary Burtschi, *Vandalia: Wilderness Capital of Lincoln's Land* (Vandalia: Little Brick House, 1963), and William E. Baringer, *Lincoln's Vandalia, a Pioneer Portrait* (New Brunswick: Rutgers University Press, 1949).

61. "Fellow Citizens of the Senate and of the House of Representatives," December 5, 1822, by Edward Coles, *Edwardsville Spectator*, December 14, 1822; Commonplace Book, volume 8, Edward Coles Collection, HSP.

62. Ibid. For the committee reports, see "In the Senate . . . report of the Committee on Slavery and Kidnapping Free Negroes," *Edwardsville Spectator*, December 21, 1822; "From the Illinois Intelligencer, December 20 . . . report," *Illinois Gazette*, January 18, 1823; "In the House of Representatives . . . views of the minority," *Edwardsville Spectator*, December 28, 1822.

4 / Crafting an Antislavery Nationalism

1. Thomas Ford, *A History of Illinois from Its Commencement as a State in 1818 to*

1847 [1854] (Urbana: University of Illinois Press, 1995), 32; and Horatio Newhall to [J. and J.] Newhall, March 22, 1823, Horatio Newhall Papers, folder 1, ISHL. See also William H. Brown, *An Historical Sketch of the Early Movement in Illinois for the Legalization of Slavery* (Chicago: Church, Goodman and Donnelley, 1865), 22–30 and 185.

2. "To the People of the State of Illinois," signed Thomas Cox, Chairman, *Illinois Intelligencer*, March 8, 1823. This address was initially reported in the *Edwardsville Spectator*, March 1, 1823, and reprinted in the *Illinois Gazette*, March 29, 1823. The other members of the committee assigned to draft the address included General Guy W. Smith, John M'Lean, Theophilus W. Smith, Emanuel J. West, Thomas Reynolds, William Kinney, Alexander Pope Field, and Joseph A. Beaird. On the central role of the idea of "the people" and the representation of their opponents as elites in the pro-convention strategy, see James Simeone, *Democracy and Slavery in Frontier Illinois, The Bottomland Republic* (DeKalb: Northern Illinois University Press, 2000), 97–132. For a more recent discussion of the role of republicanism, see Adam Rowe, "The Republican Rhetoric of a Frontier Controversy: Newspapers in the Illinois Slavery Debate, 1823–1824," *JER* 31 (Winter 2011), 671–99.

3. "To the People of Illinois," signed "Risdon Moore, . . . Vandalia, 18 February 1823," *Illinois Intelligencer*, March 8, 1823; Lippincott, "The Conflict of the Century," typescript, Thomas Lippincott Papers, ISHS. See also Merton L. Dillon, "The Antislavery Movement in Illinois, 1809–1844," Ph. D. dissertation, University of Michigan, 1951, 85–87, and E. B. Washburne, *Sketch of Edward Coles, Second Governor of Illinois, and of the Slavery Struggle of 1823–4* [1882] (New York: Negro University Press, 1969), 99–102.

4. John Reynolds to Major Reynolds, May 3, 1823, John Reynolds Papers, ISHL; John Reynolds, *My Own Times: Embracing also the History of My Life* (Chicago: Fergus Printing, 1879), 153; Brown, *An Historical Sketch*, 31–32; Edward Coles to Mary Carter, March 15, 1823, Carter-Smith Family Collection, UVA.

5. Edward Coles to Eliza Carter, March 15, 1823, Carter-Smith Family Collection, UVA; "Mark of Respect," *Edwardsville Spectator*, March 8, 1823.

6. Edward Coles to Nicholas Biddle, April 22, 1823, Papers of Edward Coles, 1786–1868, PU. Brown, An Historical Sketch, 37–38; Reverend John Mason Peck to Hooper Warren, March 27, 1855, *Free West*, May 3, 1855, reprinted in *Governor Edward Coles*, edited by Clarence Alvord (Springfield: Illinois Historical Society, 1920), 334.

7. For Coles's reception in St. Clair County, see Edward Coles to Eliza Carter, March 15, 1823, Carter-Smith Family Collection, UVA; Lippincott, "Early Days in Madison County, No. 42," typescript, Thomas Lippincott Papers, ISHS; "Address to the Board of Managers of the St. Clair Society to prevent the further introduction of Slavery in the State of Illinois," unsigned [Rev. John Mason Peck], *Edwardsville Spectator*, April 12, 1823; "Address of the Monroe Society *to the People of the State of Illinois*," unsigned, *Edwardsville Spectator*, May 31, 1823. For notices and addresses from other anticonvention society meetings and dinners, see *Edwardsville Spectator*, May 10, July 12, August 16, September 6, 20, and 27, 1823 and March 16, 1824. See also, Brown, *An Historical Sketch*, 37–38; Reverend John Mason Peck to Hooper Warren, March 27, 1855, *Free West*, May 3, 1855, reprinted in Alvord, ed., *Governor Edward Coles*, 334.

8. "Agreement," February 18, 1823, reprinted in N. Dwight Harris, *The History of Negro Servitude in Illinois and of the Slavery Agitation in that State, 1719–1864* (New York: Negro University Press, 1969), 265–66; John Mason Peck to Hooper Warren,

March 27, 1855, *Free West*, May 3, 1855, in Alvord, ed., *Governor Edward Coles*, 234–35; Thomas Lippincott, "The Conflict of the Century," typescript, Thomas Lippincott Papers, ISHS. See also Dillon, "The Antislavery Movement in Illinois," 86–87.

9. Edward Coles to Nicholas Biddle, April 22, 1823, Papers of Edward Coles, 1786–1868, PU.

10. Edward Coles to Richard Flower, April 12, 1823, "Letters of Governor Edward Coles Bearing on the Struggle of Freedom and Slavery in Illinois," *Journal of Negro History* 3 (April 1918), 167. On the fallout between Birkbeck and Flower, men who emigrated to Illinois from England together, see Mary Ann Salter, "Quarreling in the English Settlement: The Flowers in Court," *Journal of the Illinois State Historical Society* 75.2 (1982), 101–14 and Christopher D. Schroeder, "'Dreams of a Prairie Republic': Morris Birkbeck and Settlement on the Indiana-Illinois Frontier, 1764–1860," Ph. D. dissertation, University of Delaware, 2000.

11. Editorial by Hooper Warren, December 21, 1854, *Free West*, December 21, 1854, and John Mason Peck to Hooper Warren, March 27, 1855, *Free West*, May 3, 1855, in Alvord, ed., *Governor Edward Coles*, 315–16 and 135–36. Peck claimed that "for many months, the project was known only to three persons, of which the writer was one." See also Charles N. Zucker, "The Free Negro Question: Race Relations in Ante-Bellum Illinois, 1801–1860," Ph.D. dissertation, Northwestern University, 1972, 106, and Kurt E. Leichtle and Bruce G. Carveth, *Crusade against Slavery: Edward Coles, Pioneer of Freedom* (Carbondale: Southern Illinois University Press, 2011), 181. On the political importance of newspapers and editors, see Jeffrey L. Pasley, *"The Tyranny of Printers": Newspaper Politics in the Early American Republic* (Charlottesville: University Press of Virginia, 2001).

12. "Fellow Citizens of the Senate and House of Representatives," December 5, 1822, by Edward Coles, *Edwardsville Spectator*, December 14, 1822. See also Commonplace Book, Volume 8, Edward Coles Collection, HSP.

13. "Fellow Citizens of the Senate and of the House of Representatives," December 5, 1822, by Edward Coles, *Edwardsville Spectator*, December 14, 1822, Commonplace Book, volume 8, Edward Coles Collection, HSP; *Illinois Intelligencer*, January 18, 1823; Lacy K. Ford, "Making the 'White Man's Country' White: Race, Slavery, and State-Building in the Jacksonian South," *Journal of the Early Republic* 19 (Winter 1999), 713–37, esp. 719. For black population statistics, see Margaret Norton, ed., *Illinois Census Returns, 1810 and 1818* (Springfield: Illinois State Historical Library, 1935), and *Illinois Census Returns 1820* (Springfield: Illinois State Historical Library, 1934).

14. Lippincott, "The Conflict of the Century," typescript, Thomas Lippincott Papers, ISHS. See also Dillon, "The Antislavery Movement in Illinois," 85–87, and Washburne, *Sketch of Edward Coles*, 99–102.

15. Horatio Newhall to [J. and J.] Newhall, undated, Horatio Newhall Papers, folder 1, ISHS; Flower, *History of the English Settlement*, 157. For the statistics on slave ownership and proslavery views among the legislative members, see Norton, ed., *Illinois Census Returns, 1810 and 1818*, and *Illinois Census Returns 1820*.

16. The term "subordinationist" is borrowed from historian Lacy K. Ford's discussion of the Jacksonian South. See Ford, "Making the 'White Man's Country' White," 719–20. The diffusion strategy had some prominent adherents outside the state, Jefferson and Madison among them. See John Craig Hammond, *Slavery, Freedom and Expansion in the Early American West* (Charlottesville: University of Virginia Press,

2007), 36–40; William H. Freehling, *Road to Disunion: Secessionists at Bay, 1776–1854* (New York: Oxford University Press, 1990),, 121–43, and Peter Onuf, "'To Declare Them Free and Independent People': Race, Slavery and National Identity in Jefferson's Thought," *JER* 18 (Spring 1998), 1–46.

17. For the southern origin of Illinois's early American settlers, see John D. Barnhart, "The Southern Influence in the Formation of Illinois," *Journal of the Illinois State Historical Society* 32 (September 1939), 348–78; Simeone, *Slavery and Democracy*, 31–34; James E. Davis, *Frontier Illinois* (Bloomington: Indiana University Press, 1998), 159–69; Nicole Etcheson, *The Emerging Midwest: Upland Southerners and the Political Culture of the Old Northwest, 1787–1861* (Bloomington: Indiana University Press, 1996), 306; John Mack Faragher, *Sugar Creek: Life on the Illinois Frontier* (New Haven: Yale University Press, 1987), 45–46; Arthur Clinton Boggess, *The Settlement of Illinois, 1778–1830* (Chicago: Chicago Historical Society, 1908), 91–92; Solon J. Buck, *Illinois in 1818* (Springfield: Illinois Centennial Commission, 1917), 95–98. For an insightful discussion of southern non-slaveholders' views of slavery and the southern social order, see Stephanie McCurry, *Masters of Small Worlds: Yeoman Households, Gender Relations, and the Political Culture of the Antebellum South Carolina Low Country* (New York: Oxford University Press, 1995). On the racial views of this portion of the Illinois population, see Simeone, *Democracy and Slavery*, 153–56; Eugene H. Berwanger, *Frontier against Slavery: Western Anti-Negro Prejudice and the Slavery Extension Controversy* (Champaign: University of Illinois Press, 1967), and Zucker, "The Free Negro Question."

18. Simeone, *Democracy and Slavery*, 42–49. For population statistics, see Norton, ed., *Illinois Census Returns, 1810 and 1818*, and *Illinois Census Returns 1820*.

19. "A Shoal Creek Farmer," *Edwardsville Spectator*, August 20, 1823. On the impact of the panic of 1819 generally, see Samuel J. Rezneck, "The Depression of 1819–1822: A Social History," *American Historical Review* 39 (October 1933), 28–47; Murray N. Rothbard, *The Panic of 1819: Reactions and Policies* (New York: Columbia University Press, 1962); and Charles Sellers, *The Market Revolution in Jacksonian America, 1815–1846* (New York: Oxford University Press, 1991), 103–38. On the panic of 1819 in Illinois, see Simeone, *Democracy and Slavery*, 42–49. For a more specific exploration of its impact on land sales, see Malcolm J. Rohrbough, *The Land Office Business: The Settlement and Administration of American Public Lands, 1789–1837* (New York: Oxford University Press, 1968), 137–56.

20. Horatio Newhall to [J. and J.] Newhall, May 21, 1823, Horatio Newhall Papers, folder 1, ISHL; Edward Coles to Nicholas Biddle, September 18, 1823, Papers of Edward Coles, 1786–1868, PU.

21. Edward Coles to Roberts Vaux, December 11, 1823, Vaux Family Papers, HSP; "Public Meeting," "Meeting at Fairfield," "Pope County," *Illinois Gazette*, November 8, 1823, April 10 and 24, 1824; Horatio Newhall to [J. and J.] Newhall, April 14, 1824, Horatio Newhall Papers, folder 1, ISHL. See also Simeone, *Democracy and Slavery*, 140–42.

22. "To the People of the State of Illinois," signed Thomas Cox, *Illinois Gazette*, March 29, 1823; "For the Spectator," signed "A Friend to Liberty," *Edwardsville Spectator*, April 1823; and "For the Intelligencer," signed "Convention," *Illinois Intelligencer*, March 15, 1823. For an analysis of this proconvention strategy, see Simeone, *Democracy and Slavery*.

23. "Another Mob at Vandalia," extract of a letter, dated December 10, 1823, *Edwardsville Spectator*, December 13, 1823; Edward Coles to Roberts Vaux, January 21, 1824, Vaux Family Papers, HSP; Edward Coles to Morris Birkbeck, January 29, 1824, "Letters of Governor Edward Coles," 180–83.

24. Edward Coles to Roberts Vaux, January 21, 1824, Vaux Family Papers, HSP; Edward Coles to Morris Birkbeck, January 29, 1824, "Letters of Governor Edward Coles," 180–83.

25. Edward Coles at County Commissioners of Madison County, January 7, 1824, Governor Edward Coles Papers, ISHS; Edward Coles, "Sketch of the Emancipation, as Told by Him," October 1827, Edward Coles Collection, HSP. See also Edward Coles to Roberts Vaux, January 21, 1824, Vaux Family Papers, HSP, and Edward Coles to Morris Birkbeck, January 29, 1824, "Letters of Governor Edward Coles," 180–83.

26. Edward Coles to Roberts Vaux, January 21, 1824, Vaux Family Papers, HSP.

27. Edward Coles to Sarah Champe Carter, February 13, 1824, Carter-Smith Family Collection, UVA. See also Edward Coles to Morris Birkbeck, January 29, 1824, "Letters of Governor Edward Coles," 180–83.

28. "To the Citizens of Illinois, No. 1," signed "One of Many" [Edward Coles], *Illinois Intelligencer*, May 14, 1824 (original in Edward Coles Collection, HSP).

29. "Address of the Board Managers," April 12, 1823; Thomas Lippincott, "Early Days in Madison County, No. 42," Thomas Lippincott Papers, ISHS; "For the Spectator," signed, "Freedom," *Edwardsville Spectator*, June 7, 1823.

30. "To the Editor of the Illinois Gazette," signed "Jonathan Freeman" [Morris Birkbeck], *Illinois Gazette*, June 14, 1823. To be sure, other arguments in favor or against slavery emerged throughout the campaign. Participants on both sides of the contest, for example, occasionally turned to the Bible to appeal to residents' sense of humanity. For the role of divine law, see Dillon, "The Antislavery Movement in Illinois," 98–105, and Simeone, *Democracy and Slavery*, 166–96. See also the numerous editorials that appeared in the *Edwardsville Spectator*, *Illinois Gazette*, and *Illinois Republican* between July and November 1823. On the transition to Jacksonian democracy in Illinois, see Gerald Leonard, *The Invention of Party Politics: Federalism, Popular Sovereignty, and Constitutional Development in Jacksonian Illinois* (Chapel Hill: University of North Carolina Press, 2002).

31. For Coles's agricultural recommendations, see "To the Farmers of the State of Illinois," signed "A Farmer of Madison County" [Edward Coles], *Edwardsville Spectator*, October 9, 1819. And for his inaugural address, see "Fellow Citizens of the Senate and of the House of Representatives, December 5, 1822," *Edwardsville Spectator*, December 14, 1822. On Coles and land policy, see David Ress, *Governor Edward Coles and the Vote to Forbid Slavery in Illinois, 1823–1824* (Jefferson, N.C.: McFarland, 2006), 75–88. On regional economic development, see Peter S. Onuf, *Statehood and Union: A History of the Northwest Ordinance* (Bloomington: Indiana University Press, 1987).

32. "To the People of Illinois," unsigned; and "On the Convention, No. III," signed "A Plain Man," *Illinois Gazette*, July 5, 1823. For a general discussion of the proconvention strategy, see Rowe, "The Republican Rhetoric," 671–74. Regarding the defense of slavery in the East, see Larry E. Tise, *Proslavery: A History of the Defense of Slavery in America, 1701–1840* (Athens: University of Georgia Press, 1987), 97–123.

33. "To the Editor of the Illinois Gazette," signed "X," *Illinois Gazette*, January 10,

1824; "For the Advocate," signed "A," *Republican Advocate*, June 5, 1823; and Lippincott, "Conflict of the Century," ISHS.

34. "The House of Representatives . . . ," signed Conrad Will, *Edwardsville Spectator*, December 28, 1822; Lippincott, "Conflict of the Century," ISHS; "For the Spestator," signed "A Friend to Liberty," *Edwardsville Spectator*, April 12, 1823.

35. "To the Citizens of Illinois, No. 2," Edward Coles Collection, HSP; *Illinois Intelligencer* July 9, 1824.

36. "To the Citizens of Illinois, No. 4, No. 5 and No. 6," Edward Coles Collection, HSP.

37. "To the Citizens of Illinois, No. 8, No. 5, No. 2, No. 4," Edward Coles Collection, HSP.

38. "To the Citizens of Illinois, No. 6," Edward Coles Collection, HSP. See also Leonard L. Richards, *The Slave Power: The Free North and Southern Domination* (Baton Rouge: Louisiana State University Press, 2000), 63–82; Don E. Fehrenbacher, *The Slaveholding Republic: An Account of the United States Government's Relations to Slavery* (New York: Oxford University Press, 2001), 3–48; Gary B. Nash, *The Forgotten Fifth: African Americans in the Age of Revolution* (Cambridge: Cambridge University Press, 2006), 70–75.

39. *Edwardsville Spectator*, April 12, June 7, September 20, and July 19, 1823.

40. Edward Coles to Nicholas Biddle, April 22, 1823, Papers of Edward Coles, 1786–1868, PU.

41. Nicholas Biddle to Edward Coles, May 20 and 26, 1823, Papers of Edward Coles, 1786–1868, PU; Roberts Vaux to Edward Coles, May 27, 1823, "Letters of Governor Edward Coles," 171–72. Coles received two shipments of pamphlets, paid for 2,000 copies of each essay, and provided for their distribution to the residents of the state as well as their republication in the local newspapers.

42. Edward Coles to Roberts Vaux, June 27, 1823, Vaux Family Papers, HSP; "To the People of Illinois," signed "Aristides," *Illinois Intelligencer*, May 24, 1823; "Democracy," *Republican Advocate*, July 24, 1823; "To the Editor of the Illinois Gazette," signed "Jonathan Freeman" [Morris Birkbeck], *Illinois Gazette*, July 19, 1824.

43. Nicholas Biddle to Edward Coles, May 20, 1823, Papers of Edward Coles, 1786–1868, PU; Edward Coles to Roberts Vaux, June 27, 1823, Vaux Family Papers, HSP; "The Crisis, No. III," and "The Crisis, No. IV," signed "Martus," *Republican Advocate*, June 19 and July 3, 1823.

44. "The Voice of Virtue, Wisdom, and Experience, on the subject of Negro Slavery," unsigned [Edward Coles], *Illinois Intelligencer*, July 13, 1824; "Remarks Addressed to the Citizens of Illinois on the Proposed Introduction of Slavery," [Roberts Vaux, 1824], ISHL.

45. "The Crisis, No. IV," signed "Martus" ; "To the Editor of the Illinois Gazette," signed "Jonathan Freeman" [Morris Birkbeck], *Illinois Gazette*, June 14, 1823; "Democracy," *Republican Advocate*, July 24 and October 9, 1823.

46. "To the People of Illinois, No. II," signed "Aristides," *Illinois Intelligencer*, May 24, 1823; "The Crisis, No. IV," signed "Martus"; "A Letter from a member of the Christian Convention on the Wabash to Mr. Roger, of White County," signed "A Hater of Slavery and Man Stealing," *Illinois Intelligencer*, January 9, 1824; "To the Citizens of Illinois, No. 3," signed "One of Many" [Edward Coles], *Illinois Intelligencer*, May 28, 1824. Individuals who opposed the convention did not have a monopoly on this type of

language. See "Brutus," *Illinois Intelligencer*, July 5, 1823, and "On the Convention, No. III," signed "A Plain Man," *Illinois Gazette*, July 10, 1824. Regarding the importance of racial prejudice in the Old Northwest, see Berwanger, *The Frontier against Slavery*.

47. "Lawrence County Society . . . address," signed Abraham Carns, *Edwardsville Spectator*, September 16, 1823; "Fello-Citizens," signed "A Friend to Illinois," *Edwardsville Spectator*, October 4, 1823.

48. Lippincott, "Conflict of the Century," ISHS; Edward Coles to Roberts Vaux, January 21, 1824, Edward Coles Collection, HSP.

49. Theodore Calvin Pease, ed., *Illinois Election Returns, 1818–1848* (Springfield: Illinois State Historical Library, 1923), 27–29. See also, Dillon, "The Antislavery Movement in Illinois," 116; Zucker, "The Free Negro Question," 132–34.

50. Edward Coles, "History of the Ordinance of 1787," ISHL.

51. "Court Documents," typescripts, Governor Edward Coles Papers, ISHS; Edward Coles to Roberts Vaux, February 8, 1826, Vaux Family Papers, HSP; and Edward Coles, "Sketch of the Emancipation," Edward Coles Collection, HSP.

52. *Edwardsville Spectator*, November 2 and 23, 1824; "Governor's Message," Commonplace Book, volume 7, Edward Coles Collection, HSP; Ress, *Governor Edward Coles*, 161–64.

53. "A History of the Ordinance of 1787," ISHL. For a sampling of the newspaper reports describing his exploits in Illinois, see *Columbian Centinel* (Mass.), September 14, 1825; *Salem Gazette* (Mass.), February 11, 1825; *Farmer's Cabinet* (N.H.), February 19, 1825; *New York Advertiser* (undated); *Connecticut Mirror*, February 21, 1825; *Poulson's American Daily Advertiser* (undated).

5 / Antislavery Reform Denied

1. Edward Coles to Sarah Champe Carter, December 21, 1827, Carter-Smith Family Collection, UVA.

2. James Madison to Edward Coles, February 22, 1827, February 23, 1827, Papers of Edward Coles, 1786–1868, PU; Edward Coles to John Rutherfoord, May 15, 1827, John Rutherfoord Letters and Papers, 1754–1891, Duke University. See also, Catherine Allgor, *A Perfect Union: Dolley Madison and the Creation of the American Nation* (New York: Henry Holt, 2006), 351–53; Ralph Ketcham, *James Madison, A Biography* (Charlottesville: University Press of Virginia, 1992), 615–16.

3. George Forquer to Edward Coles, February 2, 1827, Papers of Edward Coles, 1786–1868, PU.

4. *Daily National Journal*, May 18 and 19, 1827; John Rutherfoord to Eliza Coles, May 21, 1827, John Rutherfoord Letters and Papers, 1754–1891, Duke University; Edward Coles to Thomas W. Gilmer, May 22, 1827, *New Hampshire Gazette*, January 15, 1828; Thomas W. Gilmer to Edward Coles, May 27, 1827, Commonplace Book, volume 8, Edward Coles Collection, HSP. Reprints of Coles's statements appeared in the *Richmond Whig, Essex Register, Rhode-Island Republican, Boston Statesman*, and *Pittsfield Sun*, among others.

5. Edward Coles to Messrs. Forquer, Breese, Ford, Prickett, McKee, Lippincott, Miller, and Todd, November 23, 1827, Commonplace Book, volume 8, Edward Coles Collection, HSP.

6. *New York Telescope*, October 1, 1825; *Western Recorder*, October 4, 1825; "Gov. Coles of Illinois," *Edwardsville Spectator*, November 5, 1825; Edward Coles to James

Madison, October 12, 1825, Edward Coles Papers, CHS; "Formation of Auxiliary Societies," *African Repository and Colonial Journal* 2 (April 1826), 62; "Extracts of Correspondents," *African Repository and Colonial Journal* 2 (June 1826), 119; "From the Hon. Edward Coles of Illinois," *African Repository and Colonial Journal* 3 (April 1827), 63; Edward Coles to Sarah Champe Carter, December 21, 1827, Carter-Smith Family Collection, UVA.

7. Edward Coles, "Sketch of the . . . Emancipation," October 1827, Papers of Edward Coles, 1786–1868, PU.

8. "Extract from a letter from Governor Coles to John Rutherfoord" (Fall 1826), in "Letters of Governor Edward Coles Bearing on the Struggle for Freedom and Slavery in Illinois," *Journal of Negro History* 3 (April 1918), 193.

9. "Colonization Society. A General Meeting of the Richmond and Manchester Society, . . . January 24, 1824, Mr. Rutherfoord's remarks," in Edward Coles, Commonplace Book, volume 7, Edward Coles Collection, HSP; John Rutherfoord to Edward Coles, April 26, 1829, John Rutherfoord Letters and Papers, 1754–1891, Duke University. For a full reprint of his colonization speeches, see *Richmond Commercial Compiler*, January 29, 1824. For biographical information on John Rutherfoord, see William B. Coles, *The Coles Family of Virginia: Its Numerous Connections, from the Emigration to America to the Year 1915* (New York, 1931), 142–44.

10. *The Constitution of the American Society for Colonizing the Free People of Color of the United States* (Washington City: Printed by D. Rapine, 1818); "To the Friends of Colonization," *African Repository and Colonial Journal* 13 (January 1828), 99; "Extracts of Correspondents," *African Repository and Colonial Journal* 2 (June 1826), 119; "Colonization Society," *African Repository and Colonial Journal* 1 (April 1825), 22, and 1 (November 1825), 257. Eric Burin, *Slavery and the Peculiar Solution: A History of the American Colonization Society* (Gainesville: University of Florida Press, 2005); Beverly Tomek, "'From motives of generosity, as well as self-preservation': Thomas Branagan, Colonization, and the Gradual Emancipation Movement," *American Nineteenth Century History* 6 (June 2005), 121–47; Ellen Eslinger, "The Brief Career of Rufus W. Bailey, American Colonization Agent in Virginia," *Journal of Southern History* 71 (February 2005), 39–74. On the Upper South and colonization, see Lacy K. Ford, *Deliver Us from Evil: The Slavery Question in the Old South* (New York: Oxford University Press, 2009), 299–328.

11. "Colonization Society," "Colonization Society," "Communication," *African Repository and Colonial Journal* 1 (April 1825), 33; 1 (November 1825), 257; and 1 (March 1825), 5.

12. "To the Friends of Colonization," *African Repository and Colonial Journal* 13 (January 1828), 99; "Extracts of Correspondents," *African Repository and Colonial Journal* 2 (June 1826), 119.

13. "Colonization Society," *African Repository and Colonial Journal* 1 (April 1825), 33, and 1 (November 1825), 257.

14. Rutherfoord served as a Jacksonian elector in 1832 and was president of Virginia's Democratic Central Committee for twenty-five years. See *Richmond Enquirer*, September 20, 1832. On the Democracy in Virginia, see William G. Shade, *Democratizing the Old Dominion: Virginia and the Second Party System, 1824–1861* (Charlottesville: University of Virginia Press, 1996).

15. John Rutherfoord to Edward Coles, February 7, 1826, John Rutherfoord Letters

and Papers, 1754–1891, Duke University. On the struggle for political reform, see Eva Sheppard Wolf, *Race and Liberty in the New Nation: Emancipation in Virginia from the Revolution to Nat Turner's Rebellion* (Baton Rouge: Louisiana State University Press, 2006), 182–85; Shade, *Democratizing the Old Dominion*, 57–63; Christopher M. Curtis, "Reconsidering Suffrage Reform in the 1829–1830 Constitutional Convention," *Journal of Southern History* 74 (February 2008), 89–124.

16. Wolf, *Race and Liberty in the New Nation*; Shade, *Democratizing the Old Dominion*, 50–77; Alison Goodyear Freehling, *Drift toward Dissolution: The Virginia Slavery Debate of 1831–1832* (Baton Rouge: Louisiana State University Press, 1982); Dickson D. Bruce, *The Rhetoric of Conservatism: The Virginia Convention of 1829–30 and the Conservative Tradition in the South* (San Marino, Cal.: Huntington Library, 1982); Christopher M. Curtis, "Reconsidering Suffrage Reform."

17. Wolf, *Race and Liberty in the New Nation*, 179–85; Susan Dunn, *Dominion of Memories: Jefferson, Madison and the Decline of Virginia* (New York: Basic Books, 2007), 15–60, and Robert P. Sutton, "Nostalgia, Pessimism, and Malaise: The Doomed Aristocrat in Late-Jeffersonian Virginia," *VMHB* 76 (January 1968), 41–46.

18. Shade, *Democratizing the Old Dominion*, 230–33.

19. For a list of the delegates, see *Proceedings and Debates of the Virginia State Convention of 1829–1830* (Richmond: Richard S. Shepherd, 1830). Watkins Leigh, Johnson, Tyler, and Tazewell all attended the College of William and Mary while Coles was a student at the school. Chapman and Tyler were probably among the friends to whom Coles first confessed his antislavery convictions. See Edward Coles, "Autobiography," April 1844, Edward Coles Collection, HSP.

20. John Rutherfoord to Edward Coles, April 26, 1829, John Rutherfoord Letters and Papers, 1754–1891, Duke University. Rutherfoord was not the only public official and friend of Coles who was reluctant to serve at the convention. John Tyler, then senator from Virginia and Coles's old college classmate, was likewise unwilling to serve. He worried that the "severe struggle for political power between the upper and lower country" and the fact that he had to represent the tidewater district, "which probably is destined under any new arrangement to lose more than any other district in the State," would undermine his national political ambitions. See John Tyler to John Rutherfoord, February 23, 1829, "Original Letters," *WMQ* 1 (January 1893), 176.

21. Shade, *Democratizing the Old Dominion*, 54–77; Freehling, *Drift toward Dissolution*, 36–81; Curtis, "Reconsidering Suffrage Reform."

22. Dolley Payne Madison to John C. Payne, December 4, 1829, and Dolley Payne Madison to Anna Cutts, December 28, 1829, in *The Selected Letters of Dolley Payne Madison*, edited by David B. Mattern and Holly C. Shulman (Charlottesville: University of Virginia Press, 2003), 280–82. For Coles's recollection, see "In conversation with Uncle Edward," September 1855, John Rutherfoord Letters and Papers, 1754–1891, Duke University.

23. "The Virginia Convention," *Genius of Universal Emancipation*, October 23, 1829; Shade, *Democratizing the Old Dominion*, 194–95.

24. "Abolition of Slavery. From the Staunton Spectator. Memorial to the Honorable Convention of Virginia," *Richmond Enquirer*, October [?], 1829, in Edward Coles, Commonplace Book, volume 7, Edward Coles Collection, HSP. See also Wolf, *Race and Liberty in the New Nation*, 185–86; Shade, *Democratizing the Old Dominion*, 59–77; Freehling, *Drift toward Dissolution*, 47.

25. "The Virginia Convention," *Genius of Universal Emancipation*, October 23, 1829; October 24, 26, and 27, 1829, *Proceedings and Debates*, 39 and 53. See also Wolf, *Race and Liberty in the New Nation*, 182.

26. October 27, 1829, *Proceedings and Debates*, 54–62.

27. October 27 and 28, 1829, *Proceedings and Debates*, 66–75.

28. November 2, 1829, *Proceedings and Debates*, 148–51.

29. October 28 and 29, 1829, *Proceedings and Debates*, 86 and 91.

30. "For the Enquirer: To James Monroe, President of the Convention, signed Jefferson [Edward Coles]," *Richmond Enquirer*, November 7, 1829, in Coles, Commonplace Book, volume 7, 81, Edward Coles Collection, HSP.

31. William Crane to R. R. Gruely, January 1, 1827, cited in Marie Tyler-McGraw, "American Colonization Society in Virginia, 1816–1832: A Case Study in Southern Liberalism," Ph.D. dissertation, George Washington University, 1980, 173; November 2 and 4, *Proceedings and Debates*, 149 and 172–73. See also Marie Tyler-McGraw, *An African Republic: Black and White Virginians in the Making of Liberia* (Chapel Hill: University of North Carolina Press, 2007), 42–45; Wolf, *Race and Liberty in the New Nation*, 161–71, and Donald J. Ratcliff, "The Decline of Antislavery Politics," in *Contesting Slavery: The Politics of Bondage and Freedom in the New Nation*, edited by John Craig Hammond and Matthew Mason (Charlottesville: University of Virginia Press, 2011), 272–73.

32. William Branch Giles, "To the Public, Mr. Jefferson's Letter, and Mr. Clay's 'great desideratum in Political Economy,'" in *Political Miscellanies* (Richmond: Richard Jeffries,1829); Shade, *Democratizing the Old Dominion*, 234–38; Drew R. McCoy, *The Last of the Fathers: James Madison and the Republican Legacy* (Cambridge: Cambridge University Press, 1989), 119–51.

33. "To the Editors of the Enquirer," signed "A Farmer," *Richmond Enquirer*, October 6, 1829. Shade, *Democratizing the Old Dominion*, 234–38; Drew R. McCoy, *The Last of the Fathers: James Madison and the Republican Legacy* (Cambridge: Cambridge University Press, 1989), 119–51; Kevin R. Gutzman, "Preserving the Patrimony: William Branch Giles and Virginia versus the Federal Tariff," *VMHB* 104 (Summer 1996), 341–72; and Donald J. Ratcliff, "The Nullification Crisis, Southern Discontents and the American Political Process," *American Nineteenth Century History* 1 (Summer 2000), 1–30.

34. Freehling, *Drift toward Dissolution*, 65–70 (quote on 69); Wolf, *Race and Liberty in the New Nation*, 190–94; Shade, *Democratizing the Old Dominion*, 76–77.

35. Gutzman, "Preserving the Patrimony," 344–53; Shade, *Democratizing the Old Dominion*, 235–43.

36. Edward Coles to James Madison, November 4, 1830, Papers of Edward Coles, Chicago Historical Society. See also McCoy, *Last of the Fathers*, 119–54. For a broader discussion of nullification, see William W. Freehling, *Prelude to Civil War: The Nullification Controversy in South Carolina, 1816–1836* (New York: Harper and Row, 1966).

37. For a discussion of Madison's nationalist perspective during the 1820s and 1830s, see McCoy, *Last of the Fathers*, 148–51. For Coles's advocacy of initiatives that would become central to Adams and Clay's nationalist vision, see "Fellow Citizens of the Senate and the House of Representatives," December 5, 1822, and "Governor's Message," December 5, 1826, Commonplace Book, volume 8, Edward Coles Collection, HSP. For Jackson's prohibition of federal aid for colonization, see Burin, *Slavery*

and the Peculiar Solution, 18. For Coles's fundraising activities, see *African Repository and Colonial Journal* 4 (February 1829), 383.

38. "To the People of Illinois," signed "Edward Coles, Edwardsville, April 12, 1831," *Illinois Intelligencer*, April 16, 1831. See also Commonplace Book, volume 8, Edward Coles Collection, HSP.

39. Edward Coles to James Madison, June 12, 1831; James Madison to Edward Coles, June 28, 1831, Papers of Edward Coles, 1786–1868, PU. Drew McCoy cites this exchange as evidence of Madison's rising impatience with Coles's unreasonable partisanship. Although his passionate objections to Jackson certainly animated his exchanges with Madison in 1834 (discussed in more depth in Chapter 6), Coles's 1831 request of Madison was not unusually animated, and Madison's response was not nearly as agitated as McCoy implies. See McCoy, *Last of the Fathers*, 158.

40. "National Republican Convention," *Constitutional Whig*, December 20, 1831. William Thomas, "Early Times: Reminiscences of Judge William Thomas," *Weekly Journal*, April 18, 1877, cited in Kurt E. Leichtle, "Edward Coles: An Agrarian on the Frontier," Ph.D. dissertation, University of Illinois—Chicago Circle, 1982, 214. On the political culture of Illinois, see Gerald Leonard, *The Invention of Party Politics: Federalism, Popular Sovereignty, and Constitutional Development in Jacksonian Illinois* (Chapel Hill: University of North Carolina Press, 2002); James Simeone, "Ninian Edwards' Republican Dilemma," *Illinois Historical Journal* 90 (Winter 1997), 245–64; and Kurt Leichtle, "The Rise of Jacksonian Politics in Illinois," *Illinois Historical Journal* 82 (Summer 1989), 93–107. On the rise the democratization of politics generally, see Sean Wilentz, *The Rise of American Democracy: From Jefferson to Lincoln* (New York: W. W. Norton, 2005). On Henry Clay and the National Republicans, see Robert V. Remini, *Henry Clay: Statesman for the Union* (New York: W. W. Norton, 1991).

41. On Illinois and Jacksonian politics, see Leonard, *The Invention of Party Politics*.

42. . Theodore Calvin Pease, ed., *Illinois Election Returns, 1818–1848* (Springfield: Illinois State Historical Library, 1923), 70–73. See also, Leichtle, "The Rise of Jacksonian Politics in Illinois," 106–107.

43. "To the General Assembly of the Commonwealth of Virginia," *Constitutional Whig*, October 17, 1831; "To the Legislature of Virginia," *Constitutional Whig*, November 10, 1831; "To the Citizens of Virginia," signed "A Native of Eastern Virginia," and "To the People of Virginia," signed "P.Q.O.," *Constitutional Whig*, November 17, 1831, and *Richmond Enquirer*, December 10, 1831; "To the Editors of the Enquirer," signed "A Freeholder of Hanover County," *Richmond Enquirer*, November 4, 1831. See also Wolf, *Race and Liberty in the New Nation*, 198–206, and Ford, *Deliver Us from Evil*, 329–389.

44. Coles recounted the late November conversation in a letter to Madison in an effort to document Madison's antislavery intentions. See Edward Coles to James Madison, January 8, 1832, Papers of Edward Coles, 1786–1868, PU.

45. Edward Coles to James Madison January 8, 1832, Papers of Edward Coles, 1786–1868, PU.

46. Edward Coles to Thomas Jefferson Randolph, December 29, 1831, Papers of Edward Coles, 1786–1868, PU; John Floyd to James Hamilton, Jr., November 19, 1831, in *The Confessions of Nat Turner and Related Documents*, edited by Kenneth S. Greenburg (Boston: Bedford Books of St. Martin's Press, 1996), 110–11; November 21, 1831, in *The Life and Diary of John Floyd*, by Charles H. Ambler (Richmond:

Richmond Press, 1918), 170. See also Wolf, *Race and Liberty in the New Nation*, 206–207.

47. Edward Coles to Thomas Jefferson Randolph, December 29, 1831, Papers of Edward Coles, 1786–1868, PU.

48. *Speech of Thomas J. Randolph* . . . (Richmond: T. W. White, 1832); Edward Coles to Thomas Jefferson Randolph, December 29, 1831, Papers of Edward Coles, 1786–1868, PU; *Speech of William H. Brodnax* . . . (Richmond: T. W. White, 1832), 10–11; *Speech of Thomas Marshall*. . .(Richmond: T. W. White, 1832), 4 and 7.

49. *Speech of Thomas J. Randolph*, 6; Edward Coles to Thomas Jefferson Randolph, December 29, 1831, Papers of Edward Coles, 1786–1868, PU; *Speech of William H. Brodnax*, 18–19.

50. *Speech of Thomas J. Randolph*, 14–15.

51. *Speech of Charles Faulkner* . . . (Richmond: T. W. White, 1832), 12; *Speech of James McDowell, Jr.* . . .(Richmond: T. W. White, 1832), 5.52. Wolf, *Race and Liberty in the New Nation*, 197–98, 229–34.

53. Adam Rothman, *Slave Country: American Expansion and the Origins of the Deep South* (Cambridge: Harvard University Press, 2005); Don E. Fehrenbacher, *The Slaveholding Republic: An Account of the United States Government's Relations to Slavery* (New York: Oxford University Press, 2001); Leonard L. Richards, *The Slave Power: The Free North and Southern Domination* (Baton Rouge: Louisiana State University Press, 2000); Paul Finkelman, *Slavery and the Founders: Race and Liberty in the Age of Jefferson* (London, M. E. Sharpe,1996); Gary B. Nash, *Race and Revolution* (Madison: Madison House, 1990); William H. Freehling, *Road to Disunion: Secessionists at Bay, 1776–1854* (New York: Oxford University Press, 1990). Several recent works have challenged the notion that slavery remained unimportant in politics during the early American republic, but they have tended to focus on national, rather than local developments. See Matthew Mason, *Slavery and Politics in the Early American Republic* (Chapel Hill: University of North Carolina Press, 2007), and Richard S. Newman, *The Transformation of American Abolitionism: Fighting Slavery in the Early Republic* (Chapel Hill: University of North Carolina Press, 2002). A few exceptions to this characterization include John Craig Hammond, *Slavery, Freedom, and Expansion in the Early American West* (Charlottesville: University of Virginia Press, 2007), Wolf, *Race and Liberty in the New Nation*, and David N. Gellman, *Emancipating New York: The Politics of Slavery and Freedom, 1777–1827* (Baton Rouge: Louisiana State University Press, 2006).

6 / Antislavery Aspirations Redirected

1. Edward Coles to Dolley Madison, November 25, 1833, Edward Coles Papers, CHS.

2. Edward Coles to Sally Champ Carter, December 21, 1827; Carter-Smith Family Collection, UVA.

3. William B. Coles, *The Coles Family of Virginia and Its Numerous Connections, from the Emigration to America to the Year 1915* (New York, 1931), 113–14. See also Russell F. Weigley, ed., *Philadelphia: A 300-Year History* (New York: W. W. Norton, 1982), especially chapters 7 and 8. On Philadelphia's associational culture, see Albrecht Koschinik, *"Let common interest bind us together": Associations, Partisanship and Culture in Philadelphia, 1775–1840* (Charlottesville: University of Virginia Press, 2007); Daniel

Kilbride, *An American Aristocracy: Southern Planters in Antebellum Philadelphia* (Columbia: University of South Carolina Press, 2006); Bruce Dorsey, *Reforming Men and Women: Gender in the Antebellum City* (Ithaca: Cornell University Press, 2002).

4. Beverly C. Tomek, *Colonization and Its Discontents: Emancipation, Emigration, and Antislavery in Antebellum Pennsylvania* (New York: New York University Press, 2011); Eric Burin, *Slavery and the Peculiar Solution: A History of the American Colonization Society* (Gainesville: University Press of Florida, 2005); Richard S. Newman, *The Transformation of American Abolitionism: Fighting Slavery in the Early Republic* (Chapel Hill: University of North Carolina Press, 2002); James Brewer Stewart, *Holy Warriors: The Abolitionists and American Slavery* (New York: Hill and Wang, 1976).

5. Dolley Madison to Edward Coles, February 10, 1834, Papers of Edward Coles, 1786–1868, PU.

6. Isaac A. Coles to John Rutherfoord, January 10, 1834, John Rutherfoord Letters and Papers, 1754–1891, Duke University. For the description of Green Mountain hospitality, see Coles, *The Coles Family of Virginia*, 108.

7. Isaac A. Coles to John Rutherfoord, January 10, 1834, John Rutherfoord Letters and Papers, 1754–1891, Duke University; Dolley Madison to Edward Coles, February 10, 1834, Papers of Edward Coles, 1786–1868, PU; and Edward Coles to James Madison, October 31, 1834, Edward Coles Papers, CHS. See also Edward Coles to Joseph Duncan, November 20, 1834, Edward Coles Collection, HSP, and Emily Ann Coles, Sally Carter, and John C. Rutherfoord to John Rutherfoord, September 9, 1834, John Rutherfoord Letters and Papers, 1754–1891, Duke University.

8. Edward Coles, "Ledger: Land Transactions, 1818–1869, Some Accounts of Hugh Roberts Estate, 1836–1866," volume 5; Account Book, 1818–1839, volume 4; Robert Wash to Edward Coles, October 31 and November 7, 1834, and February 5 and November 30, 1835, Edward Coles to Robert Wash, September 23 and November 7, 1835, Edward Coles Collection, HSP. See also George Alter, Claudia Goldin, and Elyce Rotella, "The Savings of Ordinary Americans: The Philadelphia Savings Fund Society in the Mid-Nineteenth Century," *Journal of Economic History* 54 (December 1994), 738; and Donald R. Adams, Jr., "The Standard of Living during American Industrialization: Evidence from the Brandywine Region, 1800–1860," *Journal of Economic History* 43 (December 1982), 903–17; Robert E. Gallman and John Joseph Wallis, eds., *American Economic Growth and Standards of Living before the Civil War* (Chicago: University of Chicago Press, 1992).

9. Edward Coles to Joseph Duncan, November 20, 1834, Edward Coles Collection, HSP.

10. Edward Coles to Joseph Duncan, November 20, 1834; Joseph Duncan to Edward Coles, February 25, 1835, Edward Coles Collection, HSP. His older brother Isaac likewise told Madison that though Edward lived in Philadelphia, "he still talks of the west, & has not yet made up his mind where he will permanently fix himself down." See I. A. Coles to James Madison, February 2, 1835, Edward Coles Papers, CHS.

11. Edward Coles to Joseph Duncan, March 16, 1835; Joseph Duncan to Edward Coles, March 20, 1835; Edward Coles to Robert Dyson, April 8, 1835; Robert Dyson to Edward Coles, April 9, 1835, Edward Coles Collection, HSP. See also Edward Crapol, "John Tyler and the Pursuit of the National Destiny," *JER* 17 (Fall 1997), 467–92; Christopher Leahy, "Torn between Family and Politics," *VMHB* 114 (Fall 2006), 322–55.

12. Edward Coles to James Madison, August 17 and September 15, 1834, Edward

Coles Papers, CHS; James Madison to Edward Coles, August 29 and October 15, 1834, Papers of Edward Coles, 1786–1868, PU. On Jackson and the "bank war," see Sean Wilentz, *The Rise of American Democracy: Jefferson to Lincoln* (New York: W. W. Norton, 2005), 360–74; Harry L. Watson, *Liberty and Power: The Politics of Jacksonian America* (New York: Noonday Press, 1990), 147; Merrill D. Peterson, *The Great Triumvirate: Webster, Clay, and Calhoun* (New York: Oxford University Press, 1987), 207–45; Robert H. Wiebe, *The Opening of American Society: From the Adoption of the Constitution to the Eve of Disunion* (New York: A. A. Knopf, 1984), 238–40. See also Drew R. McCoy, *Last of the Fathers: James Madison and the Republican Legacy* (Cambridge: Cambridge University Press, 1989), 119–70.

13. Edward Coles to Andrew Stevenson, January 7, 13, 16, 17, and February 4, 1835; Edward Coles to John Tyler, January 26, 1835, Papers of Edward Coles, 1786–1868, PU. See also Francis F. Wayland, *Andrew Stevenson: Democrat and Diplomat, 1785–1857* (Philadelphia: University of Pennsylvania Press, 1949). On Webster's actions, see Edward Coles to Daniel Webster, July 12, 1834, and Daniel Webster to Edward Coles, July 29, 1834, Papers of Edward Coles, 1786–1868, PU.

14. *Report of the Committee of Investigation Appointed at the Meeting of the Stockholders, January 4, 1841* (Philadelphia: J. Lippincott, 1841). The report was presented to the Board of Directors on April 5, 1841. See also Weigley, ed., *Philadelphia*, 304–306.

15. Edward Coles to Isaac A. Coles, April 11, 1840, Papers of Edward Coles, 1786–1868, PU; Andrew Stevenson to Edward Coles, May 26, 1841, Edward Coles Collection, HSP.

16. William Chambers, *Things as They Are in America* (Philadelphia: Lippincott, Crambo, 1854), 317. See also Stuart M. Blumin, *The Emergence of the Middle Class: Social Experience in the American City, 1760–1900* (Cambridge: Cambridge University Press, 1989); Weigley, ed., *Philadelphia*; Kilbride, *An American Aristocracy*.

17. Diary entry, January 7, 1844, in Nicholas B. Wainwright, ed., *A Philadelphia Perspective: The Diary of Sidney George Fisher, Covering the Years 1834–1871* (Philadelphia: Historical Society of Pennsylvania, 1969), 51. See also Weigley, ed., *Philadelphia*, 278–360.

18. *Transactions of the American Philosophical Society* 6 (Philadelphia: James Kay, Jr. and Brothers, 1839), v–vii; Kilbride, *An American Aristocracy*, 104–26.

19. Job R. Tyson, *Sketch of a Wistar Party of Philadelphia* [1846] (Philadelphia, 1898), 6–8; Kilbride, *An American Aristocracy*, 120–22.

20. Tyson, *Sketch of a Wistar Party of Philadelphia*, 6–15; Peter S. Du Ponceau, *A Brief View of the Constitution of the United States* (Philadelphia: E. G. Dorsey, 1831), http://www.constitution.org/cmt/psdp/consti.htm.

21. Edward Coles to Isaac A. Coles, December 17, March 25, and May 2, 1840, Edward Coles Collection, HSP. Diary entry, October 31, 1840, in Wainwright, ed., *A Philadelphia Perspective*, 106.

22. Sally Coles Stevenson to Edward and Sally Coles, November 14, 1840, and March 3, 1841, and Edward Coles to Isaac A. Coles, March 25, 1840, Edward Coles Collection, HSP; Edward Coles to Martin Van Buren, July 25, 1842, Papers of Edward Coles, 1786–1868, PU. For Van Buren's response and agreement, see Martin Van Buren to Edward Coles, August 9, 1842, Papers of Edward Coles, 1786–1868, PU.

23. John Tyler, "Speech of Gov. Tyler," August 22, 1835, Gloucester County Meeting, in *Letters and Times of the Tylers*, 3 vols., edited by Lyon Gardiner Tyler (Richmond:

Whittet and Shepperson, 1884), 1: 576–78, http://www.archive.org; Andrew Jackson, quoted in Leonard L. Richards, *The Slave Power: The Free North and Southern Domination, 1780–1860* (Baton Rouge: Louisiana State University Press, 2000), 129. Coles certainly read Tyler's speech in the *Richmond Enquirer*, a paper he subscribed to throughout his lifetime. They may have discussed the issue during their conversations whenever Coles visited Washington. In January 1835, Tyler confessed to Coles that "[I] recognize in you one of my oldest and longest tried friends—a friendship which had its origin in College and has continued uninterruptedly to the present day." See John Tyler to Edward Coles, January 31, 1835, Papers of Edward Coles, 1786–1868, PU.

    24. Daniel Wirls, "'The Only Mode of Avoiding Everlasting Debate': The Overlooked Senate Gag Rule for Antislavery Petitions," *JER* 27 (Spring 2007), 115–38; Richards, *The Slave Power*; William Lee Miller, *Arguing against Slavery: The Great Battle in the United States Congress* (New York: A. A. Knopf, 1996), 115–28; William W. Freehling, *The Road to Disunion: Secessionists at Bay, 1776–1854* (New York: Oxford University Press, 1990), 322–27; Don E. Fehrenbacher, *The Slaveholding Republic: An Account of the United States Government's Relations to Slavery* (New York: Oxford University Press, 2001), 81–88.

    25. *Register of Debates*, 24th Congress, 1st Session, January 7, 1836, 7: 74. Wirls, "'The Only Mode of Avoiding Everlasting Debate,'" 115–23; Richards, *The Slave Power*, 126–31; Miller, *Arguing against Slavery*, 115–28; Freehling, *The Road to Disunion*, 322–27; Fehrenbacher, *The Slaveholding Republic*, 81–88.

    26. "For the National Intelligencer," undated, Commonplace Book, volume 7, 97, Edward Coles Collection, HSP.

    27. Martin Van Buren, *Opinions of Martin Van Buren, Vice President of the United States, upon the Powers and Duties of Congress, in Reference to the Abolition of Slavery Either in the Slave-Holding States or in the District of Columbia* (Washington, D.C.: Blair and Rives, 1836). Wirls, "'The Only Mode of Avoiding Everlasting Debate,'" 124–28; Leonard, *The Slave Power*, 129–33; William G. Shade, "'The Most Delicate and Exciting Topics'" Martin Van Buren, Slavery, and the Election of 1836," *JER* 18 (Fall 1998), 459–84. See also Joel Silbey, *Martin Van Buren and the Emergence of American Popular Politics* (New York: Rowman and Littlefield, 2002), and Robert V. Remini, *Henry Clay: Statesman for the Union* (New York: W. W. Norton, 1991), 408–409 and 471–96.

    28. Edward Coles to Dolley Madison, July 6, 1836, Edward Coles Papers, CHS.

    29. John C. Payne to Edward Coles, July 18, 1836, Papers of Edward Coles, 1786–1868, PU.

    30. Edward Coles to Sally Stevenson, July 28 and November 12, 1836, Papers of Edward Coles, 1786–1868, PU. See also Catherine Allgor, *A Perfect Union: Dolley Madison and the Creation of the American Nation* (New York: Henry Holt, 2006), 381–82.

    31. Robert Wash to Edward Coles March 25, October 31, and November 7, 1834; Account Book, 1818–1839, volume 4, Edward Coles Collection, HSP; "Edward Coles in Account with Isaac Prickett," Edward Coles Papers, CHS. For the land purchases, see Illinois Public Domain Land Database, Illinois State Archives. In June 1832, Coles secured a claim to eighty acres of forfeited land stock adjacent to Prarieland. Robert Crawford purchased another eighty acres between 1832 and 1836 in the same section. Michael Lee bought forty acres in 1831 and another forty acres in 1836. Jessie Price

married Kate Crawford's oldest daughter Betsy in 1826 and moved eastward, possibly settling in Vermillion County, where a free black of that name purchased eighty acres of land in 1835. For the marriage records, see Illinois Statewide Marriage Index, Illinois State Archives.

32. Edward Coles to Robert and Kate Crawford, February 7, 1837, Papers of Edward Coles, 1786–1868, PU. See also Edward Coles to Sally Coles Stevenson, November 12, 1836, Papers of Edward Coles, 1786–1868, PU.

33. John Payne to Edward Coles, February 28 and March 15, 1837, Papers of Edward Coles, 1786–1868, PU.

34. William Chambers, *Things as They Are in America* (Philadelphia: Lippincott, Grambo , 1854), 305; Weigley, ed., *Philadelphia*, 274–310; Stewart Blumin, "Mobility and Change in Ante-Bellum Philadelphia," in *The Private City: Philadelphia in Three Periods of Growth*, by Sam Bass Warner (Philadelphia: University of Pennsylvania Press, 1987), 65–78.

35. Edward Coles to John Rutherfoord, April 9, 1837, John Rutherfoord Letters and Papers, 1754–1891, Duke University; Nicholas B. Wainwright, ed., *A Philadelphia Perspective: The Diary of Sidney George Fisher, Covering the Years 1834–1871* (Philadelphia: Historical Society of Pennsylvania, 1969), 30–31. Most of Coles's financial anxieties resulted from the depressed economy in Missouri and Illinois, where he owned a great deal of land. His agent in St. Louis reported that "the spirite of improvement & business of every description & with it the price of property is sensibly depressed." See Robert Wash to Edward Coles, May 17, 1837, Edward Coles Collection, HSP. On conditions in Philadelphia, see Gary B. Nash, *First City: Philadelphia and the Forging of Historical Memory* (Philadelphia: University of Pennsylvania Press, 2002), 144–75, and Weigley, ed., *Philadelphia*, 307–62.

36. Robert Purvis, quoted in Nash, *First City*, 167–70. See also Julie Winch, *Philadelphia's Black Elites: Activism, Accommodation, and the Struggle for Autonomy, 1787–1848* (Philadelphia: Temple University Press, 1988); Tomek, *Colonization and Its Discontents*, 225–28; Dorsey, *Reforming Men and Women*, 152; David Grimsted, *American Mobbing, 1828–1861* (New York: Oxford University Press, 1998); John Runcie, "'Hunting the Nigs' in Philadelphia: The Race Riot of August 1834," *Pennsylvania History* 39 (April 1972), 187–218; Elizabeth M. Geffen, "Violence in Philadelphia in the 1840s and 1850s," *Pennsylvania History* 36 (October 1969), 381–410.

37. *African Repository and Colonial Journal* 12 (November 1836), 360. See also Burin, *Slavery and the Peculiar Solution*, 35–45.

38. "Proceedings of the American Colonization Society," *African Repository and Colonial Journal* 12 (January 1836), 1; William Lloyd Garrison, *Thoughts on African Colonization* (Boston: Garrison and Knapp, 1832). See also Tomek, *Colonization and Its Discontents*, 93–131 and 219–38; Burin, *Slavery and the Peculiar Solution*, 21 and 84–86; Newman, *The Transformation of American Abolitionism*; Julie Winch, *A Gentleman of Color: The Life of James Forten* (New York: Oxford University Press, 2000), 248–53; and Henry Mayer, *All on Fire: William Lloyd Garrison and the Abolition of Slavery* (New York: St. Martin's Press, 1998).

39. R. R. Gurley, *Address at the Annual Meeting of the Pennsylvania Colonization Society, November 11, 1839* (Philadelphia: Herman Hooker, 1839), 10–11, 17–18.

40. Pennsylvania Colonization Society, Minute Books, 1838–1849, 28–29 and 34, Lincoln University (Pennsylvania); *Colonization Herald*, January 31, 1838;

"Proceedings of the American Colonization Society," *African Repository and Colonial Journal* 15 (January 1839), 18. See also Tomek, *Colonization and Its Discontents*, 93–131, and Burin, *Slavery and the Peculiar Solution*, 20–21 and 80–85.

41. Pennsylvania Colonization Society, Minute Books, 1838–1849, 46–65, Lincoln University (Pennsylvania); *African Repository and Colonial Journal* 15 (March 1839), 95; *An Inquiry into the Condition and Prospects of the African Race in the United States and the Manner of Bettering Its Fortunes* (Philadelphia: Haswell, Barrington, Haswell, 1839), 14–15.

42. Edward Coles, "Autobiography," April 1844, Edward Coles Collection, HSP.

43. Coles, "Autobiography," April 1844, Edward Coles Collection, HSP.

44. Coles, "Autobiography," April 1844, Edward Coles Collection, HSP.

45. Coles, "Autobiography," April 1844, Edward Coles Collection, HSP.

46. Coles, "Autobiography," April 1844, Edward Coles Collection, HSP.

47. Coles, "Autobiography," April 1844, Edward Coles Collection, HSP.

48. Coles, "Autobiography," April 1844, Edward Coles Collection, HSP. On the reluctance of African Americans to emigrate, see Tomek, *Colonization and Its Discontents*, 132–62.

49. Coles, "Autobiography," April 1844, Edward Coles Collection, HSP; Robert and Kate Crawford to Edward Coles, October 23, 1841, Papers of Edward Coles, 1786–1868, PU.

50. Young Men's Colonization Society, Executive Committee Minute Book, 1834–1841, Lincoln University (Pennsylvania). See also Burin, *Slavery and the Peculiar Solution*, 24 and 80–86; Kocher, "A Duty to America and Africa," 130–41; Eli Seifman, "The United Colonization Societies of New York and Pennsylvania and the Establishment of the African Colony of Bassa Cove," *Pennsylvania History* 35 (January 1968), 23.

51. Edward Coles to Richard Singleton, November 2, 1845, Richard Singleton Papers, UVA; Coles, Ledger: Land Transactions, 1818–1869, Edward Coles Collection, HSP; Thomas Baldwin and J. Thomas, *A New and Complete Gazetteer of the United States* (Philadelphia: Lippincott, Grambo, 1854), cited in Weigley, ed., *Philadelphia*, 310.

52. Edward Coles to Isaac Coles, August 2, 1839, Edward Coles Collection, HSP; Edward Coles to Dolley Madison, February 26, 1840 and August 29, 1841, Edward Coles Papers, ISHL; and Edward Coles to Richard Singleton, May 2, 1845, John Rutherfoord Letters and Papers, 1754–1891, Duke University.

53. Coles took his family to Virginia in 1838 for an extended visit and to attend a family wedding. He went again in 1840 to join his extended family (including those from South Carolina) at Fauquier Springs, Virginia. See Edward Coles to Isaac Prickett, July 8, 1838; Edward Coles to Isaac Coles, July 14 and August 26, 1840; Edward Coles to Dolley Madison, October 12, 1840, Edward Coles Papers, ISHL; and Emily A. Rutherfoord to John Coles Rutherfoord, September 23, 1840, John Rutherfoord Letters and Papers, 1754–1891, Duke University. For two examples of family visits to Philadelphia, see Edward Coles to Isaac Coles, December 17, 1840, Edward Coles Collections, HSP; Edward Coles to Richard Singleton, August 19, 1844, Richard Singleton Papers, UVA; Richard Singleton to John Rutherfoord, November 5, 1844 and May 2, 1845, John Rutherfoord Letters and Papers, 1754–1891, Duke University.

54. Edward Coles to John Rutherfoord, November 6, 1847, John Rutherfoord

Letters and Papers, 1754–1891, Duke University. See also Coles, *The Coles Family of Virginia*, 142–44.

7 / Antislavery Nationalism Resurrected

1. B. W. Richards to Edward Coles, Philadelphia, September 2, 1848, Commonplace Book, volume 7, Edward Coles Collection, HSP. See also Michael A. Morrison, *Slavery and the American West: The Eclipse of Manifest Destiny and the Coming of the Civil War* (Chapel Hill: University of North Carolina Press, 1999). and George B. Forgie, *Patricide in the House Divided: A Psychological Interpretation of Lincoln and His Age* (New York: W. W. Norton, 1979), 124–36.

2. Edward Coles to B.W. Richards, September 9, 1848, Commonplace Book, volume 7, Edward Coles Collection, HSP.

3. Edward Coles to B.W. Richards, September 9, 1848, Commonplace Book, volume 7, Edward Coles Collection, HSP.

4. Edward Coles to B.W. Richards, September 9, 1848, Commonplace Book, volume 7, Edward Coles Collection, HSP.

5. Morrison, *Slavery and the American West*, 66–95; Sean Wilentz, *The Rise of American Democracy: From Jefferson to Lincoln* (New York: W. W. Norton, 2005), 602–32.

6. Edward Coles to B. W. Richards, September 9, 1848, Commonplace Book, volume 7, Edward Coles Collection, HSP. Less than a month before the election, Free-Soil presidential candidate Martin Van Buren wrote Coles congratulating him for writing an "effective letter" that he predicted would add to Coles's "consistent, earnest and self sacrificing" antislavery reputation. He lamented that his earlier effort against slavery in Illinois "have not been appreciated as it deserves." He then confessed he wished he could "repeat from the housetops" Coles's arguments, but demurred because he feared doing so might "expose my motives to an uncharitable and injurious construction." See Martin Van Buren to Edward Coles, October 1, 1848, Papers of Edward Coles, 1786–1869, PU.

7. Zachary Taylor, Inaugural Address, March 5, 1849; http://www.let.rug.n1/usa/P/zt12/speeches/taylor.htm.

8. Michael Holt, *The Rise and Fall of the American Whig Party* (New York: Oxford University Press, 1999), 459–92; Morrison, *Slavery and the American West*, 105–109.

9. Edward Coles to Henry Clay, March 15, 1850, Papers of Edward Coles, 1786–1868, PU; Andrew Stevenson to John Rutherfoord, January 25, 1849, John Rutherfoord Letters and Papers, 1754–1891, Duke University; William Bigler to Henry Simpson (of Philadelphia), January 9, 1850, William Bigler Papers, HSP. Morrison, *Slavery and the American West*, 119–25; Michael Holt, *The Political Crisis of the 1850s* (New York: W.W. Norton, 1978), 76–85.

10. Edward Coles to Henry Clay, March 15, 1850; "Advice to My Country," Papers of Edward Coles, 1786–1868, PU. On the "advice" generally, see Adrienne Koch, *Madison's "Advice to My Country"* (Princeton: Princeton University Press, 1966), and David B. Mattern, ed., *James Madison's "Advice to My Country"* (Charlottesville: University Press of Virginia, 1997).

11. Francis E. Brewster, *Slavery and the Constitution: Both Sides of the Question* (Philadelphia, February 15, 1850), 5, 7, 14 and 20 [unsigned]; *Philadelphia, July 4* (Philadelphia, 1850).

12. William Gilmore Simms to Nathaniel Beverly Tucker, January 30, 1850, and William Gilmore Simms to Hon. Beverly Tucker, November 27 [1850], in Glenn M. Linden, comp., *Voices from the Gathering Storm* (Wilmington: Scholarly Resources, 2001), 46–47. See also Minisha Sinha, *The Counter-Revolution of Slavery: Politics and Ideology in Antebellum South Carolina* (Chapel Hill: University of North Carolina Press, 2000), 95–105; William J. Cooper, Jr., *Liberty and Slavery: Southern Politics to 1860* (New York: A. A. Knopf, 1983) , 233–38.

13. "Meeting," *Philadelphia Inquirer*, November 20, 1850.

14. [unsigned], *Union Proceedings of the Grand Union Meeting held . . . at Philadelphia . . . on the 21st of November 1850* (Philadelphia: F. Mifflin, 1850), 3 and 11–12. On the southern character of Philadelphia, see Daniel Kilbride, *An American Aristocracy: Southern Planters in Antebellum Philadelphia* (Columbia: University of South Carolina Press, 2006).

15. *Proceedings of the Grand Union Meeting*, 11–13.

16. Holt, *The Rise and Fall of the American Whig Party*, 542–52, and Wilentz, *The Rise of American Democracy*, 633–44. See Sinha, *The Counter-Revolution of Slavery*, 106–23; Cooper, Jr., *Liberty and Slavery*, 235–38; James L. Huston, "Southerners against Secession: The Argument of the Constitutional Unionists in 1850–52," *Civil War History* 46 (December 2000), 181–99.

17. *Proceedings of the Grand Union Meeting*, 11–13; "Speech on Kansas-Nebraska Act at Peoria, Illinois," October 16, 1854, in Abraham Lincoln, *Speeches and Writings, 1859–1865*, edited by Don E. Fehrenbacher (New York: Library of America, 1989), 314.

18. Edward Coles to Richard Singleton, January 8, 1851, John Rutherfoord Letters and Papers, 1754–1891, Duke University.

19. Edward Coles to *National Intelligencer*, and Edward Coles to Messrs. Gales and Seaton, February 20, 1851, Papers of Edward Coles, 1786–1868, PU.

20. James Buchanan to William Bigler, April 10, 1851, William Bigler Papers, 1836–1880, Historical Society of Pennsylvania.

21. [unsigned], *A Word to the Whigs of Pennsylvania* (n.p., 1850). Leonard L. Richards, *The Slave Power: The Free North and Southern Domination, 1780–1860* (Baton Rouge: Louisiana State University Press, 2000); Elizabeth Varon, *Disunion!: The Coming of the Civil War* (Chapel Hill: University of North Carolina Press, 2008).

22. Edward Coles to J. R. Poinsett, March 15, 1851, Papers of Edward Coles, 1786–1868, PU. Coles preserved a clipping of the newspaper publication of this letter. See Commonplace Book, volume 7, 105, Edward Coles Collection, HSP.

23. Edward Coles to J.R. Poinsett, March 15, 1851, Papers of Edward Coles, 1786–1868, PU.

24. Edward Coles to J. R. Poinsett, March 15, 1851, Papers of Edward Coles, 1786–1868, PU. On Douglas, see Graham A. Peck, "Was Stephen A. Douglas Antislavery?," *Journal of the Abraham Lincoln Association* 26 (Summer 2005), 1–21, http:historycooperative.org/journals/jala/26.2/peck.html.

25. Charles Sumner, "Tribute to Robert Rantoul, Jr.," August 9, 1852, in *The Works of Charles Sumner* (Boston: Lee and Shepard, 1872), 3: 75.

26. Edward Coles to Charles Sumner, August 18, 1852, Papers of Edward Coles, 1786–1868, PU. On Jefferson and the Northwest Ordinance of 1787, see Don E. Fehrenbacher, *The Slaveholding Republic: An Account of the United States Government's Relations to Slavery* (New York: Oxford University Press, 2001), 253–59; Peter S. Onuf,

Statehood and Union: A History of the Northwest Ordinance (Bloomington: Indiana University Press, 1987), 44–66; and Paul Finkelman, *Slavery and the Founders: Race and Liberty in the Age of Jefferson* (London, 1996), 34–56.

27. Charles Sumner to Edward Coles, August 23, 1852, Papers of Edward Coles, 1786–1868, PU. See also Sumner, *The Works of Charles Sumner*, 3: 81–85.

28. Charles Sumner to George Putnam, April 1848, cited in David Herbert Donald, *Charles Sumner* (New York: Da Capo Press, 1996), 134.

29. Edward Coles, "Who Was the Author of the Ordinance of 1787?," *National Intelligencer*, January 4, 1853.

30. Coles, "Was Was the author of the Ordinance of 1787?" (emphasis added).

31. Martin Van Buren to Edward Coles, January 19, 1853, Edward Coles to Martin Van Buren, January 25, 1853, and Edward Coles to Joseph C. Cabell, May 26, 1853, Papers of Edward Coles, 1786–1868, PU.

32. Joseph R. Fornieri, "Lincoln's Critique of *Dred Scott* as a Vindication of the Founding," and Allen C. Guelzo, "'Sublime in Its Magnitude': The Emancipation Proclamation," in *Lincoln and Freedom: Slavery, Emancipation and the Thirteenth Amendment*, edited by Harold Holzer and Sara Vaughn Gabbard (Carbondale: Southern Illinois University Press, 2007), 20–26 and 65–78.

33. Adam I. P. Smith and Susan-Mary Grant, eds., *The North and the Nation in the Era of the Civil War* (New York: Fordham University Press, 2003); Susan-Mary Grant, *North over South: Northern Nationalism and American Identity in the Antebellum Era* (Lawrence: University Press of Kansas, 2000); Melinda Lawson, *Patriot Fires: Forging a New American Nationalism in the Civil War North* (Lawrence: University Press of Kansas, 2002); Major Wilson, *Space, Time, and Freedom: The Quest for Nationality and the Irrepressible Conflict, 1815–1861* (Westport, Conn.: Greenwood, 1974); Paul C. Nagel, *This Sacred Trust: American Nationality, 1798–1898* (New York: Oxford University Press, 1971).

34. Wilentz, *The Rise of American Democracy*, 668–77, and Nichole Etcheson, *Bleeding Kansas: Contested Liberty in the Civil War Era* (Lawrence: University Press of Kansas, 2004), 9–27.

35. Salmon P. Chase, Charles Sumner, J. R. Giddings, Edward Wade, Gerritt Smith, and Alexander De Witt, "Appeal of the Independent Democrats," *National Era*, January 19, 1854. This "Appeal" was also republished in *Frederick Douglas's Paper*, February 10, 1854. Wilentz, *Rise of American Democracy*, 668–88.

36. *Speech of Hon. S. A. Douglas, of Illinois, in the Senate, January 29, 1854, on the Nebraska Territory* (Washington: Printed at the Sentinel Office, 1854), 5–7.

37. *Speech of Hon. S. A. Douglas, of Illinois, in the Senate, January 29, 1854*, 11.

38. "Edward Coles to Senator Douglas, February 13, 1854," *National Intelligencer*, February 18, 1854.

39. "Edward Coles to Senator Douglas, February 13, 1854," *National Intelligencer*, February 18, 1854. Douglas responded to Coles, lambasting him in severe language for so inadequately refuting his claims. See Stephen A. Douglas to Edward Coles, February 18, 1854 in *The Letters of Stephen A. Douglas*, edited by Robert W. Johannsen (Urbana: University of Illinois Press, 1961), 290–99.

40. Frank J. Klingberg and Frank W. Klingberg, eds., *The Correspondence between Henry Stephens Randall and Hugh Blair Grigsby, 1856–1861* (Berkeley: University of California Press, 1952), 1–10.

41. Edward Coles to Hugh Blair Grigsby, December 23, 1854, Edward Coles Collection, HSP.

42. Edward Coles to Hugh Blair Grigsby, December 23, 1854, Edward Coles Collection, HSP. See also Klingberg and Klingberg, eds., *The Correspondence between Henry Stephens Randall and Hugh Blair Grigsby*, 1–7.

43. Edward Coles to Nellie C. Willis, December 18, 1855, John Willis to Edward Coles, December 19, 1855, Papers of Edward Coles, 1786–1868, PU.

44. Edward Coles to William Cabell Rives, February 3, 1857, William Cabell Rives Papers, Box 85 and 89, Library of Congress.

45. Edward Coles to Richard Singleton, January 27, 1848, October 25, 1848, and January 29, 1849, Richard Singleton Papers, UVA; Edward Coles to John Rutherfoord, November 7, 1847, January 8, 1851, John Rutherfoord Letters and Papers, 1754–1891, Duke University.

46. Edward Coles to Richard Singleton, May 3, 1847, and January 27, 1848, and Edward Coles to Rebecca Singleton, April 29, 1848, Richard Singleton Papers, UVA; Sally Coles Stevenson to Edward Coles, June 8, 1847, Edward Coles to Edward Bates, July 15, 1858, Edward Coles Collection, HSP; Edward Coles to John Rutherfoord, November 6, 1847, Edward Coles to Richard Singleton, January 8, 1851, and Edward Coles to Matt Singleton, December 7, 1852, and John Coles Rutherfoord, "Slavery and Politics," September 1855, John Rutherfoord Letters and Papers, 1754–1891, Duke University.

47. Edward Coles to Richard Singleton, May 3, 1847, and January 27, 1848, and Edward Coles to Rebecca Singleton, April 29, 1848, Richard Singleton Papers, UVA; Sally Coles Stevenson to Edward Coles, June 8, 1847, Edward Coles to Andrew Stevenson, February 4, 1851, Edward Coles Collection, HSP; Edward Coles to John Rutherfoord, November 6, 1847, Edward Coles to Richard Singleton, January 8, 1851, and Edward Coles to Matt Singleton, December 7, 1852, Edward Coles to A. S. Rutherfoord, December 17, 1856, John Rutherfoord Letters and Papers, 1754–1891, Duke University.

48. Edward Coles to John Coles Rutherfoord, March 14, 1856, John Rutherfoord Letters and Papers, 1754–1891, Duke University. For the details of the case, see William A. Link, *Roots of Secession: Slavery and Politics in Antebellum Virginia* (Chapel Hill: University of North Carolina Press, 2003), 110–12 and 142–44.

49. Edward Coles to John Coles Rutherfoord, March 14, 1856, John Rutherfoord Letters and Papers, 1754–1891, Duke University.

50. Edward Coles to John Coles Rutherfoord, March 14, 1856, John Rutherfoord Letters and Papers, 1754–1891, Duke University. See Varon, *Disunion!*, especially chapters 7 and 8.

51. Edward Coles to John Coles Rutherfoord, March 14, 1856, John Rutherfoord Letters and Papers, 1754–1891, Duke University.

52. [Edward Coles], *Ordinance of 1787*, Edward Coles Papers, ISHL. Modern scholars have challenged Coles's opinion that the Ordinance effectively abolished slavery in the region. See Paul Finkelman, *Slavery and the Founders: Race and Liberty in the Age of Jefferson* (London: M. E. Sharpe, 1996), and Onuf, *Statehood and Union*. See also James Simeone, *Democracy and Slavery in Frontier Illinois, The Bottomland Republic* (Dekalb: Northern Illinois University Press, 2000), and Nicole Etcheson, *The Emerging Midwest: Upland Southern and the Political Culture of the Old Northwest, 1787–1861* (Bloomington: Indiana University Press, 1996).

53. [Coles], *Ordinance of 1787*, 20–27, Edward Coles Papers, Illinois State Historical Library.

54. [Coles], *Ordinance of 1787*, 25–32, Edward Coles Papers, Illinois State Historical Library.

55. *Portraits and Sketches of the Lives of All the Candidates for the Presidency and Vice-Presidency for 1860* (New York: J. C. Buttie, 1860), 6–8. On Lincoln and slavery, see Eric Foner, *Fiery Trial: Abraham Lincoln and American Slavery* (New York: W. W. Norton, 2010), and James Oaks, *The Radical and the Republican: Frederick Douglass, Abraham Lincoln and the Triumph of Antislavery Politics* (New York: W. W. Norton, 2007).

56. Abraham Lincoln, "Address at Cooper Institute, New York City," February 27, 1860 in *Speeches and Writings, 1859–1865*, 117, 120–123, and 129–30. See also Harold Holzer, *Lincoln at Cooper Union: The Speech that Made Abraham Lincoln President* (New York: Simon and Schuster, 2004).

57. Nicholas P. Trist to James Parton, May 31, 1860, Papers of Nicholas P. Trist, Library of Congress; Nicholas B. Wainwright, ed., *A Philadelphia Perspective: The Diary of Sidney George Fisher, Covering the Years 1834–1871* (Philadelphia: Historical Society of Pennsylvania, 1969),, 353 (May 17, 1860); *Portraits and Sketches*, 13.

58. William Cabell Rives to Green Payton, September 17, 1860, Rives-Troubetsky Papers, Box 2, UVA. On the prominence of unionism in the Upper South, see Daniel W. Crofts, *Reluctant Confederates: Upper South Unionists in the Secession Crisis* (Chapel Hill: University of North Carolina Press, 1993).

59. Robert C. Winthrop, Jr., *A Memoir of Robert C. Winthrop* (Boston: Little, Brown, 1897), 212–14.

60. "Explanation" (1861), Papers of Nicolas P. Trist, Library of Congress. On Election Day, Trist arrived at Coles's door and escorted him to the polls.

61. Grant, *North and South,* and Paul Quigley, *Shifting Grounds: Nationalism and the American South 1848–1865* (New York: Oxford University Press, 2011).

62. "Let Us Keep Cool," and "The Disturbed Condition of Things," *North American*, November 10 and 12, 1860.

63. "The Great Meeting, a Day for the Union," *Philadelphia Inquirer*, December 14, 1860; "The Union Meeting," *North American*, December 12, 1860; "The Union Meeting," *Sunday Dispatch*, December 16, 1860.

64. John W. Forney, *Anecdotes of Public Men* (New York: Harper and Brothers, 1873), 223. J. Matthew Gallman, *Mastering Wartime: A Social History of Philadelphia during the Civil War* (Philadelphia: University of Pennsylvania Press, 1990).

65. "The Presidential Reception and the Mayor's Speech," *Philadelphia Inquirer*, February 22, 1861; *Evening Bulletin*, February 21, 1861, excerpted in Joseph George, Jr., "Philadelphians Greet Their President-Elect—1861," *Pennsylvania History* 29 (October 1962), 385–86.

66. "The Arrival at the Continental," *Philadelphia Inquirer*, February 22, 1861; Edward Coles to Abraham Lincoln—Explanation, The Papers of Nicholas P. Trist, Library of Congress. See also George, Jr., "Philadelphians Greet Their President-Elect," 386.

67. "Mr. Lincoln's Speech," *Philadelphia Inquirer*, February 22, 1861. See also "Reply to Mayor Alexander Henry at Philadelphia, Pennsylvania," in Lincoln, *Speeches and Writings, 1859–1865*, 211–12. For a description of the conclusion of the evening and the

fireworks, see George, Jr., "Philadelphians Greet Their President-Elect," 387. See also Bradley R. Hock, *The Lincoln Trail in Pennsylvania* (University Park: Pennsylvania State University Press, 2001), 72–73.

68. "President Lincoln at Independence Hall," *Albany Journal*, February 23, 1861. See also "Speech at Independence Hall, Philadelphia, Pennsylvania," in Lincoln, *Speeches and Writings, 1859–1865*, 213–41. See also George, Jr., "Philadelphians Greet their President-Elect," 388–89.

69. "President Lincoln," *Philadelphia Inquirer*, February 23, 1861; "President Lincoln," *North American*, February 23, 1861. See also, Russell F. Weigley, ed., *Philadelphia: A 300-Year History* (New York: W. W. Norton, 1982), 393–94.

Afterword

1. "The Great Central Fair," *Philadelphia Inquirer*, June 8, 1864. See also J. Matthew Gallman, *Mastering Wartime: A Social History of Philadelphia during the Civil War* (Philadelphia: University of Pennsylvania Press, 2000), 146–51, and Russell F. Weigley, ed., *Philadelphia: A 300-Year History* (New York: W. W. Norton and Company, 1982), 412.

2. *Department of Useful and Fancy Articles (Home-made) in Aid of the Great Central Fair*, March 1864; diary entry, June 11, 1864, in Wainwright, ed., *A Philadelphia Perspective: The Civil War Diary of Sidney George Fisher*, edited by Jonathan W. White (New York: Fordham University Press, 2007); *A Philadelphia Perspective*, 225–26. See also Nina Silber, *Daughters of the Union: Northern Women Fight the Civil War* (Cambridge: Harvard University Press, 2005); and Judith Giesberg, *Civil War Sisterhood: The United States Sanitary Commission and Women's Politics in Transition* (Boston: Northeastern University Press, 2000).

3. "The Citizens' Volunteer Bounty," *Philadelphia Inquirer*, August 4, 1862; Philadelphia Union League, *Charter and By-Laws of the Union League of Philadelphia* (Philadelphia: Sherman, 1865), 3–15; diary entry, March 11, 1863, in Nicholas B. Wainwright, ed., *A Philadelphia Perspective: The Civil War Diary of Sidney George Fisher*, edited by Jonathan W. White (New York: Fordham University Press, 2007), 185.

4. John Rutherfoord to Edward Coles, Jr., June 5, 1863; Office of Provost Marshal General, Department of the Missouri. St. Louis, January 6, 1862; "For Civilians. Head Quarters city Guard," Provost Marshal's Office, November, 22, 1861, Edward Coles Collection, HSP; William B. Coles, *The Coles Family of Virginia and Its Numerous Connections* (New York, 1931), 86, 88, 93, 103, 111.

5. Adam Goodheart, *1861: The Civil War Awakening* (New York: Alfred A. Knopf, 2011), 295–347; Eric Foner, *The Fiery Trial: Abraham Lincoln and Slavery* (New York: W. W. Norton, 2010), 206–47; William W. Freehling, *The South vs. the South: How Anti-Confederate Southerners Shaped the Course of the Civil War* (New York: Oxford University Press, 2001), 87–114; and James Oakes, *The Radical and the Republican: Frederick Douglass, Abraham Lincoln and the Triumph of Antislavery Politics* (New York: W. W. Norton, 2007), 133–71 and 179–202. See also James McPherson, *Crossroads of Freedom: The Battle of Antietam, The Battle That Changed the Course of the Civil War* (New York: Oxford University Press, 2002).

6. "President Lincoln's Proclamation" and "An Emancipation Proclamation," *Philadelphia Inquirer*, September 23 and 30, 1862; "Proclamation Reaches Richmond," and "Effect of the President's Proclamation," *Philadelphia Public Ledger*, October 1 and

7, 1862; "National Union Meeting," and "The Dismay Caused by the Proclamation," *Philadelphia Inquirer*, October 9 and November 2, 1862; "European Views of American Affairs," *Philadelphia Public Ledger*, December 20, 1862. On Philadelphians' response, see Weigley, ed., *Philadelphia*, 407.

7. Philip S. Foner, "The Battle to End Discrimination against Negroes in Philadelphia's Streetcars: (Part I) The Background and Beginning of the Battle," *Pennsylvania History* (September 1973), 261–90; David Quigley, *Second Founding: New York City, Reconstruction, and the Making of American Democracy* (New York: Hill and Wang, 2004). For Coles's will, see Philadelphia, Philadelphia County, Pennsylvania, Will Book 63, 98–102, HSP.

Index